THE OTHER MIRROR

THE OTHER MIRROR

GRAND THEORY THROUGH THE LENS OF LATIN AMERICA

Miguel Angel Centeno and
Fernando López-Alves, Editors

PRINCETON UNIVERSITY PRESS

PRINCETON AND OXFORD

Library of Congress Cataloging-in-Publication Data

The other mirror : grand theory through the lens of Latin America / Miguel Angel Centeno
and Fernando López-Alves, editors

  p. cm.

Includes bibliographical references and index.

ISBN 0-691-05016-3 (alk. paper) — ISBN 0-691-05017-1 (pbk. : alk. paper)

1. Social sciences—Latin America—Philosophy. 2. Social sciences—Philosophy. 3. Latin
America—Politics and government. 4. Latin America—Economic conditions. I. Centeno,
Miguel Angel, 1957–. II. López-Alves, Fernando.

H53.L3 084 2000

300′.98–dc21   00-032625

This book has been composed in Sabon

The paper used in this publication meets the minimum requirements
of ANSI/NISO Z39.48-1992 (R1997) (*Permanence of Paper*)

www.pup.princeton.edu

Printed in the United States of America

10 9 8 7 6 5 4 3 2 1

10 9 8 7 6 5 4 3 2 1

(Pbk.)

To Alex, Allexa, Maya, and Tania

CONTENTS

PREFACE

THIS BOOK began as a conversation on a sunny New York after-noon a few years back. As we spoke, we realized we shared a common frustration with the provincialism of our home disciplines as well as with the antitheoretical tone of much of the work in our specific areas of study. What began as a quick walk turned into a several-hour marathon through a considerable part of Manhattan. We started with a few complaints and ended up planning a book. Several years later and thanks to very patient contributors, friends, and colleagues, we have arrived at our destination.

From the beginning, Charles Tilly was our inspiration. Both of us had come to New York to participate in his seminar, and we shared a deep admiration for his work. We discussed how useful a Tillean worldview might be for the study of Latin America but also noted how some of the expected theoretical patterns might be challenged by that particular history. While celebrating Tilly's work, our original idea for a conference also involved debunking some of his major findings, at least in light of Latin America. Generous as always, he actually encouraged us to pursue our ideas. As we added texts to our list of classics, he remained a great supporter. While he bears absolutely no responsibility for any errors one might find in this volume, his career-long commitment to the fruitful marriage of theory and fact remains our model. Thanks, Chuck.

In the intervening years, we have accumulated many debts and obligations. Our thanks to the contributors, who have seen their work forced through several drafts and at least two public presentations. Without their commitment, the project obviously would have been impossible. Other colleagues have listened more times than they might have wanted to the various versions of our ideas, criticized drafts, and helped us test titles. We especially want to thank audiences at the 1997 Latin American Studies Association meetings in Guadalajara and the subsequent 1998 conference at Princeton University. For the success of the latter, David Myhre and Rose Rivera deserve special praise. Our home institutions have also been generous with time and money. Ian Malcom at PUP has been outstanding and supportive. Finally, friends and family have been bored and ignored too many times as we spoke endlessly about "the book." There are no excuses—we just hope you understand.

In the end, our children are our best mirrors, reflecting what is good in us and teaching us the inappropriateness of our assumptions. To Alex, Allexa, Maya, and Tania we dedicate this book.

CONTRIBUTORS

JEREMY ADELMAN
Professor of History and Director of the Program in Latin American Studies at Princeton University

MIGUEL ANGEL CENTENO
Associate Professor of Sociology and Master of Wilson College at Princeton University

JORGE I. DOMÍNGUEZ
Clarence Dillon Professor of International Affairs and Director of the Weatherhead Center for Interanational Affairs at Harvard University

PAUL GOOTENBERG
Professor of History at the State University of New York at Stony Brook

ALAN KNIGHT
Chair of Latin American History at Oxford University and Fellow of St. Antony's College

ROBERT M. LEVINE
Professor of History and Director of Latin American Studies at the University of Miami, Coral Gables

CLAUDIO LOMNITZ
Professor of History at the University of Chicago

FERNANDO LÓPEZ-ALVES
Associate Professor of Political Science at the University of Pittsburgh

JOHN MARKOFF
Professor of Sociology at the University of Pittsburgh

VERÓNICA MONTECINOS
Associate Professor of Sociology at the Pennsyvlania State University, McKeesport Campus

STEVEN TOPIK
Professor of History and Chair of the Department of History at the University of California, Irvine

J. SAMUEL VALENZUELA
Professor of Sociology at Notre Dame University

THE OTHER MIRROR

INTRODUCTION

Miguel Angel Centeno and Fernando López-Alves

ACADEMIC LUMPERS and splitters are rarely seen together. The first seek widespread patterns with which to generate a universal model of human behavior, while the second emphasize the concrete specifics of singular empirical realities. While lumpers cavort among the wide areas of relatively thin knowledge, splitters take comfort in the depth and sturdiness of specialization. Only in a Borges story could one imagine a debate about which was a "better beast," the fox or the hedgehog. Yet communication across academic species too often consists of methodological sniping and theoretical disdain. Grand visionaries scoff at bean counters, and archival specialists scorn generalizations.

We believe that without having to compromise their academic principles, lumpers and splitters can learn a great deal from each other. Both as members of our respective disciplines and as students of a particular region, we are especially interested in promoting this dialogue between social science and Latin American studies. Over the past two decades, we have seen the scanty references to Latin America practically disappear from the leading political science and sociology journals. It is also true that the regional and area studies literature rarely addresses the major questions of our disciplines.[1]

We have edited this volume in order to promote a dialogue between our different academic halves. The essays engage in a dialectic between universal theory and specific history. They are meant not as yet another imperial claim to knowledge but as an expansion of the number of empirical cases considered relevant. We are not proposing a "Latin American" theory to supplant a "European" one. Rather, we merely wish to encourage including a greater variety of cases that may produce a better and truly generalizable map of the social world. We offer Latin America as "another mirror" that reflects new variations of classical theoretical themes. We hope the book will spark a wider debate about the origin and utility of historical models in general and also generate more accurate and theoretically rich representations of Latin America in particular.

The chapters in this volume conclude that grand theory, in order to remain such, needs to incorporate narratives and empirical data different from the realities that inspired its original formulation. We believe that theory should be able to adjust to these different realities in flexible ways. After all, by definition, the incorporation of new empirical evidence constitutes part of what theory is designed to do. We have learned not only that the Latin American experience was different from that of Europe but also that the analysis of that region's reality often differed from the conceptualization used by current grand theoretical formulations focusing on institutions and societal behavior. A central part of a future research agenda must include methods by which we can enrich grand theory without destroying its noble aims. By incorporating Latin America—and other areas outside Europe—we can begin presenting their experiences in the language we customarily speak when making larger comparative generalizations.

Similarly, the study of theoretical classics has taught us the limitations of contemporary efforts to understand Latin America's historical trajectory of political power and economic development.[2] Latin American studies as a field of research needs to recover a middle ground between the detailed analytic narrative and broad speculation on methodology and identity. This middle range seeks to define and test theoretical propositions regarding the various aspects of social, political, and economic life through a comparative framework. It looks for inspiration to a group of authors who have asked larger questions than can be universally established, but whose scope still allows for empirical investigation. What factors help explain differences in economic development? What role does the state play in the economy and the polity? How do states develop the capacity to rule? Whom do these states serve? What kind of obedience and loyalty do they elicit? Similar to many other regional specialties, Latin American studies has tended to concentrate on either international or local issues, with less attention paid to national questions. Our dialogue between grand theory and Latin America has pointed to the need for more serious work at the intermediate level, where the basic rules of authority and exchange are negotiated and established.

The next section places this enterprise in the specific context of Latin American studies. The section after that discusses how the chapters offer valuable lessons to academic foxes seeking generalizable and comparative claims. The one after reverses pedagogical roles and asks how this wider perspective can improve Latin American studies. Following some general conclusions, a final section describes the structure of the book.

LOOKING FOR A LATIN AMERICAN VISION

If the "cultural turn" of much of contemporary social science has taught us anything, it is that the production of knowledge is often circumstantial and constrained by institutional and social boundaries. The social sciences, and especially those dealing with comparative historical work, are still dominated by a predominently European and North American perspective. The result is that our most general models of political and social development are based primarily on a very small set of cases of questionable relevance to the contemporary world. While history may perhaps suffer less from this confusion than the social sciences, we are all used to assumptions that peasant means French, state means Germany, revolution means Russia, and democracy means Westminster.[3]

We would be less concerned with this situation if the empirical models replacing regional specializations were truly generalizable. But, as in the case of "globalization," for instance, the abandonment of local references has meant not an integration of many countries' experiences but the domination of scholarly discussions by a limited set of cases. Instead of replacing area studies with a wider comparative framework, as would be most desirable, we have increasingly restricted our study to a few empirical references masquerading as universals. In other words, as important as 1688, 1789, and 1870 may be for Europe,[4] we want to argue that 1521, 1810, 1852, and 1889 may be more critical for Latin America. The inclusion of these dates in the comparative almanac will lead to a more accurate understanding of historical processes.

Since its inception as part of the global economy in the sixteenth century, Latin America has looked elsewhere for models to understand and imagine itself or to emulate. The early philosophers of independence were inspired by the triumph of the European Enlightenment and later by the American and French Revolutions. Rare voices sought to imagine a Latin America defined in its own terms and by its own capabilities and limitations. The independence of the continent partially originated in events outside it. The countries imagined by independence leaders had little to do with the areas they inhabited and much more to do with their personal bibliographies or travels abroad; San Martín looked to Europe, while Bolívar searched north for inspiration. In most cases, the United States was the model used both to design many of the subsequent political creations and to judge their success. Few of the more localized (and indigenist) visions of independence survived the process.

The search for external models continued throughout the nineteenth century. Imitation was arguably more of a liberal habit than a conservative one. Conservatives sought their inspiration in an idealized past. Liberals, on the other hand, sought their political inspiration in Washington and their economic models in Manchester; the "Hausmannization" of practically every capital on the continent is the most concrete manifestation of their ideological triumph. Of course, some voices spoke against external emulation,[5] but the angle of view remained northward.

The collapse of liberalism in the interwar years generated perhaps the first "homegrown" regime model. While clearly influenced by both the

Popular Front Left and fascism, Latin American corporatist populism had indigenous ingredients and sought to formulate answers clearly linked to the nature of the economic, political, and social problems they were meant to solve. Yet, with some individual exceptions, this interlude lasted no more than twenty years, and by the 1950s Latin America was once again seeking to emulate other places and be other things than itself. Modernization theory represents perhaps the most explicit attempt to establish a particular historical trajectory as a universal standard. Its various manifestations stipulated a need for Latin America to transform either its culture or its history to follow more closely a British or North American model. While it had fewer adherents on the Latin American continent than outside, the theory nevertheless helped shape many of the development and political policies of the 1950s and 1960s.

In many ways, this period also served as an inspiration for *dependencia*, which is probably Latin America's most important contribution to social science theory. Yet while producing its own version of history, Latin America focused its intellectual attention on centers and actors outside the continent. Even in its more sophisticated guises, dependency theory saw Latin America as a practically passive actor in its own underdevelopment. Note was taken of what Latin America *did not have*, such as a nationalist bourgeoisie or dirigiste states. While conceived as a response to modernization theory, *dependencia* repeated the same "metadiscourse" of looking for the answers to Latin America's problems in its difference from an unstated standard.

The last twenty years have seen a return to the application of external models with neoliberalism's rise to hegemonic status. The Thatcher and Reagan revolutions and the collapse of the Soviet block firmly established the notion that there was no alternative to liberal markets and democracy. Certainly the idea of a Latin American "third way" is no longer taken seriously, nor is the last vestige of a previous alternative, Cuba. Globalization has taken the process of external orientation to its ultimate form—there is no longer an "inside" or a "local," only a universalized "global" order.

Efforts to challenge this vision are of more than purely academic concern. Work on the importance of ideas has more than adequately demonstrated that the manner in which we view the world plays an immense role in determining whether we choose to change it and how we seek to interact with it. A Latin America understood through European or North American eyes is not an accurate representation—not because Eurocentric spectacles are worse than any other but simply because they are shaped by assumptions foreign to the continent. As we see in the following chapters, notions of state, property, or race are not necessarily universal. What may be understood as the natural basis for political power, for example, may remain an illusory goal for nations on the continent. What may appear as the most normal forms of social regulation may assume different shapes in Latin America. Since the names we give to things help define them, inappropriate labeling using alien categories can and will lead to critical misreadings. The imposition of academic models, much like that of their policy counterparts, rarely succeeds. Even if they prove to be useful or productive, they need to be tempered in a debate with those visions arising from local conditions. It is the formulation of the latter that this book hopes to encourage.

Using the Wrong Lenses: What Latin America Can Teach Grand Theory

Without engaging in the provincialism against which Alan Knight's chapter in this volume aptly warns us, we wish to emphasize how the local should help redefine the supposedly universal. (We will address the reverse relationship in the next section.) This is not an argument for the specificities of case studies or historical pedantry, but for the need to continually adapt and improve scholarly generalizations. The chapters in this book emphasize a series of problems that are perhaps endemic to any attempt to formulate generalizable claims. Yet the specific experience of Latin America can teach us more than to simply mind our history.

Latin American studies offer macrosociology lessons in contextuality, contingency, and relationality. By the first we mean a greater awareness of the specific circumstances of the institutions that are the subject of macrotheoretical formulations. The laws of the state, the negotiations of the market, and the mental constructs of daily life arise in different ways and have different manifestations under different conditions. Our argument for conditionality is a repudiation of directionality or teleology in historical processes. If successful states and economies are all alike (questionable in itself), each failure has its own story. By calling for a relational approach, we hope to persuade students of historical processes to be more aware of the often critical role played by each society's structure of domestic and international relations. States at war, for instance, will develop in different ways than those whose existence is not threatened, and utilization of resources will depend on who is in charge.

Oftentimes, much grand theorizing and analysis in the social sciences focuses on a subject of study without proper consideration of where and how it fits into a larger social context. The concept of "holding all other things equal" blinds us to the interaction effects that surround any shift in a social condition. It may be obvious that no social phenomenon exists in a vacuum, but much theorizing assumes this is possible. Various authors in this volume rightly emphasize the contextual aspects of economic development and the role of politics; rules naturally reflect the economic, social, and political relations under which they were written. Position within a global, domestic, or local structure of power and privilege has significant consequences for the manner in which actions are judged and controlled. Attempts to divorce the understanding of institutions from that of social structure will result in fundamental misconstructions. These concerns are of particular interest in contemporary Latin America. The imposition of a neoliberal model often assumes that classic liberal institutions (in the widest sense of the word) already exist, and that they can tame the more predatory aspects of the market. In the absence of a working system of laws, however, theoretically productive competition and self-interest become chaos and plunder.[6]

According to Jeremy Adelman, for example, efforts to narrate and explain the Latin American past have included a number of hidden assumptions about the institutions that they examine. He concludes that institutions do not purely emerge from the bedrock of that special set of claims that we usually call "property rights." Ideology and problems of collective action do intrude. Politics acquires a special status in rule making. The distribution of power cannot be ignored. The conflicts between inclusive and exclusive forms of rule that, according to Adelman, characterize most of the history of Latin America are surely far from being apolitical. Thus, grand theory must always take into account the particular contextual forces that helped shape the construction of what appear to be representatives of universal institutions.

Stretching concepts or inappropriately applying descriptive terms with heavy historical and connational baggage is pervasive in the social sciences. For all the benefits to be had in defining a common language, we have to take into account associated costs in empirical validity. We too often assume that things called by the same name are identical or fulfill the same roles—an assumption that leads to a variety of mistakes. For example, Paul Gootenberg and Fernando López-Alves discuss how *late development* and *state* meant very different things in Latin America than in Eastern Europe or postwar East Asia. The timing of industrialization and the absence of geopolitical competition produced a very different form of industrial capitalism than Bismarckian, Meiji, or Stalinist "catch-ups." Militaries and their conflicts also played different roles. Tilly's state-making wars represent a very different form of organized violence than that seen in Latin America. Similarly, the existence of certain institutions, be they prisons or markets, does not necessarily imply that they do the same things, or do them in the same way, as their counterparts in other regions.

Nowhere is the importance of recognizing the intellectual specificity of concepts clearer than in the realm of that supposedly most universal of sciences, economics. Veronica Montecinos and John Markoff strongly argue against treating economic policies and their intellectual roots as if they arose from a vacuum. Shifts in policy priorities and models cannot be understood by allusion to a utilitarian adaptation to changing circumstances. We need references to transformations in both the intellectual roots of the economics discipline and the role played by its practitioners. Economic policy making is embedded in a set of transnational networks, of cultural biases, of scholarly paradigms, and of political openings that have to be articulated historically. A history of ideas (and of their subsequent implementation) written out of context is nonsense.

Similar concerns apply to the application of other social science models and concepts. Marxist structural analysis, for example, has faced many problems in Latin America. Political parties and interest groups in the continent did not mirror their European counterparts and did not fully express, as in Europe, class cleavages. Likewise, nation building in Latin America did not represent the victory of capitalism over feudal legacies, while in most of Europe, republican rule did. And in Latin America, the consolidation of the republican state did not express powerful class alliances connected to industrialization, as it did in Europe.

Few theories have been as "stretched" as Barrington Moore's ideas, and Samuel Valenzuela focuses on the adequacy of this framework in light of the Chilean historical record. Conservative landowners and legislators, rather than Moore's liberal bourgeois sectors, championed democratic reform in Chile. Democracy in Chile was the product neither of a bourgeois revolution nor of working-class pressures. On closer examination, the leadership that pressed for democratic reform consisted of precisely those who, given their class backgrounds, should have been antidemocratic. Of equal importance, class analysis cannot account for the battle over state-church relations, which in Chile played a profound role in creating the pressures leading to democratic reform.

Closer attention to a specific set of cases also might reveal inherent problems in the very definition of concepts. Nationalism, as Claudio Lomnitz makes clear, comes in various strands, and the very notion of nation can mean many things. Miguel Centeno, in turn, discusses the major problems with the notion of discipline, including difficulties in measurement, application after the fact, and sheer ambiguity. Both chapters emphasize the problems inherent in creating general social concepts derived from singular historical narratives.

A related problem with comparative analysis and grand theory in general is the failure to specify the functions associated with the social phenomena under study. State capacity is certainly one of the most popular objects of comparative analysis. Yet we too rarely ask, "capacity to do what?" The forms of political control required to defend a particular policy, a social interest group, or a mafia-like predation are quite different, and subsequently our discussion should take account of such differences. In his chapter Alan Knight discards some well-known theories of the state and reviews a number of paradigms to understand the evolution of the Mexican state. He notes correspondences and discrepancies between theory and empirical reality, setting out a broad framework of analysis comprising relative strength and autonomy.

The importation of new cases will do much more, however, than merely caution theorists and comparativists to tread more carefully. It also can contribute to the substantive development of such theories and comparisons by suggesting not only new wrinkles but also new causalities and outcomes. This requires that nonstandard cases not be treated as conceptual outliers that need not concern readers. When Latin America does appear in general discussions of comparative history or grand theory, it is most often as the negative counterfactual. As several authors note, the Black Legend of Latin American failures to develop economic and political institutions is elaborate and deeply ingrained in our disciplinary heritages. Yet little effort is expended in explaining these breakdowns, malfunctions, and disappointments or even analyzing whether they were indeed failures. Why not treat Latin America as simply an alternative development, with its own probabilities and variances? The inclusion of these cases will amplify the range of outcomes considered possible and make explaining this range (rather than reaching some historical end point) the main goal of theorizing. Imagining a standard outcome, no matter how unconsciously, reduces comparative analysis to medical diagnosis. Our job is not to find what is "wrong" with a patient but to understand how the body works. For that, we need a much larger sample than has been generally available.

Latin American references point out the idiosyncrasy of European and North American institutional development. Those societies (and their theorists) tend to assume that institutions capable of guarding property rights, enforcing discipline, instilling nationalism, and fighting wars would develop in a relatively linear fashion. The Latin American experience should make students of Europe and North America even more curious about why they enjoyed this institutional development. We might well ask, as did many of the founding authors of our disciplines, how did the "West" triumph?[7] This time, the question could be posed without the cultural chauvinism that once characterized it, but with a better informed empirical appreciation of a phenomenon's rarity and a theoretical recognition of its complexity.

An awareness of multiple outcomes combined with an appreciation of singular complexities would produce a less deterministic brand of theory and one that wrestled with historical conjecture. The difference between asking, "How do states grow?" and "What set of conditions produce what kind of states?" is crucial. The first assumes not only an outcome but also, because of the inherent specific reference, a set of underlying conditions. The second phrasing accepts the multiplicity of conditions and developments and allows for a more precise definition of significant factors. Similarly, to ask how peasants and landlords may have contributed to democratic governance is to assume that these categories have a universality devoid of the relationships between them. The key factor is not the essential qualities of owning or working land but the relationships that link one social position to the other.

Adding to the relevant set of cases improves our chances for identifying the significant attributes of political and economic development by increasing the variance found among both dependent and independent variables. Comparative efforts that implicitly or explicitly limit themselves to Europe or North America deny consideration of the importance of social phenomena that are uniform on the Latin American continent. These chapters here implicitly suggest two characteristics that tend to distinguish Latin America and pose the most interesting challenges to a general understanding of the rise of the contemporary world.

The first of these is the issue of race. Unlike Europe and even much more so than the United States, Latin American societies live with a permanent internal division that was codified in innumerable laws and supported by daily customs and assumptions. On rereading the social science classics, one notices that even those authors who recognized class divisions still tended to treat the societies in question as organic wholes. One could even say that the great success of the nation-state in Europe was to create precisely such a phenomenon by the twentieth century. But what of societies where such divisions have not disappeared? The Latin American experience indicates how much of subsequent history depends on the critical starting condition of ethnic or racial homogeneity.

According to Lomnitz, for example, Anderson's notion of "deep horizontal camaraderie" does not capture the experience of Latin America. Lomnitz proposes to resolve what he sees as the most fundamental problem with Anderson's definition of nationalism—that is, its (false) expectation of fraternity—by looking at "bonds of dependence" rather than bonds of fellowship. The nation turns out to be a community conceived as full comradeship only among full citizens, which explicitly excludes the disenfranchised. Unlike European experiences, the first phase of the formation of Latin American nationalism in the colonies starts with colonization. The way in which the new states of the nineteenth century dealt with this legacy profoundly shaped their sense of nation. Cultural bonds were not strong enough in terms of the construction of "the nation," and the Latin American variant of nationalism emerged from "highly unstable" formulations during the early postcolonial period.

The economic and political consequences of this colonization represent the second major challenge to comparative and historical theories. Recent work in mainstream sociology is of obvious relevance here. Mustafa Emirbayer, who arguably has done the most to push such discussions to the forefront of theoretical debates, has argued for a "relational perspective" that sees persons, for example, as "inseparable from the transactional contexts within which they are embedded."[8] Such contexts are not static or categorical but instead involve the dynamic development of relations between people and within societies. Social phenomena can no longer be treated as products of static essentialist qualities. Instead, we should emphasize much more the causal role played by the relations between the various actors under study. While the recent calls for a "relational perspective" have focused on microprocesses, a similar approach could apply to more macrosociological analyses. The relational context under which Latin American states developed and their economies grew was radically different from that found in the standard cases. By taking into account such different relations and the very different outcomes, we can better appreciate the specific contributions of institutional characteristics and contexts.

Even those not wishing to accept dependency analysis in its entirety recognize the importance of more than three hundred years of colonial history and a further two centuries of often disadvantageous dealings with the rest of the globe. Latin America's economic alternatives were at least partly constrained by its history and relationships. Stress on individual rational behavior as a sufficient and necessary condition of long-term development fails to capture the paradoxical features of the region's economic experience: well-endowed with resources and largely free of traditional fetters on market activity, Latin American performance remained at best uneven. The Latin American experience with development cannot be divorced from the pattern of transactions the region established with the world system. Similarly, the geopolitical context of Latin America was radically different from that of Europe and the United States. With relatively little intraregional competition and a legacy of external control, states developed with radically different agendas than in other areas. Theoretical analyses of European and North American developments or even more general treatments of comparative historical questions such as the rise of the state need to take into account where societies fit into a geographic and historical framework and how these positions, more than intrinsic qualities, help explain outcomes.

What Latin America offers comparative analysis and grand theory is thus not a rejection of the possibility of universal claims but a broader base from which to make these. As discussed earlier, the practically mo-nopolistic position of a set of Western European and North American cases within the comparative-historical canon has reduced the scope of possible comparisons. It has removed potentially critical variables from the analysis and has supported neglect of the transactional and relational contexts in which institutions develop. To expand the empirical scope of our research is not to replace generalizable theory with particularistic narrative. None of the authors suggest that we abandon theory—their affection and respect for the attempts herewith described are obvious. As the next section makes clear, Latin American studies needs the analytic signposts that grand theory provides. As believers in "inductive theoriz-ing," we cannot but feel that the challenge of more cases will only gener-ate better theory.

A Clearer Vision: What Latin America Can Learn from Grand Theory

If Latin America's "difference" has something to add to these theories, the classics also have much to say to Latin Americanists. The chapters in this book highlight several themes that in one way or another have been relatively neglected in the field. Perhaps more important, they also point out approaches that might benefit Latin American studies. Regional spe-cialists have much to learn from colleagues across disciplinary lines. Scholarship on Latin America may be booming, and the quality and quantity of our knowledge about practically every social phenomenon and institution have never been better. But, other than dependency the-ory, the field has not produced an articulate theoretical paradigm.[9]

Renewed emphasis on economic development and institutions under-lines the importance of middle-range theory. From this perspective, the current methodological and epistemological drift of theoretical work in Latin American studies offers little hope of a real conceptual advance. As disparate as their selection of authors, themes, and empirical references, the chapters in this book can help us reframe the classic problem of social order in Latin America. (By *order* we mean the assumed understanding that institutionalized rules will be both imposed and obeyed in a standard and universalized way.) What distinguishes the Latin American experi-ence is that despite considerable economic development and an indepen-dent political history of nearly two hundred years, the classic nineteenth-century problem of chaos and institutional weakness remains. We are struck by the consistent failure of an elite to establish a stable, hegemonic, and effective domination. The continued existence of pockets of resis-tance to formal authority implies some institutional dwarfism. And while this apparent failure was the subject of considerable discussion at earlier stages,[10] we feel that it has been abandoned of late. Interestingly, the neo-liberal message of a state overwhelming civil society appears to have been accepted by much of the academic left when, we would argue, it is the very absence of that state that may best explain the conditions of subaltern populations.

We would argue that part of the reason for the continental marginality in our professional disciplines is that the study of Latin America as a whole has been generally much more case driven than theory driven.[11] Rare is the book that begins with a large macro question divorced from the peculiarities of the field. Borrowing from Tilly's categories, Latin Americanists have privileged the "individualizing comparison in which the point is to contrast specific instances of a given phenomenon as a means of grasping the peculiarities of each case."[12] When theoretical concerns arise, they often are of such an abstract nature (e.g., epistemological puzzles or discourses on sources of identity) as to make systematic comparative analysis practically impossible. Perhaps this is an understandable concern with the peculiarities of their sample. Yet, note that those who work on the U.S. or European cases exclusively feel no need to treat them as isolated cases, viewing them instead as fully legitimate sites for tests of universal propositions. We may not wish to repeat such errors, but we may be inspired by the ambition.

Three structural characteristics may help to explain this atheoretical trend. First, while social scientists often took the lead in the early development of Latin American studies, now the field is increasingly dominated by historians whose professional training inherently suspects generalizable claims and who tend to wear their hedgehog identities with pride.[13] Second, specialization by time and region has become the standard in all academic fields, including ours. This has obviously produced a much richer understanding of the subjects of study. In some guises this specialization also became the most productive theoretical area, but it has come at the cost of the sweeping essay (à la Morse),[14] systemic comparison (Johnson),[15] and grand continental narrative (Burns).[16] These efforts sacrificed specificities for grander theoretical claims of patterns and causalities.[17] Finally, in part because of the limited resources available to Latin American states, in part because of intellectual fashion in the field, we have often lacked the kind of reliable data required by sophisticated quantitative techniques that dominate most of the disciplinary journals. Simply put, we lacked the forms of facts that rigorous theory testing requires.

Of course, simply adopting a theory will not solve these problems. In fact, too close an adherence to a single paradigm may stifle scholarship.

Paul Gootenberg argues that Gerschenkron's impact was eclipsed by the regional dependency school and that this stifled much needed questioning of the forms of economic dysfunction that pervaded the relevant societies. Deep-rooted historical traditions within the region, in addition to the ideologically charged 1960s and 1970s, managed to drive out Gerschenkron's pivotal metaphors from the imagery and conceptualization of Latin American development. Similarly, Jorge Domínguez charges that ideological discomfort prevented the wider utilization of a Huntingtonian perspective that might have better informed political analysis. Too often, it seems, "theory" in Latin American studies has meant a hegemonic model that did not allow for comparative debate. The poststructural habit of questioning the hidden ideological biases behind supposedly objective views of the world has perhaps infected our field too much. While such caution is warranted (and part of this book is predicated on such concerns), we need to stop associating a theory or its proponent with the evils under study. To consider the state worthy of analysis does not make one authoritarian, and to study political parties does not imply that they are all one needs for democracy.

The authors discussed in this volume should give us the courage to overcome the epistemological distress that has gripped all of the social sciences but has been particularly strong in Latin American studies.[18] The impossibility of knowing, or of using that knowledge constructively, the propensity to tell someone's story as appropriation and exploitation—all of the many self-indulgent habits of poststructuralism are to be seen in Latin American studies. The awareness of the limitations of our enterprise, the sensitivity to the inherent elitism of scientific analysis, and the guilt from our situation of privilege have frozen far too much of the field in a state of intellectual paralysis. Our awareness of the limitations of any speech may soon prevent us from saying anything at all. In addition, the strong awareness of our too often dark reality has precluded us from seeing different shades or even brighter lights. At times, the delayed entry of Realpolitik into Latin American studies and the return to the influence of leaders and individuals to explain politics and institutions have produced a positivist overreaction or too strong incursions into rational choice theory.[19] Our fear is that Latin American studies will devote less and less time to knowing something, and more and more to debates about how we know it or should prove it. We simply know too little about too much to afford to engage in such luxuries. This is not to argue against the importance of epistemological or methodological debates, but to wonder if given the massive holes in our basic knowledge of the continent, we might not use our resources more wisely. We believe that one way to accomplish this and at the same time improve our grasp on methodology is to compare the way we work, and the paradigms we often use, with the approaches of other scholars working on areas constructed by different intellectual traditions.

The themes left unexplored by much work on Latin American studies also make us wonder if the pendulum has perhaps swung too far in the direction of nonelites and social history. As any perusal of the new book lists of major publishers will attest, the most dynamic sector in Latin American studies is that which seeks detailed social knowledge of the poor and marginalized. While not arguing for a return to a whiggish past, we join others in wondering if more attention should not be paid to those who, for better or worse, make decisions, to organizations that define policies, and to those who implement them.

Specifically, these chapters encourage Latin Americanists to rediscover development, perhaps the most salient theme of the field during much of the past century yet one that has been sadly neglected in the last decade. Partly in response to the triumphalism of neoliberalism ("there are no more issues to discuss"), partly as a response to the difficulties of the past twenty years ("why speak about what cannot be?"), Latin American studies apparently has abandoned the study of the political economy of development. As we do in this volume, one can look far and wide to discover a significant new work that would follow in the lines of Polanyi or Gerschenkron. Other chapters remind us that the current dominant narrative of all-encompassing markets is neither new nor historically accurate. Those who studied the development of Europe and North America have previously challenged notions of self-regulating markets and societies. Laissez-faire has never really existed for Polanyi, for example, because the state has been "fundamental" in creating property rights and institutions that regulate market transactions and, ultimately, capitalist growth. Steve Topik suggests that this applies nicely to market-state relations in nineteenth-century Latin America, where weak states nonetheless played intrusive economic and social roles. As in those cases, Latin America's economy is embedded in a particular historically complex social system and needs to be studied as such. It is precisely this sensitivity to historical creation of institutions that makes theorists such as Polanyi an attractive model for future theorizing about the continent.

Institutions do matter—not as repositories of unchanging cultural legacies but as evolving creations of economic, political, and social developments. Various chapters attempt to resuscitate the study of institutions from both the culturalist determinism of the "Black Legend" and the scholasticism and jingoism of the traditional *historia patria*. Others argue that several institutions that played a major role in the development of contemporary European society are both underdeveloped and understudied in Latin America.[20] Douglass North's and Samuel Huntington's notions of institutions provide a much-needed framework for the still underdeveloped history of how political power came to pacify and centralize authority on the continent. The property rights approach discussed by Jeremy Adelman offers a fresh vision of institution making while at the same time rescuing a largely forgotten constitutional-legal-historiography approach that characterizes much classic work on Latin America. Fernando López-Alves similarly emphasizes institutional history. A striking conclusion of his chapter is that the emphasis on the late nineteenth century, which in part coincides with the developmentalist version of Latin America, must be revisited. To explain the type of states that arose in the twentieth century, one must search in the period prior to 1850. Both institutional design and different degrees of autonomy reflected prior developments tightly related to the conflicts involved in the first phases of power centralization. Miguel Centeno also notes that the institutions critical for the study of the impact of discipline in "disciplinary societies" appear to be less developed in Latin America. Similarly, Valenzuela offers an alternative to a class-based Moorian approach by suggesting that a political-institutional and organizational perspective is more appropriate for the study of regime formation. Domínguez notes that the analysis of political parties has already had a resurgence, with wonderful benefits for our understanding of the new wave of democratization.

The authors discussed in these chapters clearly demonstrate that theory does not have to be dogmatic or deterministic. The most fruitful research comes from placing the patterns of social theory over the chaos of empirical data while also recognizing historical uncertainty and the often unpredictable complexity of social interactions. What North, Huntington, and Polanyi have to tell us does not lose its value because it might not fit our case. Rather, it should teach us how to analyze our specific field of study in a different manner.

CONCLUSIONS

It should not be surprising that a volume covering such varied topics cannot and will not provide a broad theoretical synthesis that explains Latin American economic and political development. That was never our aim. There *are* key differences. If Huntington and Tilly consider political power to be best understood through the study of the state, Foucault and de Certeau look for it in everyday interactions. Polanyi and Gerschenkron clearly have different views on the role of the state in economic development, while more contemporary economic theorists have even questioned its general relevance or positive contribution.

As discussed previously, there are also some general convergences. Most important, the chapters here remind us of the importance of both analyzing the basic institutions that establish the rules for a society and studying their specific origins and progressions. The chapters share some key concerns regarding the relationship between grand theory and Latin American reality. First, they explicitly privilege the uniqueness of the Latin American narrative and present a healthy counter to the often imperial grasp of the grand theories of the day. If these theories undoubtedly help us study, order, and understand the empirical reality, specifics also serve to ground theories in a series of confirmations, exceptions, and falsifications. All the authors, however, also call for more attention to be paid to some of these theoretical issues. These new questions could inspire a new and original enthusiasm in Latin American studies, as well as providing new insights for old problems.

It is this combination that we consider the volume's most important contribution. Douglass North helps us understand or at least identify critical junctures in Argentine history. Simultaneously, the Argentine case makes us more aware of how conceptions and understandings of property rights need to be contextualized. Latin America has much to teach Huntington about political order, but this political scientist can also reframe attention paid to political parties. Nationalism in Latin America may not have followed Benedict Anderson's expected paths, but certainly our discussion of how it developed could benefit a great deal from his concepts. Foucault and Weber on discipline are far from being directly applicable to Latin American realities, but disciplinary institutions in Latin America can teach European-based models a different lesson about disciplinary societies. And although state formation was a very different process in Europe and Latin America, Tilly can inform and correct (or be corrected by) our traditional ways of understanding state building.

The key differences this volume found between the European and Latin American experiences and literatures suggest the need for a healthy shift in how we understand both grand theory and the Latin American experience. We would like to enthusiastically encourage—and make a plea for—future research that can wear the lenses of theory when looking at Latin America. Such a research agenda will inevitably lead to a restructuring and transformation of both fields of study. The "corrections" that authors suggest in this volume constitute an initial step in this direction. None of them want to abandon theory. Rather, our aim is to formulate macrohistorical patterns that could elaborate upon the specifics of areas like Latin America, therefore becoming a more truly universal—and recognizable—map of the social world. We need more specificity, and we are willing to pay for it by allowing somewhat less parsimony in the formulation of our theorizing. Yet we cannot fall in the trap of the "exceptional" or the "unique," which has been so common to some Latin American theorizing.

We return in the end to the suggested model of "relational analysis." If we may use the perhaps worn-out analogy of language, words do have particular characteristics and meanings. But they acquire sense and purpose as parts of phrases and sentences. Similarly, social phenomena need to be understood in their relationship with other events, both contemporaneous and historical. We offer a new set of cases in the hope that this new literature will enrich our understanding of the linguistic possibilities. Conversely, we suggest that despite the infinite variety of word combinations, there are some grammars that, if not necessarily universal, seem to follow clear patterns. Theoretical models provide a guide with which we can organize the flow of words into meaningful sentences.

In the end, grand theory and area studies constitute a false dichotomy similar to the equally fallacious split between quantitative and qualitative work. The best social science seeks to marry general insights with grounded empirical reality; it seeks to join analysis with narrative in exciting new ways. All the authors in this volume call for such an approach. If the book inspires others to do the same, we will judge it a success.

ORGANIZATION OF THE BOOK

We asked a number of leading scholars to analyze prominent theorists and schools in light of Latin American history. We invited them to think about whether these theories were useful, how they could adjust to Latin American reality, and what Latin American variants might look like.[21] The following chapters are the products of this collaboration.

More than one observer has noted the absent parties to our enterprise. Perhaps the most obvious are Marx and Weber. Early on in the project we decided to discourage contributors from writing on the "founding fathers" for two main reasons. First, we found that the central insights of these two men already played a major role in Latin American studies. Moreover, many of the later generation of theorists we did include continued classic themes that gave us an opportunity to return to the sources. Second, and most obviously, the breadth and scope of the relevant works would require at the very least one entire volume for each author.

Our choice of more contemporary authors was less systematic. We let the contributors choose their topics, and enough of the "usual suspects" were selected to make us hesitate to impose a research agenda on anyone. Obviously this left some holes. Perhaps the most apparent is the absence of a direct treatment of dependency theory, but here one might note the same objections as just mentioned for Marx and Weber. Other possibilities might have included Gramsci, the Frankfurt school, or (crossing various divides) Seymour Martin Lipset or Reinhard Bendix. We also might have included some of *gran pensadores* of Latin America, including, for example, Fernando Ortíz, Gilberto Freyre, José Carlos Mariátegui, or Raúl Prebisch. The selection, then, is not meant to be exhaustive. While it was not composed around an explicit theme, it no doubt reflects the biases and interests of the group of contributors who tend to favor a structuralist approach to political economy.

While we did not impose an agenda on our contributors or compose the conferences with such a schema in mind, the chapters distributed themselves quite naturally along the three classic categories of economy, polity, and society. In order to provide readers with a cognitive map of the interaction between theory and the specific cases of Latin America, we have divided the book into three parts that reflect the classic issues of social science theory: the rise of industrial capitalism, the development of the democratic states, and the diffusion of what may be called the ethos of modernity. These are also the central questions of Latin American studies. How do we explain the contradictory juxtaposition of wealth and underdevelopment on the continent? Why has governance often been so ineffective *and* authoritarian? Finally, is there something in the Iberian heritage that explains Latin America's troubled past and present?

The first part focuses on debates regarding economic processes and the best ways to understand development in a Latin American context. Adelman and Topik discuss grand theoretical accounts of the rise of the modern economy and its relationship to other social institutions. Gootenberg focuses on the analysis of late developers, and Montecinos and Markoff discuss more contemporary economic theories. If nothing else, these chapters clearly demonstrate the importance of historicizing our understanding of the economy and becoming more aware of how the distribution of power influences which social relationships are judged "natural" or productive. This part also asks us to consider how it is that some intellectual ideas become more influential than others and why some authors found a small audience on the continent.

The second part of the book explores a variety of theories that have sought to explain political behavior, specifically the development of the state and democratic rule. López-Alves compares how the different forms of warfare helped define the particular form of the Latin American state. Knight focuses on revolutionary Mexico and how notions of state autonomy and state capacity can inform and learn from this case. Domínguez considers the lost opportunity that a Huntingtonian approach might have offered Latin American studies. Finally, Valenzuela uses the Chilean case to challenge class-deterministic accounts of the rise of democracy. Once again, the importance of expanding our series of cases is made patently clear. Different relationships between states and organized violence, between private and public elites, between political interests and parties, and between conservative forces and democratic rules transform our understanding of standard categories such as war, autonomy, representation, and political order. Conversely, they offer Latin American studies new modes of framing questions of the political structures on the continent.

The contributions in the final part of this volume include treatments of a variety of themes. What are the cultural underpinnings of modernity? How to define and explain nationalism? What aspects of everyday life are most important? Centeno discusses the limitations of notions of discipline drawn from Foucault and Weber. Levine suggests how methodological and theoretical notions of "everyday life" need to be adapted to a Latin American reality but still may produce important insights. Finally, Lomnitz suggests how Latin American nationalism needs to be understood in light of the colonial legacy. The Latin American cases indicate that some of these most basic concepts are constructed around erroneous or limited assumptions. The theoretical trespassing in which these chapters engage should also encourage Latin Americanists to ask new sets of questions about their region in a comparative perspective.

NOTES

With many thanks to the contributors and referees whose comments helped improve our various drafts. We want to specially thank Deborah Kaple, Charles Tilly, and Bruce Western for forcing us to make it better. These individuals deserve the credit for what may be of value and none of the blame for the rest.

1. A search through the *Social Science Citation Index* from 1978 to 1999 located only 37 out of 3,203 articles in four major journals of sociology and political science (*American Journal of Sociology, American Sociological Review, American Political Science Review,* and *Journal of Politics*) that had an explicit reference in either the title or the abstract to Latin America or any of the individual countries. A parallel search in three Latin American studies journals (*Latin American Research Review, Journal of Latin American Studies,* and *Hispanic American Historical Review*) found only 1 article out of 727 that used the term *sociology* or *political science* in the title or abstract.

2. Obviously, combining the different experiences of countries and societies under this rubric may also produce confusion and miss critical differences. We believe, however, that enough links these cases to allow some generalization.

3. We also err in assuming that non-European means Latin America. Certainly Africa has received even less attention, and one could say the same thing for large parts of Asia. In some recent pieces, John Markoff has noted that the real division is not between regions but between the focus on "great powers" and the assumed

marginality of lesser ones. "Where and When Was Democracy Invented?" *Comparative Studies in Society and History*, 41 (1999):66–90.

4. We will be using this term as shorthand to mean the standard suspects of comparative analysis: France, Germany, Russia, and (less so) the Netherlands and Scandinavia. Obviously, within "Europe" large segments have been neglected, particularly the experience of the East but also that of the Mediterranean countries.

5. Most obviously, José Martí, Eduardo Prado, and of course, José Rodó.

6. Similar concerns apply with the use of North American and Western European models to the former socialist states. See Joan Nelson, Charles Tilly, and Lee Walker, eds., *Transforming Post-Communist Political Economies* (Washington, D.C.: National Academy Press, 1998).

7. See the series of review essays on David Landes's *The Wealth and Poverty of Nations* in the *American Historical Review* 104 (1999): 1240–57.

8. Mustafa Emirbayer, "Manifesto for a Relational Sociology," *American Journal of Sociology* 103 (1997): 287.

9. "Transitology" may be an exception, but its capacity to trespass is limited. The field was arguably founded by Guillermo O'Donnell, Philippe Schmitter, and Laurence Whitehead's four-volume *Transitions from Authoritarian Rule: Comparative Perspective and Tentative Conclusions* (Baltimore: Johns Hopkins University Press, 1987). Another exception may be gender and ethnic studies. A wonderful example of how a Latin American case can shed light on a theoretical discussion within a discipline is Peggy Lovell, "Race, Gender, and Development in Brazil," *Latin American Research Review* 29, no. 3 (1994), 7–37. For a summary of some of the work being done in gender, see Jane Jaquette, "Gender in Latin American Studies," in Peter Smith, ed., *Latin America in Comparative Perspective: New Approaches to Methods and Analysis* (Boulder, Colo.: Westview 1995), 111–34.

10. See Frank Safford, "The Problem of Political Order in Early Republican Spanish America," *Journal of Latin American Studies* 24 supplement (1992): 83–98.

11. Ironically, this may be because Latin American studies has not questioned the major "comparative" myths and has largely accepted the supposed universal patterns defined by social science.

12. Charles Tilly, *Big Structures, Large Processes, Huge Comparisons* (New York: Russell Sage, 1984), 89.

13. For a wonderful summary of recent historical scholarship, see Thomas Skidmore, "Studying the History of Latin America," *Latin American Research Review* 33, no. 1 (1998): 105–27.

14. Richard Morse, "The Heritage of Latin America," in Louis Hartz, ed., *The Founding of New Societies: Studies in the History of the United States, Latin America, South Africa, Canada, and Australia* (New York, Harcourt Brace Jovanovich, 1964).

15. John J. Johnson, *Political Change in Latin America: The Emergence of the Middle Sectors* (Stanford, Calif.: Stanford University Press, 1958).

16. E. Bradford Burns, *The Poverty of Progress: Latin America in the Nineteenth Century* (Berkeley: University of California Press, 1980).

17. Models do exist for such work. The quincentenary supplement published by the *Journal of Latin American Studies* in 1992 includes several excellent essays that successfully compare individual cases to grand themes and processes.

18. For a good example of the kind of debate this engenders, see *Hispanic American Historical Review* 79, no. 2 (May 1999).

19. Barbara Geddes, "Uses and Limitations of Rational Choice," in Smith, *Latin America in Comparative Perspective*.

20. Obviously some institutions (i.e., slavery and the church) have received much more attention.

21. We organized a series of panels on these themes for the Latin American Studies Association Congress held in Guadalajara in April 1997. The participants were then asked to reflect on what they had heard and written and were asked to prepare new drafts for a second meeting in Princeton in February 1998. These chapters represent a third round of collaborative thinking and tinkering.

PART I

CREATING AN ECONOMY

Chapter One

INSTITUTIONS, PROPERTY, AND ECONOMIC DEVELOPMENT IN LATIN AMERICA

JEREMY ADELMAN

GENERATIONS of social scientists and historians have tackled the role of institutions in Latin America's economic and political fortunes. But Latin Americanists have posed their institutional questions in particular ways. In other American societies, scholars frequently ask how social arrangements emerged and shaped the ground rules for subsequent developments, like the Industrial Revolution, the exhaustion of open access resources (like fisheries or timber), or even the outcome of wars or revolutions. In these accounts, institutional rearrangements propelled societies forward, usually implying a break with past practices and generating new theories of social life.

Latin America, however, has conventionally presented something of a quandary. Queries about the long-term effects of institutions almost always provided cover for concerns with "What went wrong?" or "Why did modernizing experiments fail?" or "Why did reforms implode?" These are questions about what did not happen, and they usually indict the institutional arrangements under study. For scholars of Latin America, their subject provided ample evidence of deviation from, and failure to live up to, a norm of change and progress. Latin America thus exemplifies the persistence of some obstacle or hindrance, the inability to adapt or modernize, or compulsive failure, especially when contrasted with other areas of the Atlantic world. In effect, efforts to narrate and explain the Latin American past have carried around a lot of hidden assumptions about the institutions they examine.

This, of course, is a somewhat simplified and overly stylized account of institutional approaches to Latin American life. But it does capture a collective mood or shared point of departure for many scholars of Latin America, and especially for non–Latin Americanists looking at the region for comparative historical lessons, as the recent work of David Landes or Stanley Engerman and Kenneth Sokoloff shows. Indeed, a recent collection of fine essays on Latin American economic history is entitled *How Latin America Fell Behind*, which of course presumes that it did. But compared with what? Brazil, as a recent work points out, had the fastest growing economy in the twentieth century.[1] This chapter, without rejecting the concern to explain failed policies, experiments, and reforms, seeks to rescue institutional stories about the Latin American past from the automatic association with nonevents or processes that did not transpire. It will try to show that institutions are not mere fetters or obstacles. But in order to show how institutions shape development, historians and social scientists need to know more about why and how institutions came into being in the first place. This chapter will argue that institutions may provide proximate explanations for economic advance or retardation. As such, they are important, but they are not ultimate causes for development or retardation. These lie in the social, political, and cultural fabrics in which institutions are embedded.

When I refer to institutions I mean collective arrangements, inspired by state policy or social initiative, to define legitimate rights and claims in society over valuable resources (cultural and material). They shape the means and method for actors' (be they individuals, families, or communities) vindications. They can be formal, even written, practices. They can also be informal, inscribed in social habits and customs. Institutions are nonneutral: they shape behavior and structure personal incentives, and in so doing predispose collective action to particular outcomes, some bad, some better.

INSTITUTIONAL LEGACIES

Where did the negative view of Latin American institutions come from? In Latin America, the disappointment with capitalist development and liberal constitutionalism led many to castigate inherited institutional structures that created malign incentives and cultures, inhibiting the "right" kind of personality for liberalism and capitalism. What made Latin America unique—as the dominant account went—was a set of institutional heritages deeply embedded in the fabric of the region's past, especially colonialism. These colonial and postcolonial structures proved resistant to human efforts to change.[2] Thus, from the start, institutionalism was associated with deep historical structures of colonialism and dependency.

The baggage of institutionalism is itself a historical by-product. In Latin America, the most common institutional formulation emerged almost on the heels of Spanish and Portuguese conquest. By subjecting new territories to the blend of autocratic absolutism, Catholic obscurantism, and preference for moneymaking through forced labor, Iberians conjured a society of downtrodden, mystical, and status-seeking people who, only having recognized the possibility of a better life, tended to rebellion. This was the Black Legend—a fabrication of sixteenth-century Elizabethan mythologizers aiming to debunk Spanish claims to sovereignty in the New World (and the wealth that flowed therefrom), which has survived the test of time and empirical verification with astounding agility. From this original founding process, Latin America has been locked into an ingrained pattern of backwardness rooted in the region's collective psychology and reproduced in public institutions and private preferences.[3]

If in the twentieth century historians like Woodrow Borah and Eugene Bolton poked away at this stubborn myth, much of it survived scrutiny. Both these scholars found a much more benign Spanish legacy. Bolton saw Spanish missionizing as a much less brutal form of inducting indigenous peoples into the Atlantic commercial and political world than the Anglo-American system of outright dispossession and exclusion. Borah's examination of the doctrines of conquest disclosed a nagging humanism and doubts about the ethics of empire—blowing holes in the conviction that Spaniards stepped onto New World soils with nothing but greedy ends and bloodthirsty means.[4] These scholars opened up new terrain for research and paved the way for a growing scholarship that dissented from Black Legending.

We now, it is safe to say, share much more nuanced views of the colonial enterprise. But when cast on a broader comparative plane, the Iberian institutional legacy still comes in for abuse and is held up as the main obstacle to development. For just as scholars—especially historians—started to reject the demonizing of the Iberian presence in the New World, two postwar turns reinforced Black Legending. The first came from modernization theory, which found in the English colonies the making of a decentralized polity resting on notions of popular sovereignty, while the Iberians trapped their colonies in centralized absolutism. When independence came along, the former easily embraced democratizing liberalism. Iberian America, on the other hand, cascaded into civil war and caudillismo. The bequest was personalism, status seeking, and rentier mentalities south of the Rio Grande, and not even robust export-led growth later in the nineteenth century could break the institutional trap. The problem, for many modernization theorists, was that Latin America inherited the *wrong* institutions, and when enlightened postcolonial statesmen sought to dismantle the fetters, they were more successful at breaking down remnants of the past than building foundations for the future. The result: weak or "capturable" public institutions, charismatic personalism, and a pliant rather than sturdy rule of law.[5]

Then, along came dependency and a functionalist brand of Marxism. By the 1960s, many historians and social scientists argued not so much that Latin America was trapped in a premodern mold, but that the institutions of rulership were unwashed instruments of class domination to preserve a certain kind of modernity. If the Left appeared to dissent from modernizationist nostrums, it added more layers of crust to the notion of deep institutional obstacles to development. Now, in this economistic turn, what went wrong was that Spain and Portugal introduced Indian and African peoples to a commercial system designed to produce for European markets at the cost of their immiserization. To keep these oppressed people in line, rulers devised authoritarian governments—regimes that enjoyed an extended life span into the twentieth century (it was not for nothing that dependency and Marxism enjoyed their vogue as Latin America took a sad praetorian turn in the 1960s and 1970s). An export economy from the sixteenth century, Latin America never hosted the emergence of its own industrial bourgeoisie because planters, miners, and plutocrats found monopoly ground rents a more lucrative mainstay for enrichment than risk-taking industrial enterprise. The language of class and global exploitation only reinforced the dominant time line of continuous institutional fetters on balanced and equitable growth.[6]

By the 1970s, accounts of Latin American development portrayed institutions as either fetters on progress or the tools of a small group of sclerotic elites. In 1966, Claudio Véliz edited *The Obstacles to Development in Latin America* just as "development studies" was emerging as a major intellectual enterprise in North American universities. Institutions were unproblematically negative. Is there an alternative approach, free from some of the pitfalls of deep-structural accounts? How can such an approach avoid presuming static, timeless characterizations of a continent overpopulated with the wrong cultural or economic predispositions for capitalism and democracy?

PROPERTY RIGHTS IN THEORY AND HISTORY

Recent work in the social sciences offers some ways to overcome the presumption of malign institutional legacies of colonialism. The property rights approach—pioneered by economists, economic historians, and more recently political scientists—presents a more elastic and more agency-attentive set of tools. There are problems—many and important ones—which I will tackle in due course, but attention to the historical-political economy of institutions, and especially the institutions governing property rights, is one way out of such a fatalistic set of narratives.

Political economists in particular have refined their understanding of institutions, paring their role to the definition and enforcement of property rights (rights of actors to exchange or use valuable assets). This recent approach was not just a response to an old Latin American heritage of asking "what went wrong" but a reaction to models forged in the North Atlantic context, which underappreciated the role of institutions altogether. Mainstream economic analysis, neoclassical economics, simply failed to capture the complexity and constraints facing economies in the throes of sweeping change. Two Nobel Prizes—to R. H. Coase and to D. C. North—helped usher in a more systematic research agenda for the study of property rights, transaction costs, and information lapses in long-term development.[7]

The work of Douglass North and what may be described broadly as the "property rights approach" may help us, with some important qualifications, to understand the problem of institutional legacies. Let me start with a synopsis of the main ingredients of this approach. In perhaps his best-known book, *Structure and Change in Economic History*, North spells out what he is reacting against: a conventional neoclassical view that treated market exchanges as frictionless operations without information costs, under conditions of complete certainty, and bearing no burdens of enforcement of the terms of exchange. The result was: (1) a tendency to presume that social and private rates of return converge (because incentives allow individuals to capture returns flowing from social investments, which compels individuals to shoulder the costs of public goods); and (2) that, over time, individuals' choices yield desired results (because decisions leading to unwanted outcomes will be reversed and better choices selected). Neoclassical thinkers were right to stress the benefits from trading and the division of labor, but they naively neglected the costs of trading. These costs, as Coase argued, could be positive and shape decision making in decisive ways. Self-interest is fine as an engine of growth, but just because everyone acts self-interestedly does not necessarily mean that a world of fluid, frictionless bargaining will emerge.[8]

This is where rules come in. Those who feel they have lost out in bargaining have incentives to free ride. Information frequently is opaque or incomplete, and seldom costless. Sometimes parties violate the terms of contracts, especially when they feel that sanctions are weak. Other times, people disagree about the meanings of the letter of contracts. Consequently, in the real world, transacting is often expensive and the results uncertain. Institutions arise as mechanisms to reduce transaction costs. These can be formal or informal, can involve cultural norms or codified statute, and can generate rules that people agree to respect, and in instances of violation imply sanctions. Rules and discipline enhance the opportunity cost of disrespect. And when people play by the same rules, they can bargain more easily, trade more, specialize and realize the promise of market diversification. Institutional rules compensate for the frictions latent to market societies and enable private contracting to occur where it otherwise would lag. They create mechanisms to resolve collective dilemmas and resolve them in contractual forms.[9]

The business of encoding legal systems to cope with transaction costs leads to a second step in North's work: creating macropolitical conditions to stabilize and ensure the rights which people have over possessions so that they may trade them at all. We can call this bundle of claims to possessions *property rights*. They span an entire spectrum, from open-access common property to exclusive freeholds. Each tends to generate particular social dynamics and conflicts. Common property often leads to resource exhaustion: no one has incentives to curb extractive appetites because others will move in and plunder the resource. When people crowd into open spaces, scarcity eventually sets it, prices rise, and people start facing incentives to mark out plots. This, more or less, accounts for the enclosure of hitherto common property.[10] Where this did not occur, as in fishing banks (like the Cheseapeake's oyster supply) or grazing grounds (like sheepherding in the Valley of Mexico), resources were exhausted. Exclusive domain, on the other hand, requires enforcement against intruders or contractual noncompliers—and this requires public authorities to levy sanctions. Modern states arise. In general, however, holding property rights enables people to trade (transact) rights rather than fight over them. In Montesquieu's image of *doux commerce*, trading bridles greedy passions, inducing people to play by a set of rules and to recognize a political sovereign who promises to uphold these rules.[11]

Definition and enforcement of property can beget wealth. Security creates the conditions for people to apply their labors, reap rewards, invest part of their earnings in more property, and so forth. Wealth then begets more property, and the virtuous cycle is on.[12] Insecurity, of course, does the opposite and can cripple the symbiotic relationship between ownership, transacting, and investing. And at its worst, weak proprietary institutions can foster pathological (but rational) behavior: free riding on the work and risk taking of others, rent seeking through cronyism. This type of mien reverses the system (and is, indeed, the prevailing account for why a resource-rich country like Argentina imploded into negative growth and intercorporate civil warring).[13]

Some historians may not greet this "property rights approach" very happily. If social scientists have been retooling, so have historians, though not in ways that foster cross-disciplinary exchange with developments in the social sciences. It may be that Alan Knight's claim in this volume is correct: that as a group, historians are congenital splitters and averse to big generalizing claims. Certainly, historians have found it increasingly uncomfortable to uphold master narratives of the past, especially as the dependency approach fell on hard times. If archives predispose analysis to complication and contingency, the recent turn to micro-history reinforces the aversion to master theories. Historians—to a very large extent—harbor justified skepticism at some of the nomothetic impli-cations of the social scientific drift, which starts with general causal claims and organizes inquiry around them. Social scientists want to ex-plain the past; historians want to interpret it.[14] This may be a healthy tension with which we should live, each side opportunistically relying on the other at best, misrepresenting each other at worst. Many social scien-tists see what historians produce as simply underanalyzed data; histori-ans see formal model builders as violators of historical complexity. The problem, of course, is that each needs the other. Besides, social scientists are themselves producers of "data," and historians seldom are the atheo-retical empiricists often imputed by social scientists.[15]

But historians' aversion to institutional explanations is more than just an unreflective idiographic bias, especially when it comes to thinking about economic matters. There is more going on than recalcitrance to apply or to test formal or informal causation. Many historians have abandoned the study of institutions altogether in favor of more "sub-ject"-centered and "agent"-centered stories because, often rightly, they saw in grand theory a juggernaut riding roughshod over people's efforts to create alternative institutional environments.

Part of many historians' dismay stems from a turn, starting in the 1960s, away from common claims that outcomes of historic processes are what required explanation. Starting in the 1960s, many historians began to question the verities of deep-structural explanations, in part out of a concern to retrieve lost or forgotten worlds. This had a great deal to do with shifting intellectual styles and a disenchantment with structural sto-ries. Social historians in particular explored how popular folk, workers, slaves—marginal sectors—often sheltered their own designs for public and private life. Even if these aspirations did not appear victorious at the end of the sequence, it did not mean they were unworthy of study. These routes-not-taken often got lost in dominant narratives of what triumphed and not what was lost. The governing matrix succeeded only at the cost of more or less suppression of alternative visions for the world. There-fore, structural explanations of outcomes were not in fact explanations at all because they could not account for how at each conjuncture, compet-ing designs clashed, with one coming out on top. Proving an outcome that observers know in advance, and thus testing a theory's predictive powers, is not itself an account of its history.

More recently, cultural historians have pushed this concern to recover alternative meanings of the past one step (or maybe even several steps) further, to try to unpack the symbolic universes of human life. Other authors in this book explore this theme more explicitly; suffice it to say that historians frequently preferred close hermeneutic analysis and narratives that more effectively captured the multiple meanings and richness of past lives. In effect, historians' aversion to structuralism animated a marked turn away from institutions altogether because institutional studies were so closely associated with timeless, dominating frames of public and private lives. Out went structuralism, and with it institutional studies. Then, when social and cultural history shook the historical imagination in the 1970s and 1980s, institutions either were ignored altogether or were set up as the aparatuses of domination or "hegemony." By then, structures were equated with institutions. All of this simply reinforced the received image of institutions-as-structures: immutable, exogenous constraints on people's lives. In Latin America, this turn away from institutional studies was even more marked, in part because it was such a dominant framing system for historiography until the 1970s, but also because such renditions had so clearly effaced histories of contestation, resistance, and some pretty creative rule breaking and rule bending.[16]

Paradoxically, while institutions recede further into the analytic background, the burden placed on them to explain Latin American malaise has, if anything, grown. So much scholarship has debunked the myths of backwardness and static institutional development that little remains of Queen Elizabeth I's historiographical progeny. Few subjects elicit more yawns than constitutional and legal history. Yet, with our neglect of the ways in which arrangements among classes, ethnic groups, and genders became encoded into a series of formal and informal rules, the appreciation of how these rules shaped subsequent bargains got lost. What, after all, were peasants, slaves, and other folk resisting, if not bequested limits on their agency? We may have purged the Black Legend from the historiographical imagination, but we have not fundamentally risen to its challenge: to offer an alternative account or approach to the long-term effects of institutional fabrics. Institutions need to be brought "back in" to the Latin American picture. On the whole, historians have given this field of inquiry (despite their frequent reliance on implied institutional explanations) a wide berth. Their distaste for Black Legending is understandable, but the Black Legend may not be the only grid for studying institutional life.

Thus, whereas social scientists examined an institutional environment's effects, they took the matrix for granted; they could not explain how institutions came into being or changed over time. Historians, meanwhile, struggled to destabilize the matrix, to show contestation and active or passive resistance to rules. How, in effect, can we return to a historical study of rule making and institutional life (looking, thereby, at structures that shape the world) without presuming that such structures are immutable, inelastic constraints on agents?

What follows is an exploration of one potential route back to a common concern for institutional roles in political and economic development. Focusing on nineteenth-century Latin America, this chapter is attuned as much to the historian as to the social scientist. This is not to suggest that the tensions between nomothetic and idiographic approaches can—or should—be bridged with casual eclecticism. There are some important and real points of disagreement. But social scientists need to be aware (as they once were) of the complicated heritages that informed the institutional milieus they study, and historians must be much more attentive to some of their causal inferences, which are all too often ad hoc and random.

PROPERTY RIGHTS IN LATIN AMERICA

What does the property rights approach offer to Latin Americanists? First is emphasizes on the political conditions of market activity. This was always something of a problem for students of Latin America who found political concerns so divorced from conventional neoclassical approaches. For the latter, "free markets" meant releasing signaling devices—the fancy contemporary term for prices—from state tampering. This was, it is worth saying, both a Hayekian dream and a Marxian telos (recalling that Marx considered capitalism a regime where property rights could reproduce themselves without state girders). What the property rights approach emphasizes is how political choices shape governing rules and the conflicts within these rules. Bargaining, no matter how materially oriented, by definition is a public proposition shaped by ground rules.

For Latin Americanists, these kinds of struggles have a manifestly political character. The regime type (absolutist, patrimonial, caudillo, populist, or authoritarian—the variations are almost innumerable) was always considered central to understanding social and economic welfare. So how does the property rights approach link regime types with social welfare? Consider Stephen Haber's study of capital markets in late nineteenth-century Brazil and Mexico. Haber found that the overthrow of the empire in Brazil in 1889 shattered a highly repressive regulatory regime: new republican rules compelled publicly held joint-stock companies to publish balance sheets and shareholder lists. With this, a financial press emerged to publicize market activity. This new transparency—compelled by public rules—opened market activity in savings and investment to newcomers. In Mexico, the legal regime of the Porfiriato (1876–1911) did not create a more liberal environment: information costs remained high because corporations did not face pressure to disclose dealings, even if they occurred in the Mexican money market. If this helped reinforce kinship-based ownership structure, the result was a smaller and more concentrated banking sector in Mexico and thus a more constrained flow of finance to industrialists. By comparison, Brazil started to look rather more like the United States.[17] Here is a good example of how attention to the legal foundations of statehood shaped the structure of incentives for private agents, how macro rules shaped micro behavior. The property rights approach need not imply a deep fissure between political foundations and market activities. Moreover, as Haber has shown, rules did change, and some of this change actually promoted more sustainable economic activity.

Second, the approach rescues the much-forgotten constitutional-legal historiography from its formalist habits. In focusing on the design of public rules, legal scholarship often obscured the effects that may not align with drafters' imagination. In effect, a long-standing tradition of Latin American legal history wrote the story of statute making, and ended the narrative there, with legal promulgation. It was simply assumed that laws functioned as intended and that the intentions of drafters were unambiguous. This may, it is worth saying, reflect the personality of the civil law tradition, which explicitly sought to reduce judicial discretion through exhaustive, objective rules. From Napoleon onward, statute (and not the messy world of common law) was meant to give rationality and clarity to the legal world. Agents were supposed to abide by such crystalline rules. Bentham was especially keen on this promise and fulminated over Blackstone's *Commentaries*. Nineteenth-century constitutionalists like Andrés Bello and Juan Bautista Alberdi shared some aspects of this view. And the legal historiography ever since often wrote the history of legal practice from the statute outward, as it were. For many early legal (and even "national") histories told the story about the eventual triumph of this or that constitution as the founding document for the nation or republic. Codes and constitutional charters were supposed to boast intrinsic and unchanging features. What mattered was the de jure and less the de facto practice of legal affairs.

Yet, the line between a legal author, statute, and people's understanding of legally permissible and forbidden acts is seldom straight. The property rights approach, by tackling the effects of rules on transaction costs, looks at the de facto history of law, not its de jure inscription. Property rights approaches examine the winners and losers and the ways in which bargaining over and within rules can alter the framers' plans. Indeed, many have remarked that what characterizes Latin American legal traditions is the deep divide between statute and practice, rhetoric and reality. For all the rules and lofty legal declarations, few respect and abide by such strictures. This does not mean that statute and rhetoric are immaterial; they simply do not suffice to account for the long-term effects of institutional life.

The gulf between de jure and de facto approaches to Latin American institutions appears in the long, complicated history of legal systems governing land use and distribution. Despite the aspirations of nineteenth-century liberal reformers, who dreamed of populating Latin American landscapes with Jeffersonian-type farmers, land, a critical asset shaping modern Latin American capitalism, wound up in the hands of largeholders. One long historical tradition simply argued that the nineteenth-century land laws gave land to a few feudal barons because a few feudal barons dominated the writing of land law. Landowners would rather satisfy their aristocratic pretensions than see public patrimony allocated to market-producing yeomanry. States simply fell capture to emerging rural oligarchies. Authors of major land law, from Benito Juárez in Mexico to Nicolás Avellaneda or Domingo Faustino Sarmiento in Argentina, promulgated laws that on the surface looked like emulations of North American homesteading, but in substance seemed to yield to a more dichotomous structure of landholding.[18]

Depicting reformers as dupes or cynics is one easy way to reconcile the gulf between the legal frame and the proprietary fact, but it flies in the face of too much evidence. To start with, before the end of the nineteenth century, large landowners were much weaker than supposed, and often too weak to unilaterally shape public policy. Indeed, it was only their bounty from new export growth after 1880 that enriched them and elevated them to a puissant elite. But to project their fin de siècle power backward to midcentury, when many of the land laws were inscribed, is simply ahistorical. The only significant exception to this pattern of gradually strengthening rural elites during the century was the slave owners, but even here, their strength has been exaggerated. Louis Pérez has described the congenital problem of the old Cuban sugar growers prior to major United States investment in the 1880s. Brazilian historians have shown that it was the selfsame planter class that backed homesteading laws to attract European settlers once slave prices began to soar in the 1850s. Hebe Maria Mattos de Castro has argued for many years that the arrangement of property rights in Brazilian slave society made way for a large stratum of freed black smallholders in the interstices of an otherwise plantation-dominated society. Michael Jiménez has shown how, even in Cundinamarca Colombia (a traditional estate region), landowners struggled to adapt to, rather than adapting, product and labor markets.[19] Furthermore, evidence is starting to mount to show that landholding patterns in areas of agrarian settlement were hardly equitable, but they were not as dichotomous as inferred by talk of a Latin American Junker class in the making. Across Latin America, small and medium-sized producers prolif-

erated. It is increasingly clear that liberal land laws of the nineteenth century—for so long seen as the crucible for emerging modern societies of the
Americas—cannot be simply dismissed as failed efforts to break with the
old colonial heritage of encomiendas and haciendas.

Still, homesteading seldom became the pattern, despite legislative intent. So how does a focus on property rights institutions reconcile the
divergence of legal intent from legal outcome if we cannot presume that
the allocation of rights was the handiwork of those who already possessed them? Part of the task requires an understanding of the difficulties
of translating goals into realities when institutional factors other than
land law affect the disbursement of land. Consider the effects of institutions governing the allocation of other factors: capital and labor. It turns
out that the institutional foundations of the land market made land supply more elastic than the girders of labor and especially capital markets.
In the nineteenth century, labor and capital scarcity was the rule, and
enormous difficulty in enlisting workers or investment, even when the
returns were high, was the pattern. This meant that landowners had to
rely on a panoply of coercive tactics to recruit labor, the infamous *engan-
che* system in Peru, debt peonage from Japan in Brazil, and encroaching
on peasant subsistence bases in Mexico.[20] Eroding the subsistence base of
former (or fugitive) slaves, eliminating village subsistence in indigenous
communities, and depriving foreign migrants of access to small plots
helped ensure (though it did not always guarantee) a less autonomous
laboring population and therefore compelled workers to seek wage
sources of sustenance. Accordingly, it was the fact that nineteenth-century workers enjoyed property rights in land, and thus withheld rights to
their labor from employers, that induced landowners to expand their possessions. Claiming large extensions of abundant land was a way of competing for scarce labor.

The operation of capital markets reinforced this propensity for property rights in land to accrue unevenly. The market for mortgages and
other long-term instruments for credit were notoriously shallow. Political
instability and fiscal indebtedness fueled a market for lucrative but risky
public bonds, elbowing out private borrowers who could not afford to
pay the higher interest on loans. Moreover, statutes of incorporation
hobbled private financial institutions and prevented firms from constitut-
ing joint-stock operations. Local private banks often operated under very
repressive conditions; local stock markets were inhospitable venues for
floating stocks.[21] Thus, the legal and institutional regimes girding capital
markets choked long-term capital flows to private borrowers. Instead,
capital flowed through informal channels, and merchant capital became
an important financial agent. Personal relations between merchants and
planters helped large landowners gain access to a money market. Often,

marriage between urban merchant families and rural landed ones created kin ties, and thus channels for the flow of investible funds. Other times, merchant families bought into the land market as a means to diversify asset portfolios and managed such operations as fictive or real extended patriarchal units. Either way, personal connections, family relations, and informal networks made up for the lack of public information.[22] And this system worked to the decided advantage of those with larger holdings—though it should be said that chocking up debts to merchants could also inspire the wrath of landowners against their creditors. So, as technological change intensified as the century wore on, and as the cost of land and labor also rose, possessors of larger expanses enjoyed better access to capital markets and therefore could meet the challenge of export competitiveness. Capital markets reinforced unequal distribution of rural property rights. Indeed, for many Latin American estate owners, it was extensive property rights in land that enabled them to gain access to labor and capital at all. The inelasticity of capital and labor markets undermined the prospects for a more homesteader-friendly pattern of rural development.

So, two implications flow from the property rights approach. First, the possessors of property rights cannot be treated as possessors before these rights even exist. This means that historians and social scientists who want to account for the rise of a landed class have to contend with a much messier exchange between formal rule making and enforcement, and the construction of certain interests around these rules. Second, interests in one domain such as land cannot be isolated from other domains. Thus, in handling the issue of transaction costs in decisions to trade or produce, the property rights approach presents a more comprehensive understanding of the rationality of agents—embedded as they so often are in a multiple, and not always reinforcing, set of economic relationships.

This excursion into the matter of land distribution shows why de jure approaches (or what I have called, for lack of a better term, formalistic accounts) to institutional development and practice can miss many of the real effects of laws and rules. For all Latin American efforts to colonize frontiers, often borrowing straight from United States settlement patterns, liberal laws provided the juridical bases for quite different proprietary regimes. This excursion also shows how interlocked property rights are—in this case between land, labor, and capital.

The property rights approach does one more thing: it enables historians and social scientists to treat the rationality of actors more delicately than dismissing them as either premodern feudal folk (as in the case of the peasant who, allegedly, spurns private landownership in favor of communal possession) or all-powerful oligarchs stomping around the Latin American countryside. While oligarchs may have consolidated and peasants remained hemmed into village holdings, the property rights approach does not presume that the outcome was rooted in nonrational psyches even before the process of capitalist development. The approach does not presume a naturalized condition of Latin American actors even before their histories began—it shifts the attention to the micro level of economic and social activity to explore how agents behave under constraints and in relationship to other agents. What I have been saying thus far implies that agents not be depicted as any less rational or purposive (by which I mean that agents align means to ends with a minimum of friction between both) just because the outcome seemed less than desirable.

Let us revisit the land question once more. By century's end, the hue and cry about the maldistribution of land and the immiserization of rural folk was heard across Latin America. And the critics were often right: landownership patterns did not tend to favor the small and medium-sized holder. In their invective, however, critics found it convenient to stylize their detractors as greedy aristocratic pretenders, who were uninterested—so the critique went—in sustained capitalism, technical change, and a robust domestic market. Landowners were treated as irrational status seekers and not rational utility maximizers. And while it may be true that uneven distribution of land eventually strangled technical change and bifurcated concerns of domestic production from domestic consumption, landowners did not necessarily intend things that way. In effect, an unfortunate outcome need not be treated as the result of defective rationality on the part of asset holders. Where land was an abundant asset and capital and labor short, extensive production systems made sense (by maximizing the productivity of labor and especially capital). And ownership in large tracts enabled owners to diversify production within the estate, forestalling declining yields by making crop rotation easier and handling world price changes by shifting land uses to the more lucrative product. Smallholders enjoyed no such economies of scale. This was certainly the case in nineteenth-century Argentina, the country with the best chance of realizing the homestead model and the one that faced the greatest obstacles to sustaining growth. Abundant land, ease of export of cattle and later sheep by-products, and popular gaucho preferences to maintain their autonomy and thus their reluctance to enter into long-term contractual relations with owners (by leases) or the state (by settlement) meant that open frontier land was cheap and appropriable by a small group. In turn, estate owners mixed their land use and enjoyed a higher yield on capital investments than their competitors in North America. Rising ground rents then enriched this landed circle.[23] All this means not that *estancieros* (landowners) were less rational than homesteaders but that their rationality differed because incentives and rewards differed.

The property rights approach shifts attention to the rationality of agents, rather than presuming that there is only one form of behavior that is rational. And while the collective outcome may be disappointing—even irrational—it was the unintended consequence of aggregated individual rational choices. Thus, a deep paradox of Latin America's nineteenth century may have been that open markets and privatized property created rather than dismantled regional oligarchies whose own economic activities to maximize their wealth bequeathed fetters on twentieth-century industrialization.[24]

All this adds up to a major challenge to the Black Legend tradition that presumed an overwhelmingly malign influence on Latin American public life. The property rights approach sees legal rules and norms as enabling as well as disabling.[25] It has been possible to explore, as some have, how proprietary arrangements yielded positive wealth-enhancing effects; under some circumstances, they can even align wealth-enhancing with democratic aspirations.[26] These are not necessarily incompatible. Yet, while this tool set is quickly occupying pride of place in the social scientific battery, we should be attentive to some important problems. For Latin Americanists in particular, there are hidden pitfalls.

THE PITFALL OF POLITICS

Rule making is fundamentally a political process. And while the property rights approach calls attention to the ways that rules shape behavior (through incentives and transaction costs), the approach is less helpful at understanding the reverse process. How are rules themselves created, interpreted, and enforced? According to the property rights approach, the state's primary role is to defend the proprietary institutions that contribute to social and personal wealth and to dismantle those that do the opposite.[27] This is certainly the doctrine that informs current constitutional approaches to "transitional" societies and the drive to dismantle populist regulatory regimes. Indeed, a recent survey in the *Economist* validated this view. The magazine's editors correlated the security of property rights with wealth and found that the greater the former, the higher the latter.[28] This of course begs the question: If institutions strangle economies, how do they survive? Even more vexing, how did they get there in the first place?

The approach is unhelpful because it presumes that rule makers make rules to beget wealth. Such a functional account narrows the spectrum of what may be considered "rights." Should we give *property* rights a keystone—as Carol Rose has queried—status to trump all other rights? Should constitutions be parsed to serve economic wealth-enhancing purposes and not other roles?[29] What about aspects of public life that are not reducible to material transactions? While these are normative issues raised by the property rights approach for current policy, they also speak to historical problems of how regimes themselves are formed. Rules may operate functionally to help agents realize goals. But this need not imply that regimes operate the same way. Nor need this infer that regimes emerge *as* systems to reinforce agents' disaggregated material aspirations. In Latin America (and elsewhere), the histories of state and regime formation are not easily reduced to a functional explanation.

Ideology and other principles of collective life intrude. The construction of public authority, never a seamless process in even the most whiggish of historiographical settings, was fraught with tension in Latin America. Warring over ecclesiastical sovereignty, fighting over the balance of central or local authority, or conflict over loyalty to rival rulers condemned emerging republics and imperial Brazil to a century of institutional instability and constitutional discord. Much of the conflict was conducted over terms that had little to do with wealth-enhancing strategies. Indeed, what is remarkable is just how much consensus there was over trade policy, the privatization of land, and—at least among the white elites—the allocation of rights over slaves.[30] And, in the case of abolition, once slave prices began to rise and the specter of self-emancipation on the part of slaves began to loom, slave owners started experimenting with alternatives. This does not discount the role of slaves in the transformation of slavery, but it does imply that public debates involved much more than discussion of rules to maximize rents. Thus any account of public institution formation will have a hard time presuming that conflict rages over how best to use rules to allocate and enforce property rights. Indeed, it is more likely that rights were allocated and enforced depending on the outcome of struggles over contending visions for the political community.

From at least the late eighteenth century, social forces have pursued profoundly different projects of the political community—the components of which are not easily reducible to squabbles over state powers to determine private rights. A whole range of ethical and cultural issues shaped imaginings of political affairs, as Claudio Lomnitz shows in his chapter in this volume. Latin American constitutional debates were the occasion for wrestling between conservatives (organic, Catholic, and hierarchical sentiments), liberals (more individualist advocates, believing in persuasive powers of reason and the potential for laws to guide local societies from their "unfortunate" habits), and radicals (usually federalists, often calling for decentralized regimes with local autonomy, and appealing to more plebeian sectors). In such a context, rules governing property rights are *derivative*, that is, the consequence of conflicts that are not themselves solely reducible to disagreement over these rights. As one recent study of Mexico shows, nineteenth-century instability (and the loss of a great deal of territory) had deeply ideational and social origins—and was not a mere contest of access to the spoils of public office. Even in Argentina, where conservativism was such a weak political force, a half century of civil turmoil engulfed the country over the principles of statehood.[31] This is an important concern because the civil strife, especially during the long nineteenth-century process of encoding rules, was so deep and bitter that the animosities cannot be explained by referring to individual interests. Not least: the costs of civil war were so high that even the winners, as John Coatsworth has shown in the case of Mexico, were losers.[32] In this context, why fight at all if making concessions could reap high dividends?

Moreover, ideology and concepts of public right and wrong must be understood as a contest over defining membership in the political community. Much of the conflict across the region involved a struggle over inclusive versus exclusive forms of governing—and, as a rule, the latter prevailed over the former. Until the 1850s, the contest yielded no clear winner, with armies of peasants fighting for regional sovereignty within a liberal constitutional carapace in Mexico, and with ample room for public electoral participation irrespective of property or color distinctions in Brazil.[33] Beginning at midcentury, state builders began inching back on the suffrage proclamations of the early days of independence, when the revolutionary rhetoric of inclusion was in full flight. Notions of what it took to belong inside the political community began to harden. Ethnicity and race became sharper markers of political entitlement; the roguish habits of the caudillos were increasingly treated with disdain, unfit for the emerging customs and manners of republican discourse. A less capacious spirit of liberalism eventually animated the "reformist" generation of the 1850s and 1860s. Stabilized regimes also became more exclusive ones. For their part, the excluded recognized and contested such regimes when and where they could, but consolidation of state power narrowed these possibilities over time. In other words, building the public institutions of government was a nonneutral proposition about whose voice would be represented in government.

Why make so much of this business about political context and milieu? What is remarkable about the nineteenth century in Latin America is just how much political life was about contested meanings of public life. What is more, civil unrest, warfare, and the sheer economic cost suggest that making public institutions to govern private property rights cannot presume that it was the stakes in private rights that motivated the discussion over institutions and the fighting over the constitutions that would back them. If ever there was a consequential tail wagging the causal dog, it is here. Parsed functional accounts of institutional development fail to appreciate the autonomy of the political field and the ways in which politics creates legal universes and languages that enable new rights to emerge and adhere—even property rights.

Politics matters in accounting for change. And politics is more than about rule making; it is about state and regime formation, which then shape the possibility for certain rules while excluding others. If constitutions are precommitment devices to compel political actors to play by certain norms as they inscribe specific rules, writing and revising them was—and is—a process that causally precedes the definition and enforcement of rights. This means the following: the analysis of the role of institutions (what the property rights approach emphasizes) should be disentangled from a theory of their emergence.[34] If more goes into rule making and institution formation than utilities, we have to look much more closely at the *process* and not just the outcome of change.[35] Either way, the process cannot be explained by the outcome. This, for historians at least, is something of a relief, since it points to the centrality of contingencies and unanticipated consequences in decision making and collective struggles. As any historian of nineteenth-century Latin America knows, there are simply too many twists and turns in the saga of institutional development—starting with Napoleon's invasion of the Peninsula—to skate over the complexities and indeterminacies of politics.

The first pitfall of the property rights approach reduces the story of public institutional development to a flattened, apolitical account of the emergence and conflict over the shape of the political community.

Change, Stability, and Equality

The second problem has to do with explanations of change over time. In his earlier work, North tended to suggest that rules change spontaneously in response to exogenous shifts (like demographic growth, discovery of new lands, technological breakthroughs) that alter relative factor prices. As the price of one factor tends to rise, agents respond to incentives to possess those rights and will devise new rules to stake their claims. Change tends to be cumulative and evolutionary.

Here, I think, the authors who work within the property rights approach reveal a bias derived from their cases. If most metatheorizing about macrosocial development emerges out of "core" society studies, it is clear that the property rights approach carries with it some indelible marks of an Anglo-American historiography when it comes to accounting for how things change over time. I will not query whether this is an accurate portrayal of the development of capitalism in the United States or

England, though many doubt whether evolutionary tales work even in these modular societies. But it is a general hallmark of the approach that where institutional change seemed to unfold with less friction, the approach could offer evidence for plausible cumulative stories.

Latin Americanists will find this dissatisfying. The problem is important to them because they study a region that appears so resilient to change for long periods of time. Institutions outlast their utility, they hamper progress, and then they are toppled in violent démarches. Such is the common frame for institutional change; evolutionary models clearly do not fit.[36] To explain institutional effects on social and economic life also requires an account of why institutions do not change despite rising pressure against rules and regulations.[37]

Consider two institutional bottlenecks, both derived from the effects of nineteenth-century struggles, the legacies of independence. First, Latin Americanists have long been concerned with the recurrent difficulty of using local savings to mobilize resources for domestic capital formation. As Carlos Marichal has shown in an important book, Latin America's debt crises did not erupt in the late twentieth century. They have a long prehistory, rooted in the early formation of local capital markets.[38] Not until late in the nineteenth century did private lending institutions begin to form, and even then they often were weak, commanded only a small share of national savings, and invested primarily in public securities or merchandising. Even the major exporting houses, with a few exceptions, did not turn to financial institutions to fund their enterprises. Industrialists were even more marooned. And yet the demand for funds was high. The rate of growth after 1860 required massive mobilization and infusions of capital. As a result, some niches turned to foreign sources of funds—especially in the public securities business and infrastructure (the most celebrated being the case of railways)—to make up for the institutional shortfall at home. Others relied on internal savings within households and extended kinship networks that operated as "firms," effectively using family obligations to reduce transaction costs. This was especially the case in the dynamic rural sector, where internal family savings obtained as much in peasant as in large estate agriculture. How do we account for the *continuity* of an institutional environment unconducive to local private investment when the demand for an alternative arrangement was so high? This remains a vast underexplored terrain, but it suggests that evolutionary approaches will not work.

A second example of where stasis, and not evolution, is what requires explanation is the difficulty Latin America faced when making the transition from agrarian and export-driven growth to industry-led growth. Few would disagree anymore that export-led growth was at least comprehensible during the golden age of multilateral free trade before 1929 (though it remains debatable how the model served certain sectors or classes at the expense of others). Yet there remain two interlocking concerns: Why did Latin American societies not use the proceeds of export growth to diversify around the staple base, as Australia, Canada, and even the classic formulation of Douglass North's economic history of the United States show? And why was the shift from staples to industry so disharmonious? Instead of maximizing linkages between exports and other market activities, general segregation was the rule in Latin America. Many authors have recently argued that we are not dealing with enclaves, that links did exist—but in comparative terms the rate of diversification around the staple base was slow despite the precocious activity. The costs of persistent segregation erupted when the world market for staples failed in the 1930s and Latin American economies had to make the lurching switch to service the domestic market with local manufacturing. Even then, what is remarkable about the 1930s is how long Latin American societies tried to shore up their export sectors in the face of an internationally hostile environment. By the 1940s, subsequent import-substitution industrialization frequently had to finance itself at the expense of the export sectors. The costs of this choice became painfully obvious by the 1950s.[39]

Two interrelated factors help account for these persistences. Neither can be fully understood in the functionalist property rights approach because institutions are supposed to be instrumental for maximizing the returns to asset holders; if not, they are revised and altered. The first is that public policy reinforced stasis and not change. This is usually the case; only in the late twentieth century, or in unusual developmental moments, like Meiji Japan, or in avowedly transformationist regimes have statists seen public policy as an instrument for future-oriented goals. But some public policies, and this is true for Latin America's other exporting cousins, enable or even encourage the transfer of resources to other sectors that can grow in the export interstices and then flourish when exports wane. Such policies, for the most part, did not obtain in Latin America. Policies encouraged resource allocation into a narrow band of activities. According to the property rights approach, rules define and defend property rights; they mutate when they are obsolete, yielding to optimal ones. Such an account is not, however, an explanation of how choices are made in public policy making; it is a consequentialist leap. To the extent that we know anything about public policy making in these frictional moments of political and economic change, it is that policy choices are not the smooth handmaidens of a new order. New industrial or financial regimes more often emerged in spite of, not because of, policy change.

This brings us to a factor that parallels the concern about belonging and exclusion from the political sphere. An ingredient that is missing from the property rights approach is a treatment of the effects of the distribution of property itself, conflict over unequal entitlements, and the social relations that give meaning to the rights themselves. Much of the property rights approach focuses on the clarity, definition, and enforceability of claims rather than their distribution. Yet distribution of power to lay claims comes before the actual rule making. Accordingly, coalitions form around rival claims and jostle—and sometimes battle—to encode these claims in law. In this fashion, distributional conflicts shape the evolution and change of institutions.[40] What makes Latin America so suggestive for students of long-term comparative development is the starkness of coalition formation, and how sharp the lines were and are between winners and losers. This process, without the seemingly universal and legitimated public infrastructure of other liberal societies, is highly contested and combative. If in some societies the covering laws of state experienced little fundamental challenge, Latin America's were challenged from the start. Thus, what often began as a private distributional conflict within a set of rules could mutate into a broader conflict over the pillars that supported the rules. The reverse also happened: victors ensured that rules and their pillars helped channel resources in their favor. Property, in effect, need not be purely understood as an individual claim—a right—over resources. Property also involves claims over other individuals, with more or less ability to negotiate. So, just as rules about public membership are anything but neutral, so too are private claims. It was the confluence of both that fueled the long and deep civil wars of the nineteenth century.

Property matters so much that it should not be reduced to the language of individual efforts to maximize returns but rather should be viewed as the concerns around which actors mobilize collectively to create rules that favor them or disfavor others. Individuals clearly do matter, and any explanatory approach worth its weight should, as Jon Elster has argued, narrow the gap between individual choices and social consequences. But individuals realize this process collectively and try to formalize it institutionally. And this deliberation over rule making is far from a consensual process. Latin Americanists have been making this case for generations, and this intellectual heritage is worth recalling. Furthermore, property rights derive from alignment of relational and distributional forces. Rights flow from relations, and not vice versa. This comes as no surprise to Latin Americanists, and it is a departure point for a dynamic approach to explorations of institutional effects on political and economic life.

CONCLUSIONS

The property rights approach offers some very clear breakthroughs. Perhaps most important, it rescues the study of institutions from purely negative and deep static explanations; it helps specify more clearly and rigorously the stakes involved in changing rules of political and economic bargaining; it gets us out of the circular determinism of the Black Legend; and helps students focus on the complex effects of rules and the rationality of agents.

On its own, however, the approach is insufficient. For while it invites us to examine competing claims and how negotiations over them are resolved, it does not account for where people stand (nor, for that matter, what they own, how they feel about ownership, what they envision) before they bargain. For students of convulsed societies like nineteenth-century Latin America—where discontinuities are as important as continuities, where change is more lurching than smooth—it will be necessary to explore the cultural, economic, and political stakes people held before they were thrown together to negotiate over collective rules. Just as important was how people understood these stakes. Otherwise the convulsions make little sense; Latin American state formation and institutional development become a saga of pointless bloodshed over meaningless projects.

Understanding property offers a bridge between the concern for agency and binding constraints (and inducements) of structures. But property transcends atomized claims. Just as it is relational and social, so too the rules that govern property, and the institutions that realize these rules, invoke processes of sharpening power relations. And this is a dynamic process whose outcomes are hard to predict. Admitting the importance of contingencies and indeterminacies of collective action, and side-stepping the functionalism of the property rights approach, institutions can be seen as fields that shape and are shaped by human activity. Specifically, if the institutions governing property can be seen as part of a set of relational conditions—of which nineteenth-century Latin Americans were so aware—historians and social scientists can tackle the social and political backdrop against which economic activity unfolds.

NOTES

1. Stephen Haber, ed., *How Latin America Fell Behind: Essays on the Economic Histories of Brazil and Mexico, 1800–1914* (Stanford, Calif.: Stanford

University Press, 1997). In particular, consult the essay by Stanley L. Engerman and Kenneth Sokoloff, "Factor Endowments, Institutions, and Differential Paths of Growth among New World Economies," 260–304; David Landes, *The Wealth and Poverty of Nations: Why Some Are So Rich and Some Are So Poor* (New York: Norton, 1998); William R. Summerhill, *Order against Progress: Government, Foreign Investment, and Railroads in Brazil, 1854–1913* (Stanford, Calif.: Stanford University Press, forthcoming).

2. Stanley J. Stein and Barbara H. Stein, *The Colonial Heritage of Latin America: Economic Dependency in Historical Perspective* (New York: Oxford University Press, 1970). For a longer treatment of the making of this tradition, see Jeremy Adelman, "The Problem of Persistence in Latin American History," in Adelman, ed., *Colonial Legacies: The Problem of Persistence in Latin American History* (New York: Routledge, 1999), 1–13.

3. Charles Gibson, "Introduction," in *The Black Legend: Anti-Spanish Attitudes in the Old World and the New World* (New York: Knopf, 1971), 3–27. Perhaps the most sweeping version of this is Octavio Paz, *The Labyrinth of Solitude* (New York: Grove, 1961). Of late, there has been a recrudescence of this deep cultural explanation of Latin American difference. Claudio Véliz, *The New World of the Gothic Fox: Culture and Economy in English and Spanish America* (Berkeley: University of California Press, 1994); Glen C. Dealy, *The Latin Americans: Spirit and Ethos* (Boulder, Colo.: Westview, 1992).

4. David J. Weber, "Turner, the Boltonians and the Borderlands," *American Historical Review* 91 (1986): 66–81; John Francis Bannon, *Herbert Eugene Bolton: The Historian and the Man, 1870–1953* (Tucson: University of Arizona Press, 1978).

5. Richard M. Morse, "The Heritage of Latin America," in Louis Hartz, ed., *The Founding of New Societies: Studies in the History of the United States, Latin America, South Africa, Canada, and Australia* (New York: Harcourt Brace Jovanovich, 1964), 123–77; John J. Johnson, *The Military and Society in Latin America* (Stanford, Calif.: Stanford University Press, 1964).

6. Immanuel Wallerstein, *The Making of the Modern World System*, vol. 1 (New York: Academic Press, 1974). For extended comments, see Ernesto Laclau, "Feudalismo y capitalismo en América Latina," in Carlos Sempat Assadourian, *Modos de producción en América Latina* (Mexico City: Siglo XXI, 1986), 23–46; Steve J. Stern, "Feudalism, Capitalism, and the World System in Perspective of Latin America and the Caribbean," *American Historical Review* 93 (1988): 829–72.

7. See Lee J. Alston, Thráinn Eggertsson, and Douglass C. North, eds., *Empirical Studies in Institutional Change* (New York: Cambridge University Press, 1996), for a taste of recent applied work.

8. Douglass North, *Structure and Change in Economic History* (New York: Norton, 1981), 5–11.

9. Douglass North, "The New Institutional Economics and Third World Development," in John Harriss, Janet Hunter, and Colin M. Lewis, eds., *The New Institutional Economics and Third World Development* (London: Routledge, 1995), 17–26.

10. Douglass North and Robert Paul Thomas, *The Rise of the Western World: A New Economic History* (Cambridge: Cambridge University Press, 1973), 12–16.

11. Carol M. Rose, *Property and Persuasion: Essays on the History, Theory, and Rhetoric of Ownership* (Boulder, Colo.: Westview, 1994); Jeremy Adelman, "Property Rules or the Rule of Property?" *Law and Social Inquiry* 21, no. 4 (1996): 101–20.

12. Gary D. Libecap, "Property Rights in Economic History: Implications for Research," *Explorations in Economic History* 23 (1986): 227–52.

13. Carlos S. Nino, *Un país al margen de la ley* (Buenos Aires: Emecé, 1992); Carlos Waisman, *The Reversal of Development in Argentina: Postwar Counterrevolutionary Policies and Their Structural Consequences* (Princeton, N.J.: Princeton University Press, 1987); Paul H. Lewis, *The Crisis of Argentine Capitalism* (Chapel Hill: University of North Carolina Press, 1990).

14. Clifford Geertz, "Thick Description: Toward an Interpretive Theory of Culture," in his *Interpretation of Cultures* (New York: Basic Books, 1973), 3–30.

15. See, for instance, the rendition by Robert Bates, "Introduction," in *Analytic Narratives* (Princeton, N.J.: Princeton University Press, 1998), especially his distinction between political scientists who analyze data and historians who "merely describe."

16. This was especially so in the study of slavery, which went from focusing on a system of domination—which it was—to examinations of slaves' own abilities to resist and negotiate the terms of their bondage. A good example is Rebecca Scott, *Slave Emancipation in Cuba: The Transition to Free Labor, 1860–1899* (Princeton, N.J.: Princeton University Press, 1985).

17. Stephen Haber, "Regulatory Regimes, Capital Markets and Industrial Development: A Comparative Study of Brazil, Mexico and the USA, 1840–1930," in Harriss, Hunter, and Lewis, *The New Institutional Economics*, 265–82; Stephen Haber, "Financial Markets and Industrial Development: A Comparative Study of Governmental Regulation, Financial Innovation, and Industrial Structure in Brazil and Mexico, 1840–1930," in Haber, *How Latin America Fell Behind*, 146–78.

18. For examples, see Bradford Burns, *The Poverty of Progress: Latin America in the Nineteenth Century* (Berkeley: University of California Press, 1980); James R. Scobie, *Revolution on the Pampas: A Social History of Argentine Wheat, 1860–1910* (Austin: University of Texas Press, 1964).

19. On Cuba, see Louis Pérez Jr., "Toward Dependency and Revolution: The Political Economy of Cuba between Wars, 1878–1895," *Latin American Research Review* 18 (1983): 127–42; on Brazil, see Hebe Maria Mattos de Castro, "Beyond Masters and Slaves: Subsistence Agriculture as a Survival Strategy in Brazil in the Second Half of the Nineteenth Century," *Hispanic American Historical Review* 68 (1988): 461–90; Emilia Viotti da Costa, *The Brazilian Empire: Myths and Realities* (Chicago: Dorsey, 1985), 78–92; for Colombia, see Michael F. Jiménez, "Travelling Far in Grandfather's Car: The Life Cycle of Colombian Coffee Estates, the Case of Viotá, Cundinamarca (1900–1930)," *Hispanic American Historical Review* 69 (1989): 185–219; for Costa Rica, see Marc Edelman, *The Logic of the Latifundio: The Large Estates of Northwestern Costa Rica since the Late Nineteenth Century* (Stanford, Calif.: Stanford University Press, 1992).

20. Freidrich Katz, "Labor Conditions on Haciendas in Porfirian Mexico," *Hispanic American Historical Review* 54 (1974): 1–47; Florencia Mallon, *The Defense of Community in the Peruvian Highlands* (Princeton, N.J.: Princeton University Press, 1983).

21. Carlos Marichal, *A Century of Debt Crises in Latin America: From Independence to the Great Depression, 1820–1930* (Princeton, N.J.: Princeton University Press, 1989); Javier Pérez Siller, "Crisis fiscal y reforma hacendaria en el siglo XIX mexicano," *Siglo XIX*, 35 (1988): 223–40.

22. João Fragoso and Manolo Florentino, *O arcaísmo como projeto: Mercado Atlantico, sociedade agrária e elite mercantil no Rio de Janeiro, c. 1790–c.1840* (Rio de Janeiro: Diadorim Editora, 1993), 71–89; Jorge F. Sábato, *La clase dominante en la Argentina moderna* (Buenos Aires: GEL, 1988), 95–114.

23. Hilda Sabato, *Capitalismo y ganadería en Buenos Aires: Fiebre del lanar, 1850–1890* (Buenos Aires: Sudamericana, 1989); Jeremy Adelman, *Frontier Development: Land, Labour and Capital on the Wheatlands of Argentina and Canada, 1890–1914* (Oxford: Oxford University Press, 1994). The same appears to have been true in parts of Mexico. See Simon Miller, "Mexican Junkers and Capitalist Haciendas, 1810–1910: The Arable Estate and the Transition to Capitalism between the Insurgency and the Revolution," *Journal of Latin American Studies* 22 (1990): 229–63.

24. Yet there remains a problem: these arrangements may be efficient at one stage and less so later. How does this approach tackle inefficiency? Why don't agents just alter institutional arrangements? Answers to these questions require a distinction between individual rationality and collective efficiency. Rationality is about purposive, utility-maximizing behavior under constraints. Agents apprehend their circumstances and try to do the best they can within confines. Efficiency—and there is an enormous debate on this concept, just as there is about rationality—is about the effects of these choices and can be gauged by their Pareto optimality (where no one would defect from a given arrangement without inflicting losses on another) or, perhaps more satisfying, ensuring free flow of resources should returns be higher by putting assets to work in alternative uses. Either way, people may behave rationally, and a system may have a logic of its own. This logic need not generate efficient results. Contracting can be both effective and defective. Inefficient rules might arise, and then interest groups can adapt to these rules and create entrenched obstacles to reform. All of this can be told in narratives that do not rely on timeless cultural categories (which, all too often, smack of racism). To date, we have no studies of long-run institutional effects to test this proposition in Latin America, although anecdotal evidence abounds.

25. Cass R. Sunstein, "On Property and Constitutionalism," *Cardozo Law Review* 14 (1993): 907–35.

26. Donald Wittman, "Why Democracies Produce Efficient Results," *Journal of Political Economy* 97 (1989): 1395–424.

27. In a pioneering study with Barry Weingast, North explored the process of constitutional change in seventeenth-century England. When the sovereign enjoyed unrivaled powers to devise the rules by which he or she must act, the apex of political power faced few constraints. This could have deleterious effects over the long run. People fear abusive exactions and arbitrary whims; their

expected rates of return fall; investment is cramped. But when the sovereign had to reckon with rival sources of political power—like Parliament—it could not act unilaterally. Instead it had to generate credible commitments to its subjects through responsible behavior (like protecting them against intruders) and not violating promises (like paying back loans—a constant source of ennui for ancien régime creditors). With arbitrariness braced thanks to a new constitutional system (the upshot of the Magna Carta and the Glorious Revolution), property rights became more secure, transaction costs dropped, and contracting became easier. England became a commercial powerhouse. This model illustrates how institutional change can ensure secure contracting across time—and the authors make a very open pitch at the end of the essay for Third World constitutionalism. North and Weingast, "Constitutions and Commitment: The Evolution of Institutions Governing Public Choice in Seventeenth-Century England," *Journal of Economic History* 49:4 (1989): 803–32; Hilton L. Root, *The Fountain of Privilege: Political Foundations of Markets in Old Regime France and England* (Berkeley: University of California Press, 1994). For an important, pointed critique, see Patrick O'Brien, Trevor Griffiths, and Philip Hunt, "Political Components of the Industrial Revolution: Parliament and the English Cotton Textile Industry, 1660–1774," *Economic History Review* 44 (1991): 395–423.

28. *The Economist*, October 11–17, 1999, pp. 27–29, of their survey of the twentieth century. For more discussion, see Sunstein, "On Property and Constitutionalism."

29. Carol M. Rose, "Property as a Keystone Right?" *Notre Dame Law Review* 71 (1996): 329–30.

30. There is an important exception—and it is the one that proves the rule: Peru. On the debate over free trade, see Paul Gootenberg, *Between Silver and Guano: Commercial Policy and the State in Post-independence Peru* (Princeton, N.J.: Princeton University Press, 1989). To be sure, debates over commercial and fiscal policy in Mexico also raged in the press, but there is less evidence of large policy shifts as governments flowed in and out of power.

31. Donald Fithian Stephens, *Origins of Instability in Early Republican Mexico* (Durham, N.C.: Duke University Press, 1991); Jeremy Adelman, *Republic of Capital: Buenos Aires and the Legal Transformation of the Atlantic World* (Stanford, Calif.: Stanford University Press, 1999).

32. John Coatsworth, "Obstacles to Economic Growth in Nineteenth-Century Mexico," *American Historical Review* 83:1 (1978): 80–100.

33. Leticia Reina, *Las rebeliones campesinas en México, 1819–1906* (Mexico City: Siglo XIX, 1980); Peter Guardino, "Barbarism or Republican Law? Guerrero's Peasants and National Politics, 1820–1846," *Hispanic American Historical Review* 75 (1995): 185–213; Richard Graham, *Patronage and Politics in Nineteenth-Century Brazil* (Stanford, Calif.: Stanford University Press, 1990).

34. Robert H. Bates, "Contra Contractarianism: Some Reflections on the New Institutionalism," *Politics and Society* 16 (1988): 387–401.

35. And here, path dependency will not suffice. Much better at explaining how people "lock in" to a set of arrangements in which the perceived opportunity cost

of change exceeds the anticipated flow of rents from staying loyal to the system, path dependency helps account for persistence and for some cases of change, but it is not especially good at explaining how we arrive at these sets of arrangements. Mark Roe, "Chaos and Evolution in Law and Economics," *Harvard Law Review* 109 (1996): 641–68.

36. North has tried to account for the lumpiness of change by turning to path dependency. Acknowledging his debt to W. Brian Arthur and Paul David's work, North invokes the notion of path dependency to explain how agents and societies crystallize around sets of rules. Institutions need not create socially efficient results. In the long run, bargaining strength affects both the rules themselves and the balance of power within the rules. Where the rules enhance the bargaining power of one agent so clearly over other agents, the former enjoys incentives to perpetuate the system, even if it starts to calcify trade and resource allocation. While polities define and enforce property rights, they are also prone to "capture," so that the process of definition and enforcement serves the interests of the few rather than the community as a whole. Changing the institutional fabric can involve deep, discontinuous ruptures, even revolutions over mutually exclusive projects for designing social rules and norms. For an early incarnation of this formulations, see Douglass North, "A Theory of Institutional Change and the Economic History of the Western World," in Michael Hechter, ed., *The Microfoundations of Macrosociology* (Philadelphia: Temple University Press, 1983), 190–215; and North, *Institutions, Institutional Change and Economic Performance* (New York: Cambridge University Press, 1990), 84–95.

37. There is a logical trap as well. These accounts for the existence of social rules and norms tend to be consequentialist. The property rights approach treats rules as parametric for behavior—they set the ground rules for contracting. The approach also wants to explain how these rules come into being. The origins and evolution of the institutions are explained in terms of their consequences. Kaushik Basum, Eric Jones, and Ekkehart Schlicht, "The Growth and Decay of the Commons: The Role of the New Institutional Economics in Economic History," *Explorations in Economic History* 24, no. 4 (1987): 1–21. This also applies to functional approaches to legal history, say of Morton Horwitz's *The Transformation of American Law, 1780–1860* (Cambridge, Mass.: Harvard University Press, 1977). For a comment, especially tackling the development of riparian rights, see Rose, *Property and Persuasion*, chap. 6.

38. Marichal, *A Century of Debt Crises*; John Coatsworth, "Economic and Institutional Trajectories in Nineteenth-Century Latin America," in John Coatsworth and Alan M. Taylor, eds., *Latin America and the World Economy since 1800* (Cambridge, Mass.: David Rockefeller Center for Latin American Studies/Harvard University Press, 1998), 33–39.

39. For a superb recent effort to explore this failure to calibrate the shifts to more historically apposite growth models, see Victor Bulmer-Thomas, *An Economic History of Latin America since Independence* (Cambridge: Cambridge University Press, 1994). On Argentina, see Carlos Díaz Alejandro, *Essays on the Economic History of the Argentine Republic* (New Haven, Conn.: Yale University Press, 1970), esp. chap. 2.

40. Gary D. Libecap, *Contracting for Property Rights* (Cambridge: Cambridge University Press, 1989), 1–4; Lee Alston, Gary D. Libecap, and Bernardo Mueller, "Property Rights and Land Conflict: A Comparison of Settlement of the U.S. Western and Brazilian Amazon Frontiers," in Coatsworth and Taylor, eds., *Latin America and the World Economy since 1800*, 55–84.

Chapter Two

HIJOS OF DR. GERSCHENKRON: "LATECOMER" CONCEPTIONS IN LATIN AMERICAN ECONOMIC HISTORY

PAUL GOOTENBERG

ALEXANDER GERSCHENKRON, the great Russo-Cantabrigian economic historian, is not a household name in Latin American studies. Historical sociologists of the state and industrialism are more likely to recognize Gerschenkron as one of the century's striking thinkers about "backwardness" and comparative development, especially through his seminal conceptions of European "latecomer" industrialization. I ask: Why did Gerschenkron's compelling political-economy stance not win more attention, application, and adherents among Latin American economists, economic historians, and historical sociologists during the "development decades" of the 1960s to 1990s? This exercise may lend clues as to how fitting (or ill-fitting) theories become useful or ultimately useless for illuminating Latin American social realities.

The opening section sizes up Gerschenkron's larger conceptions, followed by a survey of his scattered "*hijos*" (progeny) about Latin American studies, particularly the extraordinary contribution of Albert O. Hirschman, who has worked a half century to translate Gerschenkron into developmental possibilities. The working assumption is that Gerschenkron *might* have been an attractive thinker here, given his broad affinities with the dominant postwar nationalist or statist model of industrialism in Latin America. The next two sections analyze his relatively scant impact, first, by pondering the Eastern European—Latin American big comparison and then by considering the (political) power of economic metaphors: the neutral chronological imagery of Gerschenkron versus the hotter aesthetics of the "dependency" school. Gerschenkron's conceptions, I argue, enjoyed a limited snob appeal that could hardly compete in the ideologized 1960s and 1970s with a more populist—and in some ways historically deeply rooted—discourse about Latin American *under*development. Finally, I will speculate whether the time has finally come for Gerschenkron's seed to take and bloom.

GERSCHENKRON FOR BEGINNERS

Albert Fishlow—who did become a Latin Americanist—calls Alexander Gerschenkron, his teacher, the "doyen" of American economic history.[1] Born in Russia and trained in central Europe, Gerschenkron established his pulpit at Harvard, where he dominated economic history and Slavic studies during the 1950s and 1960s and, among other honors, served as president of both the American Economics Association and the Economic History Association. Biographically and intellectually, Gerschenkron was part of that remarkable cohort—Bert Hoselitz and Albert O. Hirschman among them—of European émigré scholars who left an indelible mark on the nascent field of development economics in the postwar United States. In contrast to the others, Gerschenkron's orientation was overwhelmingly historical.

Gerschenkron was a highly prolific, eclectic, and sometimes rambling writer whose most widely admired work is the 1962 essay collection *Economic Backwardness in Historical Perspective*, taken from the title essay of a decade before.[2] In the revelatory title essay, Gerschenkron takes readers on a twenty-five-page whirlwind tour of "late" (nineteenth-century) eastern European industrialisms, exposing in historical fashion their relativist deviations from the liberal paradigm of Industrial Revolution in England. For macroeconomic history, Gerschenkron lays out a way of thinking analogous to that of a more celebrated middle European, anthropologist Karl Polanyi.[3]

Others have refined Gerschenkron's themes as a model.[4] There were some six essential grand findings from the European "latecomer" experience—those economies that industrialized between the 1870s and 1930s. First, the more "backward" the economy when it began to develop, the more rapid its initial impulse and rate of industrialization and growth. Gerschenkron inelegantly labeled this the "spurt" and maintained it was much more than a baseline phenomenon. Second, in situations of relative backwardness, the scale of institutions, firms, and plants tended to loom larger. The industrial firms of modern Germany dwarfed little England's; Soviet factories were humongous. Third, financing this costlier industrialism tended to shift onto other institutions, such as banks, cartels, and later the state, growing in size and intensity all the way. Fourth, industries (in what is often termed the "second" industrial revolution) tended toward producer and capital goods over consumption goods. This was achieved mainly at the expense of consumption, by various modes of forced savings, taxation, and investment. Fifth, agriculture played an increasingly modest part in the later industrialisms, and Gerschenkron consistently downplayed commonsense notions of agrarian constraints to in-

dustrial progress. Finally, over time European states and societies revealed mounting recourse to powerful ideologies to justify delayed industrial drives, from French Saint-Simonianism to Soviet Communism. In
these ways, industrialism could mobilize widely and proceed rapidly
across a diverse topography of institutional and cultural contexts.

Underlying these propositions were two core concepts and a host of
lesser ones. One was the paradoxical Veblenish "advantages of backwardness."[5] For example, countries that tardily industrialized could import advanced scientific and industrial techniques that put them on the
cutting edge of world product cycles and competition. The other was the
general notion of "substitutes." If an element or prerequisite for growth
were lacking—for example, formal capital markets—European societies
proved highly adept at concocting new institutions, such as financial
trusts or state industrial banks. Later, this was conceived as fast skipping
stages in growth. Throughout his thinking, Gerschenkron privileged historical discontinuity over linearly conceived continuities and traditions.
He was also explicitly relational: later industrializers were different precisely because they were affected, often through demonstration effects, by
the first-comers. Finally, Gerschenkron, unlike most liberal economists,
strove to analyze rather than minimize the role of the state in development, which he judged to be a normal function in history.

Gerschenkron may sound anachronistic to today's readers. First, the
enormous stress on heavy industrialism seems odd in the 1990s, when
agricultural adaptability, productivity, trade, "upgrading," risk, and information technology are deemed more vital. Second, if highly empirical,
Gerschenkron also relied on discourse of historical or statist forces or
tensions that can seem overly philosophical or teleological to non-European ears. Gerschenkron's world also tends toward the "closed economies," potentially limiting its utility in a commercially opening or trad-
able universe. And, of course, there have been ongoing quandaries over
how to measure and rank relative backwardness, which is not always so
obvious, and whether to use national economies as the proper units of
analysis.[6]

Latin Americanists can still best grasp Gerschenkron's project in the
context of his merciless critique of Walt Whitman Rostow's *Stages of
Economic Growth* (1960) and, by extension, most forms of North American (Parsonian) modernization theory. Broadly, Rostow's cold-warrior
model posited, in the inverted capitalistic fashion of Marx himself, that
all developing countries had passed through five stages Rostow derived
from the British experience of industrial revolution—replete with strict
"prerequisites" and "thresholds" for savings, investment, and so on
along the way.[7] For contrast, Gerschenkron took the latecomer, fast-de-
veloping late nineteenth-century central and eastern European economies

as his paradigm and assumed their links and involvement in a larger system. Economic history revealed relative backwardness overcome by novel strategies and pathways to industrialism and accelerated growth. History rode roughshod over any neat recipes of prerequisites and takeoffs. Rostow was mistaken. There were no prescriptible progressions, and alternative possibilities were eminently thinkable in economic development.

History, so far as I can tell, has been kind to Gerschenkron, though he is still far from an intellectual celebrity. Influence and prestige garnered in European economic history live on, even as particular assertions have come under heavy scrutiny. The major cross-national survey of European economic history—Clive Trebilcock's *Industrialization of the Continental Powers*—roundly judges Gerschenkron the knockout winner in his debate with Rostow, proposing "anti-models" as the ideal for European research. Others have amended his concepts with other European cases (e.g., even tardier Scandinavian developers), adding factors such as education and human capital to the question of backwardness, or have sought out distinctive non-Western cases like Japan's.[8] Today's renewed interest in institutional economic history and hidden pathways to growth owes much to Gerschenkron.[9]

Finally, let me add something about the intellectual sensibility of Gerschenkron, which should recommend him to fellow Latin Americanists. Gerschenkron's writings reveal a mind of remarkable erudition, intellect, irony, and interdisciplinary range. Here was an economist who could conceptualize history but resisted all dogmas (including economism) and its iron laws of "continuity." Here was an economist, steeped in Continental historicism, who maintained that history, sociology, institutions, politics, philosophy, and even literature belonged with his craft. He conducted specialized research not only on Russia but also on Italy, Austria, Germany, and even Bulgaria. Gerschenkron was as comfortable in qualitative historical, sociology (analyzing dictatorship or social movements) and intellectual history as in empirical studies of tractor prices and index numbers (a special statistical conundrum carries his name) or even in interpreting *Doctor Zhivago* and the Soviet novel. Nothing seems further from the technocratic, mathematical, and one might say reductionist culture that has overcome both mainstream economic history and development in recent decades.[10] Can that Gershenkronian spirit be revived?

HIJOS OF DR. GERSCHENKRON

On one point, however, Gerschenkron resisted eclecticism: repeatedly and emphatically he declined to draw comparisons between backwardness in European history and the developmental condition of the then just-discovered Third World. This comes across as a principled objection—that history offers no easy predictable formulas—but we can gather that Gerschenkron was aware of the implications of his very public feuding with the Rostowians.[11] In this sense, he left no open or legitimate *hijos* for Latin Americanists.

Nonetheless, a handful of scattered intellectual progeny have appeared who have tried to apply "Gerschenkronian" notions to development studies and to Latin American industrialism and state building. This section analyzes those writers who explicitly extended Gerschenkron's ideas, though not exhaustively, leaving for later the broader arena of parallel developmental concerns and reinvented ideas. Their influence, I argue, has been restrained due to the elegant ambiguity of Gerschenkron's models, but even more so by shifting political climates and timing.

The remarkable heir apparent is economist Albert O. Hirschman. Hirschman, of course, hails from a comparable Middle-European tradition, a generation after. He befriended Gerschenkron on arriving in the United States and for a time was a close colleague at Harvard.[12] Hirschman's erudite, humanistic, historical, metaphoric, "metatheoretical," and essentially irreproducible modeling style resembles Gerschenkron's.[13] They are clearly kindred souls.[14]

Specifically, Hirschman has striven throughout his lifework to translate—or actively "trespass," to use his metaphor—some of Gerschenkron's core historical insights into developmental ones, apt for Latin America. Hirschman's heterodox "unbalanced" theory of economic growth of the 1950s (*The Strategy of Economic Development*), his provocative policy essays of the 1960s (of *Journeys Towards Progress*), and his later refined conception of "linkages" can all be understood as putting Gerschenkron's unorthodox substitutes and stage skipping into the messy praxis of development. A paradox-embracing essay, "Obstacles to Growth: A Classification and a Quasi-Vanishing Act" (1965), argues à la Gerschenkron that Latin American structuralists and modernizationists alike had hooked into illusory rigidities about developmental prerequisites. In the real world of development, they are highly elusive or evadable. Another pivotal article, "Ideologies of Development in Latin America" (1960), develops Gerschenkron's theme of latecomers' needful invention of militant industrial ideologies.[15] While by the 1950s Latin America had embraced one with Prebischian *desarrollismo*, Hirschman found that, prior to the 1930s, pessimistic "self-incrimination" ruled over developmental mobilization—a notion that unconsciously prompted this historian to write an entire book, based on fresh nineteenth-century evidence, as a reply.[16] Even in the 1990s (and his own eighties), Hirschman drew from the well of Gerschenkron's historical perspective, as in the rich essay "Industrialism and Its Manifold Discontents: West, East, and

South." In it, the typical lament of Latin Americans that their industries suffer as "light" and consumerist contrasts sharply with the plaint from the ex-socialist economies of Eastern Europe that they failed for being too "heavy," too into producer goods. In all, Hirschman's politics of "possibilism" exudes the empowering optimism in the face of adversity that Gerschenkron's history foretold.

The most salient statement is Hirschman's now-classic essay "The Political Economy of Import-Substituting Industrialization in Latin America" (1968), which boldly evaluates "late development" from a Latin American perspective.[17] Hirschman finds spiritual affinities but in reality less direct application than he would have hoped. Save for the exceptional Brazilian or Mexican miracles, modern Latin American industrialism has not been marked by dramatic spurts. These latecomers lack a European élan, no small psychopolitical dilemma for aspiring and often foreign-born industrial classes. Moreover, the initial scale of plant and supporting institutions (if any) in the region has hardly been outlandish. Most industrial sectors began with modest factories, geared to meeting light consumer wants previously satisfied by mass imports. With such variance from Gerschenkron's predictions, Hirschman deploys a new Gershenkronian category of "*late*-late industrializers." It focuses on the challenges of import-substituting industrialization (ISI), clearing a space for the *open-economy* industrialism of Latin America. If you are very late, Hirschman suggests, you forfeit many of the advantages of backwardness and even suffer tangible drawbacks in industrial structure. Even gains from imported technology can seem inappropriate. Core dilemmas of the postwar economy—chronically overvalued exchange rates or tolerance of creeping inflation—were read as Gerschenkronian substitutes for resolving more intractable quandaries. But the chief drawback of ISI is how it had trapped the Latin American cases into tightly sequential "stages." For example, economies seemed unable to shift into high-gear industrial exports or producer goods, in sharp contrast to Gerschenkron's flexible stage skippers. Hirschman's analysis put a finger on the dilemmas of ISI by the 1960s, yet one that raised an array of strategies over and around the constraints that became widely misinterpreted as the "exhaustion" of industrialism.[18] Yet few Latin American economies (in contrast to the Asians) have proved supple enough to overcome their impasse.

In sum, Hirschman's oeuvre finds inspiration in Gerschenkron even as it suggests some Latin American limits to his model. These point, arguably, to an even greater, not lesser, need for economic history, for example, in grasping how nineteenth-century developments framed the circumstances that Hirschman terms late-late.[19] The still relatively undeveloped historiography of modern Latin American industrialism would itself make a revealing arena for analysis, and not all economic historians would consent to Hirschman's particular interpretation of ISI.[20] For sure, there are not many *hijos* or *hermanos* of Hirschman around, at least not within the economics profession. Albert Fishlow, who personally studied with Gerschenkron, is a shining exception, as manifest in his serious passion for economic history and his healthy refusal to banish the state and policy from Latin American development. Some of his work has historically complicated even Hirschman's grasp of ISI. Werner Baer, another respected Brazilianist, also trained with Gerschenkron and readily admits the influence on his view of Brazilian developmental institutions.[21] Whatever the case, Albert O. Hirschman's brilliant and paradox-rich mode of thinking had a refreshing impact *outside* of the Latin Americanist fold.[22] Yet, I am afraid to say, it works less effect on the core of our craft, pulled off in other directions since the 1960s.

For the 1970s and beyond, I have stumbled upon a few isolated attempts to deploy "historical backwardness." The noted economic historian of Mexico, John H. Coatsworth, was never enamored of 1970s dependency thought and has pursued several Gerschenkronian leads. His underground classic, "From Backwardness to Underdevelopment" (a lamentably unpublished history of viceregal and nineteenth-century Mexico) centers on its titular preoccupation of distinguishing the discontinuity between mere colonial "backwardness" and modern underdevelopment. A striking and by now famous finding is the fact that Mexico, and by extension much of Latin America, was not so far behind the "West" in 1800 in terms of measurable productivity or technological and factor endowments. Underdevelopment thus *developed* during Mexico's painful nineteenth century, which by the Porfirian era (1876–1911) came replete with Gerschenkronian catch-up efforts and developments in scale. Other catch-up effects intensified or were instituted under an expansive postrevolutionary state. One still wonders whether the influx of foreign capital to late-nineteenth-century Latin America is best construed as a form of substitution (for missing capital, entrepreneurs, markets, technology) or as a continuity in long-exposed ex-colonial economies, which may lend them qualitatively distinctive historical dynamics.[23]

From political science of the early 1980s, also against the dependency current, one can highlight Hewlett and Weinert's volume *Brazil and Mexico: Patterns in Late Development*, which adopts Gerschenkron's lexicon. Of note is their comparative focus and stress on timing. Bennett and Sharpe's test case of the Mexican developmental state is the most overtly Gerschenkronian of the lot, and perhaps of all Latin American social science. Gerschenkron suggests a robust description of the expansive productive roles of the postrevolutionary state in quasi-entrepreneurial slots like industrial finance. But they also find the theory unduly functionalist and teleological, for assuming more than explaining the causal logic of

Mexico's then (pre-1982) secular upward trend in economic activism.[24] A thicker historical and class analysis is applied, in a relational story of "last-resort" institutional substitution. This Mexicanist affinity for Gerschenkron seems no accident.

But the closest and most logical kin to the family of Gerschenkron is the larger "bureaucratic-authoritarian" school of sociology from the latter 1970s. In highly Latin Americanized terms this approach focused on the political consequences of delayed development, many of which were seen as adverse. Guillermo O'Donnell's contributions, and his critics, are too numerous and complex to recount here: suffice it to say that this was a serious turn toward a regionally embedded political economy. It blended questions of timing and comparative political culture with a Barrington-Moorish analysis of the authoritarian regimes then peaking in the region, especially in the oppressed Southern Cone. O'Donnell argued, at his simplest, that these novel forms of military government in Argentina, Brazil, Uruguay, and Chile were purposefully out to "deepen" industrial (and related labor-repressive) structures, in a grand push toward capital-goods linkages to take them beyond an exhausted and politically polarized ISI. To bureaucratic-authoritarian theorists, this looked suspiciously like a long-range or institutionalized project. An innovative institutional strategy of sorts, it was heavy with dire political and social implications. Bureaucratic authoritarianism, as theory, shared common roots of reaction against Panglossian modernization ideas and also was the sharpest Latin American alternative of note to dependency theory, given its tremendous stress on the autonomy of Latin American states and actors. The founding father, O'Donnell, indeed does credit Gerschenkron in a footnote of *Modernization and Bureaucratic-Authoritarianism*, though the parallel with latecomer theory was not finely drawn.[25]

Hirschman, among others, reacted vigorously against the bureaucratic-authoritarian thesis (though not its basic concerns) for its exaggerated economic determinism and for its literal reading of the "exhaustion" of import-led industrialism. Critics discovered embarrassing empirical holes, though the key to its short life as Latin American sociology, thankfully, was the exhaustion of the authoritarian regimes themselves in motley crisis-driven transitions of the 1980s toward democratization.[26]

Finally, jumping to the historiographical present (I will return to a vital skipped stage), the rise of a postdependency, recovering-Marxist "new" political economy in the 1990s has "brought the state back in" (à la Skocpol) without bringing in much of Gerschenkron himself. Peter Evans's sociological and comparative *Embedded Autonomy* nods to Gerschenkron as the pioneer in identifying "embedded autonomy"—modern Third World polities that get just the right mix of industrial will and civil-society and market constraints. This marks an important shift from basically crude state-autonomy models of development to Polanyi-like notions of socioeconomic embeddedness. But Latin America, in Evans's postdependency universe, appears relegated mainly to the statist middle road or netherworld of chronically ineffectual developmental politics and policies.[27]

Arguably the newest cohort of "political economists," formed during the dramatic crisis of the 1980s, Latin America's "lost decade" of development, is the lost generation of Gerschenkron *nietos*. The terms of debate among these recent thinkers has shifted refreshingly far from liberalism and Marxism's state versus market, into interrogating how these two intersect institutionally and their mutual efficacies—an advance Gerschenkron would have blessed. More interesting work has seemed to be emerging out of politics than from economics as disciplines, tackling quandaries of political timing or the workability of developmental institutions. Evans himself is a prime example. An overlooked and insightful book by Steven Sanderson explores *"political* terms of trade" in contemporary Latin America and ends up (using Hirschman) in a vintage economic historicism. Kathryn Sikkink comparatively studies what made the ideologies of "developmentalism" tick—in one case miraculously for a while—in her innovative institutional and ideational analysis of Argentina and Brazil during the fifties and sixties. Carlos Waisman roams the "developmental tracks" of postwar Argentina, taking to task the *excessive* autonomy of the Argentine state and its rushed reversal to its (Peronist) form of autarkic industrialism.[28] Here, in eclectic sociologizing, the lament becomes the developmental *"disadvantages* of modernity," a reversal of Gerschenkron that might have used his helping hand.

As the long-sought developmental capacities of most Latin American states radically imploded after the 1980s, along with a de facto neoliberal *de*-industrialization, different issues arose. Merilee Grindle, for example, has lately compared Latin America with Africa (Mexico and Kenya, to be precise), rather than to any corner of Europe, in exploring how even in "downsizing" conjunctures innovating institutions can emerge more capable or responsive. The virtual *nieta* of Gerschenkron, Judith Tendler (she is one of Hirschman's few known students) recently published the hopeful *Good Government in the Tropics*. Privileging the local institutional branches of the Brazilian state, Tendler sheds a humanistic light on public developmental efforts, in a 1990s climate in which generally the "state" has become totalized or vilified by economists and their institutional hosts.[29]

Still, by the 1990s, the invidious huge comparisons of our time, in Evans, Gereffi and the like, lie not with historic European first-comers or latecomers but with the leapfrogging Asian *Tigres del Este*. These dynamic "newly industrializing states" had somehow truly taken advantage of their lags, deprivations, and relative backwardness, in several cases with surprising state-assisted strategies. I am not sure how much this line of questioning will tell us ultimately about Latin American development per se, or how much the reputation of the East Asia model will now fluctuate with the fortunes of the Asian stock markets, but Stephan Haggard's *Pathways from the Periphery* makes a good start for students of state building. Here, in studied comparisons between Brazil, Mexico, Korea, and Taiwan, postwar industrialisms are politically deconstructed into three types of transitions, not to nineteenth-century-style heavy industry but to flexible exports, high-tech, and self-sustaining growth. Here, the sad Latin American cases barely jump out of the rigidly inward ISI cage framed by Hirschman three decades ago.[30] Postmortems on the age of Latin American developmentalism, these make the most distantly recognizable scions of Gerschenkron.

DUELING PERIPHERIES

One transitional line of inquiry might ask: How apt and useful are the ostensible developmental and historical comparisons between eastern Europe and Latin America? Latin Americanists seem recurrently drawn into such comparisons, for both zones, albeit in differing ways, are related offshoots of western and southern European capitalism, "peripheries," as it were. For example, the Chilean Cristóbal Kay, before moving into regional economic thought, left a massive thesis comparing the evolution of the Latin American hacienda to feudal manorialism east of the Elbe, particularly under their latecomer experiences of export agriculture. In this area, the Polish scholar of feudalism Wiltold Kula also left a mark on our colonial "modes-of-production" debates. A recent tome of sociological analysis by Stephens, Huber, and Reuschemeyer pieces together bits of Marx and Moore to explore the relations between authoritarianism and dependent capitalism, mainly across these two regions. If rumors are acceptable, Zbigniew Brzezinski, Carter's notorious national security chief, supposedly composed a policy paper recommending the stable yet dependent Polish (party-state) "model" as the modernization route for Mexico and Latin America! Others have explored historical consumption patterns across both regions, pursuing the culturally impacted demonstration effects of European industrialism. James Kurth's various "tales from the peripheries," drawing explicitly on Gerschenkron, also bridge the two regions, along with his other attempts to compare the ex-Soviet and North American imperium. Yet by the 1980s no less than Immanuel Wallerstein may have inadvertently quelled this broad type of comparative field by geographically tagging eastern Europe as "semi-periphery" in his evolving "world-system"—as opposed to Latin America, stuck in a labor-coercive "periphery" position since its colonial conquest-incorporation in the sixteenth century. Only the latest world transformation, the collapse of "socialism" in the east, has again raised comparisons, with predictions this time of a "Latin Americanization" of decrepit civic cultures and industries in nations like Poland and Romania.[31]

For purposes of analysis here, the most compelling of such comparisons are found in Joseph Love's provocative recent book *Crafting the Third World: Theorizing Underdevelopment in Romania and Brazil* (1996). Contrasting regional contexts and economic ideas, Love argues for a palpable link between Romanian developmental debates (in their latecomer stage, 1880–1940) and later (post–*Estado Novo*) Brazilian and Latin American heterodoxies from imported northern European liberalism. Here, he finds Eastern European influences on Raúl Prebisch and Celso Furtado's Comisión Económica para América Latina (CEPAL) structuralism of the 1940s and 1950s, and through them to the neo-Marxism and dependency movements of the sixties and beyond. These were the exemplars of state-centered or state-conscious thought in modern Latin America. Love contends that the Latin Americans, given broadly similar neocolonial conditions, were reliving European mode-of-production debates of the early twentieth century, as national-capitalist and socialist standards for industrialism.[32]

There is much to recommend here, such as Love's grasp of the role of central European talent in the making of metropolitan developmental economics. But my reading of the book is that it fails to establish its central point—a direct overseas intellectual transmission to Latin America via the corporatist thought of Romanian economist Mihail Manoilescu. Maynard Keynes, I would venture, makes a more likely enabler here, though we lack strong research on the consumption and developmentalist transformations of Keynesian ideas across postwar Latin America. It makes sense that this book's setting is Brazil, a historically broader economy where statist thinking took early root among industrialists, the military, and varied intellectuals alike. But in trying to play up a strained external transmission thesis, Love tends to overplay images of pre-1930s Latin America as a pristine tabula rasa of unfettered and imported economic liberalism.[33] It thus underplays what may be long-felt and widely dispersed domestic national deviations from economic liberalism in the Americas. It might even underestimate the originality of Latin American figures like Prebisch, who might be reconsidered as the Gerschenkron of the Latin open economies.

Some of Love's ideas do stand out well in distinguishing *Cepalista* Latin American heterodoxy from the East's: the mounting claims of "commercial" exploitation (as in postwar terms-of-trade arguments for forced industrialization) and the geoeconomic distinctions (traceable to at least Prebisch himself) of "core" and "periphery" in the world economy. These terms were to become ammunition in the explosion of dependency thought in the 1960s. Gerschenkron, of course, was not a major player in this exchange, but such metaphors of commerce may help explain why.

METAPHOR, VISION, AND FALLING BEHIND

A conversation is becoming more audible on the outskirts of mainstream economics about the function of "rhetoric" and "metaphor" in economic analysis (notably, in the works of Dierdre McCloskey, a former economic historian and yet another Harvard student of Gerschenkron). Alternatively, from the economics Left, as in Heilbroner and Milberg's recent book *The Crisis of Vision in Modern Economic Thought*, we find a renewed interest in political "vision," viewed as far more than a mere ideology, in fact, as the unseen power source in modern economic theory.[34] Developmentalists such as Rostow, Gerschenkron, and masterfully Hirschman work and play potently with economic metaphors throughout their works: "takeoffs," "spurts," and "linkages" are but three of the most obvious and effective ones. Can such perilously "postmodern" notions about economic discourse help untangle the strange tale of Gerschenkron among the Latin Americanists?

In broaching this possibility, we need to consider another peripatetic European scholar—André Gunder Frank—who by the late 1960s came to exert untold intellectual power over large visions of Latin American history and development. Here I digress beyond writers who purposely use and cite Gerschenkron into the wider developmental and cultural Zeitgeists of Latin America, or these as read by the Latin Americanists themselves. Frank, who in fact studied economic development with Arnold Harberger at Chicago, defined himself in a similar milieu as Gerschenkron: in resistance to liberal diffusionist modernization paradigms, then peaking in the U.S. academy of the mid-1960s.[35] Why did one rhetoric gain so much prominence while the other—Gerschenkron's—remained largely at the margins?

While it now seems so easy to deride Frank, there is no question that his initial work, *Dependency and Underdevelopment in Latin America* (1967), carried a deep resonance at the time. And even decades after Frank declared himself intellectually dead, it is still hard for many to recover from his wake. The wide notion that European "capitalism," from October 12, 1492, onward, had deformed and progressively "*under-developed*" the whole of Latin America, through exploitative monopoly chains of "metropolitan-satellite" commercial ties, won instant credibility among a huge and credulous audience, north and south, including a fair number of competent historians. Here was a clear response to Latin American modernizationists and diffusionists, even those on the Left who would soon decry Frank's "circulationist" and "stagnationist" errors.[36] As grandiose metaphor if not grand theory, it revolved around facile binaries: "inward" and "outward" orientations, "national" and "collaborationist" interests. Mere economic backwardness became relational historical processes of underdevelopment, a chronic condition that had only worked (in this zero-sum globe) to advantage imperial European capitalism. Politically—and the politics was indispensable here—the damning characterization of the Latin American "national bourgeoisies" as failed "lumpens" assailed not only modernization advocates but also nationalist and progressive *desarrollismo* and its hypothetical Gerschenkronian alliances of the national state and local elites. Not just Frank-and-sons, but far more sophisticated and nuanced constructions (Wallerstein's "world-systems" or Cardoso and Faletto's "dependency *and* development") rested on comparable kinds of economic metaphors.[37]

To be sure, there were vital discrepancies among dependency writers, their inspirations, assumptions, and tropes. Though rarely spelled out and scrutinized, the central dependency "counterfactual" (especially for the nineteenth century) was analogous to Gerschenkron's core Bismarckian case—that Latin Americans *should have* emulated that strong state-heavy industrial path but were precluded by free-trade imperialism, their entrenched "comprador" elites, neocolonial social structures, or other such obstacles.[38] Beyond this were bifurcations between those vaunting long-run *continuities* from early Iberian colonialism (versus a stress on the capitalist *discontinuities* of the liberal post-1850 export era) and the famously byzantine theoretical factionalism in modes of production controversies. The basic divide quickly surfaced between Frank's full-fledged anticapitalist posture and the kind of critical support for "national" or "state" capitalism implicit in works like Fernando Henrique Cardoso and Enzo Faletto's *Dependency and Development in Latin America*. For Cardoso and his followers, a "dependent situation" could still allow for a good measure of development, if given a robust enough alliance of national elites and strong state to overcome (i.e., substitute for) the structural constraints of global dependency. In this sense, this contra-Frank position *was* indeed a strain of the dominant *Cepalista* tradition of postwar industrializing Latin America, right before bureaucratic authoritarianism changed the terms of this developmentalist alliance for good.[39] In any case, this longer embedded statist ethos and the terms of these debates are what make relative neglect of Gerschenkron during these development decades so particularly mysterious.

In retrospect, we might dismiss dependency as a spurt of socialist developmental thought "that failed" or even as an exaggerated "ideological substitute" for economic and political reality, to frame it in Gerschenkron's core terms.[40] Condemnation comes easy these days, but it is much harder to find an intellectually convincing account of how motley *dependentistas* came to so overwhelm Latin Americanist discourse by the 1970s. This was not just a mad case of sloppy social science reasoning, as some now have it. Others ironically suggest dependency as favoring rent-seeking national elites: it made an intellectually conducive blanket justification of grandiose state building and extreme protectionism of the 1970s, à la Echeverría's Mexico or Velasco's Peru. We also need to recall the ideological contests and contexts of the Latin American 1960s.[41] Industrialization per se was far from an alluring or studied topic for scholars in this heated context, even as the region was becoming definitively transformed by it by the late 1970s. Other signifying metaphors crept in around industrialism: about "frustrated," "incomplete," "distorted," or "reversed" development instead.[42] The attractions of the dependency critique were unevenly felt among struggling Latin American intellectuals (striving to salvage some space as authoritarians shook their universities and appropriated the standard of development) and among affluent North American academic "consumers" (Cardoso's appellation), consolidating their Latin Americanist field in a guilt-ridden metropole.

But I wish to stress two other points instead. First, that in the ideologically charged 1960s and 1970s this sort of dependency positioning (by a kind of Gresham's law of intellectual goods) drove out the finer metaphors and research or policy agendas raised in Gerschenkron's or Hirschman's line of thought. But second, this intellectual displacement was not driven by a free-floating "sphere of circulating metaphors" alone but seems related to deep-seated *historical* conceptions within the region itself.

Gerschenkron's pivotal metaphor seems to me about *time* (being "late," "behindness"), and consequently about the followers "catching up." While entirely relational, as backwardness is determined by the others arriving before, it embraces the hopeful notion that a little tardiness even carries certain advantages. Timing becomes opportunity here. And while there are certain costs to telescoping temporal stages of development in Gerschenkron's view, a notion of exploitation it is not. These are cool, neutralist conceptions. The hotter dependency economic metaphor centers around colonized "space" and a vast social geography of exploitation: inward, outward, metropole-satellite, core/semi-periphery/periphery. Location becomes *destiny*. Without overabstracting, this seems the opposite rendering of historical time: the longer one had been behind (as in, say, northeast Brazil or Upper Peru), the longer "incorporated" into the (world) system, the more hopeless and disadvantaged appeared the developmental possibilities.[43] The sole escape route was total flight from geographically privileged world capitalism. Only later did many historians respond to what a deterministic, uncultured, and unpeopled vision of the past this made.

Despite these speculations, I am not satisfied this puzzle is truly resolvable in the linguistic or discursive sphere alone. What still begs explanation is the attraction, timing, or force of certain metaphors and visions over others. We can probe even deeper and wider into cross-regional historical realities to grasp why dependency gained such mental power over its alternatives.

Gerschenkron's late industrialism (of a Russia, Germany, or Italy) was set among reactive state builders (and large-scale industrializers from above) along the frontiers of Europe. These were countries, nations-in-formation that, if sharing some of the patchwork characteristics of nineteenth-century Latin America (imperial fragments, multiethnicities), suddenly found themselves in proximate competition with expansive industrial capitalisms. If long a part of a European states system, nationalist competition here took on a threatening urgency—of an escalating militaristic and imperialist nature—by the late nineteenth century. To be late or backward (in technology or mobilization capacities) in this context fast endangered the state and nation gathering under its wings. If now recognized by a range of historical sociologists, the contributions of *warfare* and its preparations to European state building and vertical organization, as well as to associated strategies and ideologies of industrialism, were not very explicit in the work of Gerschenkron himself.[44] In this way, even the dramatic "war communism" of the early Soviet Union appears as either a bland substitute for missing institutions or an extremist variant of Western industrial ideology. In the rest of the globe, only Japan (which has undergone its Gerschenkronian analysis) possessed a strong and cohesive enough state to compete, with factories as well as tanks and planes.

"Latin America"—as its imported nineteenth-century nomenclature suggests—incubated for three long centuries as a colonial and commercial outpost of southwestern Europe. It inherited not only a distinct state tradition (more absolutist yet with fewer of those European advantages) but also an ideological crust, disseminated by Creole nationalists, of thinking about (geographically) "external" and "commercial" exploitations. By the mid–nineteenth century, as I have argued at length elsewhere (in a book called *Imagining Development*), even among staunch liberals this colonial history translated, Gerschenkron-style, into utopian longings for economic independence, industrial modernity, and more vigorous states. If cited and read, Adam Smith was rarely an unambiguous

hero down there. We need to reflect on these deeply nationalist conservative and liberal thinkers—the Alamáns and Antuñanos of Mexico, the
Cisneros and Pardos of Peru—and weigh their distinctions with the more
strategic Listeans of Europe, for they were different, especially in answer-
ing to the *commercial* vulnerabilities of their wide-open national economies. This was long before such imagery and its genealogy in the mid–
twentieth century became reworked by regional developmentalists and
seems to me an embedded and often popular basis for the passionate
appeal of the *dependentista* metaphors met and interrogated earlier.[45] Although there was some strategic thinking about falling "behind" the industrializing West, much of that was soon dissipated by the swift advantages left by later nineteenth-century commodity trades (guano being a
fine example), a *sweet* commerce that by and large helped consolidate
stronger elite states by the 1870s. It was also buffered by Creole memories
that, in core culture zones at least, their societies were hardly "new"
(backward) or at least as venerable as industrial upstarts like Cincinnati
or Chicago. Attitudes toward progress were ambivalently and colonially
mapped.

Second, with due respect to M. A. Centeno, the "strategic" metaphor
and motive never became terribly pronounced in postcolonial Latin
America. While there was much diffuse violence (and hierarchy), actual
interstate conflict was rare, with economy-debilitating internecine caudillismo the rule and a major factor in industrial lags to 1870. Nowhere did
a militaristic state-building project exert the sort of pressures felt in eastern Europe, and the zone was remote from the pressures of the final European scramble for formal empires. Indeed, the two possible exceptions—a
Bismarckian triumphal Chile and a disintegrating, frontline, and defeated
pre-Porfirian Mexico—were the only states, I would venture, to react
with the kind of top-down power, extractive, or scale considerations
worthy of full Gerschenkronian analysis. The more statist or developmental traditions of contemporary Brazil would likely find distinctive
roots.[46] The remainder of the region—indulging in one huge generalization—would suffer relatively "weak" European-style states, officially operating on the light economic principles of free trade, primary exports,
and invisible hands. No wonder that Latin Americans looking back upon
themselves from the 1950s and 1960s saw not active, dirigiste states to
explain or rationalize (the essence of European latecomer analysis) but
instead the opposite: a long history of dwarfish, sleepy, and supposedly
liberal ones. Not until recently has this image changed, among citizenries
and academic specialists alike, with the rise of the neoliberal critique.
Whatever the case, neither the exigencies of Latin American postcolonial
history nor the ideological imaginings it spawned would make fertile
ground for Gerschenkron's grand theory.

A New Late Political Economy?

I began this chapter hoping that the economic history perspectives of an Alexander Gerschenkron might be found "useful" for modern Latin America, for there is much to be admired in his intellectual scope and sensibilities. I am now less sure or realize that the most literal applications of latecomer analysis will not do. Rather than pursue the short question of whether Gerschenkron's theories of relative backwardness fit Latin American reality, I tried in longhand to see how they have been (timidly) applied before and why they were seemingly shunted during the polarized development decades of the 1960s and 1970s. Along the way, some fitful insights emerged as to how the theory does or does not relate, some welling up from Latin American history, but such realities themselves are fast changing.

Is the 21st century at last a delayed opportunity? Though I ought to brim with Hirschmanian possibilism, knowing that now we are supposed to be "postdependency," post-Marxist, and postmodern to boot, I don't. "Development" has been in deep political, and some feel epistemological, trouble for well over a decade now, starting even before Latin America's debt and developmental crashes of the 1980s, with the military repressions of the 1970s. It is hard to grasp, however, how we can simply march back to some pristine methodological Eden before dependency and still later critiques of modernization.[47] But the historical Left—normally the dominant carrier of integrative political economy traditions—is abandoning this field in droves, as if sore losers, substituting for it a strange and ahistorical wonderland of "identity" politics. Anything that bespeaks of economics, state discourse, praxis, or development is labeled "economistic" or worse, while the entire notion of modern "master narrative" (i.e., most social theory) is still in retreat before a different species of continental drift.[48] Paradoxically or not, this at a time when material uplift and material destitution have never meant more, and with a more global immediacy, to Latin American peoples themselves. Not coincidentally, our coeval northern crisis of multidisciplinary "area studies" would also dim chances for revival of a Gerschenkronian-inspired political economy, which intrinsically belongs with geographically and culturally embedded disciplinary traditions.

The modest "right" in our disciplines, if perennially antistatist, has never been historical as it worked to reduce economic traditions to rational choice theory, mindless quantification, and liberal-market dogmas—almost the mirror image of the eclectic, fluent historical sensibility of Gerschenkron's cohort of Continental political economists. Alas, by this juncture, the majority of Latin American economic and policy elites have roundly convinced themselves of the inevitability, if not desirability, of ideological neoliberalism. The postwar national developmental coalitions and *Cepalista* currents that at least implied Gerschenkronian ways have de facto dried up in the region.[49] Thus, save for their mutual demonization of the Latin American state, there seems little creative ground for cross-fertilization between left and right "visions," methodologically or politically. Ironically, Gerschenkron himself has very lately shown up, in academic cameos, as a scapegoat of sorts—a shared target of our Latin Americanist Right and Left, such as they are.[50] Just as strange, while caught in crossfire from both politico-academic wings, a dynamic assertive role for the Third World state has been recently rediscovered by none other than the multilateral development agencies, most notably the World Bank.[51]

The refuge of "new" political economy is the sociological current engaged in comparative and pragmatic "state-centered" studies—such as the Evans and Haggard works encountered earlier. There are also the occasional political scientists still drawn to questions of political timing and cultures. They might be invigorated by renewed economics interests in institutions (as in Douglass North's Polanyi-like historicism or so-called economics path dependence, the fancy new name for historical perspective). So far, the big comparisons for Latin Americanists have been aimed largely at Asia, not always fitting (save to policy elites), and sociological history has not ventured much deeper than the 1930s. The intellectual gene pool may become too small to support a healthy resurgence of historical political economy. But if a resurgence ever comes, it is likely to be born from the multidisciplinary study of the "deviant" Western cases, such as those found in Latin America's long history. We could still have a long wait before Gerschenkron becomes a household name among the Latin Americanists.

NOTES

I thank Atul Kohli, Héctor Lindo-Fuentes, Richard Salvucci, Sarah and Albert Hirschman, Silvana Palermo, and Ricardo Salvatorre for insightful criticisms; the Russell Sage Foundation, where this first got drafted; as well as enthusiasts of Guadalajara's "Other Mirror," Miguel Centeno, Fernando López-Alves, and Gerry Munck among them. I dedicate this chapter to the memory of my politically incorrect friend, Daniel Nugent.

1. See Albert Fishlow, "Gerschenkron," in *The New Palgrave: A Dictionary of Economics* (London: Macmillan, 1987), 518–19, for a fine intellectual biography. Cf. "Backwardness."

2. Alexander Gerschenkron, *Economic Backwardness in Historical Perspective: A Book of Essays* (Cambridge, Mass.: Belknap/Harvard University Press, 1962); another less renowned collection is *Continuity in History and Other Essays* (Cambridge, Mass.: Belknap/Harvard University Press, 1968); Gerschenkron, *El atraso económico e industrialización* (Madrid: Ariel, 1970), containing three core essays, introduced his work to Latin America.

3. Polanyi, however, attracts more friends in the afterlife; for example, he (not Gerschenkron) made it into Theda Skocpol's *Vision and Method in Historical Sociology* (New York: Cambridge University Press, 1984), in the chapter by Fred Block and Margaret Somer, "Beyond the Economistic Fallacy: The Holistic Social Science of Karl Polanyi," 47–85.

4. See Fishlow, "Gerschenkron"; or Gerschenkron's own synthesis, "The Approach to European Industrialism: A Postscript," in *Economic Backwardness*, 353–66.

5. Biographers overlook the American institutionalist Thorstein Veblen's parallel concept in his 1915 *Imperial Germany and the Industrial Revolution*, subtitled *The Advantages of Backwardness*.

6. Throughout his career, Gerschenkron felt energetically moved to defend his constructs against myriad critics, in such succinctly titled articles as "The Discipline and I," (*Journal of Economic History* 27 (1967): 443–59. This provides interesting reactions to the rise of "New Economic History." See M. Falkus, "Backwardness," in *The New Palgrave*, 170–71 (as well as "German Historical School"), for a feel for Gerschenkron's legacy and vestiges of Schumpeter and Toynbee. The "new" economic sociology, despite similar interests, seems less indebted to Gerschenkron: N. Smelsor and R. Swedberg, eds., *Handbook of Economic Sociology* (New York: Russell Sage, 1994), esp. Fred Block, "The Roles of the State in the Economy."

7. W. W. Rostow, *The Stages of Economic Growth: A Non-Communist Manifesto* (Cambridge: Cambridge University Press, 1960); Gerschenkron, "Reflections on the Concept of 'Prerequisites of Modern Industrialization,'" chap. 2 or "An Approach to European Industrialization: A Postscript" of *Economic Backwardness*; Albert Fishlow, "Empty Economic Stages?" *Economic Journal* 65, no. 297 (1965): 112–25—a superb review and critique; or radical and youthful John H. Coatsworth's "Walt W. Rostow: The Stages of Economic Stagnation" (SDS pamphlet, Madison, Wisconsin, 1967?). For Latin American context, see Joseph A. Kahl, *Modernization, Exploitation, and Dependency in Latin America: Germani, González Casanova and Cardoso* (New Brunswick, N.J.: Transaction Books, 1976). For many Latin Americanists of the 1960s, Rostow's formulas seemed little more than vulgar or Eurocentric justifications for the era's foreign aid strategies, and they became a sounding board for the antidiffusionist and ultimately autarkic vision of dependency theory.

8. Clive Trebilcock, *The Industrialization of the Continental Powers, 1780–1914* (London: Longman, 1981); Lars G. Sandberg, "Ignorance, Poverty and Economic Backwardness in the Early Stages of European Industrialization: Variations on Alexander Gerschenkron's Grand Themes," *Journal of European Economic History* 11 (1982): 675–97; Henry Rosovsky, "Japan's Transition to

Modern Economic Growth, 1868–1885," in Henry Rosovsky, ed., *Industrialization in Two Worlds: Essays in Honor of Alexander Gerschenkron* (New York: Wiley, 1966), 91–139.

9. Douglass North and Robert Thomas, *The Rise of the Western World: A New Economic History* (Cambridge: Cambridge University Press, 1976); or E. L. Jones, *The European Miracle* (Cambridge: Cambridge University Press, 1981) and *Growth Recurring* (New York: Oxford, 1988), which move to post-Gerschenkronian stress on gradual shifts in economic history. See J. Adelman, this volume, for new institutionalism and Latin America.

10. For a taste, browse the contents of essays in *Economic Backwardness* and *Continuity*; for intellectual history, see the key essay A. Gerschenkron, "History of Economic Doctrines and Economic History," *American Economic Review* 59, no. 2 (1969): 1–17.

11. For example, Gerschenkron, "The Discipline and I," 448–49, or *Continuity*, 7–8.

12. Personal Communication, Sarah Hirschman and Albert O. Hirschman, Princeton, February 1998; before this chat, I somehow assumed no direct relationship. In fact, Gerschenkron helped Hirschman land his first postwar job at Berkeley and a later one at Harvard; in the 1960s, however, they parted ways, as one of them progressively embraced the rhetoric of reaction.

13. I hesitate to call them "coreligionists," though this, too, could be a factor. For Hirschman's larger heterodoxy, consult *Essays in Trespassing: From Economics to Politics and Beyond* (New York: Cambridge University Press, 1981); for revealing biographical essays, see his more recent *A Propensity to Self-Subversion* (Cambridge, Mass.: Harvard University Press, 1995). Volumes that explore Hirschman's influence are: Simón Teitel's *Towards a New Development Strategy for Latin America: Pathways from Hirschman's Thought* (Washington: IDB, 1992) (for Latin America); and A. Foxley, M. McPherson, and G. O'Donnell, eds., *Development, Democracy and the Art of Trespassing* (Notre Dame, Ind.: University of Notre Dame Press, 1986).

14. Though I think Peter Evans goes too far by flatly conflating them into a "Gerschenkronian-Hirschmanian vision" on states in development. "Predatory, Developmental and Other Apparatuses: A Comparative Political Economy Perspective on the Third World State," *Sociological Forum* 4 (1989): 567–69.

15. Albert O. Hirschman, *The Strategy of Economic Devlopment* (New Haven, Conn.: Yale University Press, 1958); Hirschman, *Journeys towards Progress: Studies in Economic Policy-Making in Latin America* (New York: Norton, 1973); "Obstacles" and "Ideologies," both reproduced in Hirschman's *A Bias for Hope: Essays on Development and Latin America* (New Haven, Conn.: Yale University Press, 1971), chaps. 13, 14; Hirschman, "Industrialism and Its Manifold Discontents," *Propensity to Self-Subversion*, chap. 17.

16. Paul Gootenberg, *Imagining Development: Economic Ideas in Peru's "Fictitious Prosperity" of Guano, 1840–1880* (Berkeley: University of California Press, 1993), which argues that utopian yearnings for industrialism pervade nineteenth-century thought. I just recently realized this Hirschmanesque forward (intellectual) linkage.

17. Albert Hirschman, "The Political Economy of Import-Substituting Indus-

trialization in Latin America," *Quarterly Journal of Economics* 82 (1968): 2–32; reprinted in *Bias for Hope*.

18. Ibid.

19. In 1988, David Landes convened a Gerschenkronian-tinged conference at Harvard—"Why the Lag in Latin American Industrialization?'—to tackle such questions, but the volume (prelude to his recent book, *The Wealth and Poverty of Nations*) never appeared, save for Stephen Haber, "Assessing the Obstacles to Industrialization: The Mexican Economy, 1830–1940," *Journal of Latin American Studies* [hereafter *JLAS*] 26 (1994): 1–33; and Arnold Bauer, "Industry and the Missing Bourgeoisie: Consumption and Development in Chile," *Hispanic American Historical Review* [hereafter *HAHR*] 70 (1990); 227–54. I recall Latin Americanists questioned the "lag" as problematic.

20. As economic history, Hirschman's characterizations from 1968 stir varied discrepancies. For example, José Gabriel Palma's "Growth and Structure of Chilean Manufacturing Industry from 1830–1935" (Ph.D., diss., Oxford University, 1979) found that in sectoral terms, "producer" goods prove vital in export economies; Haber's "Assessing the Obstacles to Industrialization" argues that factory scale early reached overcapacity (due to "capital market imperfections"); T. Rosemary Thorp, "A Reappraisal of the Origins of ISI, 1920–1950," *JLAS* 24 (1992): 181–97, credits foreign capital (during the 1950s) for distortions Hirschman deems intrinsic.

21. Albert Fishlow, "Brazilian Development in Long-Term Perspective," *American Economic Review* 70, no. 2 (1980): 102–8; Fishlow, "The Latin American State," *Journal of Economic Perspectives* 4, no. 3 (1990): 61–74; and his critique of Rostow's aggregates "Empty Economic Stages?" cited in note 7. Interestingly, Fishlow and Coatsworth both began their careers scrutinizing with "New Economic History" one of Rostow's "leading sectors": railways, U.S. and Mexican. Personal communication, W. Baer, Lima, June 1998.

22. Witness the wide reverberations of his generalist works like *The Passions and the Interests* and *Exit, Voice and Loyalty*.

23. John H. Coatsworth, "From Backwardness to Underdevelopment" (ms., Chicago, 1977); findings widely disseminated in "Obstacles to Economic Growth in Nineteenth-Century Mexico," *American Historical Review* 82 (1978): 80–100; see note 7 for Coatsworth's early Rostowian aim. The explicit comparative focus in Coatsworthian analysis is also very Gerschenkronian. Although Coatsworth was my mentor, he never brought up Gerschenkron per se; my worn copy of *Economic Backwardness* was aptly the gift of a college girlfriend studying *European* economic history. Haber might be read as one simplified Coatsworth spinoff.

24. Sylvia Ann Hewlett and Richard S. Weinert, *Brazil and Mexico: Patterns in Late Development* (Philadelphia: Institute for the Study of Human Issues, 1982); Douglass Bennett and Kenneth Sharpe, "The State as Banker and Entrepreneur: The Last Resort Character of the Mexican State's Economic Intervention, 1917–1970," *Comparative Politics*, 12 (1980): 165—89; cf. briefer treatment in their *Transnational Corporations versus the State: The Political Economy of the Mexican Auto Industry* (Princeton, N.J.: Princeton University Press, 1985), 40–41. This is neglecting a similar (Marxist and non-Marxist)

literature on Latin American "state capitalism" (e.g., E. K. Fitzgerald on Peru in the 1960s–1970s).

25. Guillermo A. O'Donnell, *Modernization and Bureaucratic-Authoritarianism: Studies in South American Politics* (Berkeley: Institute of International Studies, University of California, 1973), 89 n. See David Collier, ed., *The New Authoritarianism in Latin America* (Princeton, N.J.: Princeton University Press, 1979), for relevant roundup. I thank Geraldo Munck for pressing here on issues of bureaucratic authoritarianism.

26. At least one scholar, James Kurth, coming out of Comparative Politics, has fruitfully continued to press the bureaucratic-authoritarianism school's Gershenkronian theses, integrating insights of Hirschman as well, largely in relation to the political development of southern and eastern Europe. Like Mediterranean "corporatism" and "patrimonialism," Kurth's allied interests, these theories do travel the seas. In fact, continuing analysis of delayed development today, given our discontinuities with economistic bureaucratic authoritarianism, focuses mainly on *political* rather than industrial implications. Albert O. Hirschman, "The Turn to Authoritarianism in Latin America and the Search for Its Economic Determinants," 61–98, and James R. Kurth, "Industrial Change and Political Change: A European Perspective," 319–62, both in Collier, *The New Authoritarianism*. See also Kurth, "A Tale of Two Peripheries: Southern Europe and Eastern Europe," and "A Tale of Four Countries: Parallel Politics in Southern Europe," both in J. Kurth and James Petras, eds., *Mediterranean Paradoxes: Politics and Social Structure in Southern Europe* (Providence, R.I.: Berg, 1993). A recent sample, besides Kurth's, is Francisco Panizza, "Late Institutionalisation and Early Modernisation: The Emergence of Uruguay's Liberal Democratic Political Order," *JLAS* 29 (1997): 667–91.

27. Peter Evans, "Predatory, Developmental, and Other Apparatuses"; Evans, *Embedded Autonomy: States and Industrial Transformation* (Princeton, N.J.: Princeton University Press, 1995); cf. Block, "Roles of the State in the Economy," for allied approaches. Evans's work is hard to evaluate historically: along the lines of bureaucratic-authoritarian theorists, or Moore, I would surmise that states of great autonomy are more willing to take the risk of extreme authoritarianism (as Soviet Russia or Nazi Germany); it is also hard to see in a policy sense how the right embedded "class" influence is achieved.

28. Steven E. Sanderson, *The Politics of Trade in Latin American Development* (Palo Alto, Calif.: Stanford University Press, 1992); Kathryn Sikkink, *Ideas and Institutions: Developmentalism in Brazil and Argentina* (Ithaca, N.Y.: Cornell University Press, 1991); Carlos H. Waisman, *Reversal of Development in Argentina: Postwar Counterrevolutionary Policies and Their Structural Consequences* (Princeton, N.J.: Princeton University Press, 1987).

29. Merilee S. Grindle, *Challenging the State: Crisis and Innovation in Latin America and Africa* (New York: Cambridge University Press, 1996); Judith Tendler, *Good Government in the Tropics* (Baltimore: Johns Hopkins University Press, 1997); her first book, in Gerschenkron mode, was on the "big" Brazilian (energy) industry. This group dramatically contrasts with bureaucratic-authoritarian theorists as well as neoliberals.

30. Stephan Haggard, *Pathways from the Periphery: The Politics of Growth*

in the Newly Industrializing Countries (Ithaca, N.Y.: Cornell University Press, 1990). Haggard, less "Skocpolean" than Evans, is drawn to markets as well as state building. G. Gereffi and D. Wyman, eds., *Manufacturing Miracles: Paths of Industrialization in Latin America and East Asia* (Princeton, N.J.: Princeton University Press, 1990). In the course of preparing this chapter, I have encountered a few newer scholars fascinated with Gerschenkron. Two examples are Emiliano Corral, a University of Chicago doctoral student with a remarkable comparative study of industrialization and labor in the U.S. South and Mexico (and an interest in Myrdal and Gerschenkron), and José Antonio Sánchez, at the Instituto Ortega y Gasset in Madrid, who works Gerschenkron into the nineteenth-century Argentine agrarian development.

31. Cristóbal Kay, "Comparative Development of the European Manorial System and the Latin American Hacienda System" (Ph.D. diss., Sussex, 1971); J. Stephens, E. Huber, and D. Reuschemeyer, *Capitalist Development and Democracy* (Chicago: University of Chicago Press, 1992); see also Nicos Mouzelis, *Politics in the Semi-periphery: Early Parliamentarism and Late Industrialism in the Balkans and Latin America* (London: Macmillan, 1986); Benjamin Orlove, ed., *The Allure of the Foreign: Imported Goods in Postcolonial Latin America* (Ann Arbor: University of Michigan Press, 1997), 18–23; J. Kurth and Jan Triska, eds., *Dominant Powers and Subordinate States: The United States in Latin America and the Soviet Union in Eastern Europe* (Durham, N.C.: Duke University Press, 1986); or cross-regional fertilization in theoretical works of Adam Przeworski (*Democracy and the Market*, [New York: Cambridge University Press, 1991]). On Moore, see E. Huber and F. Safford, eds., *Agrarian Structure and Political Power: Landlord and Peasant in the Making of Latin America* (Pittsburgh: University of Pittsburgh Press, 1995). Immanuel Wallerstein, *The Modern World-System* (New York: Academic Press, 1977), vol. 1.

32. Joseph Love, *Crafting the Third World: Theorizing Underdevelopment in Rumania and Brazil* (Stanford, Calif.: Stanford University Press, 1996).

33. Ibid.; critiqued in a review for *The Americas* 53, no. 2 (1997). The liberal portrayal of the pre-1930 era contrasts with Love's own collection (with N. Jacobsen), *Guiding the Invisible Hand: Economic Liberalism and the State in Latin American History* (New York: Praeger, 1988). Salvucci (personal communication) views Prebisch this way.

34. Donald [Dierdre] McClosky, *The Rhetoric of Economics* (Madison: University of Wisconsin Press, 1985); Robert Heilbroner and William Milberg, *The Crisis of Vision in Modern Economic Thought* (New York: Cambridge University Press, 1995); Albert O. Hirschman, "Rival Views of Market Society: Civilizing, Destructive, or Feeble?" in *Rival Views of Market Society* (New York: Viking, 1986), chap. 1, for multiple metaphoric insights; Gerschenkron, *Economic Backwardness*, 363, reflects on metaphors. On colonial history, P. Gootenberg's mixed-metaphoric "On Salamanders, Pyramids and Mexico's 'Growth-without Change': Anachronistic Reflections on a Case of Bourbon Mexico," *Colonial Latin American Review* 5, no. 1 (1996): 117–27.

35. André Gunder Frank, *Capitalism and Underdevelopment in Latin America* (New York: Monthly Review Press, 1967), which begins on his reaction against modernization. In Chicago lore, Harberger (of later Pinochet infamy)

saved Frank from voracious departmental colleagues because Frank's father had been his favorite German mystery writer. Paul Baran's 1950s essays (not Gerschenkron) are cited inspirationally by dependency writers, for his Marxist conception of "deformed" neocolonial collaborator elites.

36. André Gunder Frank, *Lumpenbourgeoisie and Lumpendevelopment in Latin America* (New York: Monthly Review Press, 1972); Frank, "Dependence Is Dead, Long Live Dependence, and the Class Struggle: A Reply to Critics," *Latin American Perspectives* 1 (1974): 89–106; E. Leclau reply, "Feudalism and Capitalism in Latin America" *New Left Review* (1971). It can be jolting to revisit literatures churned out during those hot years—for example, R. Chilcote and D. Johnson, eds., *Theories of Development: Mode of Production or Dependency?* (Beverley Hills, Calif.: Sage, 1983).

37. Another metaphor was frankly sexual: the one of "dependent," "weak," "supine," feminized "national markets"—"penetrated" by a desirous and vigorous European capitalism, a kind of racialist rape fantasy of the sort Franz Fanon might have gloried in (and in broad contrast with the desexualized, depoliticized consensual idea of commerce in mainstream trade theory).

38. Two explicit critiques later on this problematic are sociologist Maurice Zeitlin's *The Civil Wars in Chile, or the Bourgeois Revolutions That Never Were* (Princeton, N.J.: Princeton University Press, 1984); and my own *Between Silver and Guano: Commercial Policy and the State in Postindependence Peru* (Princeton, N.J.: Princeton University Press, 1989).

39. Fernando Henrique Cardoso and Enzo Faletto, *Dependency and Development in Latin America* (Berkeley: University of California Press, 1979); note page xix, a possibly veiled referent to Gerschenkron himself. See also Cardoso's fine essay on the intellectual issues, "The Originality of the Copy: The Economic Commission for Latin America and the Idea of Development," in *Towards a New Strategy of Development* (New York: Pergamon, 1979), 53–72; or his well-known "The Consumption of Dependency Theory in the United States," *Latin American Research Review* [hereafter *LARR*] 12, no. 3 (1979): 7–24. Cardoso, of course, is now *leading* that Brazilian state, if brandishing a new set of metaphors: Brazil is no longer an underdeveloped society but a more simply "unjust" one.

40. Gerschenkron, "History of Economic Doctrines" and "Realism and Utopia in Russian Economic Thought," both in *Economic Backwardness* (188–97), stress how economic ideas need not have *direct* relation with realities; indeed, the opposite is more likely true. For regime infatuation with dependency (Velasco), see Rosemary Thorp and Geoffrey Bertram, *Peru: 1890–1977: Growth and Policy in an Open Economy* (London: Macmillan, 1978), chap. 15. On dependency as "bad science," see Stephan Haber's "Economic Growth and Latin American Economic Historiography," in Stephan Haber, ed., *How Latin America Fell Behind: Essays on the Economic Histories of Brazil and Mexico* (Palo Alto, Calif.: Stanford University Press, 1997), 7, in which even Gerschenkron (!) gets implicated in the *dependentista* plague.

41. Graphically detailed in Gary Gerrefi and Peter Evans, "Transnational Corporations, Dependent Development, and State Policy in the Semiperiphery: A Comparison of Brazil and Mexico," *LARR* 16, no. 1 (1981): 31–64; reprinted in Hewlett and Weinert, *Brazil and Mexico*.

42. Juan Carlos Korol and Hilda Sábato, "Incomplete Industrialization: An Argentine Obsession," *LARR* 25, no. 1 (1990): 7–30—a suggestive survey, replete with Argentine exceptionalism (fascinations with staple and modernization theory). Eventually, Hirschman was moved to protest that such intellectual frustrations obscured the growth achievements of the postwar era, in "The Political Economy of Latin America: Seven Exercises in Retrospection," *LARR* 22, no. 3 (1987), 7–36.

43. For geopolitical poetics: Fernando Coronil, "Beyond Occidentalism: Toward Non-imperial Geohistorical Categories," *Cultural Anthropology* 11, no. 1 (1996): 51–87; or Barry Eichengreen, "Geography as Destiny: A Brief History of Economic Growth," *Foreign Affairs* 77 (1998): 128–33 (on Landes's reposing of Gerschenkron's dilemmas). Cf. Steve Stern, "Feudalism, Capitalism, and the World System in the Perspective of Latin America and the Caribbean," *American Historical Review* 93 (1988): 829–72.

44. Michael Mann, *States, Wars, and Capitalism* (London: Blackwell, 1988); Charles Tilly, *Coercion, Capital and the European State, A.D. 990–1990* (London: Blackwell, 1990); William McNeil, *The Pursuit of Power* (Chicago: University of Chicago Press, 1982); Jones, *European Miracle*; John A. Hall, "States and Economic Development: Reflections on Adam Smith," in *States in History* (London: Blackwell, 1986), 154–76—here, growing stress is placed on feudalism as priming European states' affinity with competitive capitalism.

45. Gootenberg, *Imagining Development*; such developmental utopianism was striking. This story contrasts with E. Bradford Burns's celebrated dependency text *The Poverty of Progress: Latin America in the Nineteenth Century* (Berkeley: University of California Press, 1980); see Tulio Halperín's exegesis of Latin American liberalism/statism, "Backward Looks and Forward Glimpses from a Quincentennial Vantage Point," *JLAS* 24 (1992): 219–34. See Gootenberg, *Between Silver and Guano*, 141, for economic nationalism as reactive (Gerschenkronian) "state-building" phenomena in early nineteenth-century Peru. Cf. Sanderson, *Politics of Trade*, chaps. 1–2, for similar commercial genealogies.

46. Miguel Angel Centeno, "Blood and Debt: War and Taxation in Nineteenth-Century Latin America," *American Journal of Sociology* 102 (1997): 1565–605; "weak" is quoted for obvious difficulties of measuring such things (states) on any unilinear scale. For a compelling differing view of state capacities (in analytic relation to export economies), see Steven Topik, "The Economic Role of the State in Liberal Regimes: Brazil and Mexico Compared," in Love and Jacobsen, *Guiding the Invisible Hand*, 117–44.

47. Hirschman "The Rise and Fall of Development Economics" (1981), in *Essays in Trespassing*, 1–24; note that Hirschman himself (even in 1981) was hardly brimming with possiblism. Cf. Haber's celebration of growth "Science" and methodological purity in *How Latin America Fell Behind*.

48. See, for a sample, Arturo Escobar's disappointment with developmentalism in *Encountering Development: The Making and Unmaking of the Third World* (Princeton, N.J.: Princeton University Press, 1995).

49. Ian Roxborough, "Neoliberalism in Latin America: Limits and Alternatives," *Third World Quarterly* 13 (1992): 421–40, foil to the *oficialista* "Neoliberalism: Curse or Plague?" line among Latin Americanists. I see these as

ponderable if pessimistic points. Does today's generalized state bashing result from a mutual exhaustion of traditional pre-1980s "targets" (landed estates, bourgeoisies, and imperialism on one side; socialism, interventionism, and redistribution on another?) or from a genuinely shared distrust of the state's repressive or parasitic roles? Is this a (trendy) phase or a genuine trend (postmodernity, the end of history)? What I cannot fully buy is the suggestion (in Harvey, Eagleton, and the like) of postmodern irreality as a cultural logic itself of globalization or ideological exhaustion.

50. On the "Right," Haber seemingly confounds Gerschenkron with Latin American "structuralism" then doubly conflated with "dependency" (*How Latin America Fell Behind*, 7). On the "Left," see Caren Addis, "A Clash of Paradigms: Recent Interpretations of Brazilian Development," *LARR* 32, no. 3 (1997): 123–39, where Gerschenkron signifies a "traditional" statist, top-down, large-scale optic on development—in contrast to labor history, feminism and other "emerging" paradigms.

51. See the remarkable *World Development Report 1997: The State in a Changing World* (Washington, D.C.: World Bank, 1997)—and its virtually Gerschenkronian ad copy. See Eichengreen, "Geography as Destiny" for a similar eye on disciplinary possibilities.

Chapter Three

KARL POLANYI AND THE CREATION OF THE

"MARKET SOCIETY"

STEVEN TOPIK

S INCE THE END of the cold war, Latin America has found itself in
a theoretical quandary. Guiding principles such as import-substituting industrialization (ISI) modernization and dependency have
been discarded or vastly modified. Certainly Marxism has declined in
popularity since the fall of the Berlin Wall, the ouster of the Sandinistas
in Nicaragua, and the decline of Cuba. There is no truly hegemonic
worldview. Instead, there is a sharp divide.

In the academy, particularly in political science and economics, scholars posit societies composed of economically rational people who attempt
to maximize their individual welfare. This is very much the modernist
vision, with a teleological belief in progress (i.e., capitalist development
and "democratic" political systems) through the diffusion of Eurocentric
reason. This has carried over to the world of politics, where we have
leaders such as Brazil's president, Fernando Henrique Cardoso (a social
democrat and one of the originators of dependency theory), Carlos
Menem (standard-bearer of the formerly nationalist Peronist Party), and
Mexico's officially institutionalized revolutionary party, the Partido
Revolucionario Institucional (PRI), headed by Ernesto Zedillo, crafting
policies aimed at privatization, attracting foreign investment, and establishing free trade.

We are told that we are in a new era where new rules obtain. The
demise of socialism, it is asserted, means that the market and private
property are the route to freedom and prosperity; the state is a parasite
that retards individual self-realization while capitalism is the only feasible
model.[1] The elevation of the market has reasserted economics as the dominant discipline.[2]

The opposition is much less sure of itself. While not entirely rejecting
Marxism, it is sometimes a Marxism that is so modified as to become
virtually unrecognizable. Rather than stressing structural relations to the
means of production and the dependence of the ideological and political
superstructure on the material base, theorists of the Left today attack

some of the central precepts of Marxism: class analysis has been modified by introducing issues of gender, race, and nationalism.[3] Identity is seen as deriving from traditions and cultural practices as much as from relations to the means of production.[4] The agency of individuals and their ability to resist the dominant trends, even if only in small, symbolic ways, are studied rather than the state's ability to assert the forces of history.[5] Culture and the linguistic turn have overshadowed materialism.

Opposition theories, whether they be postcolonial, subaltern, or feminist studies, are guided by a critique of the dominant paradigm but not by any unifying theory. Indeed, there is something of an epistemological crisis in which subjects are destabilized, points of view are decentered, and causality is made suspect. "Complicating" reality, rather than positing elegant models, has become the goal. The critiques tend to shun what Quentin Skinner called "grand theory" or Hayden White "metanarratives." Rather, there is a postmodern tendency to adopt an eclectic approach, mixing and matching theoretical tools depending upon the question at issue.[6]

This chapter suggests that many of the aspects of oppositional stands can be coherently united by accepting the insights of Karl Polanyi, an iconoclastic theorist who has not been much used of late by Latin Americanists outside of anthropology.[7] He offers a unified vision, though his studies of primitive, archaic, and capitalist societies have been generally studied in isolation. His best-known work, *The Great Transformation*, a Christian socialist manifesto, offers a critique that can benefit scholars, including Latin Americanists, interested in both subaltern and peasant studies, as well as political economists critical of "neoliberalism."[8] But his other, less well known works also form part of a coherent whole.

Scholars from different disciplines tend to stress different aspects of Polanyi's thought; they often treat him as if he were two different theorists, one concerned with the development of capitalism and the other with precapitalist social relations. I will argue, however, that his thought was unified, focusing on the central question of the changing place of economies and the construction and consequences of markets in archaic, primitive, and capitalist societies. Consequently, he speaks directly to a wide range of phenomena that interest students of Latin America, where markets have many "imperfections," even though ideologically the market has become supreme.[9]

Although much influenced by structuralists such as Max Weber, Karl Marx, and Émile Durkheim, many aspects of Polanyi's thought are consonant with postmodernist tendencies. Polanyi constructed a metanarrative, but it was a metanarrative that was more theological than teleological, concerned with ethics and freedom rather than materialism or scientific laws. He believed in contingency and human agency but argued that humans were fundamentally social beings. Tradition weighed heavily in decision-making. Communities, not individuals, moved history: "In our century the great ideas of world history are not written by great minds, scholars, artists, not even great politicians, but rather by the people."[10] Originally used to attack both fascism and Soviet state communism, his views have become important in a different battle: the struggle against neoliberalism and commodification. The global coherence of Polanyi's thought allows Latin Americanists to see the interrelationship of many apparently remote concepts and issues such as concerns with precapitalism both in archaic civilizations and later, less complex peoples, the household economy and sexual division of labor, the evolution and consequences of markets, the emergence of the global dominance of finance capital, the importance of religion, and the role of the state.[11] He provides a possible solution to the culture wars with his hopeful, humanistic vision that is, at the same time, not deterministic. He bridges the gulf between culture and economics, which are not competing explanations but aspects of the same human condition: "The outstanding discovery of recent historical and anthropological research is that man's economy, as a rule, is submerged in his social relationships."[12]

OVERVIEW OF POLANYI'S THEORETICAL CONTRIBUTIONS

Although written more than half a century ago as an analysis of the death of nineteenth-century liberalism and the rise of fascism, *The Great Transformation* has tremendous current relevance. Indeed, it reads as if it were written today. Polanyi was ahead of his time in combining an interest in subaltern and "primitive" peoples with a concern with global commodification. He cared about both exploitation and alienation. Greatly influenced by the anthropology of Bronislaw Malinowski and Richard Thurnwald but trained in neoclassical economics, Polanyi challenged materialist structuralism, the separation of the political, economic, and social spheres, and the specialization of disciplines.[13] A socialist, he was as interested in praxis as in theory.

His work affected many disciplines. Polanyi was a founder of economic anthropology, much influencing such prominent Latin Americanists as Eric Wolf, Frank Cancian, Rhoda Halperin, and Michael Taussig in their uses of reciprocity and redistribution and the social "embeddedness" of economies to study ancient and less complex peoples.[14] Polanyi's work anticipated E. P. Thompson's concept of "moral economy," and Charles Tilly's and James Scott's insistence on the importance of collective action and popular resistance, all of which have been influential in

Latin America. Earlier than two other central European economists, Albert Hirschman and Alexander Gerschenkron, Polanyi underlined the social and intellectual dimensions of economics and the central role of the state.[15]

Similarly, the study of the informal sector, which is viewed as a late capitalist phenomenon in places such as Brazil, Mexico, and Peru, takes inspiration from Polanyi's study of less complex people.[16] As with subaltern studies, he stressed the historical role of the inarticulate and unheard masses. Concentrating on the rise of capitalism in its most advanced center, England, he nonetheless expounded theories resembling the later work of André Gunder Frank and Samir Amin, useful to students of noncapitalist peoples and to understanding the nature of social destruction brought about by imperialism, as well as the very different faces the world economy has worn in different settings: "External trade is originally, more in the nature of adventure, exploration, hunting, piracy and war than of barter. It may as little imply peace as two-sidedness."[17] He noted that "markets are not institutions functioning mainly within an economy but without."[18] Long-distance trade was not a natural outgrowth of domestic development but rather preceded domestic trade. It resulted from geographic difference in which goods were obtained "as much akin to robbery and piracy as what we regard as trade."[19] Consequently, the growth of trade did not necessarily expand the domestic market or bring about monetary relations. Numerous disciples of world-systems analysis who have written on Latin America, such as Terence Hopkins, Peter Evans, Immanuel Wallerstein, Giovanni Arrighi, and Walter Goldfrank, have taken inspiration from Polanyi.[20]

In addition to the many more orthodox social scientists who borrow perspectives from him, some postmodernists apply key concepts central to Polanyi's view. In particular, Polanyi discarded the infrastructure-superstructure dichotomy, believing that ideology and politics were central to understanding the economic. He was extremely concerned with the concept and process of commodification, reification, and alienation, ideas that would come to us from the Frankfurt school. Indeed, the "myths" of commodities and the "metaphysics" of economics were central concerns, which has made him attractive to modern-day critics of consumer culture.[21]

Polanyi also had a postmodern view of time. His view was a dialectic based on freedom and ethics, not "scientific laws." Indeed, it is not teleological.[22] In this he disagreed with the German historical school of Hegel and Marx. Polanyi preached: "Never has there been such an absurd superstition as the belief that the history of man is governed by laws that are independent of his will and action. The concept of a future which awaits us somewhere is senseless because the future does not exist, not now or later. The future is constantly being remade by those who live in the present."[23] Thus he stressed human agency. Human actions are not simply dictated by material laws and necessities; people have the freedom to make ethical choices for which they bear responsibility both as individuals and as members of society. He noted: "Economic motives *per se* are notoriously much less effective with most people than so-called emotional ones."[24]

The bulk of Polanyi's work on archaic and less complex people was intended to demonstrate the historically exceptional nature of market society. Indeed, not only was all of history *not* conspiring to create capitalism, but in fact capitalism was an unexpected surprise: "The emergence of the idea of self-regulation was a complete reversal of the trend of development."[25] Presumably if history took this one sharp turn, it could do so again in the future. There is no reason to believe that today's fascination with free trade and laissez-faire is the end of history or that the future is predictable.

Another implication of Polanyi's notion of time is that there is no reason to believe that what is most recent is best. Much can be learned from past societies and their practices. The indigenous peoples of the Americas are not remnants, stragglers of history, but rather rich reservoirs of knowledge and practice. History has no definite direction. Indeed, he noted that Egypt two thousand years earlier was richer than Europe at the end of the Middle Ages. Writing two years before his death, he mused: "In the last sixty years we experienced the dialectic of radical breaks, unmediated contradictions and repeated returns to already discarded positions which make it difficult, if not impossible, to discern the underlying logic of advance."[26]

He specifically rejected a stages-of-development notion of history. His is neither a dialectical view of thesis, antithesis, and synthesis with directionality nor an equilibrium model. History is open-ended, created by human agency, though people are not free to make it any way they wish, for they find themselves under conditions not of their own choosing.[27] He rejected the sort of reasoning that saw different social relations (often synonymous with different ethnicities) as products of different historical epochs, as Jacques Lambert posited for Brazil or Mario Vargas Llosa for Peru. Polanyi particularly dismissed practitioners of modernization theory who saw modern and backward social segments or even different countries or regions belonging to different centuries.

BIOGRAPHY AS CRITICISM

Polanyi's almost postmodern bent derived in part from the milieu in which he was raised. Born Jewish in Vienna, he was both privileged and an outsider, an intellectual with social concerns living in a bourgeois family. He was a contemporary of Sigmund Freud, Eric Fromm, and Ludwig Wittgenstein, whose work regarding the difficulty in understanding material "reality" because of individual histories, the collective subconscious, and the problems of semantics no doubt drove young Karl to question the accepted scientific "truths" of both liberalism and Marxism. His doubts led Polanyi to engage in seminal intellectual debates.

Raised from an early age in Budapest, he grew up in an Austro-Hungarian empire that was a western outpost on the border of eastern Europe. It is easy to understand why young Karl, living in a conglomerate of different nationalities and ethnicities, wondered about the glue that held societies together. Growing up in colonized and relatively underdeveloped Hungary, he adopted the skeptical approach of other central Europeans. It is not by chance that these views would have a major impact on Latin American intellectuals who also believed they needed to catch up to more developed and powerful neighbors.[28]

However, he did not fully subscribe to developmentalism, sometimes being swayed by the romantic communitarianism that was popular in the Balkans. Polanyi's father was an affluent railroad contractor, but his mother was a leftist intellectual who conducted one of the city's most active salons, at which Georg Lukacs was a frequent visitor. Although Karl disagreed with Lukacs on many particulars, both were concerned with commodity fetishism and alienation. Critical of capitalism, Polanyi also became disillusioned by the Hungarian Communist regime of Béla Kun and communism in general. Polanyi was involved in the Hungarian National Bourgeois Radical Party for a short while but soon returned to Vienna, where he became a journalist and refrained from direct political action.[29]

However, his commitment to social reform never wavered. His wife, Ilona Duczynska, was a revolutionary in Hungary, worked for the Comintern in Russia, and later joined the Austrian Communist Party before breaking with it. Karl himself was a non-Marxist revolutionary socialist. Although he sometimes resembled a German Liberal such as Max Weber or a Social Democrat à la Karl Kautsky, he in fact was closer to the Narodniks of prerevolutionary Russia in his stress on community and communal relations. In this he was similar to some of his contemporaries in Latin American such as Haya de la Torre and José Carlos Mariategui of Peru and Antonio Soto y Gama and José Vasconcelos of Mexico. However, he did not have a romantic attachment to the past, and he believed technical advance was inevitable and necessary. The machines could not be stopped; they had to be harnessed to human and humane needs.

Polanyi's distrust of liberal market society led him to debate in the press Ludwig von Mises, one of the founders of the Austrian school of neoclassical economics. This debate was an early rehearsal of the arguments today between Latin American social democrats and neoliberals. Polanyi argued that value was not simply derived from markets, and indeed that price-setting markets were not necessary for society because historically people had successfully exchanged through other, nonprice mechanisms such as reciprocity and state redistribution. Great civilizations had existed in which the price-determining market was a subordinate and marginal element. Von Mises countered that only market society could efficiently distribute resources by setting prices. Other forms of exchange denied the freedom and property rights of the individual and impaired rational economic decision-making by introducing social considerations.[30] Another Austrian, F. A. Hayek, today the darling of many neoclassicists, also directly controverted Polanyi's notion of the social embeddedness of the economy and the need for state assistance by arguing that fascism, not greater social justice, was the result of departures from self-regulating markets.[31] That is, state economic involvement disturbed the price-setting mechanism, requiring greater state interference and thereby undercutting personal freedoms, leading to fascism. Polanyi countered that fascism was not a perversion of capitalism caused by avoidable state interference but rather a foreseeable, logical, and perhaps unavoidable outcome of capitalism. Capitalism's inequities created social unrest, which had to be crushed by a strong state.

Then Polanyi encountered fascism firsthand in the form of Austrian Nazism. He lost his position at the journal *Osterreichische Volkswirt* and had to flee to London by 1933. Spending thirteen years in England teaching workers, he developed what his wife called "the roots of a sacred hate," the hate of market society and commodification.[32] This led him to begin, at age fifty, to study and write economic history. In the United Kingdom he wrote *The Great Transformation*, based largely on the development of capitalism in England. After the end of World War II, he moved to the United States, where he taught at Columbia University from 1947 to 1957. In the United States he began his research into less complex and archaic societies for the foundations of a comparative economic history that would reveal the various relationships between societies and markets. He died in 1964, and many of his works were published posthumously.

It was Polanyi's experience with Marxism, the Austrian liberal school, polyglot Austro-Hungary, fascism, and the Anglo-Saxon welfare state that shaped his theory and have made him so useful for us today. He never visited Latin America, but his views can easily be extrapolated to fit the Latin American realities. His experiences with communism and fascism led him to deplore authoritarian regimes and command economies. Yet the Great Depression caused him to disdain laissez-faire liberalism. He had strong communitarian principles, believing that Robert Owens was the nineteenth century's greatest thinker. Like his contemporary

Herbert Marcuse, Polanyi aspired to understand how a society could protect both individual freedoms and its social unity.[33]

POLANYI'S THOUGHT

To many students Polanyi's writing seems to be divided into two quite distinct areas: the study of archaic and less complex societies, and the development of capitalism in the nineteenth and twentieth centuries. In the first area he examined ancient Near Eastern civilizations such as Assyria and Babylonia, the economic theories of Aristotle, and the nineteenth-century slave trade in Dahomey. In the second he studied, in his classic work *The Great Transformation*, the rise and decline of what he termed "market economy," that is, industrialization, finance capital, and commodification. The two seem very separate not only in time but also in topic and conception. Economic anthropologists have been inspired by the first body of work, while historians, historical sociologists, and political scientists read and use the second.

In fact, the two are merely different sides of the same concern. At base, Polanyi was arguing against the liberal notion of human nature and history, which has returned to favor in Latin America in the 1990s. In his studies of archaic and less complex societies, he sought to demonstrate the historically exceptional nature of the self-regulating market (the idea that an equitable and efficient distribution of goods could be best made by individuals seeking to maximize their benefits in a price-setting market with a minimum of state involvement). Liberals believed in "Homo economicus," the individual who sought to improve his own material gain through competition, and the notion that economic calculation was the basis of all human action. This was phrased by von Mises as "all rational action is economic, all economic activity is rational action."[34] Lionel Robbins expanded this idea by stressing that economic rationality is instrumental economic rationality, that all people seek to improve their material condition.[35] The individual, in the liberal view, is faced by scarcity and opportunity costs. He calculates his resources based on his preferences and assumptions of individual optimal results.[36] Markets are essential to establishing prices for goods and opportunity costs and are also natural, as is, in Adam Smith's words, the "urge to barter, truck and exchange."[37]

Instead, Polanyi argued that human motivation was not so much individual as socially conditioned (which he termed "social embeddedness"): "The goals for which an individual will work are culturally determined."[38] That motivation varied according to the context. He noted that many societies existed with markets occupying a minor role. Humans were basically cooperative, not competitive. Their societies were based on concepts such as "reciprocity" (just exchanges of goods and services, often based on kinship, custom, or status rather than material gain); "redistribution" (the state gathering goods and redistributing them according to individual needs, not according to prices); "household economy," in which the household is virtually self-sufficient; and "exchange," which did not necessarily imply exchange of commodities, since most exchanges throughout history were bartered. Before the nineteenth century, markets, prices, and money were not central to most people's decision making. This is not to say that markets did not exist but that custom, notions of moral economy (Aristotle's idea of the just price), and the state impinged greatly on economic decision-making and that economic concerns were often subordinated to other social ones.[39]

This describes not only earlier societies but also many contemporary peasant societies. Peasants have constituted a large portion, if not a majority, of most Latin American countries well into the twentieth century. Polanyi's notion of peasant economics has been useful to students of subsistence growers.[40] While recognizing that many peasants lived in a noncapitalist world of redistribution and reciprocity, he also recognized—as have, for example, Frank Cancian, David McCreery, William Rosebery and Carol Smith—that peasants were also involved in the market.[41] His idea that exchange was done through a number of social conventions and institutions and that culture, society, and politics have to be considered in conjunction with economic variables is similar to the Marxian "modes of production" analysis that was widely employed in Latin America in the 1970s and 1980s and still has a significant residue in social thought.[42] A recent issue of *Latin American Perspectives*, which focuses on the historical development of markets in Latin America, reflects Polanyi's influence.[43]

Markets, for most of human existence, were subsidiary; humans were social beings who found their authenticity in social interaction, while market relations were artificial. Hence, rather than man being naturally economically rational, economic rationality was artificial and removed people from nature. That is, markets were usually either relatively unimportant or administered or ritualized in some way that was not purely governed by the mechanisms of supply and demand. Indeed, because market society often led to great social dislocations and hardships as well as ecological disasters, Polanyi did not think that it was particularly rational. Without social or state interference, the market society would destroy itself. In fact, he ridiculed market society and neoliberal "science": "Science itself is haunted by insanity."[44]

His concern with the ecological consequences of capitalism set him off from most pre-1960s social thinkers. In his environmental concern, he differed sharply with most students of capitalism such as Max Weber and Karl Marx, as well as Latin America's development economists of the 1960s such as Raul Prebisch, Walt Rostow, or Celso Furtado, who saw capitalism causing rationality to overcome superstition and tradition.[45] They saw capitalism solving problems and eliminating waste rather than creating them. As products of the Enlightenment, they believed in social perfectibility. Although Polanyi was ultimately optimistic, he did not believe that more complex societies were more likely to master problems, particularly because the process of commodification obfuscated the authentic relationship of people to people and people to nature: "But no society could stand the effects of such crude fictions even for the shortest stretch of time unless its human and natural substance as well as its business organization was protected against the ravages of this satanic mill."[46] He noted the contradictory nature of economic growth: "Unheard-of wealth turned out to be inseparable from unheard-of poverty."[47]

Moreover, Polanyi disagreed about the central importance of economic wants and decisions. Scarcity, for example, was not a universal state because many less complex people, while materially "deprived," had even lower wants and expectations. That is, scarcity is not a natural notion but a socially determined one. And social goods that conferred status or marked celebrations could weigh more heavily than material ones. A society could be richer in the sense of perceived welfare despite having fewer material goods. Thus the focus of economics on problems of scarcity is too limited; it ignores the social dimensions of abundance. Some markets are governed by "magic and etiquette" rather than supply and demand.[48]

Economic anthropology divided into two warring camps over Polanyi's distinctions. Polanyi's followers were in the "substantivist" school, while the "formalists" believed that all societies, independent of their level of complexity, followed the basic market principles of economic value and accumulation. Interestingly, the formalists included not only followers of neoclassical economics but also what would seem their opposites: Marxists.[49]

Many Marxists rejected Polanyi because he seemed to have rejected Marx. Polanyi, who drew much inspiration from Weber, began his analysis by examining forms of distribution, not production (though Marx began *Capital* in exactly the same way). Moreover, his rejection of "Homo economicus" led him to reject the necessary dependence of the ideological and cultural superstructure on the material base and, indeed, to question the labor theory of value. Polanyi believed that this theory was not just too materialistic, valuing only palpable goods, but also too anthropocentric; it argued that all things had value only insofar as they were worked by and for people. This would lead to ecological disaster. His concern with the environment foreshadowed some seminal works on Latin America such as those by Cook, Crosby, Dean, Kiple, and Melville, who have come to see the environment and disease as historical actors, not simply backdrops.[50]

Despite these fundamental differences with Marx and his repudiation of communism, Polanyi's thought resonated with much of early Marx, and many New Left Marxians have come to find him useful. Arriving in England in 1933, he encountered the writings of young Marx, which only the year before were first translated into English and circulated among Marxists by Mayer and Landshut. This more humanist vision that would later influence the New Left in the United States and Europe and Latin American revolutionaries inspired by the Cuban Revolution, especially by Che Guevara, was shared by Polanyi. To him, Marx's great contribution was to foresee the tendencies of capitalism and to show that "the forms of consciousness induced by the condition of things under the capitalist system were analyzed and shown to be the inevitable results of the private ownership of the means of production under modern capitalism (fetishisation, the self-estrangement of man, the pseudo-reality of economic objectification like commodity value, capital, and so on)."[51]

Moreover, Polanyi did not disagree with Marx's analysis of social relations in the nineteenth century, when, he believed, the self-regulating market came to dominate in western Europe and North America. At that point in Europe and the "developed" world, Marx's materialist assumptions pertained. But Polanyi would not abstract from that particular historical epoch to the past, to the less developed world, or to human nature. Although Marx's theory might have been more "scientific" in the sense that it was supposed to be universally applicable, Polanyi's was more historical, noting that different rules and relationships obtained in different historical epochs and, indeed, in societies at different levels of complexity during the same epoch.[52]

Polanyi's second body of work, which is best known, is represented by his study of the rise of "market society" in the nineteenth century. In *The Great Transformation* he came to grips with the specific problematic that Marx analyzed: industrialization. The work is usually valued as a historical analysis of the role of finance capital in the creation of the Hundred Years' Peace. In fact, the study is not a triumphalist account of the spread of capitalism but rather an examination of the rise *and fall* of the self-regulating market. Fascism was a logical result of the disaster created by laissez-faire. Polanyi intended for his book to be entitled *Liberal Utopia: Origins of the Cataclysm*. But because North Americans would misinterpret "liberalism" as meaning New Deal politics rather than neoclassical ones, it was changed to *The Great Transformation* and the subtitle to *The*

Political and Economic Origins of Our Time; this caused readers to misunderstand his intention.[53] Polanyi's central concern was to reveal the utopian nature of nineteenth-century liberalism and the discursive fictions upon which it was based. The supposedly hard-headed rational materialists were in fact dreamers who based their worldview on myths. This is as true for today's neoliberals who preside over Latin America's economic policies.

The key myth of liberals was the self-regulating market and market society. According to Polanyi, markets had long existed as subordinate institutions to states and societies. Only in the nineteenth century, with the advent of industrialization and finance capital, did market society come into existence. Although he usually refrained from using the word *capitalism*, Polanyi agreed with Weber and Marx that in the nineteenth century, society in western Europe and North America came to function under qualitatively new rules. The transformation was brought about by machines that created a vast increase in demand for raw materials (commodifying land), labor, and consumption. To the extent that machines generated social change, Polanyi was a structural materialist. However, people had choices about the nature and pace of the changes, so that politics guided economics. In the short run it appeared that now politics and society were subordinated to the market. Indeed, in market society economics, politics, and social questions became distinct areas, with the latter two subject to the former. Polanyi saw the transition very much in the concept, if not specifically the terms, of the Tonnies' move from gemeinschaft, or organic face-to-face status society, to gesellschaft, or impersonal rule-bound, institutionalized, contractual social relations. However, even at its height, the self-regulating market was not completely hegemonic. Other forms of social integration such as reciprocity, state, redistribution, and even household economy continued to have importance.[54]

Liberals came to believe that market society acted under scientific rules that would eventually benefit all participants as long as the state did not intervene to distort the economy. Civil society dominated the state, and the most economically rational and adept dominated civil society, maximizing productivity and wealth through their entrepreneurship and efficient use of resources. Land, labor, and capital became conceived of as commodities, natural things that the economy manipulated through the magic of the market. (Liberal fetishism is reflected in the market's "magic.")

Polanyi denounced this liberal worldview, arguing that markets could not be self-regulating because on their own they led to miserable wages, concentration of wealth, and ecological disaster. Only the "double movement" of social pressure to mend the economy's destructive ways, through either state action or acts by civil society, prevented liberals from self-destruction. The defensive movements were taken by "society" as a whole, a concept he believed was invented only in the nineteenth century as an answer to the mechanistic self-regulating market.[55] This should not be confused with Keynes's contemporary formulation of the necessity of state interventions to compensate for inadequate demand. Polanyi saw the double movement as motivated by social concerns and instituted by the masses, not "scientific" economic principles enforced by a techno-cratic elite as did Keynes.

Polanyi did not believe that only specific classes undertook political actions, but rather what another contemporary, Antonio Gramsci, called "historical blocks." Hence, while Polanyi agreed with Marx that conflict was the central historical creative force, he did not believe that class conflict was the engine of history. Rather, the principal clash was between a more organic society and the commodification of market society. Ideology and culture were more important as historical forces to Polanyi than objective class interests. He noted that by the 1930s even states with sub-stantially different political orientations and objectives were forced to in-tervene in the market to avoid being "annihilated by the action of the self-regulating market."[56] By the 1930s the self-regulating market mecha-nism had failed because land, labor, and money could no longer even sustain the pretense of being commodities. "The market has been the out-come of conscious and often violent intervention on the part of govern-ment which imposed the market organization on society for non-eco-nomic ends."[57]

To ensure social peace, land became dominated by social determi-nants, and food prices were put under state control; labor protected itself from the market through unions and state aid; and currency went off the gold standard, so its price began to correspond to state policies set for political purposes rather than acting as a stable marker for value and exchange. The state had to replace the market's price-setting mechanism as the means of allocation of scarce resources.

The exact mechanisms of this adjustment are vague in Polanyi's writ-ing because Polanyi did not specifically define either civil society or the state. Civil society seems to have come into existence only in the nine-teenth century as more traditional, organic, face-to-face relationships broke down and people needed other institutions to defend themselves against the forces of market society. Thus he anticipated Habermas's no-tion that civil society was created by capitalism and the rise of the bour-geoisie. But civil society continued to be influenced by earlier forms of sociability that centered on family, tradition, or magic.

States, of course, have existed since time immemorial. Some were au-tonomous, such as the Dahomey kingdom or those of ancient Assyria and

Babylonia; others were instrumental. Some based their authority on communal values and traditions, others on patrimonial or patriarchal power. Having studied primitive and archaic states, Polanyi was more conscious of the wide range of state forms and sorts of state power that had existed historically. He does not seem to have believed that capitalism necessarily brought one form of state; fascism and communist authoritarianism, liberal decentralization, and a welfare-state societal regulator state were all possible outcomes of economic development dictated more by political struggles than by the abstract logical necessities of capital accumulation or reason working through history. Peasant communities could be tied together by more traditional, organic bonds.

The state was essential to resolve clashes between various social interests. For Polanyi, laissez-faire had never existed because the state had been fundamental in creating institutions and property rights necessary for capitalism to flourish and to overcome its built-in contradictions. In this he anticipated more recent findings about the actions of the liberal state in Latin America. Numerous historians and economists such as Winston Fritsch, Paul Gootenberg, Stephen Haber, Joseph Love, Steven Topik, Allen Wells, and Richard Weiner, who have studied the nineteenth and early twentieth centuries have shown that even states in relatively underdeveloped countries philosophically dedicated to laissez-faire played intrusive economic and social roles. The issue is not whether under capitalism the economy operates better through market forces or through the state. This is a false dichotomy; both need to work together to provide social efficiency and equity.[58] And even if the economies do not function efficiently or equitably, the interests of contending groups within the countries and external to them demand both state action and market responses.

Karl Polanyi's importance does not lie only in his precursor role as a social theoretician. More important, he is one of the few intellectuals who constructed a theory that united the many insights that today often are studied in isolation. He provides a nonmaterialist structuralism that values individual perceptions and actions while at the same time privileging social, collective action. Culture and political action are crucial, but they cannot be understood in isolation from the economy. While deconstructing the master narrative of nineteenth-century liberalism, he constructed another master theory, but one that allowed, indeed required, contradictions and variation, hegemony and resistance. To the extent that one can distinguish these spheres, society works through the state to affect the economy. General material structures circumscribe the realm of the possible, but those structures are more culturally determined and socially constructed than they are objective conditions. Since groups of people communicate and act through shared culture, society's struggle to defend itself through the "double movement" has a wide range of possible goals and outcomes. In this schema, group identities become political rallying points that can be vital for affecting the unfolding of history. Resistance is not merely a heroic afterthought, a curiosity along the highway of "modernization" (a concept Polanyi neither used nor care for). Rather, resistance is necessary for society's continued survival. Even if groups such as the Luddites ultimately failed, they helped slow the pace of the transformation toward market society, hence permitting society in general more time to adapt to new conditions. The same holds for the Mexican Revolution or other Latin American social movements. Their importance is not measured just by their ability to take political power or affect a social revolution. To fight the good fight is not just a romantic tilting at windmills or the morally correct thing to do. It can change perceptions, identities, and values. In this sense, Polanyi folds together objective and subjective conditions, giving people and the environment in which they operate formative power. Thus not just the direction of change but also its pace are important. The struggles are fought not just in the factories, fields, and streets; they are fought over ideas, over meanings, over concepts. Rituals, traditions, and notions of morality are all ammunition in the historic struggle. The socially conceived interpretation of events is fundamental to the impact that events will have.

WORLD HISTORY

This brings us to the last question: What scale do we apply to "society," and how did the different parts of the globe interact historically? This is difficult to discern in Polanyi's writing because *The Great Transformation* is a fundamentally Eurocentric document that touches only briefly on questions of colonialism and "primitive" peoples, as well as peasants in western Europe. Only late in life did Polanyi concern himself at all with questions of underdevelopment.

There are carryovers from nineteenth-century European thought in *The Great Transition*. Polanyi refers, for example, to the European "race" and to "outworn cultures" and "primitive peoples," as well as to "weaker countries."[59] Although he expressly rejects a theory focusing on stages of development, he in fact employs it when he discusses the advance of the European economy from archaic to feudal to mercantilist to capitalist. And he argues that the rest of the world was sucked into the European world economy: "By the time it reached its maximum extent, around 1914, every part of the globe, all of its inhabitants and yet unborn generations . . . were comprised in it. A new way of life spread over the planet with a claim to universality unparalleled since the age when

Christianity started out on its career, only this time the movement was on a purely material level."[60]

His Eurocentrism is evidenced by his discussion of Christianity rather than Islam, which had an equally far-reaching spread. This spread, however, should not be taken as a victory for virtue or technology: "Business success involved the ruthless use of force against weaker countries and the use of underhand measures of gaining ends familiar to the colonial and semi-colonial jungle."[61] But although he objected to the violence of imperialism, he still named the nineteenth century the "Hundred Years' Peace."[62] He believed that European and North American countries had a "*mission civilatrice*" to bring civil liberties and order to the "semi-colonial and colonial jungle." Late in life Polanyi reflected back, "My life was a world life. . . . my work is for Asia and Africa, for the new peoples. The West should bring them spiritual and intellectual assistance."[63] On the other hand, he hated the economic developmentalism of Walt Rostow and Arnold Harberger, whom he called "enemies." He believed that the economists neglected the social embeddedness of economies, assuming a monotonous uniformity of all societies' path to development. Although Polanyi was a cultural absolutist when it came to matters of individual civil rights, he was a cultural relativist in other areas, especially in market relations. The three most fundamental values were "knowledge of death, knowledge of freedom, knowledge of society."[64] This translated into being a Christian democratic socialist or a belief in morality, individualism, and communitarianism.

Although Polanyi did not expressly speak to the problems of the Third World in general, much less to Latin America, his approach is useful for scholars in many areas. He does not provide a blueprint, a formula. Instead, he problematizes categories and relationships in imaginative and open-ended ways. Although he did not specifically examine peasants, his insistence on the substantist view of social embeddedness and multiple forms of social integration—reciprocity, redistribution, household, and exchange—has inspired most studies of peasants.

His reading of primitive societies such as the Trobriand Islanders of western Melanesia, studied by Malinowski and Thurnwald, led him to think not only about the sexual division of labor but also about gendered power inherent in reciprocity and redistribution. This is an area of great and growing importance in the study of Latin America. Scholars such as Liz Dore, Heather Fowler-Salamini, Mary Kay Vaughn, Carmen Diana Deere, Verena Stolcke, Heidi Tinsman, and Steve Stern have interjected the issue of gender into the market and politics. Looking at state power as small-scale local transactions, as well as the acts of centralized nation-states, Polanyi touched on the political, social, and economic power of women and the regionalized, fragmented nature of state power.[65]

By rejecting a stage theory, he provided a notion akin to Trotsky's "combined and uneven development" or modes-of-production analysis. That is, any society is constituted by local as well as national cultures. The local are not homogenized into uniform proletarians by the market but rather retain forms of reciprocity, redistribution, and household in a variety of combinations. The nature of market and social relations cannot be structurally predicted because it is largely a result of historical political struggles. These struggles might have very different forms and meanings in different societies so that, for example, the principles of the French Revolution could have very different ramifications in France and in Haiti.[66]

Ideology also does not flow out of specific relations to the means of production as wine out of a bottle. Traditions, ecological variations, and shared understandings shape ideas and meanings. These subaltern groups make important contributions to broader social life and to the economy. Because Polanyi did not believe maximization of capital accumulation and efficiency were the goals of society, but rather survival and freedom were, he valued the peasants and the less complex peoples of the Third World. He was a prophet of multiculturalism.

Today, with the resurgence of neoliberalism, Polanyi's critique of the self-regulating market is also of great import. He explodes both the myth of the magic of the market and the notion that the state is counterproductive. State economic action is both necessary and inevitable. But states can be harmful as well as protective. Society, the collective action of groups from many areas of social life, must force the best state action.

NOTES

I would like to thank Frank Cancian, Mark Poster, Ken Pomeranz, Dennis Kortheuer, Miguel Centeno, and Fernando Lopez-Alves for their helpful comments.

1. This view is discussed and ultimately rejected in David Smith, Dorothy Solinger, and Steven Topik, eds., *State and Sovereignty* (London: Routledge, 1999).

2. C. Fred Bergsten, "The Primacy of Economics," *Foreign Policy* 87 (summer 1992): 3–24. A contrasting view is presented in the World Bank's *World Development Report, 1997: The State in a Changing World* (Oxford: Oxford University Press, 1997). Two recent examples of this approach are Stephen Haber, ed., *How Latin America Fell Behind* (Stanford, Calif.: Stanford University Press, 1997); and Barbara Geddes, "Uses and Limitations of Rational Choice," in Peter H. Smith, ed., *Latin America in Comparative Perspective* (Boulder, Colo.: Westview, 1995).

3. See the twenty-fifth anniversary issue of *Latin American Perspectives*

(November 1998) for views on where the Left in Latin America is and where it is going. A good review essay of recent trends is Susan Deans Smith, "The Secret History of Gender," *Latin American Research Review* 33, no. 1 (winter 1998): 257–78. For examples of historical studies, see Emília Viotti da Costa, *Crown of Glory* (New York: Oxford University Press, 1994); Robin Blackburn, *The Making of New World Slavery* (London: Verso, 1997); and Steve Stern, *The Secret History of Sex* (Chapel Hill: University of North Carolina Press, 1995).

4. For example, William Beezley, Cheryl English Martin, and William French, eds., *Rituals of Rule, Rituals of Resistance* (Wilmington, Del.: Scholarly Resources, 1994), which was inspired by Benedict Anderson, *Imagined Communities* (London: Verso, 1992); Eric Hobsbawm and Terence Ranger, eds., *The Invention of Tradition* (Cambridge: Cambridge University Press, 1983); Eric Hobsbawm, ed., *Nations and Nationalism since 1780* (Cambridge: Cambridge University Press, 1990).

5. For example, Gilbert Joseph and Daniel Nugent, eds., *Everyday Forms of State Formation* (Durham, N.C.: Duke University Press, 1988), which was inspired by James C. Scott with *Weapons of the Weak, Everyday Forms of Peasant Resistance* (New Haven, Conn.: Yale University Press, 1985).

6. Quentin Skinner, ed., *The Return of Grand Theory in the Human Sciences* (Cambridge: Cambridge University Press, 1985); Hayden White, *Metahistory* (Baltimore: Johns Hopkins University Press, 1973).

7. Enzo Mingione observed in *Fragmented Societies: A Sociology of Economic Life beyond the Market Paradigm*, trans. Paul Goodrick (Cambridge, Mass.: Blackwell, 1991): "It is the very radicalism of Polanyi's criticism of the self-regulating market paradigm and his elaboration of devastating historical evidence against it that make this author fashionable today when the market paradigm is in crisis, after he had been almost forgotten during the decades of the Fordish golden age" (21). In addition to *The Great Transformation* (Boston: Beacon, 1944), Polanyi also wrote, with A. Rotstein, *Dahomey and the Slave Trade: An Analysis of an Archaic Economy* (Seattle: University of Washington, 1966), and edited three volumes, with Conrad M. Arensberg and Harry W. Pearson, *Trade and Markets in the Early Empires* (Glencoe, Ill.: Free Press, 1957); with John Lewis and Donald K. Kitchin, *Christianity and Social Revolution* (London: Gollancz, 1935); and with Ilona Duczynska, *The Plow and the Pen: Writings from Hungary (1930–1956)* (London: P. Owen, 1963). Some of his writings were collected in *Primitive, Archaic, and Modern Economies: Essays of Karl Polanyi* (Garden City, N.Y.: Anchor Books, 1968); *The Livelihood of Man*, ed. Harry W. Pearson (New York: Academic Press, 1977); and *Fascism: Democracy and Industrial Civilization*, ed. Kari Polanyi-Levitt and Marguerite Mendell (Budapest: Gondolat, 1986). Polanyi's decline in the 1960s is evidenced by the fact that he is not even mentioned in Philip Wiener, ed., *Dictionary of the History of Ideas* (New York: Scribner's, 1974).

8. See, for example, Kari Polanyi-Levitt, ed., *The Life and Work of Karl Polanyi: A Celebration* (Montreal: Black Rose Books, 1990); E. S. Gudeman, *Economics as Culture* (London: Routledge and Kegan Paul, 1986); Marshall Sahlins, *Stone Age Economics* (Chicago: Aldine-Atherton, 1972); Claus Offe,

Contradictions of the Welfare State (London: Hutchinson, 1984); and Geoff Hodgson, *The Democratic Economy* (Harmondsworth: Penguin, 1984).

9. Polanyi was so taken by the study of the market because, as he pointed out in *The Great Transformation*: "The 'market' turns out to be a junction-point between social, economic and intellectual histories, and a sensitive metaphor for many kinds of exchange" (257). The market was not simply a place, a force, or a concept; it was a field of power.

10. Quoted in ibid., xviii.

11. Polanyi used the term *primitive* rather than *less complex* to refer to peoples with less complex material culture. That word has fallen into disrepute as racist and implying a moral and material gradient of societies. Many anthropologists have come to question whether these societies are actually less complex as greater study reveals previously unrecognized layers of sophistication. A good case in point is Sahlins's *Stone Age Economics*, especially chap. 1.

12. Polanyi, *The Great Transformation*, 46.

13. Bronislaw Malinowski, *Argonauts of the Western Pacific* (London: Routledge and Kegan Paul, 1922); Richard Thurnwald, *Economics in Primitive Communities* (London: Oxford University Press, 1932).

14. Frank Cancian, *Change and Uncertainty in a Peasant Economy: The Maya Corn Farmers of Zinacantan* (Stanford, Calif.: Stanford University Press, 1972), 1, 2, 189, 192; Eric Wolf, *Peasants* (Englewood Cliffs, N.J.: Prentice-Hall, 1966), 12–17; Wolf, *Europe and the People without History* (Berkeley: University of California Press, 1982); Michael T. Taussig, *The Devil and Commodity Fetishism in South America* (Chapel Hill: University of North Carolina Press, 1980); M. L. Finley, *The Ancient Economy*, 2d ed. (London: Hogarth Press, 1985); Philip D. Curtin, *Cross-Cultural Trade in World History* (Cambridge: Cambridge University Press, 1984), 13–14, 87; George Dalton, "Writings That Clarify Theoretical Disputes over Karl Polanyi's Work," in Polanyi-Levitt, *The Life and Work of Karl Polanyi*, 183–87; Sahlins, *Stone Age Economics*; Rhoda Halperin, "The Substantive Economy in Peasant Societies," in Rhoda Halperin and James Dop, eds., *Peasant Livelihood: Studies in Economic Anthropology and Cultural Ecology* (New York: St. Martin's, 1977), 1–16; and Halperin, *Economies across Cultures: Towards a Comparative Science of the Economy* (Houndmills, Basingstoke, Hampshire: Macmillan, 1988).

15. E. P. Thompson, *Customs in Common: Studies in Traditional Popular Culture* (New York: New Press, 1993); Alexander Gerschenkron, *Economic Backwardness in Historic Perspective* (Cambridge, Mass.: Belknap Press of Harvard University Press, 1962); James C. Scott, *Weapons of the Weak: Everyday Forms of Peasant Resistance* (New Haven, Conn.: Yale University Press, 1985); Charles Tilly, *The Contentious French: Four Centuries of Popular Struggle* (Cambridge, Mass.: Belknap Press of Harvard University Press, 1986); Albert Hirschman, *The Passions and the Interests: Political Arguments for Capitalism before Its Triumph* (Princeton, N.J.: Princeton University Press, 1977); Michel Foucault, *The Archaeology of Knowledge*, trans. A. M. Sheridan Smith (New York: Pantheon, 1972).

16. Alejandro Portes, M. Castells, and L. Benton, *The Informal Economy: Studies in Advanced and Less Developed Countries* (Baltimore: Johns Hopkins

University Press, 1989); Enzo Mingione, *Fragmented Societies: A Sociology of Economic Life beyond the Market Paradigm,* trans. by Paul Goodrick (Cambridge, Mass.: Blackwell, 1991).

17. Polanyi, *The Great Transformation,* 59. The importance of unequal trade and piracy is underlined in Kenneth Pomeranz and Steven Topik, *The World Trade Created* (Armonk, N.Y.: M. E. Sharpe, 1999).

18. Polanyi, *The Great Transformation,* 59.

19. Ibid.

20. Samir Amin, *Le Developpment inegal: Essai sur les formations sociales periphique* (Paris: Minuit, 1973); Walter Goldfrank "Fascism and World Economy," in B. H. Kaplan, ed., *Social Change and the Capitalist World Economy* (Beverly Hills, Calif.; Sage, 1978), 91–92; Fred Block, "Marxist Theories of the State in World Systems Analysis," in Kaplan, *Social Change and the Capitalist World Economy,* 36; Giovanni Arreghi, *The Long Twentieth Century: Money, Power and the Origins of Our Times* (London: Verso, 1994); Terence Hopkins, "The Study of the Capitalist World-Economy: Some Introductory Considerations," in Walter L. Goldfrank, ed., *The World-System of Capitalism: Past and Present* (Beverly Hills, Calif.: Sage, 1979), 21–52; Attila Agh, "The Hundred Years' Peace: Karl Polanyi on the Dynamics of World Systems," in Polanyi-Levitt, *The Life and World of Karl Polanyi,* 93–97. Fernand Braudel criticized Polanyi in volume 2 of *Civilization and Capitalism, Fifteenth through Eighteenth Centuries: The Wheels of Commerce* (New York: Harper and Row, 1979), 226–27, for not distinguishing between exchange and trade and distinguishing the economic from the political. In fact, Braudel misinterprets Polanyi and, indeed, Braudel's conclusions in volume 3, *The Perspective of the World* (New York: Harper and Row, 1984), 601–9, are very similar to Polanyi's.

21. Polanyi quoted in Marguerite Mendell and Daniel Salee, eds., *The Legacy of Karl Polanyi: Market, State and Society at the End of the Twentieth Century* (New York: St. Martin's, 1991): "The struggle which had to be waged against religion long ago must now be waged against metaphysics" (xviii). See, for example, Fredric Jameson, "Postmodernism and the Market," in *Postmodernism, or, the Cultural Logic of Late Capitalism* (Durham, N.C.: Duke University Press, 1991), 260–78), which closely resembles Polanyi's view without citing him. Jameson takes much of his direct influence from Marx's *Grundrisse.* See also Anthony Giddens, *A Contemporary Critique of Historical Materialism* (Berkeley: University of California Press, 1981).

22. Gregory Baum, *Karl Polanyi on Ethics and Economics* (Montreal: McGill-Queen's University Press, 1996), 6–7, 21, 24. A key postmodern text, Guy Debord's *The Society of the Spectacle,* trans. Donald Nicholson-Smith (New York: Zone Books, 1994), notes: "The spectacle corresponds to the historical moment at which the commodity completes its colonization of social life" (29). Trent Schroyer, "Karl Polanyi's Post-Marxist Critical Theory," in Mendell and Salee, *The Legacy of Karl Polanyi,* argues that "Polanyi anticipated some crucial parts of Habermas' synthesis of Marx and Weber within his critique of economism" (68–70).

23. Quoted in Kari Polanyi-Levitt, "Origins and Significance of the Great Transformation," in Polanyi-Levitt, *The Life and Work of Karl Polanyi,* 118.

Marx sometimes took this view, too, for instance: "History does nothing, it does not 'possess immense riches, it does not fight battles.' It is men, real, living men, who do all this, who possess things and fight battles. History is nothing but the activity of men in pursuit of their ends." Quoted in Anthony Giddens, *A Contemporary Critique of Historical Materialism* (Berkeley: University of California Press, 1981), 74.

24. Polanyi, *The Great Transformation*, 219. Stressing agency, he also observed that political events "are the core of history" (219).

25. Ibid., 68.

26. Quoted in introduction to Mendell and Salee, *The Legacy of Karl Polanyi*, xvii.

27. This is, of course, a paraphrase of Marx. Where the two differ is that Polanyi sees ideas being less time-bound and enjoying some autonomy and, indeed, command over material conditions. On stages of development, see Polanyi, "The Economy as Instituted Process," 256.

28. See Joseph Love's study of the origin of development theory in central Europe: *Crafting the Third World* (Stanford, Calif.: Stanford University Press, 1996).

29. Erzsebet Vezer, "The Polanyi Family," 18, 20, 29; Gyorgy Litvan, "Karl Polanyi in Hungarian Politics," 33, 34; Doug Brown, "Karl Polanyi's Influence on the Budapest School," 44, all in Kari Polanyi-Levitt, *The Life and Work of Karl Polanyi*.

30. Ludwig von Mises, *Die Gemeinwirtschaft: Untersuchung über den Sozialismus* (Munich: Philosophia Verlad, 1981), argued that "where there is no market there is no price control; without price control there is no economic calculation" (111).

31. F. A. Hayek, *The Road to Serfdom* (Chicago: University of Chicago Press, 1944).

32. Illona Ducyznska Polanyi, "Karl Polanyi," in Polanyi-Levitt, *The Life and Work of Karl Polanyi*, xvi.

33. Herbert Marcuse, *One Dimensional Man* (Boston: Beacon Press, 1964); Abraham Rothstein, "The Reality of Society and Karl Polanyi's Philosophical Perspective," in Polayni-Levitt, *The Life and Work of Karl Polanyi*, 99, 108.

34. Von Mises, *Die Gemeinwirtschaft*, 83.

35. Lionel Robbins, *An Essay on the Nature and Significance of Economic Science* (London: Macmillan, 1932). An excellent summary of the Liberal position is K. Polanyi, C. Arensberg, and H. Pearson, "The Economy as Instituted Process," in *Trade and Market in the Early Empires*, 243–70.

36. Gerald Berthoud, "Toward a Comparative Approach: The Contribution of Karl Polanyi," in Polanyi-Levitt, *The Life and Work of Karl Polanyi*, 196. Robbins, *Essay on the Nature and Significance of Economic Science,* said: "[Economic science] focuses on a particular *aspect* of behavior, the form imposed by the influence of society. It follows from this, therefore, that in so far as it presents this aspect, any kind of human behavior falls within the scope of economic generalization. We do not say that the productivity of potatoes is economic activity and the production of philosophy is not. We say rather that, in so far as either kind of activity involves the relinquishment of other desired alternatives, it has its

economic aspect. There are no limitations on the subject-matter of Economic Science save this" (17).

37. Polanyi disagreed with many historians of economic thought in that he placed Smith in the "societal approach" rather than the "economistic." For Adam Smith, whom he considered "the founder of political economy," economic life was only one aspect of national life; the nature of the society and the state, not just the atomistic individuals, were important. See "The Place of Economies in Societies," in George Dalton, ed., *Primitive, Archaic, and Modern Economies. Essays of Karl Polanyi* (Garden City, N.Y.: Anchor, 1968), 127–28.

38. Polanyi, *The Great Transformation*, 158.

39. Neil Smelser, "A Comparative View of Exchange Systems," *Economic Development and Cultural Change* 7 (1959): 173–82; S. C. Humphreys, "History, Economics and Anthropology: The Work of Karl Polanyi," *History and Theory*. (1969): 165–212; Lucette Valensi, "Economic Anthropology and History: The Work of Karl Polanyi," *Research in Economic Anthropology* 3 (1980); Anne Mayhew, "Culture: Core Concept under Attack," *Journal of Economic Issues* 21, no. 2 (1987): 587–603.

40. William Roseberry, *Anthropologies and Histories* (New Brunswick, N.J.: Rutgers University Press, 1989); Elizabeth Dore, ed., *Gender Politics in Latin America* (New York: Monthly Review Press, 1997); Rodolfo Stavenhagen, *Agrarian Problems and Peasant Movements in Latin America* (Garden City, N.Y.: Doubleday, 1970).

41. Polanyi said in *The Great Transformation*: "By the fourth quarter of the nineteenth century world commodity prices were the central reality in the lives of millions of Continental peasants" (18). Frank Cancian, *The Decline of Community in Zinacantan* (Stanford, Calif.: Stanford University Press, 1992); David McCreery, *Rural Guatemala, 1760–1940* (Stanford, Calif.: Stanford University Press, 1994); William Roseberry, *Coffee and Capitalism in the Venezuelan Andes* (Austin: University of Texas Press, 1983); Carol A. Smith, ed., *Guatemalan Indians and the State: 1540–1988* (Austin: University of Texas Press, 1990).

42. For theoretical statements, see Ron Chilcote, *Theories of Development, Mode of Production or Dependency* (Beverly Hills, Calif.: Sage, 1983); Ciro Cardoso, *Agricultura, Escravidão e Capitalismo* (Petrópolis, Brazil: Vozes, 1979); Cristobal Kay, *Latin American Theories of Development and Underdevelopment* (London: Routledge, 1989). A fine application is Florencia Mallon, *Defense of Commuity in Peru's Central Highland* (Princeton, N.J.: Princeton University Press, 1983).

43. "Creating Markets in Latin America" *Latin American Perspectives*, 104, 26:1, January 1999.

44. Karl Polanyi, "Our Obsolete Market Mentality," *Commentary* 3 (February 1947): 110.

45. H. H. Gerth and C. Wright Mills, *From Max Weber: Essays in Sociology* (New York: Oxford University Press, 1946), passim, esp. 50–51; Reinhard Bendix, *Max Weber: An Intellectual Portrait* (New York: Anchor, 1962), 52, 68–69; Celso Furtado, *A Fantasia Organizada* (Rio de Janeiro: Paz e Terra, 1985); Raul Prebisch, *La obra de Prebisch en la CEPAL* (Mexico City: Fondo de Cultura Economica, 1982); Walt W. Rostow, *The Stages of Economic Growth* (Cambridge: Cambridge University Press, 1960).

46. Polanyi, *The Great Transformation*, 73.

47. Ibid., 102.

48. Ibid., 50.

49. For a cogent discussion of the formalist-substantivist debate, see Stuart Plattner, "Introduction," *Economic Anthropology* (Stanford, Calif.: Stanford University Press, 1989). See also Halperin, *Economies across Cultures*. Frank Cancian reconciles the essentials of the two warring camps in a brief, elegant discussion, "Maximization as Norm, Strategy and Theory: A Comment on Programmatic Statements in Economic Anthropology," *American Anthropology* 68 (April 1966): 465–469. In a paper delivered at a meeting of the American Anthropology Association in Washington, D.C., in November 1997, Cancian shows the similarities among—and some differences in—Polanyi's concept of redistribution, Sahlin's views on primitive exchange, Wallerstein's world systems, and Eric Wolf's modes of production which center on how socially embedded economic exchanges are.

50. Noble David Cook, *Born to Die* (Cambridge: Cambridge University Press, 1998); Alfred Crosby, *Ecological Imperialism* (Cambridge: Cambridge University Press, 1986); Warren Dean, *With Broadax and Firebrand* (Berkeley: University of California Press, 1995); Kenneth Kiple and Stephen Beck, eds., *Consequences of European Expansion* (Brookfield, Vt.: Ashgate/Variorum, 1997).

51. Karl Polanyi in Lucille Beaudry, Christian Deblock, and Jean-Jacques Gislain, eds., *Un siecle de Marxisme* (Sillery, Quebec: Presses de l'Universite du Quebec, 1990), 124.

52. Trent Schroyer, "Karl Polanyi's Post-Marxist Critical Theory," in Mendell and Salee, *The Legacy of Karl Polanyi*.

53. Kari Polanyi-Levitt, "Introduction" in Polanyi-Levitt, *The Life and Work of Karl Polanyi*, 7.

54. Polanyi, *The Great Transformation*, 37, 46; Polanyi, Arensberg, and Pearson, "The Economy as Instituted Process," 256.

55. Hannah Arendt made the same distinction later in *The Human Condition* (Chicago: University of Chicago Press, 1958) 46. See also Jurgen Habermas, *The Structural Transformation of the Public Sphere: An Inquiry into a Category of Bourgeois Society*, trans. Thomas Burger and Fredrick Lawrence (Cambridge, Mass.: MIT Press, 1961), 16–26.

56. Polanyi, *The Great Transformation*, 249; "The fate of classes more often determined by the needs of society than the fate of society is determined by the need of classes" (152).

57. Ibid., 250.

58. Ibid., 253–58; Winston Fritsch, *External Constraints on Economic Policy in Brazil* (Pittsburgh: University of Pittsburgh Press, 1988); Paul Gootenberg, *Imagining Development* (Berkeley: University of California Press, 1993); Stephen Haber, *Industry and Development* (Stanford, Calif.: Stanford University Press, 1989); Joseph Love, *Crafting the Third World: Theorizing Underdevelopment in Rumania and Brazil* (Stanford, Calif.: Stanford University Press, 1996); Joseph Love and Nils Jacobsen, eds., *Guiding the Invisible Hand: Economic Liberalism and the State in Latin American History* (New York: Praeger, 1988); C. Peloso and Barbara Tenenbaum, *Liberals, Politics and Power* (Athens: University of Georgia Press, 1996); Steven Topik, *The Political Economy of the Brazilian State,*

1889–1930 (Austin: University of Texas Press, 1989); Steven Topik and Allen Wells, *The Second Conquest of Latin America* (Austin: University of Texas Press, 1998); Allen Wells and Gilbert Joseph, *Summer of Discontent, Seasons of Upheaval* (Stanford, Calif.: Stanford University Press, 1996); Richard Weiner, "Demons and Deities: Market Discourse in Porfirian Mexico" (Ph.D. diss., University of California, Irvine, 1999). For a discussion of the New Institutional Economics, see John Harriss, Janet Hunter, and Colin M. Lewis, eds., *The New Institutional Economics and Third World Development* (London: Routledge, 1995).

59. Polanyi, *The Great Transformation*, 6, 13.

60. Ibid., 130.

61. Ibid., 13.

62. Ibid., 16.

63. Kari Polanyi-Levitt, "The Origins and Significance of the Great Transformation," in Polanyi-Levitt, *The Life and Work of Karl Polanyi*, 112.

64. Polanyi, *The Great Transformation*, 258.

65. Ibid., 46–55; Carmen Diana Deere, *Household and Class Relations* (Berkeley: University of California Press, 1990); Dore, *Gender Politics in Latin America*; Heather Fowler-Salamini and Mary Kay Vaughan, eds., *Women of the Mexican Countryside* (Tucson: University of Arizona Press, 1994); Verena Stolcke, *Coffee Planters, Workers and Wives* (New York: St. Martin's, 1988); Steve Stern, *The Secret History of Gender* (Chapel Hill: University of North Carolina Press, 1995); Heidi Tinsman, *Unequal Uplift: The Sexual Politics of Gender and Labor Struggle in the Chilean Countryside 1950–1973* (Durham, N.C.: Duke University Press, forthcoming).

66. He noted in *The Great Transformation* that "the same needs of society which benefitted democracy in the New World strengthened the influence of the aristocracy in the old," (185).

Chapter Four

FROM THE POWER OF ECONOMIC IDEAS TO THE POWER OF ECONOMISTS

Verónica Montecinos and John Markoff

GOVERNMENT OFFICIALS, contenders for office, investors, union leaders, consumers, workers, voters, revolutionaries, not to mention professional economists, all have ideas about how economies work, could work, or should work. Such ideas guide actions—government policy, investment decisions, electoral campaign strategies, union action or inaction, consumers' propensities to spend or save, voters' choices, and the organization of insurrections—with the most profound consequences for both the fate of states and the circumstances of daily life; and these ideas about how economies work, could work, or should work are, in turn, reshaped as those attempted actions encounter recalcitrant realities.

These are truisms everywhere, but in Latin America the economic arena also has tended to be the central object of politics to a degree unsurpassed in other places. Its interstate wars have been few compared with Europe's, its twentieth-century intellectuals and political elites less inclined to stake out a cultural battleground over the place of its distinctive civilization in a modern world or a global economy than is the case in Islamic countries or Asia, and views about the role of the state in regulating moral and religious life are less a determinant of voter choice than in North America. Of course, this is merely a *comparative* statement: the Paraguayan or Gran Chaco wars were full of consequences, some Mexican or Andean intellectuals have been absorbed in claiming a significant precapitalist heritage, and growing conversions to Protestantism raise significant political issues in a number of countries. But, we contend, if ever there was a broad region where the economy can be held responsible for almost all major political twists and turns in the twentieth century, it would be Latin America.

It is hardly surprising, then, that Latin America's own economists have been profoundly involved in reflecting on their societies in broad, innovative ways and, over a number of decades, as we shall describe later, were developing a distinctive body of ideas. We shall also describe how that intellectual movement lost its élan. So what is interesting is not whether economic ideas have had an impact in Latin America—of course they have—but how the ideas that have been dominant have changed, and how the ways in which those ideas have had an impact have changed. An important theme in our account—made up of several intertwined but distinguishable strands—will be the radically changing role of professional economists.

First, the broad economic notions that have informed Latin American economic policy in the twentieth century have undergone two radical shifts. The early twentieth century saw a widespread adherence to liberal doctrines of a limited state, gently assisting the natural movements of economic life whose relation to the world economy was, and ought to be, summed up by notions of comparative advantage. If one may broadly call the ideals, policies, and associated doctrines of that moment "orthodox," the great economic and political crisis of the 1930s was the context for a shift to a more activist state pursuing "heterodox" ideals with appropriate policies. Latin American economists became important participants in the development of heterodox economic ideas, although they were participating in a discussion among economists that extended far beyond Latin America. One of the central tenets of this heterodoxy was the very notion that Latin America was a region with its own distinctive character, issues, histories, cultures, and economies, and as such needed distinctive economic policies. The crafting of these policies provided the context for the development of a distinctive body of theory. By contrast, the more recent crisis that we shall consider, which we may locate in the 1980s, led to another turn of the wheel and a radical re-embrace of orthodoxy. One of the central tenets of this re-embrace was the notion that what Latin America needed was the same policies as anywhere else, which at a more abstract level suggested and was suggested by the repudiation of anything resembling a distinctive body of theory.

The second major strand of our story is the changing role played by economists themselves, for the political impact of that profession has grown enormously. An important part of why the economic theory informing the policies that came out of the 1980s was so different from and in many ways a repudiation of the ideas that came out of the 1930s was the far greater role played by economists in shaping political life during the more recent period. We may, a bit overschematically, summarize our discussion by contending that while the crisis of the 1930s reshaped economics, the economics profession reshaped the crisis of the 1980s.

WHOSE ECONOMIC IDEAS MATTER?

A striking observation of Joseph Love: "Industrialization in Latin America was fact before it was policy, and policy before it was theory."[1] In the late nineteenth and early twentieth centuries, Latin American governments were not pursuing growth-oriented policies. In this, their policy makers (or might one say policy nonmakers?) were much in tune with those currents of economic thought that paid little attention to issues of growth or development. H. W. Arndt's survey depicts the economics mainstream in broad strokes: "Hardly a line is to be found in the writings of any professional economists between 1870 and 1940 in support of economic growth as a policy objective."[2] Writing in the mid-1950s of an even longer time span, Arthur Lewis observed that "no comprehensive treatise on [growth] has been published for about a century."[3] We might question such sweeping generalizations about such a long stretch of time, particularly if we move away from the English-speaking world. But if some Marxists were continuing Marx's focus on "the law of motion" of capitalism (the translation of *Capital* may well have been the point where the term *development* entered into English-language discussions of economics),[4] few others were doing so.[5]

If the mainstream in early twentieth-century economics had little interest in issues of growth, Latin American governments had little concern for promoting some conception of "development." The keystone of relevant theoretical wisdom drew on Ricardo's notion of comparative advantage, and Latin American economies were to find prosperity in exporting primary products to resource-hungry industrializers whose factories needed raw materials and whose workers needed food. Images of the "natural" abounded: it was natural to use the resources provided by nature, rather than those shaped by planned action; it was natural for owners of resources to make their fortune and artificial for government to strive for change; it was natural for lush tropical gardens to produce tropical products and artificial for them to deliberately aim at industry.[6] Government policy aimed at supporting such export economies, and one could find ample room for ironic commentary on whether it was not as "artificial" for Brazilian policies to keep up coffee profits as it would have been to promote factories. The upshot of such theory-supported practice was that demand for the products of industry was to be satisfied by importation.

As World War I and then the Great Depression disrupted established patterns of trade, some Latin American entrepreneurs found golden opportunities in moving into industrial production for domestic markets no longer adequately supplied with imported goods. The long history of import-substituting industrialization had begun, largely without benefit of state planning at all, and in defiance of rather than subservience to the prevailing wisdom of the economics profession. The relevant economic ideas that drove change at this moment, then, were not primarily the ideas of politicians nor of economists, but of businessmen, including export-oriented landowners who pragmatically seized the available opportunities.[7]

Political elites then began to discover a whole array of possibility in *deliberately* promoting import-substituting industrial growth through disrupting transborder commerce by policy. Import quotas and tariff barriers, coupled with a variety of policies favoring industrialists and the development of an urban factory proletariat (subsidized urban public transportation, say), were appealing to a whole generation of political leaders, who could put together a broad national coalition of industrialists, factory workers, employees of the rapidly growing state ministries, providers of services to expanding urban populations, lawyers employed in writing and interpreting regulations, and even military officers pressing for domestic arms industries (not to mention all the politicians' cousins and in-laws who could be given posts). In this second industrializing moment, the key economic ideas were those of political leaders, cementing broad-based multiclass political support. As political elites began to build broad coalitions around policies of import-substituting industrialization, in which state action played a considerable role, professional economists began to find important places as advisers to government.

It was against this background that some Latin American economic thinkers began to develop an anti-Ricardian theoretical critique of notions of comparative advantage as they would play out in what was not yet called the Third World. Intimately involved in advising governments busy pursuing some variant of import-substituting industrialization, but also a part of the global community of economists, an innovative group of Latin American economists after World War II formed what came to be known as the CEPAL school (from Comisión Económica para América Latina); we shall return to the ideas of these economists later.

Now, and increasingly so, the economic ideas infusing change were beginning to be the ideas of professional economists, as much as, or more than, the ideas of businessmen or politicians. At first entrepreneurs and then politicians had brought about change in defiance of the ideas of many economists, and in particular the body of ideas we may label, approximately, as "orthodoxy." State-sponsored development created opportunities for economists with views that differed from this orthodoxy, however. Increasingly it was these professional economists who were the carriers of the politically potent economic ideas about development, ideas we may label, approximately, as "heterodoxy." To follow this crucial shift more closely, we need to explore the roots of developmentalist ideas among economists in and out of Latin America, as well as the growth of the Latin American economics profession.

Twentieth-Century Crises

Determining the proper sphere of, and modalities of, state action was something about which economists, like everyone else, could disagree throughout most of the nineteenth century. But the Russian Revolution of 1917 provided a powerful stimulus to statist currents. For pre-1917 socialists, revolution was long seen as one of the most important *fruits* of development, as a maturing industrial working class seized control of the potentially liberating modern technology. Most Marxists, for example, had expected the center of revolution to be the industrial powerhouses of the world, with a possible revolution in Russia thought of as at most a sideshow. After 1917, for socialists who, much to the surprise of many of them, found themselves in charge of that huge country, which they themselves regarded as culturally, politically, and economically backward, and for fascinated but not always friendly socialists elsewhere, socialism suddenly had to be reconceived as the *path* to development.

As Russian revolutionaries were now inventing one kind of developmentalism, economists and political leaders in the West were suddenly groping for some alternative but equally compelling model, especially some proposal to control the business cycle, much feared as the source of recruitment into radical movements. The Keynesian revolution in macroeconomic thought promised the tools for state-managed manipulation of crucial variables without socialism. We leave it to a rapidly developing specialist literature to sort out the role played in this revolution by the theories of professional economists and the improvisations of political elites; the pressures of social movements and the innovations of governmental bureaucracies; fear of socialist revolution and concern for immediate crises; and the specific contribution of Keynes, as opposed to economists elsewhere on independent but convergent intellectual paths.[8]

With Keynesianism supplying a vital intellectual rationale, four successive crises provided fertile opportunities for an increasing penetration of the new economic ideas into government, and along with those ideas came the economists who believed in them:

- The struggle for recovery from the Great Depression of the 1930s.
- The management of wartime economies, 1939–45.
- The deeply successful effort by the Western powers for postwar industrial recovery, defined to embrace even the defeated enemy

powers, a task made urgent by the U.S.-Soviet rivalry. The continued appeal of Keynesianism and its offshoot, "growth economics," was spurred by revived fears of revolutionism and significant communist voting strength in some Western countries. The slide from a specifically postwar "reconstruction" to a broader "development" is encapsulated in the designation of one of the central institutions of the moment, the International Bank for Reconstruction and Development (an important source of financing for infrastructural projects).[9]

• The end of western empire. As western Europe and Japan prospered, the new challenge of decolonization raised the specter of the forms national liberation might take. Now "development economics" blossomed as the Western powers, especially the United States, sought to continue and extend the now-established tradition of state-run economic management, with an eye to warding off Third World revolution. Not only was it desirable that West Germany outshine East Germany, South Korea was to surpass the North, and Taiwan was to surpass China; more generally, the promise of Third World developmentalism was held high. In the former colonial powers, moreover, developmentalism, as Frederick Cooper and Randall Packard have suggested, provided a rationale for continuing involvement in the affairs of former colonies.[10]

By the 1960s, economists had secure places as government advisers on long-term developmental issues as well as short-term crisis management, and they were staffing a variety of government agencies (and international agencies also); this had occurred in the prosperous Western states and in the Third World. Developmentalism, then, was a transnational idea, rooted in transnational processes. The decolonizations that followed World War II, the rivalry of the United States and the Soviet Union, and the establishment of such international financial institutions as the World Bank and the International Monetary Fund cemented developmentalism on virtually a global scale. As states in the Soviet orbit pursued their own developmental strategies, the United States supported, through the Marshall Plan, the reindustrialization of its major allies. One might speak of the Marshall Plan as a transnational variant of state macroeconomic intervention. And in many a poorer country, the hope that state policies might lead toward a national industrial future blossomed: to this end, Third World governments could seek support from Eastern socialists, Western Keynesians, or both in succession.

The Third World aspect of developmentalism was not only of particular significance for Latin America, but Latin Americans played their own, significant role in shaping this body of economic ideas. A long tradition of dealing with foreign economic advice going back to the nineteenth century[11]—advice sometimes welcomed, sometimes not—was now updated in the form of nearly continual dealings with the postwar financial institutions of developmentalism, and Latin American economists were perforce active in drawing up required developmental plans and mediating between national political elites and such transnational institutions. The pinnacle of this process was reached with the Alliance for Progress, launched in 1961. The proponents of this project saw it as a shift in the focus of inter-American relations from issues of hemispheric security to the promotion of democracy and modernization. This new Alliance included financial and technical support for industrialization, agrarian reform, housing, health, and education, as well as government planning and regional integration.[12]

Meanwhile, another of the institutions of postwar recovery, the United Nations, provided a base and resources for economists to address broad developmental issues, an opportunity used with particular creativity by Latin Americans.

Latin American Economists Embrace Developmentalism

Latin American economists shaped their own approach to developmentalism. In Latin America, neoclassical economic doctrines had been widely propagated since the mid–nineteenth century. The idea that free international trade generated benefits to all participants came to be widely taken for granted, part of the common sense of economics. In some quarters, foreign commerce had even been held to be a civilizing process, as it came to be considered in the context of debates among Latin Americans about their culture. To those who, following the Argentine Sarmiento, saw a struggle between polar forces that could be summed up as "civilization" and "barbarism," commercial relations with Europe could figure as a channel along which civilization would flow into Latin America.[13] Nonetheless, liberal ideas were by no means unchallenged. At a moment when the principal participants in debates about economic policy included business interests, landholders, government officials, and foreign economic advisers, it is probably fair to say that policy in practice grew out of the economic interests of the powerful and politicians' political needs for support. Economists' ideas were only a small and frequently ignored part of the picture. Indeed, there was hardly much of a Latin American profession at all, and the relevant economists were largely temporary visitors from abroad.

The devastating impact of the Great Depression of the 1930s brought dramatic changes into Latin American discussion of economic policy. But some of the new trends had institutional and intellectual roots that antedated the world economic crisis.[14] The economic disruptions associated with World War I, as noted earlier, produced some of the same effects later deliberately crafted by governments. Less dramatically, urban growth provided markets not wholly satisfied by imported goods; so did extractive activities like mining, which tended to generate all sorts of demand for infrastructure (e.g., railroad construction between mine and port). Some export-oriented agriculture also tended to nurture processing industry (e.g., sugar). The industrial sector was already significant in some places by 1929 (23 percent of gross domestic product in Argentina, 14 percent in Mexico).[15]

Quite apart from openings for industrial growth, the web of international financial connection encouraged governmental economic management. Paul Drake has shown that the boom of foreign lending to Latin America in the 1920s permitted large increases in government spending and the financing of infrastructural investment and other public projects. In some places, governments were involving themselves in economic management despite an official liberalism. Steven Topik has shown in the case of Brazil that extensive dealing with foreign investors went beyond *permitting* government action in the economy and virtually *impelled* government management as responsible politicians, however liberal their credentials, found themselves having to placate foreign creditors (who might be backed by foreign gunboats).[16] Institutions and procedures thus established under liberal auspices would become, under statist auspices, "major instruments of national development."[17]

In Mexico, the revolution had opened the way to new sorts of projects as intellectuals with various socialist and nationalist visions offered their advice to one or another party contending for power. The 1917 constitution had formally sanctioned a mixed-economy approach. Jesús Silva Herzog, a Marxist of independent mind, traveled to Moscow as ambassador and later became one of the founders of Mexico's first economics program. José Vasconcelos, education minister in the 1920s, became a key spokesman for a regional, "Latin American" perspective on developmental issues.[18]

In Chile, major economic and administrative reforms were also introduced in the second half of the 1920s. Under the leadership of Finance Minister Pablo Ramírez, a committed nationalist, a generation of capable engineers was brought in to staff the growing public bureaucracy. The newly created Central Bank and the General Comptroller's Office—an agency overseeing the legality of state actions—guided the crafting of interventionist policies that included extensive public works, industrial promotion, fiscal and monetary restructuring, anticorruption measures, and the regulation of foreign trade. Ramírez proudly declared in 1929 that "our government is exclusively technical; the engineer, the banker, and the expert in economic affairs have replaced the politician."[19]

With the abrupt end of export-led prosperity, the doctrines of economic liberalism became widely discredited. Although sociological references to paradigm shifts are generally overblown, this expression does not seem excessive as a description of what was happening in economic debate. The orthodoxy of free-market ideas seemed an inadequate guide to understanding the new economic context and seemed unhelpful in suggesting routes out of the crisis. Alternative interpretations were developed, alternative policies came to be favored, and alternative institutions for the making of economic policy began to be set up.

Latin Americans were taking a close look at experiences elsewhere. Various arguments in favor of state-promoted industrialization were gaining favor in the economic debates of the 1930s. Latin Americans (not just Mexican Marxists) were paying close attention to Soviet practices, debating the works of corporatist theorists, receiving technical assistance and academic advice from French missions, discovering German social thinkers, and talking to Spanish refugees. A fertile, diverse mix of economic ideas from diverse sources was under intense discussion. The Chilean-German Ernst Wagemann and the Romanian Nicolai Manoilescu seem to have had a stimulating impact on many of those looking for new policies.[20]

Over the next several decades, a broad consensus emerged regarding the need for greater insulation of the national from the transnational economy, industrialization came to be embraced as virtually the hallmark of economic success, state action came to be heralded as the engine of industrialization, and economic planning came to be seen as a crucial vehicle for rationally guiding that state action.

Initially, economists were still playing a secondary role in this shift. It was the loss of export markets and the disappearance of foreign imports, foreign credit, and foreign investment that spurred the political elites of Latin America to develop new ways of dealing with this changed situation. Without benefit of some new theoretical framework, the sometimes desperate search for a more self-reliant pattern of domestic production generated improvised solutions and ad hoc arrangements. The major players in putting together the new policies were usually politicians, industrialists, lawyers, engineers, and sometimes military officers or labor leaders. In the course of seeking political support, managing an economic crisis, groping for national economic independence, and generally trying to make it possible for state action to manipulate the national economy, they both developed the state bureaucracy and sought to assure themselves of secure positions within it.

In the following decades, more systematic, technically inspired proposals began to supplement and then supplant what was initially a pragmatic coping with crisis. Now an enlarging body of professional economists came to develop increasingly sophisticated, audacious, and heterodox rationales to justify and guide what Hirschman has called a "barrage of structural reforms."[21]

Economics had hardly been established as an autonomous profession in Latin America when economic liberalism was dethroned from its previous hegemonic position. At this time only a handful of training programs in economics even existed in the region, perhaps the best of which was at the University of Buenos Aires.[22] Many of these programs were adjuncts of other professional schools. In Chile, for example, the Catholic University set up its School of Economics and Business Administration in 1924. For the next two decades, this school was largely devoted to training in accounting and commerce. The Mexican Escuela de Economía became a separate school in 1935, offering courses that had been taught at the Escuela de Jurisprudencia since 1929. The mission of this program was the training of economists for government service on behalf of economic development. In Brazil before the 1940s, economics was taught in law, engineering, and military programs; it was established as an independent academic discipline in 1945 in the Facultade Nacional de Ciênciais Ecônomicas of the Universidade do Brasil. The picture elsewhere was similar.[23] Those teaching these early generations of economic specialists were themselves often self-taught economists, frequently high-level government officials who had managed to acquire some economic knowledge.[24] Latin America, moreover, had no tradition of empirical economic research, and the specialized publications of its economists dealt mostly with monetary and other policy issues.[25] We may take this as an indication that economists, like other actors in economic debates, were largely reacting to the problems of the moment rather than acting at the behest of some broad, theoretically articulated vision.

So there were no strong institutions committed to preserving the old free-trade consensus as sacred doctrine. In the 1930s, Raúl Prebisch, along with some other members of the still tiny community of Latin American economists, abandoned an initial allegiance to neoclassical theory and, as he later put it, began to "convert to protectionism."[26] The diffusion of protectionist doctrines encountered little organized resistance and was rapidly embraced by both government bureaucracies and business associations. Protectionism soon became the dominant body of ideas within the emerging economics profession. So the crisis of the 1930s was reshaping Latin American economic thinking, including the thinking of economists.

In the 1940s, more programs in economics achieved academic recognition and were able to set themselves up somewhat independently from other programs. In addition, curricula were brought up to date, and some younger economists were pursuing graduate training in Europe and the United States. Nonetheless, Latin Americans were not doing much by way of developing economic theory. During this period, several research and training programs in economics were inaugurated by government agencies (sometimes in collaboration with universities, sometimes independently). These institutes, however, were mainly oriented to professionalizing public administration, collecting basic statistical information, and giving more coherence to the ongoing state interventionism that had been developing in a pragmatic, piecemeal fashion.[27]

Someone trying to discover what it was that Latin American economists had on their minds in the 1940s would have paid attention to what was probably the most cosmopolitan group among them: those who functioned as delegates at international meetings of economists and those who belonged to the network of financial specialists, including those involved in the operations of central banks. What these economists were using their intellects for seems primarily to have been issues of monetary and exchange policy. As recalled by Felipe Pazos, a prominent figure in this early generation of Latin American economists, economic theory was then little more than an intellectual exercise. It "had nothing to do with our reality. . . . We had to study concrete problems, looking for commonsense explanations and solutions."[28] But something else was happening as well. It was at the first meeting of the region's central bankers, in Mexico City in 1946, that Prebisch first presented in writing his influential and innovative conceptualization of center-periphery relations in the course of illustrating his general argument that neoclassical theories of trade did not serve the interests of Latin America.[29] The following year Prebisch published his introduction to Keynes.[30]

The rapidly growing literature produced by Latin American economists was still overwhelmingly focused on practical rather than theoretical issues. A broad public of entrepreneurs, academics, and public officials, as well as economists, took part in debates over the virtues and defects of industrial protectionism.[31] Newly founded economics journals, such as the Mexican *El Trimestre Económico*, were also devoted primarily to policy questions. These journals "did not attempt to compete with foreign professional publications," for it was thought that "in countries that must devote all their intellectual energies to the solution of urgent problems, pure scientific creation is a luxury that we cannot afford."[32]

But if Latin American economists were not devoting themselves to theoretical contributions, this does not mean that they were uncritical devotees of theory produced elsewhere. Many of them seem to have been deeply skeptical about the validity and relevance of imported economic doctrines. The generally nationalist flavor that infused the economic policies in which they were participants encouraged a critical stance toward the enormous influence that foreign "money doctors"—the economic advisers to Latin American governments who were virtually emissaries of foreign banks, foreign investors, and foreign governments—had been able to exert in earlier decades.

Edwin Kemmerer and other missionaries of economic orthodoxy, acting as financial consultants to regional governments, had encouraged various legislative and administrative actions, or "reforms," as such changes were generally known. Latin Americans had been urged to "modernize" their accounting practices, as well as their collection of tariffs and taxes; they were urged to adopt the banking and fiscal practices that were standard in the "more advanced" countries. Such steps, it was held, would reduce financial instability, make economic policy more effective, and improve access to foreign loans and investment.[33]

In response to decades of such injunctions and admonitions, the increasingly active economists of Latin America were beginning to draw on their own experience in the service of governments committed in an atheoretical way to heterodox protectionist policies. They were convinced that among the lessons of the crash and the Great Depression were indications that orthodoxy did not have all the answers, and certainly did not have answers with any relevance to their own countries' situations. With experience in public service came increased willingness to assert the soundness of their own judgment. Serving governments devoted to national economic autonomy and in varying degrees unhappy with national economic dependence—to invoke a word soon to be much used—they wanted to break the grip of their own professional dependence on the claims of foreign economists to be the interpreters of the timeless and universal wisdom of the science of economics. They wanted to claim for themselves the autonomy, prestige, and prerogatives that foreign economists enjoyed. They needed a theory, their own theory.

United Nations Economic Commission for Latin America (CEPAL)

Thus, in the postdepression years, economic recovery was accompanied by a mixture of intense pragmatism and theoretical uncertainty. It was only in the late 1940s and 1950s that a theoretically grounded justification for import-substitution industrialization emerged. In 1948 the United Nations Economic Commission for Latin America (CEPAL) was established. Its economists, under the leadership of the already famous Prebisch, launched a comprehensive strategic proposal for a development model that was, to use a much-repeated phrase, inward-looking and that took industrialization as its goal. CEPAL's theoretical framework for economic development was part of an ambitious project that amounted to nothing less than the establishment of a new school of economic thought that would provide the theoretical underpinnings of new policies already adopted and from which newer policies would flow.

CEPAL's "structuralism," as its approach came to be known in summary, offered to meld its own economic theory and policy advice in ways that no foreign theory could. It was argued that both neoclassical economics and Keynesianism presupposed institutional structures (labor markets, firms, state agencies, and exchange mechanisms) that were typical of advanced capitalist countries but were largely absent in Latin America.[34] Unlike orthodox economic theory, a specifically "Latin American economics" would be able to uncover the deep structural roots of economic phenomena, addressing such intractable issues as inflation and balance-of-payments problems through a careful examination of a country's historical and sociopolitical reality. Neoclassical economics held that there was a "homo economicus," and that there was therefore an economic science whose laws applied in richer and poorer countries alike, a "monoeconomics," to use A. O. Hirschman's felicitous expression.[35] By contrast, the *cepalinos* took as central historical differences in institutions. For some these differences were produced by the power relations between different parts of the world, so that there was, as Prebisch held, a great difference between the ways "core" economies worked and the ways "peripheral" economies worked. Policies based on Ricardian notions of comparative advantage, moreover, were held to work to the comparative disadvantage of peripheral economies, consigned by Ricardian neoclassicists to the role of producers of primary commodities, because agricultural products were subject to declining terms of trade (a central proposition for CEPAL). In short, the *cepalinos* took the heterodox view that what was sauce for the goose was poison for the gander, and they developed a theoretical grounding for their support for different economic policies for Latin America than might be appropriate for the wealthy countries of the core. Their analyses, moreover, called attention to the varying ways national economies were shaped by history and culture, the role of power disparities between core and peripheral countries in shaping their economies differently, and the positive role that might be played by peripheral states in protecting their national economies from the nefarious consequences of these power imbalances.

The new theoretical vision never severed its connections with the practical concerns that had been the daily preoccupation of the Latin

American economists who had been involved in forging concrete development policies. That vision promised to add a theoretical dimension that might serve to inspire, guide, and inform their concrete recommendations. At a moment when much prestige among professional economists in core countries accrued to the elaboration of abstract mathematical models, the CEPAL group proposed more attention to history, institutions, and national and regional differences, as well as continuing attention to practical concerns. The new economics, moreover, would furnish a basis for the rejection of what were held to be the "stereotypes" and other deficiencies often found among foreign economic advisers.[36]

CEPAL prescriptions offered a theoretical orientation to guide the building of more diversified, less vulnerable national economies. By exposing the ideological biases of neoclassical economics, structuralist analyses encouraged efforts to redress what were now to be understood as unjust asymmetries between an industrial core and the peripheral exporters of primary commodities. For some time, Latin American economists already had been advising governments embarked on such policies; CEPAL now provided a theoretical rationale. In so doing economists were asserting their own claims within a profession in which theoretical work has generally carried far more prestige than public service.[37] As these Latin American economists were contending that they, too, had a theoretical vision, that vision was one that called attention to the transnational embeddedness of their countries' economies. Its insistence that trade represented a vehicle for exploitation suggested a very different outlook on international questions than the classical embrace of comparative advantage. Rather than go with such opportunities as "naturally" accrued to places endowed with primary resources, planning for industrialization now found its own theoretical basis. To look at international trade under this new lens, moreover, was to support a regional sense of common identity in relation to core countries, and thereby help strengthen Latin America's bargaining power within the international economic system.

These ideas had a powerful impact. In a sense, it has been argued, Prebisch "created Latin America."[38] CEPAL became "the recognized spokesman for Latin American economic development,"[39] and CEPAL's theories served to legitimate the existing direction of policy. In several countries, as we have repeatedly suggested, an earlier generation of modernizing state managers had already introduced some of the institutions and techniques (infrastructural programs, tariffs, subsidies, and loans) through which states could advance the industrialization drive. As Prebisch said in an interview in 1985, "CEPAL's merit was to demonstrate that theoretically [these ideas] were correct."[40]

CEPAL combined a militant proselytism for its theoretical vision with an avowed neutrality on many issues that were profoundly divisive in Latin American political life. First of all, it avoided party identifications in national political conflicts. Second, it avoided taking positions on some particularly conflictual issues (land reform, social security, and military expenditures) while taking cautiously middle-of-the road positions on others (foreign ownership of national resources). Cardoso refers to CEPAL as "[a] UN agency often dependent upon somewhat unprogressive governments," noting that "some issues were left in the shade."[41] CEPAL's middle-of-the-road flavor was attractive to those hoping to find a third road, between socialism and laissez-faire capitalism, another of the points of convergence between CEPAL and First World Keynesianism. Its ideas helped cement a broad intellectual and political consensus.

CEPAL was able to propagate its branch of economic heterodoxy through advisory missions to governments, textbooks, and publications of research on specific countries. It sponsored a new research agenda for the economics profession and, looking to its own ideas for guidance, began to discourage newer generations from attending economics training programs abroad.[42] To this latter end it organized its own economics courses and seminars that were attended by hundreds of economists—and other government officials—throughout Latin America.[43]

CEPAL's heterodox position saw state planning (euphemistically referred to as "programming") not as antithetical to market mechanisms and private initiative but as working in conjunction with them, yet another of the many ways in which *cepalinos* converged with the Keynesianism that was so important in the post-World War II core countries. Nonetheless, some powerful conservative academics and business groups, in Latin America and elsewhere, strongly attacked the emphasis on state planning as a sign that CEPAL was functioning as an agent of communism,[44] rather paralleling the right's attacks on the antisocialist Keynes. Nonetheless, the intellectual repute of CEPAL (due in part, we have been suggesting, to the economic ideas influential at the time in the First World) and its affiliation with the United Nations allowed it to continue to attract external support.

It may be worth recalling that many Latin American countries had strong traditions of conceiving of government in a managerial role, as an active shaper of social relations and morality, that long preceded the twentieth-century significance of the economics profession. Centralized decision making guided by expert advice was hardly something new; nor were notions of a state as in some sense the guardian of a collectivity (by contrast, for example, with Anglo-American notions of a state as the arena where individuals and collectivities fought and with luck harmonized their separate interests).[45] One thinks, for example, of the power of positivism in late nineteenth-century Brazil or the *científicos* around Mexico's Porfirio Díaz. While for an earlier generation, an engineering background often could provide the proper technical credentials, now it was beginning to be economists who were looked to.

SANTIAGO, 1964–73

Economic ideas, like other ideas, do not get born, grow, intertwine, change, and die apart from the interconnections among human beings and the contexts in which those interconnections exist. It is therefore worth pausing over the place CEPAL was located and considering as well the particular moment. CEPAL was centered not in Buenos Aires, Rio de Janeiro, Mexico City, nor other imaginable locations but in Santiago, which meant that a very important part of its environment was the tremendous Chilean drama from the election of Eduardo Frei to the presidency in 1964 to the military coup that ended the presidency and life of Salvador Allende in 1973.

CEPAL's first meeting in Santiago took place in 1948. The United Nations had already established two regional commissions to deal with the reconstruction of war-torn regions. Latin American diplomats persuaded UN officials that their region should not be excluded from aid programs. (They argued that their countries had contributed to the war effort and had been indirectly affected by the war.) This broadening of the geography of postwar aid enlarged its purpose from "reconstruction" to "development." Chile's prominence in the diplomatic discussions may have contributed to CEPAL's installation in Santiago.[46]

Whatever brought CEPAL to Chile, Chile brought something to CEPAL. In the 1960s, Chile became a hothouse of political, social, and economic ideas. Chilean political forces on the center and left competed with each other to develop, and embody, correct revolutionary ideas, while conservative forces remained very much in contention. Frei's Christian Democrats were divided by the degree of radicalism they espoused. The rival major parties of the left competed with each other to show themselves more radical still than the leftist Christian Democrats. Within each of the major parties, established leaderships struggled to contain the youthful partisans of factions more radical than the party mainstream. Foreign supporters of one or another grouping provided assistance as they tried to guide the Chilean drama in one or another direction. CEPAL's prestige as a forum for intergovernmental consultation, data gathering, and technical training had brought to Santiago a large contingent of international academics and development experts. And as coups or other repressive developments took place elsewhere in Latin America, political exiles from neighboring countries gravitated to Santiago, attracted by democratic freedoms, an open and vigorous university life, emerging opportunities for policy experimentation, the hope of revolution ended by bayonets at home, and the immunity and prerogatives that came with positions in the expanding international civil service that

CEPAL and other international organizations were bringing to Santiago.[47] An important group of Brazilians, for example, was working there, including Fernando Henrique Cardoso, Maria da Conceição Tavares, José Serra, and Theotonio dos Santos.

Although Prebisch, who had headed CEPAL since 1950, moved to a new UN position in 1964, that date hardly marked an end to CEPAL's influence. The new Chilean presidency of Eduardo Frei galvanized the hopes of those who sought some route to development that would be an attractive alternative to the revolutionary Cuban model. (Some looked to Yugoslavia for inspiration.) Animated by the principles of "communitarian socialism" and CEPAL-inspired developmentalism, the Frei government sponsored a program of agrarian, educational, and tax reform and a general openness to social change carried out in collaboration with private investments.

Many in Europe and the United States took note and provided support to one or another Chilean body. By the mid-1960s, Chile's two leading universities were developing rival programs in economics that aimed to attract students from all over Latin America. The more radical program (ESCOLATINA) was established at the University of Chile, the more conservative (PREL) at the Catholic University. This latter program was supported by the Ford Foundation and academics from the University of Chicago. (It was typical of the moment that the Catholic Church itself was divided, with a left encouraged by the anticapitalist rhetoric of the Frei government and an at least equally active anticommunist wing as well, both supported by foreign clerics and foreign social scientists.) The election in 1970 of Salvador Allende continued the sense of Chile as a laboratory for social experiment, now open to some of the more radical theories of development that were being nurtured in Santiago's intellectual circles. And, to complete the picture, Allende's overthrow in 1973, and the authoritarian period that followed, brought another group of experimenters to the fore. In all these mutations, Chile was serving as a test case for a variety of social and economic theories; providing material support for a large and cosmopolitan group, the producers of these theories; providing intellectual stimulation in the encounters of a multinational group of social theorists and social activists; and providing a sense of the possibility of translating radical theories into policy.

DEVELOPMENT ECONOMICS IN AND OUT OF LATIN AMERICA

In the postwar years, economic development acquired a prominent role among those who sought to ground a more peaceful world on "reconstruction," a notion extended by some beyond repairing a devastated Europe to addressing the economic problems of poorer countries. As mentioned earlier, the role that fears of socialist revolution played in all this was considerable. Foreign aid and technical assistance programs, so their proponents asserted, were intended to reduce international differences in wealth and social well-being, thereby discouraging political radicalization in the poorer countries.

This was the moment when the new field of "development economics" flourished in universities in Western Europe and the United States. The field was powerfully shaped by economists with origins in Central and Eastern Europe, many of them Jewish, who relocated to England and the United States, where they participated in the rising tide of Keynesianism (among them Michał Kalecki, Paul Rosenstein-Rodan, and Nicholas Kaldor).[48] Like their counterparts in Latin America, they advocated planned state support for industrialization as the route to development. They held that the social, political, or cultural circumstances of poorer countries made conventional neoclassical prescriptions inapplicable, even perverse, and that the application of policies predicated on notions of uniform economic processes was seen as a formula for persistent failure. Like the CEPAL structuralists, they contended that the specific problems of the periphery demanded a new kind of economics. And distinguishing themselves from those who tended to see freer markets as all-purpose remedies to problems, they tended to focus on what they saw as market failures.

In underlining the importance of the unorthodox claim that a different kind of country might need to be understood through the lens of a different kind of economic theory, A. O. Hirschman has emphasized the parallelism with the Keynesian attention to the distinctive properties of industrial economies with underutilized capacities. The Keynesian revolution, as he puts it, had already broken "the ice of monoeconomics."[49] So the prestige of Keynesianism in the First World helped in conferring intellectual legitimation on the ideas now being crafted in Latin America. The success of the Marshall Plan in Western Europe also bolstered the conviction among economists, in various parts of the world, that investment planning, together with infusions of capital, could spur growth. As a striking instance of convergence of economic ideas, we may note that Raúl Prebisch in Santiago and Hans Singer in New York at virtually the same historical moment published their seminal papers on declining terms of trade for agricultural goods.[50]

Despite some collaborative work involving CEPAL and those establishing development economics in the core countries,[51] the Latin Americans tended to downplay the influence of Keynesianism. Asserting their own originality, they claimed to be advancing into "uncharted lands."[52] Distinguishing which ideas were borrowed from abroad, which adopted with significant alterations, which were developed in response to and in opposition to foreign ideas, which were developed in parallel, and which were developed in total independence is a fruitless exercise. What can be said with certainty is that Latin American economists were major participants in the intellectual debates and were very far from being simply importers of foreign ideas forged in the First World. Indeed, to refer to the "First World" origins of ideas propounded in London or New York is to overlook the degree to which many of the most important propounders were themselves from Central and Eastern Europe; and Love's work points to some direct connections between ideas originating in Eastern Europe and Latin America that did not even pass through New York.[53] To further complicate the picture of the geography of intellectual innovation, we might r ecall that CEPAL was established under UN auspices.[54]

The Decline and (Perhaps) Fall of Development Economics: World Trends

The vision of a tamed market, state regulation, public spending as the key to economic management, citizenship rights conceived in very large part as claims on portions of state spending, and nationally oriented conceptions of economic growth went hand in hand. But since the 1970s this complex of ideas has pretty much fallen apart. European communist states are no more, the Soviet Union, Yugoslavia, and Czechoslovakia literally disintegrating in the 1990s and the German Democratic Republic literally vanishing; the International Monetary Fund and the World Bank are attempting to support the dismantling of state-led developmental programs in favor of privatization; the sacralization of the marketplace, for which labels like Reaganism and Thatcherism are stand-ins, dominates the political life of Britain and the United States and is a major challenge to the surviving statist welfarism of others; and economic nationalism is scorned as hopelessly inefficient when measured against the promise of opening the national economy to the world.

The collapse of the old developmentalist vision had many components, including the following:[55]

- Relocation of much industrial production from First World to Third World sites, coordinated by transnational corporations and transnational financial networks. Conspicuous success in this late-twentieth-century developmental pattern went to Asian countries pursuing export-oriented production that broke down the distinction between the national and global economies, rather than to countries following the policies advocated by the champions of nationally oriented development. The "Asian tigers" have been seized on as exemplars of the wisdom of integration into the global marketplace by those who criticized economic nationalism in the name of economic liberalization (while the extent of state activism in the various Asian "miracles" and egalitarian redistributive policies such as Taiwan's extensive land reform have entered far less into such discussions).[56]

- The failure of development projects to alter social inequalities in many places, while at the same time increasing radically national indebtedness and the political power of transnational sources of credit. These failures helped inspire critiques of developmentalism from the Left (and from the Right as well). Discussing these changing ideas, Kathryn Sikkink calls attention to the persuasive power of a simple two-by-two table prepared in the 1980s by a participant in CEPAL's self-critical discussions. The table's dimensions were (1) rapidity of growth and (2) equity; the entries in the cells were countries. For Latin America, after three decades of import-substituting industrialization, the cell for growth with equity had no cases. The empty cell was more striking because elsewhere growth and equity had co-occurred.[57]

- The collapse of European communism, which eliminated not only a major variant of developmentalism directly but also the fear of socialism, one of the main sources of upper-class acquiescence in Keynesian policies in the Western countries. As the remaining communist states embraced the global marketplace, monetarists, supply-siders, and antistatists became the economists with influence on First World and Third World governments alike, while Latin American leftists rethought many of their positions.

- The debt crises of the 1980s refocused the managers of Third World economies, as well as their creditors, toward debt management. This produced a further convergence toward development strategies geared to export earnings for debt repayment (to the extent, in Chile and Argentina, of accepting a significant measure of deindustrialization). By contrast, the surfeit of their petrodollars in the 1970s had led banks to encourage development projects to sink their funds into. But in the 1980s, as interest rates rose and Latin America's terms of trade deteriorated, the bankers suspended the flow of financial resources. We might say that the bankers' demand for development projects evaporated.

- The new technologies of electronic communications enhanced the financial integration of what was becoming known as a "global" economy and contributed mightily toward making economic autonomy seem not merely inadvisable, as economic liberals had long contended, but impossible.

- The limitations of Keynesianism as an intellectual construction,[58] which had long stimulated technical critiques whose political force was insignificant as long as an antisocialist doctrine of state management was desired and was working. The most fundamental theoretical issue was the micro-macro gap. Many economists were (and are) committed to core assumptions of methodological individualism and believed that in principle properties of larger systems should be understandable as the aggregate consequence of the behavior of individual rational actors. Despite the expenditure of much intellectual energy, however, no one managed to produce an account of Keynesian macroeconomic propositions along these lines that achieved any general assent among economists. A leading textbook writer said he did microeconomics and macroeconomics on separate days.[59] No doubt some theorists were more comfortable when the collapse of political support for Keynesian policies relieved them of their intellectual conundrum.

THE DECLINE (AND PERHAPS) FALL OF DEVELOPMENTALISM: LATIN AMERICA

The success of the rapidly evolving subdiscipline of development economics as an intellectual enterprise, signaled by prestigious faculty appointments in First World universities, professional conferences on developmental themes, papers accepted in leading scholarly journals, and success in competing for research grants, buttressed the optimism of development planners everywhere. But the euphoria was short-lived. The market-versus-plan debate was recast once again as it became evident that Latin American economic development was proving something less than a panacea. By the late 1950s and early 1960s, Latin America's external dependency had not only not been reduced; it actually was aggravated through the use of capital-intensive technologies in conjunction with import-substituting industrialization. In a nutshell, as Latin American industries moved into consumer goods production, the financing of the factories and infrastructural projects from roads to electricity had to come from somewhere—so did the machines used in the factories. Rather than find the autonomy sought after by economic nationalists since at least the 1930s, Latin Americans were discovering the extent to which this new industrial investment and production took the form of the multinational corporation.

The result was such a dramatic increase (not decrease) in foreign indebtedness and in some places even of foreign control over local resources that some observers were now writing of Latin American industrialization as "dependent development."[60] It would be hard to claim success when unemployment remained high, exports were discouraged, agricultural production neglected, and inflation unrelenting. Although it had been hoped, and at optimistic moments expected, that greater growth rates would improve living standards, the problem of income inequality actually seemed to be worsening. To the extent that developmentalism was supposed to bring social peace by warding off social radicalism, it was hardly encouraging that the social crises in many countries were instead, by the 1960s, producing a wave of military coups.

Many economists, including some of the most prominent of the *cepalinos*, began to have second (or third) thoughts. Some began to argue that policies of industrial protection had not been targeted with sufficient precision, leading to the sorts of abuses and "distortions" that attracted orthodoxy's scorn. Prebisch, in a retrospective autobiographical essay, reported his own growing disenchantment.[61] Others felt that they had wound up recommending the same sort of policies they had so ardently criticized.[62] Just like the First World advisers whose advice was rejected, so this line of self-criticism went, they had been overattentive to quantifiable indicators and underattentive to the complexity of social and political phenomena; they utilized simplistic models of economic growth (in which capital scarcity was the basic cause of underdevelopment); they had paid inadequate attention to the limited administrative capabilities of state institutions and to the political uncertainties of implementing policies.[63] While they had attempted to avoid "the reification of economics," they had placed other social sciences "side by side" with economics, which led to a "mere interdisciplinary approach by aggregation" rather than an integrated social science.[64]

In the social polarization that led to, and continued under, the military regimes of the 1960s and 1970s, some of those who had participated in the construction of Latin American developmentalism were coming to doubt their original critiques of orthodoxy, while others were coming to argue that developmentalism had not been heterodox enough. While orthodox, neoclassical critiques came to seem increasingly forceful and cogent to some of those impressed by developmentalism's many failures, others moved to embrace a more radical critique of the international order. The growing critique of developmentalism from the left, in which such developmentalist luminaries as Furtado and Sunkel participated, generated the dependency model. As A. O. Hirschman has pointedly noted,[65] developmentalism was under attack both from conservatives who, among many more specific complaints, ridiculed the fundamental notion that different sorts of countries needed different sorts of economic theory and from an increasingly radical group contending that CEPAL's view of the international economic order and of the political barriers to development at home was not nearly critical enough.

The dependency critique was of some influence in Allende's Chile (1970–73) and in the Sandinistas' Nicaragua (1979–90),[66] although its adherents acknowledge that it did not provide them with concrete economic programs.[67] Moreover, it proved the most successful Latin American intellectual export in the economic field, having considerable impact on social science in North America and Western Europe, far more than the structuralism out of which it emerged and against which it partly defined itself.[68] It deserves an extended discussion that we cannot undertake here, other than to note that it again provides ample evidence that in the economic domain,[69] Latin Americans were doing far more than consuming imported ideas.

Under attack from left and right, Latin American developmentalism, and developmentalism generally, faltered. The celebration of their own intellectual originality began to fade as many Latin American economists lost faith in the notion that a distinct economic theory was what they needed. Indeed, development economics itself began to lose ground as an autonomous field as fewer stars within the profession were contributing to the subdiscipline and the most heterodox voices suffered increased marginalization.

In the face of these challenges, some sought to maintain the general lines of the structuralist vision while allowing more scope to the market; the general notion was that there had been an indiscriminate and inappropriate overuse of protectionist measures as well as the setting of unrealistic exchange rates. Another proposal in the 1960s was the promotion of regional integration in the hope that enlarged markets would make import substitution more efficient and reduce external vulnerabilities. But intraregional trade did not rise significantly;[70] the principal beneficiaries of such policies were the transnational corporations whose cross-border activities were thereby facilitated. (The successful outward-oriented strategy of the Asian tigers did not figure as a contrast to structuralist prescriptions in these discussions until the late 1970s.)

THE U.S. MAGNET

In the 1970s, much of the intellectual credibility and policy effectiveness of the Latin American developmentalist consensus had eroded. Debates between orthodox and heterodox critics of developmentalism took place against a background of the coups that gave an almost uniformly military cast to South American governments by the early 1970s. The new regimes were promoting a radical shift to freeing, and internationalizing, the market. Structuralists, not to mention adherents of the dependency model, were engaged in criticizing what they saw as an excessive reliance on market forces and the high social costs imposed by rapid trade liberalization and anti-inflationary priorities.

The intellectual debate among economists was played out within an increasingly transnationalized environment. The case for economic orthodoxy was being propagated in Latin America through academic exchange programs and scholarships to U.S. universities;[71] the tightened links with transnational financial institutions that mounting debt crises brought in their wake provided a mechanism for those institutions to play a pedagogical role as well.[72]

At the same time, Latin American heterodoxy was gaining a wide audience abroad. Bureaucratic and academic purges, and other sources of political exile, led many economists, as well as other intellectual figures, to move from country to country ahead of military coups, as well as to seek temporary or even permanent careers in North America and Europe; for graduate students with leftist or even centrist sympathies, the attractions of study abroad were particularly strong. Social scientists of the center and the left were strengthening personal and professional ties with counterparts from other countries in Latin America, as well as with their colleagues in the First World. Institutional support came in the form of think tanks, international conferences, and research projects funded by First World governments and private foundations.[73] So while orthodox economics reentered Latin America with renewed vigor, intellectual refugees from barbaric regimes injected new forms of social criticism into First World academies. (We will refrain from commenting on who got a better deal from this particular international exchange.)

One important consequence of all these cross-border movements of people and ideas was that many economists who opposed the ascending neoliberal trend were attending the same institutions in which their opponents had been, or were being, trained. The attraction of graduate economics education in prestigious U.S. universities has continued to run strong for fledgling economists, regardless of their national origins, their initial political leanings, or their views on economics. A doctoral degree is now universally considered the sign of professional membership, and a U.S. degree a sign of prestige within that profession. By the late 1990s, more than half the students enrolled in doctoral economics programs in the United States were foreigners, up dramatically from 20 percent in 1972.[74] The Latin American contribution to this flow of students may be explained by the shortage of Latin American programs relative to the number of young people now seeking careers as economists (a career path coming to rival a legal career as a route to power) and by the rapid erosion of the prestige of non-U.S. degrees. Economists looking for careers in government and politics are now seeking the clout that goes with a Ph.D. despite the fact that U.S. doctoral programs notoriously lack emphasis on practical skills and lay heavy stress on economic theory and quantitatively esoteric techniques.[75] As an indication of what the political class sees as the credentials of the future, we note the degree to which children of prominent political figures go abroad to seek degrees in economics. Centeno, for example, points out that members of the younger generation of Mexican technocrats are likely to combine prestigious professional training with the cultural capital provided by their prominent political families.[76]

Such biographical backgrounds were coming to have a significant impact on the emergence of a market-oriented economic consensus in post-military Latin America.[77] Not only did those of dissenting views have long periods of immersion in economic orthodoxy, but the comradeship of graduate school, research project, and professional conference forged personal ties that facilitated a pattern of negotiation across party lines that helped pull parties on the left to the right on economic questions. An example of this trend is Chile's continuation of market-oriented policies under the center-left Concertación coalition in the 1990s.[78]

The new proliferation of private universities in Latin America since the 1970s has contributed substantially to the flourishing of free-market ideas (and vice versa). Curriculum and faculty credentials resemble those in U.S. universities, often as part of formal agreements with those U.S. universities. (Arnold Harberger, of the University of Chicago and then UCLA, played a major role in Latin American economics education over four decades.) In some countries, the business sector has generously funded faculty salaries, research projects, scholarships, and building construction. Although tuition is higher than in public universities, student enrollment has been growing rapidly. Graduates tend to find well-paid positions or to pursue graduate training in the United States. Such programs include the Instituto Tecnológico Autónomo de México (ITAM), Instituto Tecnológico de Estudios Superiores de México (ITESM), the Centro de Estudios Macroeconómicos de Argentina (CEMA), the Universidad de San Andrés and Universidad de Belgrano in Argentina, and the Universidad Gabriela Mistral and Universidad Finis Terrae in Chile.[79]

Leading students of the trends in North American economics beyond the 1950s point to the growth of stricter standards of technical rigor, declining interest in policy issues, and conformity to an internal hierarchy of prestige in which highly mathematized versions of theory were at the pinnacle. "Abstract, ahistorical, amoral, mechanistic metaphors" dominated.[80] It came to be accepted that "good economists do not go into government, or, if they do they do not stay good for long, since they rapidly suffer from professional obsolescence."[81] Thus the search for professionalism led to academicism. Knowledge of institutions was replaced by elegant theory. One economist who studies his profession argues that "the art of economics was lost."[82] The emphasis on esoteric technique aggrandized professional prestige,[83] and students caught on. A path-breaking survey of graduate students in top U.S. economics departments by Klamer and Colander shows that a majority of those students regarded mathematical excellence as "very important" for professional success, while a scant 3 percent regarded "having a thorough knowledge of the economy" as similarly significant.[84]

Development economics had been considered "the least orthodox field in economics" because of its advocacy of planning, its core notion of a distinct body of theory for specific institutional circumstances,[85] and its mistrust of self-regulated markets. Although some had expressed hope that the subfield would recast economics,[86] it became relegated to a second-class specialty within academic departments in the United States. One economist, writing in 1973, attributed the low status of development economists to their violation of tribal taboos barring association with political scientists and sociologists.[87] At the same time that U.S. theories, techniques, professional standards, and methods of training were becoming widely adopted throughout the world,[88] in U.S. economics departments in the 1990s it was mostly students from the Third World who were taking the development courses.[89]

After Developmentalism?

But this is running just a bit ahead of our story. Let us return to the great crisis of the 1980s. The enormous flow of external resources in the form of investments and loans that had been part of the developmentalist model not only halted but went into reverse. Large trade imbalances, huge budget deficits, and astronomical foreign indebtedness were no longer manageable when new loans to cover old debts were no longer forthcoming. As foreign loans dried up, exports declined, inflationary pressures grew out of control, unemployment jumped, poverty deepened,[90] and transnational financial networks shifted from the promotion of developmental projects to debt management. In the 1980s, Latin America transferred more than $223 billion abroad to service the debt and pay dividends on foreign investment.[91] The "lost decade" of the 1980s in Latin America rivaled the 1930s in its devastation and accelerated the already considerable decline of developmentalism. Latin America turned away from industrial protectionism and toward the economic orthodoxy of the international lenders. In exchange for access to external financing, policy makers, with various degrees of enthusiasm, followed the leadership of the International Monetary Fund and the World Bank by moving toward austere fiscal policies and toward trade and financial liberalization.

In the 1980s, there were some unsuccessful attempts to retard such a radical policy shift. The possibility of a "debtors' club," advocated by Cuba's Fidel Castro and Peru's Alan García, was discussed and dismissed at a regionwide ministerial meeting in 1984.[92] Heterodox stabilization packages were implemented in Argentina, Brazil, and Peru in the mid-1980s. These measures, however, no longer seemed part of a long-term strategy that had been the distinctive trait of structuralism—these "neo-structuralist" proposals were stopgap responses to immediate problems.[93] The tide was running toward orthodoxy, whose champions were the ones insisting on the need to implement structural changes.[94]

By the early 1990s, adoption of the new direction was widespread. The external sector was seen as the engine of economic growth, and tariff barriers fell. The return of capital inflows created something of an investment boom, and components of the "outward-looking" development model began to be endorsed even by those associated with the previous program. Enrique Iglesias, for example, formerly head of CEPAL and currently president of the Inter-American Development Bank, contended that "the force with which transnationalization has advanced in today's world makes it imperative for all societies to face up to these changes and either eliminate or reduce the likelihood of embarking on development paths that are radically divergent or isolated."[95]

This dramatic shift coincided with another one, equally dramatic: the relinquishment of formal power by militaries all over Latin America and the reconstruction of democratically legitimated regimes. Although the diffusion of liberal economic ideas was spearheaded largely by an increasingly homogeneous and transnationalized community of professional economists, the technical issues of liberalization became intertwined with the politics of democratization. Champions of economic change needed to secure the support of presidents and the acquiescence of electorates rather than the support of generals. The broad consensus that had been reached among academic and government economists in Latin America and abroad greatly facilitated the consolidation of a new economic strategy within a globalized system.[96] And some were now urging Latin America's economists to do a great deal of thinking about politics.[97]

Indeed, one might argue that they were becoming new kinds of politicians, as they ascended to ministerial positions and became significant figures within the political parties.[98] Older discussions of the role of technical experts as advisers to powerful policy makers became out-moded as professional economists became powerful policy makers them-selves (a process hardly confined to Latin America).[99]

DEVELOPMENTALISM REBORN?

In 1981, A. O. Hirschman published an essay explaining how the until recently flourishing field of development economics had been grievously wounded as "the blows from Left and Right that fell upon the fledgling and far from unified subdiscipline left it, indeed, rather stunned."[100] The mounting critiques that we have noted in this chapter provide much evi-dence for this diagnosis; nonetheless, many would dissent from the prog-nosis that seems to follow. As Amartya Sen observed in response to Hirschman, "The time to bury traditional development economics has not yet arrived."[101] Nearly two decades after Hirschman's article ap-peared, development economics is still in existence, in at least three differ-ent forms.

First of all, as we have seen, its original champions did not always abandon the developmental ship when it threatened to run aground (al-though some jumped off to left or right) but instead tried to correct its course. By the early 1990s, a Latin American "neostructuralist" synthesis had defined itself. This neostructuralism conceded error but held that rad-ical antistatism was sure to produce its own problems. Its exponents ar-gued that what is needed is avoidance of the "artificial dilemmas of the past" (exclusively promoting industry or agriculture, the domestic or the international market, government or private enterprise, planning or mar-ket). Its advocates insist on regaining and renewing Latin America's rich tradition of autonomous and independent thinking on development, much of which, they fear, is already lost to the younger generation of economists whose education pays that tradition no attention whatsoever, a state of affairs that in Sunkel's view "has undoubtedly contributed to the absence of adequate and creative responses on the part of these econo-mists to the demands of Latin American society in its current crisis."[102]

Second, the critics of the developmentalist policies of the past, now in power, have themselves been creating their own version of development economics. Perhaps one might say that "economic development" was an idea that could not be ignored; it could merely be redefined or sought by other means. For those who think this a too idealistic explanation of the "new development economics," we offer an alternative set of hypotheses:

- Having come to hold positions of power in many a government, some of the critics of the state action of the past have now discovered that the state is useful after all, and what is needed is not an indiscriminate hostility to states and all their doings but a more discriminating use of state power (a point of significant agreement with the neostructuralism we have just described).

- Personal responsibility for policy decisions with human consequences is a different matter than crafting an abstract argument for a lecture or a journal, and it leads some in power to favor a less radical break with recent practice.
- The pull and tug of politics does not cease when politicians are also economists. (Indeed, some economists in power have even discovered politics to be not just a nuisance but a stimulating new subject for their intellects.) And at this democratizing moment, a finance minister may even find himself thinking about how his party will win electoral majorities, or about how he himself might gain control of the party machinery,[103] as well as about how to impress his professional colleagues.

On the theoretical plane, this movement calls for a "new institutional economics,"[104] because economic decisions are not made in the context of idealized markets but are constrained by institutions (which also implies some attention to history). Attention to institutions readily shades off into attention to power; in the 1990s, economists of this theoretical persuasion have been discovering, as we noted earlier, some common grounds with political scientists, particularly with political scientists who subscribe to the methodological individualism of the "rational choice" school.[105] We cannot pursue this important subject here other than to note the resultant multidisciplinary flavor of the academic component of this new political economy of development.[106]

Third, there is an emerging reconceptualization of "development" that places great stress on distributional issues. In the same essay in which Sen contended that reports of the death of development economics were premature, he insisted that notions of development needed to get away from aggregate growth and consider what sorts of lives people were able to live. To assess development properly means understanding human capabilities, the possibilities open to people, "e.g., the ability to be well nourished, to avoid escapable morbidity or mortality, to read and write and communicate, to take part in the life of the community, to appear in public without shame."[107] Of course, this means going beyond economics as narrowly understood: "A study of entitlements has to go beyond purely economic factors and take into account political arrangements."[108] In the 1990s, others were insisting that economists take into account the differential impact of economic policies. As one insisted, "Throughout the Third World, women, peasants and tribals are struggling for liberation from 'development' just as they earlier struggled for liberation from colonialism. . . . [D]evelopment itself was the problem."[109] And opening up yet another way of bringing distributional issues to the forefront, a significant literature was emerging that argued that poverty, inequality, or both constituted barriers to growth.[110] No one doubted that the 1980s had seen an increase in Latin American poverty and inequality, or that these problems persisted in the late 1990s; now some were arguing that these conditions were impediments to economic development even as conventionally defined.

In light of the foregoing, it would be an error to describe the post–1980s scene as simply a return to the pre-1930s past. The new development economics criticized what was seen as the naive institutional assumptions of the old model, particularly its vision of a wise and beneficent state readily capable of correcting the undesirable consequences of markets. The focus on market failure, it was now said, "diverted attention from the dangers of government failure."[111] The proponents of the new course held that the postwar "dirigiste dogma"[112] had been unduly influenced by nationalist and anticolonial ideologies, too pessimistic about private domestic entrepreneurship, wrong to dismiss the employment potential of agricultural activities, and complacent regarding foreign borrowing and inflationary financing as remedies for capital scarcity. Some were going beyond such specific critiques to a generally antistatist position, in which the state was seen as inherently prone to "rent seeking" (a common charge), corruption, and the irrational distortions produced by the inevitable combination of bureaucratic power and the self-interest of bureaucrats. In this view, what was desirable would be a minimalist state, stripped of entrepreneurial and redistributive functions, that would be devoted to the protection of private property rights, the enforcement of contracts, the rule of law, and the maintenance of a generally stable framework for the smooth operation of markets; within such a framework, the markets could run themselves. But this extreme, and utopian, antistatism is only a part of a more complex picture.

A new set of policies were emerging which, their advocates contended, would lead to a wide variety of desirable ends. Strict official commitment to fiscal austerity and stabilization would increase investors' confidence. Fixed exchange rates would enhance government credibility. Low and uniform tariffs would increase governmental transparency, reduce lobbying for concessions, and expand trade. The privatization of state enterprise would spread ownership, attract foreign investors, improve efficiency, raise revenues, and ease state deficits. More autonomous central banks would reduce the impact of short-term political considerations on economic policy. Financial deregulation would increase savings and make investment decisions more rational. Labor-intensive export activities would open employment opportunities. Labor market deregulation would result in a more mobile and more productive workforce. Social policies focused on education, nutritional programs, and other specifically targeted services would increase human capital, reduce poverty, and promote productivity gains.[113]

Some had doubts. It may be that the financial downturn triggered by the Asian crisis of the late 1990s, will cool the exuberant expectations of marketeers and suggest to some of those in and out of Latin America who have been damning one or another country for not being more like the Asian tigers in its policies that there are problems in the Asian model as well. On the other hand, perhaps the Asian crisis will be made into an object lesson of what happens if countries are not market-oriented enough, and allow a politicized capitalism to impede natural market forces. In the late 1990s, the dominant view was running in favor of more market, less state;[114] doubters suggested that whatever the long-term prospects of growth, the question of the distribution of well-being would keep alive issues of social justice, and sooner or later lead to intensified social conflict.[115] We shall see.

THE ASCENT TO POWER OF PROFESSIONAL ECONOMISTS: THE 1990s IN LATIN AMERICA

We may distinguish two moments in the relationship of economists' ideas to power: an earlier moment in which economic advisers sought the support of those elites and established specialized agencies for some of the tasks of economic management; and a more recent moment in which professional economists have entered the political elites themselves and have been assuming a very broad array of governing tasks at the highest positions of formal authority. We might represent different facets of that first moment by the increasing employment of economists in statistics-gathering roles in the United States from the 1930s to the 1950s, the role of economists as high-level advisers in wartime Britain or Germany after 1939, and the activities of numerous economists drawing up developmental plans in Latin America in the 1960s. We might represent that second moment by the recent frequent appointments of economists to prime ministerships, to high-level positions in foreign affairs and defense ministries, and to top positions in political parties, where they are plainly assuming roles well beyond that of giving technical advice and well beyond any narrow definition of economic management.[116]

While various versions of socialism and Keynesianism propelled economists to the forefront as technical advisers worldwide, the dismantling of statist programs—should we say here "remarkably"?—has not led to a retreat of economists back to the university and the private sector, but to considerably greater influence within the very states that are privatizing, downsizing, outsourcing, and deregulating. The crisis of the 1930s drew economists into government service, where they enjoyed significant influence as advisers to political elites committed to development projects. More recently they have entered the political elites. By the 1990s, the theory-bearers were now often the finance ministers, and sometimes the presidents or leaders of the opposition. In the Chilean elections of 1989, the two leading presidential candidates held economics degrees. Keynes's comment that "practical men who believe themselves to be quite exempt from any intellectual influences, are usually the slaves of some defunct economist" comes out of another era; living economists exercise visible power over economies at the end of the twentieth century and have become the practical men (and, occasionally, women) of the moment.

Coming out of the crisis of the 1930s and the opportunities of the postwar world, the vision forged by Latin American economists was a theoretical response to policies already in place and a rationale for what many political figures were already engaged in doing. But at the end of the twentieth century, it would be a very difficult task to decide whether policy changes were responding to the new theoretical vision or the reverse: through the persons of economists in command, the two appear more or less fused.

The Latin American variant of development economics put its economic thinkers in the forefront of a challenge to previous economic wisdom. Latin American economists could enjoy a sense of their own creative independence from, and innovation within, the world economics community as they advocated a theoretical position that stressed the distinctiveness of histories, the economic consequences of differential power, and the virtues of some level of national autonomy. Latin American economists in the 1980s and beyond have been enjoying their lack of distinctiveness as they embrace pretty much the same views as other economists and discover the timeless principles of economic life the attempted defiance of which is folly. Even those who are not completely convinced of the virtues of the market may be reluctant to publicize their dissent. "It is dangerous to be outside the mainstream," commented Sunkel in an interview with one of the authors in January 1998. "There are many elements of dissidence, but they have not come together in a single current. . . . Even those who practice neostructuralism do not call it such."[117]

A comparison of the part played by economists in the crises of the 1930s and the 1980s reveals more than a dramatic increase in their political influence. The politically active members of this profession are central players, with much higher public visibility and much greater intellectual and ideological clout, and they are much more integrated into the political elite than their predecessors ever envisaged only a few decades ago.

While the old economic planners relied mainly on the support of those they regarded as the progressive politicians, remaining themselves backstage in the political dramas of the day, the technopols of the new brand, from the right to the left, have been aggressively trying to reshape the rules of politics. Some have moved to the political frontstage by vilifying traditional political leaders and institutions for their petty feuding, corrupt practices, and ineffectual policies. Others have created new political parties or orchestrated the technification of existing party organizations. Many politically active economists claim to have elaborated new interpretations of long-standing social cleavages and to offer new ways to resolve deep-rooted ideological and social conflicts. A few have decided to participate directly in electoral contests, presenting themselves to the voters as the carriers of a modern, nonconfrontational political style, appropriate for dealing with the economic challenges and institutional complexities imposed by a globalized world.

In both their old and new versions, economic managers have displayed a distinctive preference for putting technical criteria ahead of political bargaining, and they have attempted to insulate the policy process from societal pressures and public debate. But in recent years, as they have acquired the habits of governing and, in some countries, of involvement in party politics, they show many signs of thinking about the issues much as political scientists might, considering such factors as the distributional implications of economic measures, the dynamics of corporatist arrangements, and the mutual influence of economic policy and electoral cycles. In order to make market reforms effective, credible, persuasive, and lasting, they are thinking about the timing and sequencing of economic measures in relation to the reactions of other key players (and not just what their old economics professors or professional colleagues might think), as well as about how to engineer electoral and legislative majorities or how to create new channels of consultation with business or labor organizations. This creates many opportunities for consulting by political scientists, and for conferences and seminars that bring economists and political scientists together. The essentially unsuccessful efforts made in the 1950s and 1960s to integrate the economic and noneconomic dimensions of structural reforms are now being pursued in a more coherent, deliberate manner. In ongoing struggles to conciliate democratic rule with market-oriented policies, we observe media campaigns, social pacts, and party alliances that often seem to follow the admonitions contained in a growing academic literature on the political economy of policy reforms. (Depending on their overall evaluations of this state of affairs, sociologists may note with regret or with pride that in most countries they have not been invited to join in.)[118]

At the same time as political science concepts are entering into the conceptual universe of economists in power, those economists find their communication with other major political actors in and out of their own country greatly facilitated by the degree to which those other actors, too, employ their own economists as emissaries. This easy communication, moreover, is enhanced by the degree to which all of these economists have attended pretty much the same sorts of graduate programs abroad and have spent part of their careers in international banks or private firms. Even the linkages of economists in government and labor organizations have become strengthened, as the unions, too, have their own economic advisers and have found their own negotiations run more smoothly when their negotiating teams are endowed with their own economic expertise. Large corporations, moreover, are increasingly likely to be populated by executives with U.S. MBAs, many of whose programs have been designed with significant input from economists, and who therefore tend to inhabit the same mental universe. (And, we may add, many business interests are pleased with the scaling down of the activist, regulatory, and redistributive state, which, having once raised economists to power, is now being altered by them.)[119]

This description may remind one of the political role of lawyers in a past generation, when they functioned as a sort of social lubricant, easing the meshing of organization and organization. But we might speculate that these linkages run more smoothly now than earlier because the training of all these economists has become so much more uniform and because many economists are committed as much to the service of what they take to be the principles of a science as they are to the defense of some client. Legal training, moreover, socialized one into a set of nationally distinct concepts; economic training socializes one into a largely denationalized body of thought (especially with the triumphal revival of monoeconomics).

Economists are no longer content to control the most technically oriented agencies within the state. Instead of concentrating their efforts on the operation of central banks and planning offices, they have stretched their intellectual and bureaucratic domain over the entire state apparatus, including poverty programs, labor market regulations, health care, social security, education, and even foreign policy—not to mention the possibilities of coordination suggested by occupancy of party chiefships and prime ministerships. Under these new arrangements, it seems conceivable that coherence and coordination in policy may be achieving a level never managed by the planners of the past, who had to contend with the logics of the lawyers, the agronomists, the physicians, the engineers, and even the sociologists. Or it may be that the rosy picture proclaimed by the champions of technical rationality will, in retrospect, turn out to have been another mirage, sustained by hopes of rationality but ultimately undermined by the pull and tug of political conflict among competing interests, as always, including the interests of the technocratic elites themselves. In the 1990s, those political conflicts were unfolding against a background of recent transitions from authoritarian rule—how far from authoritarian rule being a matter of considerable variation from place to place. So an important part of the context for the future unfolding of the new role of professional economists in national political life is going to be the inherent tensions between technocratic policy making and all the many things that go with democracy: accountability to publics (not just to scientific principles), representation of interests (not just optimal solutions), and pressures from social movements (not just dispassionate calculation). We merely pose this big, big issue here.

CONCLUSIONS

Appalled by French revolutionary horrors and disgusted at the champions of the systematic application of reason to human affairs whom he held in large part responsible, Edmund Burke, in 1790, summed up the transition to a new social world: "But the age of chivalry is gone.—That of sophisters, oeconomists, and calculators, has succeeded; and the glory of Europe is extinguished for ever."[120] Two centuries later, it would hardly take an impassioned wake-up call to a complacent British elite to suggest the political power of economic ideas. In the 1980s and 1990s, holders of degrees in economics have actually headed a diverse array of governments, including those of Greece, Turkey, Ireland, Holland, Taiwan, India, Mexico, Colombia, Guyana, Italy, and Rwanda. But this very diversity gives some pause for thought. The collection of presidents and prime ministers includes champions of the free-market right and the socialist Left, people reputedly corrupt and people reputedly honest, and even one who has confessed to genocide before an international tribunal.[121] In short, many political leanings and political actions are represented. Consider one candidate for the Philippine Senate in 1998, describing his qualifications for office: "I'm a singer, a guitar player and an economist"; according to the *New York Times*, he "also wowed crowds by demonstrating his karate kicks."[122]

  With such diversity, can it be said that the increased presence of economists in power has any distinguishable consequences? Are economists in politics different from any other political figures? Is there something to be learned from their much more dramatic presence on the world political scene of the 1980s and 1990s, as compared with the long-standing influence of economic ideas already excoriated by Burke two centuries back? We would answer yes to all these questions.

We have suggested that one of the most important things to consider in assessing the impact of economic ideas in Latin America was how the ideas that shape policy are increasingly the ideas of economists. We examined the two great shifts in dominant economic notions in the twentieth century—the shift toward state-orchestrated developmentalism, for which the crisis of the 1930s was a critical context; and the shift away from state-orchestrated developmentalism, a worldwide process that in Latin America drew its force from the crisis of the 1980s. One of the big differences in what happened in these two challenges to received economic policy was the role of economists. The crisis of the 1930s drew them into policy-advisory positions and thereby changed the character of the profession and challenged its orthodoxy. The crisis of the 1980s came upon states in which economists, already having considerable political clout, were dealing with foreign governments and transnational financial institutions in which economists were similarly situated. This gave the economists, who by then had largely rejected the developmentalism that originally brought them into public service, a considerable capacity to be in the forefront in the redesign of institutions, and not only in Latin America.

Rather than talk about the "influence of economic ideas" in a social vacuum, we think it essential to note the transnational networks connecting economist and economist within and between national states. And when we look at professional life, with English as the dominant language of economic analysis; when we look at the locales where economists are trained and the consequent ties of colleague and colleague, teacher and student, it seems a fair summary that the future of economics, more than ever before, is being forged in the United States. When we read in the newspapers that the International Monetary Fund or the World Bank is negotiating conditions for loans with some country, we should recognize that these organizations and that state are very likely in communication through established professional ties. An economist in the Finance Ministry (maybe it's the finance minister) is on the phone with an old graduate student comrade, now a World Bank official (or perhaps it is a former professor, or student, or friend from academic conferences). The policy decisions of today—and tomorrow—are shaped in part by the professional socialization of economists in increasingly homogeneous graduate programs in a single country. And they are shaped as well by the reinforcement of those policies in the everyday give-and-take within the network of economists across institutional and national frontiers. The transnational character of their professional life may receive further nourishment by the re-embrace of the predevelopmentalist orthodoxy, particularly the tendency to theorize about the behavior of "homo economicus," whose lack of specific cultural, emotional, intellectual, class, or gender characteristics is powerfully congruent with the policies that are ascendant in our era of transnationalized economies. Economics today is a profoundly transnational profession socialized in a body of thought that to a considerable degree is skeptical of the claims of culture and history, and that has re-embraced the sacralization of the unimpeded market and the unchallenged integration of the national into the global economy. As such, economists are among the most important carriers of a profound challenge to notions that national states could or should control their own economies, negotiate with (or go to war with) one another as sovereign entities, follow their own cultures, and operate as self-governing political communities. Just where this leaves the future of class relations, the interstate system, cultural traditions, and democratic political practice as we try to peer ahead into the twenty-first century constitutes a whole series of very big questions that we merely point to by way of conclusion.

NOTES

For challenging comments on an earlier draft, we thank A. W. Coats and Michael Jiménez.

1. Joseph L. Love, *Crafting the Third World: Theorizing Underdevelopment in Rumania and Brazil* (Stanford, Calif.: Stanford University Press, 1996), 120.

2. H. W. Arndt, *The Rise and Fall of Economic Growth: A Study in Contemporary Thought* (Chicago: University of Chicago Press, 1978), 13.

3. Quoted in Gerald M. Meier, *Emerging from Poverty: The Economics That Really Matters* (New York: Oxford University Press, 1984), 127.

4. H.W. Arndt, "Economic Development: A Semantic History," *Economic Development and Cultural Change* 29 (1981): 458–59.

5. The great exception is Schumpeter in his *Theory of Economic Development*, published in 1912. Joseph A. Schumpeter, *Theorie der wirtschaftlichen Entwicklung* (Leipzig: Duncker and Humblot, 1912.

6. For the Brazilian version of these discussions, see Nícia Vilela Luz, *A luta pela industrialização do Brasil* (São Paulo: Editora Alfa Omega, 1975).

7. A more nuanced statement would acknowledge some variation in time and space. In the 1920s, for example, political upheavals had favored state-organized developmental projects in Russia, Italy, and Mexico. The Mexican Revolution led to policy emphases at an early date that were distinctive in Latin America.

8. On many of these questions, see Peter A. Hall, *The Political Power of Economic Ideas: Keynesianism across Nations* (Princeton, N.J.: Princeton University Press, 1989).

9. Barend A. de Vries, "The World Bank as an International Player in

Economic Analysis," in A.W. Coats, ed., *The Post-1945 Internationalization of Economics* (Durham, N.C.: Duke University Press, 1997), 225.

10. Frederick Cooper and Randall Packard, "Introduction," in Frederick Cooper and Randall Packard, eds., *International Development and the Social Sciences: Essays on the History and Politics of Knowledge* (Berkeley: University of California Press, 1997), 7.

11. Paul Drake, *Money Doctors, Foreign Debts, and Economic Reforms in Latin America from the 1890s to the Present* (Wilmington, Del.: Scholarly Resources, 1994).

12. Enrique V. Iglesias, *Reflections on Economic Development: Toward a New Latin American Consensus* (Washington, D.C.: Inter-American Development Bank, 1992), 7–9.

13. Joseph L. Love, "Structural Change and Conceptual Response in Latin America and Romania, 1860–1950," in Joseph L. Love and Nils Jacobsen, eds., *Guiding the Invisible Hand: Economic Liberalism and the State in Latin American History* (New York: Praeger, 1988), 9.

14. Rosemary Thorp, ed., *Latin America in the 1930s: The Role of the Periphery in the World Crisis* (London: Macmillan, 1984).

15. Celso Furtado, *Economic Development of Latin America*, reprinted in Peter F. Klarén and Thomas J. Bossert, eds., *Promise of Development: Theories of Change in Latin America* (Boulder, Colo.: Westview, 1986), 139.

16. Drake, *Money Doctors*, xxix; Steven Topik, *The Political Economy of the Brazilian State, 1889–1930* (Austin: University of Texas Press, 1987).

17. Drake, *Money Doctors*, xxix.

18. Roderic A. Camp, *La formación de un gobernante: La socialización de los líderes políticos en el México post-revolucionario* (Mexico City: Fondo de Cultura Económica, 1986), 193, 197, 207, 212; Sarah L. Babb, "The Evolution of Economic Expertise in a Developing Country: Mexican Economics, 1929–1998," (Ph.D diss., Northwestern University, 1998), 58.

19. Patricio Silva, "Pablo Ramírez: A Political Technocrat Avant-la-Lettre," in Miguel Angel Centeno and Patricio Silva, eds., *The Politics of Expertise in Latin America* (New York: St. Martin's, 1998), 70.

20. Among the influenced: Raúl Prebisch. See Joseph Hodara, *Prebisch y la CEPAL: Sustancia, trayectoria y contexto institucional* (Mexico City: El Colegio de México, 1987), 135, 137; Love, *Crafting the Third World*, 102, 134.

21. Albert O. Hirschman, "The Turn to Authoritarianism in Latin America and the Search for Its Economic Determinants," in Albert. O. Hirschman, *Essays in Trespassing: Economics to Politics and Beyond* (Cambridge: Cambridge University Press, 1981), 119.

22. Love, *Crafting the Third World*, 122.

23. Verónica Montecinos, "Economics and Power: Chilean Economists in Government, 1958–1985" (Ph.D. diss., University of Pittsburgh, 1988), 409; Babb, "Evolution of Economic Expertise," 54–61; Maria Rita Loureiro, *Os Economistas no governo: Gestão econômica e democracia* (Rio de Janeiro: Editora Fundação Getúlio Vargas, 1997), 34–35; Paulo Roberto Haddad, "Brazil: Economists in a Bureaucratic-Authoritarian System," in A. W. Coats, ed., *Economists in Government: An International Comparative Study* (Durham, N.C.: Duke

University Press, 1981), 320–21; Catherine Conaghan, "Stars of the Crisis: The Ascent of Economists in Peruvian Public Life," Centeno and Silva, *The Politics of Expertise in Latin America*, 144–45; Lauchlin Currie, *La enseñanza de la economía en Colombia. ¿Cómo? ¿Para quién? ¿Sobre qué? ¿Por qué?* (Bogotá: Ediciones Tercer Mundo, 1965), 9.

24. Roderic Ai Camp, "The National School of Economics and Public Life in Mexico," *Latin American Research Review* 10 (1975): 142.

25. Love, *Crafting the Third World*, 150

26. Raúl Prebisch, "Five Stages in My Thinking on Development," in Gerald M. Meier and Dudley Seers, eds., *Pioneers in Development* (New York: Oxford University Press, 1984), 173–91. Prebisch, a graduate of the Facultad de Ciencias Económicas of the University of Buenos Aires, was serving as delegate to the League of Nations in Geneva in 1932–33 when, according to one biography, he began to see Argentina as a "dangerously isolated and vulnerable" player in the world economy. Edgar J. Dosman and David H. Pollock, "Raúl Prebisch, 1901–1971: La Búsqueda constante," in Enrique V. Iglesias, ed., *El Legado de Raúl Prebisch* (Washington, D.C.: Banco Interamericano de Desarrollo, 1993), 23. In 1935, he founded and became the first director of Argentina's new Central Bank. When the rising Peronist movement secured his removal in 1943, he accepted an invitation from the Mexican Central Bank and then went on to advise other central banks in Latin America. In this period of exile he moved from his Argentine concerns to a truly Latin American perspective.

27. Two important examples of these early forms of economics education are Brazil's Itamaraty under Vargas and Chile's Corporación de Fomento de la Producción (CORFO) during the Popular Front governments. See Kathryn Sikkink, *Ideas and Institutions: Developmentalism in Brazil and Argentina* (Ithaca, N.Y.: Cornell University Press, 1991), 129–30; Montecinos, "Economics and Power," 165.

28. Felipe Pazos, "Pensamiento económico en la América Latina," *El Trimestre Económico* 4 (1983): 1918, 1928.

29. Love, *Crafting the Third World*, 128.

30. Raúl Prebisch, *Introducción a Keynes* (Mexico City: Fondo de Cultura Económica, 1947).

31. On the influential Brazilian debate on this issue, for example, see Loureiro, *Os Economistas no governo*, 32–33.

32. Pazos, "Cincuenta años de pensamiento económico," 1916.

33. Drake, *Money Doctors*.

34. Osvaldo Sunkel, "The Development of Development Thinking," in José J. Villamil, ed., *Transnational Capitalism and National Development: New Perspectives on Dependence* (Atlantic Highlands, N.J.: Humanities Press, 1979), 22.

35. Albert O. Hirschman, "The Rise and Decline of Development Economics," in Hirschman, *Essays in Trespassing*, 3.

36. James H. Street, "The Latin American Structuralists and the Institutionalists: Convergence in Development Theory," in James L. Dietz and James H. Street, eds., *Latin America's Economic Development: Institutionalists and Structuralists* (Boulder, Colo.: Lynne Rienner, 1987), 106; Dudley Seers, "Why Visiting Economists Fail," *Journal of Political Economy* 70 (1962): 325–38.

37. This point and other matters relating to the economics profession are elaborated in John Markoff and Verónica Montecinos, "The Ubiquitous Rise of Economists," *Journal of Public Policy* 13 (1993): 37–68.

38. Dosman and Pollock, *Prebisch*, 30.

39. Albert O. Hirschman, "Ideologies of Economic Development in Latin America," in Albert O. Hirschman, ed., *Latin American Issues: Essays and Comments* (New York: Twentieth Century Fund, 1961), 13.

40. Sikkink, *Ideas and Institutions*, 88.

41. Fernando Henrique Cardoso, "The Originality of a Copy: CEPAL and the Idea of Development," *CEPAL Review*, no. 63 (1997): 27.

42. Aníbal Pinto and Osvaldo Sunkel, "Latin American Economists in the United States," *Economic Development and Cultural Change* 15 (1966): 79–86.

43. Verónica Montecinos, "Economists in Political and Policy Elites in Latin America," in Coats, ed., *The Post-1945 Internationalization of Economics*, 289.

44. Sunkel, "The Development of Development Thinking," 24.

45. See, for example, James M. Malloy, "Policy Analysts, Public Policy, and Regime Structure in Latin America," *Governance* 3 (1989): 315–38.

46. Hodara, *Prebisch y la CEPAL*. If it is hardly obvious why the choice fell to Santiago, it may at least be observed that other imaginable urban sites could not have so readily represented the goals of regional stability and antirevolutionary democratic politics espoused by the Western victors in the war. Buenos Aires was tainted by Axis ties, Bogotá and Caracas by political instability, Rio—despite the wartime alliance with the United States—combined Vargas's *Estado Novo* with cultural distinctiveness, and Mexico may perhaps still have seemed too close to its own revolutionary past (and in any event got a branch office in 1950 to deal with Mesoamerica and the Caribbean). While the United States was less than keen on setting up CEPAL at all, promoting the Organization of American States as its own preferred form of regional association (founded almost simultaneously with CEPAL in 1948), it was probably easier to accept a CEPAL based in a country that had just demonstrated that it was the right kind of antirevolutionary democracy by banning the Chilean Communist Party in 1947.

47. The international offices set up in Santiago were an impressive collection of acronyms: FAO, UNICEF, FLACSO, CELADE, and PREALC, among others.

48. H. W. Arndt, *Economic Development: The History of an Idea* (Chicago: University of Chicago Press, 1987), 47. Love, *Crafting the Third World*, 6, has some interesting observations on the Central and Eastern European roots of a longer list of major development theorists, including Thomas Balogh, Hans Singer, Alexander Gerschenkron, Kurt Martin, Peter T. Bauer, Gottfried Haberler, and Paul Baran. Schumpeter's first teaching position, incidentally, was in Bukovina.

49. Hirschman, "The Rise and Decline of Development Economics," 6–7.

50. Love, *Crafting the Third World*, 130–33.

51. Ibid., 113, 161.

52. Celso Furtado, *La Fantasía organizada* (Buenos Aires: Eudeba, 1988), 82.

53. Love insists that the "history of ideas is notoriously international" and calls attention to the "transit of theorizing about unequal exchange, dependency and other issues of underdevelopment from East Central Europe to Latin Amer-

ica" (*Crafting the Third World*, 13, 101). Love's work strikes us not only as among the most insightful writing on the modern history of Latin American economic ideas but also as an exemplary treatment of the role of semiperipheral places as sources of intellectual creativity. For some discussion of other forms of such creativity as well, see John Markoff, "Where and When Was Democracy Invented?" *Comparative Studies in Society and History*, 41 (1999): 660–90; and Markoff, "From Center to Periphery and Back Again: Reflections on the Geography of Democratic Innovation," in Michael Hanagan and Charles Tilly, eds., *Extending Citizenship, Reconfiguring States* (Lanham, M.D.: Rowman and Littlefield, 1999), 229–46.

54. In trying to define the distinctive contributions of Latin Americans to development economics, it would be an interesting exercise to study comparatively the activities and ideas of the other regional economic commissions set up by the United Nations in addition to CEPAL.

55. Philip McMichael, *Development and Social Change: A Global Perspective* (Thousand Oaks, Calif.: Pine Forge Press, 1996); Rajani Kanth, ed., *Paradigms in Economic Development: Classic Perspectives, Critiques, and Reflections* (Armonk, N.Y.: M. E. Sharpe, 1994).

56. For varying lessons drawn from the Asian tigers, see Bela Balassa, "Exports, Policy Choice, and Economic Growth in Developing Countries after the 1973 Oil Shock," *Journal of Development Economics* 18 (1985): 23–25; Stephen Haggard, *Pathways from the Periphery: The Politics of Growth in the Newly Industrializing Countries* (Ithaca, N.Y.: Cornell University Press, 1990); Alice Amsden, "Why Isn't the Whole World Experimenting with the East Asian Model to Develop?" *World Development* 22 (1994): 627–33.

57. Kathryn Sikkink, "Development Ideas in Latin America: Paradigm Shift and the Economic Commission for Latin America," in Frederick Cooper and Randall Packard, eds., *International Development and the Social Sciences: Essays on the History and Politics of Knowledge* (Berkeley: University of California Press, 1997), 244.

58. John R. Hicks, *The Crisis of Keynesian Economics* (New York: Basic Books, 1975); Paul Krugman, *Peddling Prosperity: Economic Sense and Nonsense in the Age of Diminished Expectations* (New York: Norton, 1994); Robert Heilbroner and William Milberg, *The Crisis of Vision in Modern Economic Thought* (Cambridge: Cambridge University Press, 1995).

59. Michael Carter, "Intellectual Openings and Policy Closings," in Cooper and Packard, *International Development and the Social Sciences*, 124.

60. Fernando Henrique Cardoso and Enzo Faletto, *Dependency and Development in Latin America* (1973; Berkeley: University of California Press, 1979); Fernando Henrique Cardoso, "Associated-Dependent Development: Theoretical and Practical Implications," in Alfred Stepan, ed., *Authoritarian Brazil* (New Haven, Conn.: Yale University Press, 1973); Peter B. Evans, *Dependent Development: The Alliance of Multinational, State and Local Capital in Brazil* (Princeton, N.J.: Princeton University Press, 1979).

61. Prebisch, "Five Stages in My Thinking on Development."

62. Osvaldo Sunkel and Pedro Paz, *El subdesarrollo latinoamericano y la teoría del desarrollo* (1970; Mexico City: Siglo XXI, 1982), 36.

63. Carlos Matus, "Planeación normativa y planeación situacional," *El Trimestre Económico* 3 (1983): 1721–81.

64. Sunkel, "The Development of Development Thinking," 27.

65. Hirschman, "The Rise and Decline of Development Economics."

66. Robert Packenham would add Velasco's Peru (1968–75), Echeverría's Mexico (1970–76), Manley's Jamaica (1972–1980) and Bishop's Grenada (1979–83). See Robert A. Packenham, *The Dependency Movement: Scholarship and Politics in Development Studies* (Cambridge, Mass.: Harvard University Press, 1992), 194.

67. See, for example, the discussion of the retrospective views of Pedro Vuskovic (Allende's economy minister) in Björn Hettne, *The Voice of the Third World: Currents in Development Thinking* (Budapest: Institute for World Economies of the Hungarian Academy of Sciences, 1991), 36. See also Packenham, *The Dependency Movement*, 205.

68. Cristóbal Kay, *Latin American Theories of Development and Underdevelopment* (London: Routledge, 1989).

69. Some would not want to accept CEPAL's dependency offspring as belonging to economics. See Albert Fishlow, "The State of Latin American Economics," in Christopher Mitchell, ed., *Changing Perspectives in Latin American Studies: Insights from Six Disciplines* (Stanford, Calif.: Stanford University Press, 1988), 97.

70. Víctor L. Urquidi, "Free Trade Experience in Latin America and the Carribbean," *Annals of the American Academy of Political and Social Science* 526 (1993): 58–67.

71. Juan Gabriel Valdés, *Pinochet's Economists: The Chicago School in Chile* (New York: Cambridge University Press, 1995).

72. Miles Kahler, "External Influence, Conditionality, and the Politics of Adjustment," in Stephan Haggard and Robert R. Kaufman, eds., *The Politics of Economic Adjustment: International Constraints, Distributive Conflicts, and the State* (Princeton, N.J.: Princeton University Press, 1992).

73. Jeffrey Puryear, *Thinking Politics: Intellectuals and Democracy in Chile, 1973–1988* (Baltimore: Johns Hopkins University Press, 1994).

74. Nahid Aslanbegui and Verónica Montecinos, "Foreign Students in U.S. Doctoral Programs," *Journal of Economic Perspectives* 12 (1998): 171–82.

75. On the symbolic power of economists' credentials, see Markoff and Montecinos, "The Ubiquitous Rise of Economists." On Ph.D. programs, see Ann O. Krueger et al., "Report of the Commission on Graduate Education in Economics," *Journal of Economic Literature* 29 (1991): 1035–53.

76. Miguel Angel Centeno, *Democracy within Reason: Technocratic Revolution in Mexico* (University Park: Pennsylvania State University Press, 1994), 107, 115.

77. In stressing the transnational character of the late-twentieth-century economics profession in Latin America, we do not mean to deny a transnational aspect to politically crucial professions of earlier eras, especially law and engineering. Many nineteenth-century Brazilian lawyers, say, were educated at Coimbra, and many nineteenth-century Colombian lawyers influenced by Bentham. But the combination of more or less similar foreign training for economists from

many countries; the continuing interaction of those economists, in and out of office, across national frontiers; and a mainstream theoretical tradition that downplays national difference seems to us well beyond the transnational aspects of previous political professions.

78. Verónica Montecinos, *Economists, Politics, and the State: Chile, 1958–1994* (Amsterdam: CEDLA, 1998), chap. 5.

79. Glen Biglaiser, "U.S. Influence in the Economics Profession in Latin America" (paper presented at the meetings of the American Political Science Association, Boston, September 1998). For a detailed study of Mexico's ITAM and its contrast with the older, more statist program of UNAM, see Babb, "Evolution of Economic Expertise."

80. Arjo Klamer, "Academic Dogs," in David Colander and Reuven Brenner, eds., *Educating Economists* (Ann Arbor: University of Michigan Press, 1992), 57.

81. A. W. Coats, "Economics as a Profession," in A. W. Coats, ed., *The Sociology and Professionalization of Economics: British and American Essays* (London: Routledge, 1993), vol. 2, 401.

82. David Colander, "The Microeconomic Myth," in Colander and Brenner, *Educating Economists*, 115; and Colander, "The Art of Economics by the Numbers," in Roger E. Backhouse, ed., *New Directions in Economic Methodology* (London: Routledge, 1994), 35–49.

83. Warren J. Samuels, "Galbraith on Economics as a System of Professional Belief," in Warren J. Samuels, ed., *Essays in the History of Heterodox Political Economy* (London: Macmillan, 1992), 293–307.

84. Arjo Klamer and David Colander, *The Making of an Economist* (Boulder, Colo.: Westview, 1990), 18.

85. "Development economists are essentially institutionalists whether they know it or not." See Philip A. Klein, "An Institutionalist View of Development Economics," in Philip A. Klein, *Beyond Dissent: Essays in Institutional Economics* (Armonk, N.Y.: M. E. Sharpe, 1994), 228.

86. Dudley Seers, "The Limitations of the Special Case," *Bulletin of the Oxford Institute of Economics and Statistics* 25 (1963): 77–98, cited in Hirschman, "The Rise and Decline of Development Economics," 6.

87. Axel Leijonhufvud, as quoted in Carter, "Intellectual Openings and Policy Closings," 141 n. As we suggest later, the taboo against political scientists seems to have loosened a quarter century later.

88. A. W. Coats, "Introduction," in Coats, *The Post-1945 Internationalization of Economics*, 3–11.

89. Amitava Krishna Dutt, "Two Issues in the State of Development Economics," in Amitava Krishna Dutt and Kenneth P. Jameson, eds., *New Directions in Development Economics* (Brookfield, Vt.: Edward Elgar, 1992), 7

90. For data on individual countries, see CEPAL, *Balance preliminar de la economía de América Latina y el Caribe 1996* (Santiago: Naciones Unidas, 1996).

91. Enrique V. Iglesias, *Reflections on Economic Development: Toward a New Latin American Consensus* (Washington, D.C.: Inter-American Development Bank, 1992), 55.

92. Enrique V. Iglesias, "Economic Reform: A View from Latin America," in

John Williamson, ed., *The Political Economy of Policy Reform* (Washington, D.C.: Institute for International Economics, 1994), 494.

93. Nora Lustig, "From Structuralism to Neostructuralism: The Search for a Heterodox Paradigm," in Patricio Meller, ed., *The Latin American Development Debate: Neostructuralism, Neomonetarism, and Adjustment Processes* (Boulder, Colo.: Westview, 1991), 38.

94. Alejandro Foxley, *Latin American Experiments in Neoconservative Economics* (Berkeley: University of California Press, 1983), 16.

95. Iglesias, *Reflections on Economic Development*, 125.

96. Iglesias, *Reflections on Economic Development*; John Williamson, "In Search of a Manual for Technopols," in Williamson, *The Political Economy of Policy Reform*.

97. Haggard and Kaufman, *The Politics of Economic Adjustment*; Stephan Haggard and Steven B. Webb, eds., *Voting for Reform: Democracy, Political Liberalization and Economic Adjustment* (New York: Oxford University Press, 1994).

98. Jorge I. Domínguez, ed., *Technopols: Freeing Politics and Markets in Latin America in the 1990s* (University Park: Pennsylvania State University Press, 1997).

99. Markoff and Montecinos, "The Ubiquitous Rise of Economists."

100. Hirschman, "The Rise and Decline of Development Economics," 19.

101. See Amartya Sen, "Development: Which Way Now?" in Rajani Kanth, ed., *Paradigms in Economic Development: Classic Perspectives, Critiques, and Reflections* (Armonk, N.Y.: M. E. Sharpe, 1994), 220. Sen's essay was originally published in 1982.

102. Osvaldo Sunkel, "Introduction: In Search of Development Lost," in Osvaldo Sunkel, ed., *Development from Within: Towards a Neostructuralist Approach for Latin America* (Boulder, Colo.: Lynne Rienner, 1993), 4.

103. In Chile, Alejandro Foxley's tenure as finance minister under Aylwin (1990–94) was followed by his winning the presidency of the Christian Democratic Party and subsequently a seat in the Senate.

104. John Harris, Janet Hunter, and Colin M. Lewis, eds., *The New Institutional Economics and Third World Development* (New York: Routledge, 1995).

105. These intellectual developments have also had an impact on the writing of Latin America's economic history, a subject we cannot pursue here (but see John H. Coatsworth and Alan M. Taylor, eds., *Latin America and the World Economy since 1800* [Cambridge, Mass.: David Rockefeller Center for Latin American Studies/Harvard University Press, 1998]).

106. For a challenge to some of the central notions of this new institutionalism, see Milan Zafirovski, "Socioeconomics and Rational Choice Theory: Specification of Their Relations," *Journal of Socioeconomics* 27, no. 2 (1998).

107. Amartya Sen, "Gender and Cooperative Conflict," in Irene Tinker, ed., *Persistent Inequalities* (Oxford: Oxford University Press, 1990), 126; quoted in Gale Summerfield, "Economic Development in Introductory Textbooks," in Nahid Aslanbegui and Michele I. Naples, eds., *Rethinking Economic Principles: Critical Essays on Introductory Textbooks* (Chicago: Irwin, 1996), 182.

108. Sen, "Development: Which Way Now?" 226.

109. V. Shiva, "Development, Ecology and Women," in Kanth, *Paradigms in Economic Development*, 244; see also James Ferguson, *The Anti-politics Machine: Development, Depoliticization, and Bureaucratic Power in the Third World* (Cambridge: Cambridge University Press, 1990).

110. For an insightful account of this line of argument, see Roberto Patricio Korzeniewicz and William C. Smith, "Poverty, Inequality and Growth in Latin America: Searching for the High Road to Globalization" *Latin American Research Review* 35, no. 3 (2000): 7–54.

111. James A. Dorn, "Introduction—Competing Visions of Development Policy," in James A. Dorn, Steve H. Hanke, and Alan A. Walters, eds., *The Revolution in Development Economics* (Washington, D.C.: Cato Institute, 1998), 13.

112. Deepak Lal, "The Transformation of Developing Economies: From Plan to Market," in Dorn, Hanke, and Walters, *The Revolution in Development Economics*, 55.

113. For a comprehensive treatment of the promises of marketization, see Sebastián Edwards, *Crisis and Reform in Latin America: From Despair to Hope* (New York: Oxford University Press, 1995).

114. Two very useful discussions of issues in the state-market debate are Peter Evans, "The State as Problem and Solution: Predation, Embedded Autonomy, and Structural Change," in Stephan Haggard and Robert Kaufman, eds., *The Politics of Economic Adjustment: International Constraints, Distributive Conflicts, and the State* (Princeton, N.J.: Princeton University Press, 1992), 139–81; and Merilee S. Grindle, "Sustaining Economic Recovery in Latin America: State Capacity, Markets, and Politics," in Graham Bird and Ann Helwege, eds., *Latin America's Future* (New York: Academic Press, 1994), 303–23.

115. Graham Bird and Ann Helwege, "Introduction," in Bird and Helwege, *Latin America's Future*, 1–9. For some very interesting speculation on the political possibilities of a revival of social democratic policies around the distributional issues connected to growth, see Korzeniewicz and Smith, "Searching for the High Road to Economic Growth."

116. Domínguez, *Technopols*; Verónica Montecinos, "Economists in Party Politics: Chilean Democracy in the Era of the Markets," in Centeno and Silva, *The Politics of Expertise in Latin America*, 126–41. For the contrasting experience of Peru, see Conaghan, "Stars of the Crisis."

117. Perhaps this is one manifestation of a lasting legacy of hostility toward theoretical and methodological pluralism that some think enveloped the North American economics profession during the McCarthy period, when the habits of "self-censorship" ran strong, a legacy still bearing fruit abroad. See Reuven Brenner, "Making Sense Out of Nonsense: Economics in Context," in Colander and Brenner, *Educating Economists*, 42; Winton U. Solberg and Robert W. Tomilson, "Academic McCarthyism and Keynesian Economics: The Bowen Controversy at the University of Illinois," *History of Political Economy* 29 (1997): 55–82.

118. Is it perhaps a symptom of Brazilian departure from some important elements of the overall picture sketched in this chapter that the Brazilian president in the late 1990s was a former president of the International Sociological Association? But let us note, *a contrario*, that it was not his success in the ISA that

propelled him into his country's presidency, but his success in curbing inflation as Brazil's finance minister.

119. One major treatment of the relationship of technocrats and business interests within the context of democratizing transitions is Catherine M. Conaghan and James M. Malloy, *Unsettling Statecraft: Democracy and Neoliberalism in the Central Andes* (Pittsburgh: University of Pittsburgh Press, 1994).

120. Edmund Burke, *Reflections on the Revolution in France* (1790; Garden City, N.Y.: Doubleday, 1961), 89.

121. *New York Times*, May 2, 1998, A1.

122. *New York Times*, May 12, 1998, A3.

PART II

THE STATE AND DEMOCRACY

Chapter Five

THE TRANSATLANTIC BRIDGE: MIRRORS, CHARLES TILLY, AND STATE FORMATION IN THE RIVER PLATE

FERNANDO LÓPEZ-ALVES

URING the nineteenth century, wars and conflict resolution carved state and nation out of the Spanish colonial map in the Americas. Such a context of state making compels a reference to Charles Tilly's work on state formation in sixteenth- and seventeenth-century Europe and his view that revolutions and state formation intertwined to craft the nation-state.[1] This chapter does not attempt to "apply" Tilly's argument to Latin America. Rather, it suggests that the Spanish-American and European experiences can talk to each other through a Tillean view of state making. While Tilly's claims are not fully applicable to Latin America, this chapter suggests that the conceptualization and assumptions that inspire his work are.

The chapter concentrates on two cases, Argentina and Uruguay, which shared a long list of cultural, economic, and geographic features but differed in the types of states they constructed during the nineteenth century.[2] This alone suggests that factors other than similar economic structures, postcolonial institutions, and inherited cultural patterns (derived from similar waves of immigration) were at work. Within the widespread pattern of guerrilla warfare that embraced the whole of Spanish America, Uruguay and Argentina express two different modes of conflict, and I argue two paths of state building. While until 1904 the Uruguayan state remained almost besieged by constant guerrilla warfare and relied on a practically nonexistent central army to enforce rule making, by the 1870s Argentina had overcome a similar pattern of guerrilla conflict and had constructed a centralized military. The consequences for the types of political systems that were to emerge were great: Argentina more militaristic and prone to military takeovers, Uruguay less militaristic and with a political elite who managed, for most of the twentieth century, to keep the professional army out of politics.

This chapter argues that a dialogue between European and Latin American cases based on the Tillean world of war, coercion, and capital can contribute to the construction of a better model of state making and nation building. It also suggests a shift in the research agenda on nation building in Latin America, from the late nineteenth and early twentieth centuries to the first half of the 1800s. Finally, it argues for comparative studies of army building and taxation.

THE LATIN AMERICAN STATE

Two broadly defined groups can be distinguished within the literature on the Latin American state. In the more established tradition, historical, sociological, and literary work blended together to provide historically grounded accounts of nation building. In a newer group, a renewed interest in the nineteenth century has sharpened the theoretical focus on the state per se, bringing it "back in" as an independent category of analysis and adding subaltern perspectives into the mix as well.[3] The sharpest difference between these two groups lies not necessarily in the period in which the work was produced but in the degree to which authors explicitly declare the approach they employ. What I see as a more established tradition did not speak in an explicit theoretical language, while the newer literature does.[4] A chief problem affecting both traditions remains methodological and conceptual. Categories of analysis often are confusing, concept stretching is of dubious applicability, and broader comparative connections with work on state formation in Europe, North America, or elsewhere remain scarce.

Authors in the more traditional group usually wrote from an implicit institutionalist and culturalist standpoint, with most scholars emphasizing the influence of the colonial era.[5] They made a well-known claim: that the centralizing character of colonial institutions, and the political culture they generated, to a great degree determined the path followed by the Latin American states.[6] Recent literature has seriously challenged these claims. For instance, in Peru, a country that traditionally has been regarded as possessing a strong colonial heritage, the postcolonial state turned out to be weaker than expected.[7] All these arguments beg, of course, the question of how long legacies can last, how to measure their influence, and how to define them[8].

Estructuralistas of the Marxist persuasion could be considered exceptional within this more established group because they have been quite explicit regarding the approach chosen. Yet they have not really focused on the state. Speaking the language of class analysis, they either neglected the state or perceived institutions as mere instruments of class domination.[9] The picture that emerged was rather gloomy: a dependent state, with low capacity and scarce autonomy. In part, the Latin American nation-state seemed to confirm the Black Legend of Latin American history. Sooner or later, these states would become repressive and corrupt, antidemocratic and authoritarian.[10]

Within the less established tradition neo-institutionalism has acquired some popularity. Rational choice theory, as well as mild versions of neo-classical economics, became popular as well.[11] Others have continued to study the state through its capacity to handle economic crises. Rather than labor relations or the mode of production, this newer literature has underscored the (rational) choices of individuals and the transaction costs associated with the economics of state building. Not surprisingly, this switch reflects the dominant trends in the social sciences during the last fifteen years or so. Of course, one finds exceptions.[12] Indeed, a preference for writing history from the bottom up remains a central characteristic of recent efforts.[13]

State autonomy continues to be a central concern of political scientists. Nora Hamilton and others studying the Mexican state have long placed state autonomy at the center of their efforts.[14] The connection between state building and regime outcomes, a favorite of the more established literature, is still unresolved. Searching for clues, some authors have revisited classic arguments about democracy and nation building in Europe.[15] And, similar to the direction taken in this chapter, Miguel Centeno has devoted much attention to revisiting the impact of war on state formation, especially on state finances.[16]

One can conclude that renewed interest in the state has sharpened old disagreements regarding methodology and categories of analysis, types of argument, and interpretation of data. Nonetheless, on two issues, work on the Latin American state has reached a rough consensus. First, most literature has assumed that ideas—especially the ideology of state makers—strongly shaped the state.[17] Second, most literature has coincided in the timing of state consolidation, placing it in the last two decades of the nineteenth century.

IDEAS, TIMING, AND DEVELOPMENT

Similar to many nineteenth-century writers, traditional and newer literature has found in the philosophical tenets and biographies of the state makers a valuable clue to understanding outcomes and institutions. During the 1960s and 1970s, Latin American Philosophers stressed that a history of ideas best explained institutions and politics. In the 1990s, the most sophisticated and critical versions of the approach argued for a thorough revision and questioned the very foundations of its application. Yet the traditional argumentation remains quite influential. Even dependency theory, the homegrown structural theory generated among *Latinoamericanistas*, highlighted the importance of cultural imperialism and ideology. Historians agreed, supporting a larger consensus on the importance of ideas in state making.[18] Shumway, for instance, has revisited the influence of the founding fathers' political philosophy in the building of the Argentine state. For him and many others, political ideas that emerged in a prior and different historical era still shape contemporary politics.[19] Francois-Xavier Guerra agrees. He has placed a heavy emphasis on the influence of the French Revolution to explain independence, as well as the character of the institutions emerging in the republics of the nineteenth century.[20] Renewed interest in Max Weber, Foucault, and *historias de vida*, in addition to postmodern discourse analysis, have all strengthened this old consensus about the importance of cognitive processes. Even mainstream Latin American historians of the structuralist persuasion have shifted to family histories, biographies, and the conceptualization of the "modern." The state becomes the product of a new kind of discipline, a *disciplina modernizante*.[21] Here the processes studied are psychological and ideological rather than social or structural. For example, the transition from the traditional to the modern state is a by-product of the assimilation of external mechanisms of social control into internal ones. In addition, a strong Hegelian undercurrent has come alive in exploring the notion of *national identity*, at least by authors coming from disciplines such as English or Latin American literature. The nation, interpreted as a universal category, would emerge when the general (the central power) confronts the particular (the individual citizen). Institutions would rise to resolve this tension.[22]

The problem for a history-of-ideas approach is that it must either assume a correspondence between ideas and final outcomes or be able to explain deviations between the two. Why did liberal ideas, shared by most nineteenth-century state makers, generate different political institutions and degrees of power centralization? As we shall see in the next section, a closer look at a Tillean combination of war, capital, and coercion can provide better answers. While for this literature intellectual constructs have guided the visible hand of state making, we will learn that conflict and its unintended consequences direct the invisible hand.

Theories of state building have also reached consensus regarding the timing of state consolidation: the argument is that one can speak of nation-states only by the end of the nineteenth century. This consensus is based on good empirical evidence. By the late 1800s, Latin American economies were fully integrated into the world economy, and coalitions uniting the economic and the political elite consolidated. State expansion and a wave of power centralization followed.[23] Persuasive as it is, many things are wrong with this picture. First, structural theories of state formation have left out military conflict. A combination of economics, collective action, and war making can offer a richer and more accurate theoretical scenario. Second, despite the findings of many historians to the contrary,[24] most of this literature views the early and mid-nineteenth century only as a chaotic period of war making.[25] Yet there was order in chaos. It was precisely during this earlier phase that the most fundamental steps were taken in terms of institutional design

Basically, the literature has mistaken the *pace* of state growth for the *type* of resulting state. There is no doubt that during the last decades of the 1800s the state expanded and grew. Yet if one wants to account for the major defining characteristics of these states, a turn toward the war-ridden and confusing independence and postindependence decades is needed. It is at this point that I want to explore a Tillean argument of state formation.

TILLEAN LATIN AMERICA

Tilly has defined routes to state formation that combine war with different stages of capitalist development. Unlike the literature on the Latin American state, ideas and the influence of founding fathers have a lesser role to play. And unlike the emphasis on structures and economy, he has presented a combination of war, collective action, and capitalist development. In *Coercion, Capital, and European States*, Tilly studies how, starting in the tenth century, military power and capital crafted the European nation-state and opened different routes of power centralization. None of the routes that he submits for Europe were predetermined, and there was nothing inevitable about the triumph of the nation-state. He places much emphasis on the unintended consequences of state making, an almost inevitable conclusion for an argument that stresses the central role of conflict in institution building. He proposes three modes of state building that result from the combination of war, coercion, and capital.[26] These modes relate to the process of modernization and therefore are not disconnected from one another; indeed, in the process of state formation, both Tilly and Michael Mann observe a continuum from coercion to capital-intensive modes.[27]

The first, or *coercion-intensive*, route taken by Brandenburg-Prussia and Russia seems alien to Latin America as a whole. In this mode, states, urged by the requirements of war, were able to increase revenues and enlarge their bureaucracies by forcing taxation upon their rural populations. Given the absence of a central army, intense rural resistance, and the resulting weak bureaucracies, Latin American states could not easily force taxation upon their rural population. And, depending on agreements with the landed elite or rural caudillos, at different points in their development many states did not wish to. In Tilly's argument, the coercion-intensive route prevailed in regions that featured few cities and an agricultural system in which direct coercion played a significant part in production. After the wars of independence, and despite their agrarian characteristics, most states in Latin America did not resemble this mode. Systems of coerced labor did exist, but not in combination with a bureaucratized system of rural taxation.

Paraguay under Gaspar de Francia is a possible exception. Placing Paraguay within this framework contributes to a better comparative understanding of both this case and the region. Unlike Argentina or Uruguay, Paraguay could not profit from controlling a port and custom duties. Thus, the extraction of state revenue required more organized forms of coercion than in societies with a city-state structure. The government found an appealing solution in state-controlled slavery. There existed a large indigenous population that could be used as forced labor, and the dominant type of crop (the yerba mate) lent itself to a plantation economy structure. If the state owned its own slaves, then the problematic task of enforcing taxation on private slave owners or other landowners could be avoided altogether. All depended, however, on the magnitude of this enterprise in relation to the rest of the rural economy, and the experiment rendered mixed results. At this point, Paraguay detached itself from its European counterparts. Labor coercion in the yerba mate hacienda remained an important but limited source of state revenue and did not really help to establish a full-fledged tax system.

The resemblance between Paraguay and some of the European coercion-intensive cases finds an explanation in Tilly's suggestions about the combination of war and coercion in state making, and the importance of the army as a crafter of the state. As in most of Europe, in Paraguay a central army emerged almost at the same time as the state, and the prevailing pattern of conflict, the *guerra de guerrillas*, took a milder form. Preparation for war against neighbors became, in Paraguay, a more defining feature of state formation than domestic warfare. While during the first half of the nineteenth century Paraguay suffered more from the *threat* of external aggression than from actual war, this was strong enough to convince the elite to invest in the army at the onset of state formation.

In the late nineteenth century, a few Latin American states took something similar to the *capital-intensive* route defined by Tilly for Europe. Capital holders, in wealthy city-states such as Venice, the Dutch Republic, or Genoa, dominated the military and carved a distinct path of state making. The dominance of seagoing city-states with powerful merchant classes in this mode immediately brings to mind important seaports such as Buenos Aires and Montevideo. Like European states in this category, these rapidly evolved into an area of "many cities and commercial predominance."[28] Along this route, state makers and capitalists struck a bargain by which they exchanged resources for protection. In Tilly's argument, such agreements characterized city-states, city-empires, urban federations, and other forms of fragmented sovereignty.[29] The River Plate region, with its high degree of urbanization and thriving cities, definitely seems to fit. Merchant classes and rural capitalists usually controlled resources and thus had something to offer to the state or the military. Owners of capital, as in Europe, asked for and obtained protection.

Argentina, because of its wealthy landed elite and its urban merchant class engaged in seagoing enterprises, as well as its more organized military, came the closest to this pattern. In the Province of Buenos Aires, which was militarized earlier as a response to the British invasions of the early 1800s and retained a more professional military force than the rest of the continent, owners of capital felt more secure and contributed more to building the central army.

Divergences between Argentina and Uruguay within this Tillean category, and contrasts between these Latin American cases and the European ones, point to crucial differences that can generate a better model of state formation *on both continents*. A lesson Europe could learn, for instance, is that strong rural commercial capitalism does not necessarily foster state making, even when the interests of exporters can theoretically be best protected by this investment. Even in wealthy Argentina, the contribution of capitalists to the state remained modest; in Uruguay, it was minimal. The same applies to most of the region as a whole.[30] Why was landed capital so reticent? To a great extent, capitalists' behavior finds a sound explanation in the prevailing pattern of conflict. Capitalists, particularly rural producers, did not invest in strengthening the state because they perceived this to be too risky an enterprise in the context of continuous guerrilla warfare, or because they had already invested in local rural militia. It was a vicious circle. The state was too weak a partner to impose law and order, and it remained weak because upper-class financial support was not forthcoming.

A second contrast teaches Latin Americanists a useful lesson, that goes back to armies and the timing of their creation. As in most regions of Latin America, Argentine and Uruguayan capitalists could not control the army and therefore did not encourage state building because there was no professional military over which to exert control in the first place. The vicious circle described for the state applies to the army. City-states like Buenos Aires and Montevideo, supported almost exclusively by custom duties, could not muster the social and economic resources to create a loyal army at the onset of state building. Or they did not wish to. In the Province of Buenos Aires, the state initially decided to invest in a more professional military; but owners of capital and politicians, threatened by the unruly nature of recruits, had second thoughts about how to secure their loyalty. Similar doubts haunted other state makers in the region, especially in Uruguay, Colombia, and Venezuela.

Another lesson is that unlike the European equivalents of Renaissance Italy, Latin American city-states did consolidate into nations. Differences in the inter-state context of conflict in which states emerged on both sides of the Atlantic, plus their use of coercion and capital to gain control of national territories, help explain this disparity in outcomes. Neither Buenos Aires nor Montevideo had to confront the external threats that faced Italian city-states. When Montevideo lost control of its hinterland as a consequence of a prolonged siege, for example, the rivalry between Brazil and Argentina and subsequent British intervention favored Montevideo's cause.

As a whole, Latin America seems to fall more easily under Tilly's mode of *capitalized coercion*, in which state makers used both coercion *and* capital to centralize power. This path, Tilly shows, was also the primary one in Europe and paved the way for Western world domination in the eighteenth and nineteenth centuries. France and England provide classic examples. They used capital to mobilize for war and war to generate capital; at the same time, within these states, the representatives of one or the other struggled for political power. In so doing, they mobilized large parts of their populations into the process of state building. This gave these states great cultural and social vitality; it is not surprising that they became the models for the development of the modern nation-state. Tilly argues that those political entities that evolved into modern nation-states did so because along the way they adopted at least some of the characteristics of capitalized coercion. Indeed, those who did not, disappeared as state projects.

The capitalized coercion path relies on the availability of large sums of commercial capital to pay for the costs of war. While the Latin American states had less cash than European rulers, they did have access to foreign loans. Like European monarchs, they also borrowed money from the upper classes. Indeed, similar to Europe, Latin American governments contracted a considerable amount of debt with the merchant and landowning classes. One can conclude, then, that dependence on local private capital, especially commercial capital, was great on both sides of the ocean. On both shores, states spent money in reconstructing the economy, buying the loyalty of local lords and army officers, establishing bureaucracies (including a system of taxation), and trying to secure the support of the economic elite. Part of the state budget also went to placate local revolts, and, on occasion, smaller sums were distributed among the populace.

In Latin America, states spent money buying the loyalties of caudillos, creating a bureaucracy devoted to collecting custom duties, and painfully reconstructing economies often ravished by guerrilla wars. Purchasing caudillo loyalty through land grants, pensions, or cash was comparable to the situation in Europe, in which army officers and local lords received similar incentives to remain loyal to the crown. But, while in Europe large sums went into the creation of royal armies and systems of taxation, this was not the case in Latin America. Systems of revenue collection and armies, therefore, played different roles in Europe and Latin America as they emerged along the path of capitalized coercion. Through foreign loans—and perhaps also through custom duties—Latin American states perhaps had an easier time tapping into sources of revenue other than taxation.[31] They therefore avoided something that the vast majority of European kings could not: the need to subjugate the upper classes.[32] Thus, the coercion part of the equation was different: tighter in Europe, more relaxed in Latin America.

The two sets of cases also differ in the relationship between taxation and the military. France teaches us that if a strong army participates in the making of the state, we can expect central taxation and a stronger bureaucracy. Latin American states that by the end of the nineteenth century came somewhat closer to France—Argentina, Venezuela, and Paraguay— did so only in regard to the strong weight they placed on the military, but they scarcely relied on their armies to subdue the upper classes or enforce taxation. The power of the central government, thus, remained weak in regard to taxation and the control of the regions via a central bureaucracy.

Great Britain could come closer to Latin America in that account, for royal power was limited. The creation of Parliament as the joint representative of landowners and bourgeoisie apparently limited the power of the head of state, while in Latin America the local caudillos and congress did. Moreover, for some time Great Britain did not count on a central army either. Similarities end right there, however. Contrasts with Great Britain convey three important lessons to be learned. One goes back to the importance of domestic capital as a financier of state making. In England, unlike most of Latin America, commercial capital and a powerful and growing industrial bourgeoisie did collaborate vigorously in constructing the state. Second, Britain was much more efficient at taxing than were Latin American states. A third lesson takes us back to the timing in the construction of the army: Great Britain built a central army at an earlier stage in the formation of the modern state.

Finally, from a Tillean perspective, Europe and Latin America differed in terms of the connection between war and capital. In Europe, war often generated capital; in Latin America, it very seldom did. War between state makers and indigenous populations over the control of natural resources translated into the annexation of Indian territory and the extermination of native peoples. Despite the loss of human resources, war in these situations ended up generating some capital. A great majority of these wars, however, took place at the time of the colony, and very few of them were fought as part of the process of formation of the modern state—the conquest of the "desert" in Argentina is one of those exceptions. Domestic conflict in the form of guerrilla warfare almost always meant huge losses in property and population, with terrible consequences for economic development and capital accumulation. Indeed, most of the time war caused capital and labor flight. Foreigners as well as Creoles or Native Americans, and at times even entire communities, abandoned regions affected by war and either left the country or sought refuge somewhere else. This also meant that many states in desperate need of labor and capital constantly failed when trying to attract European immigrants.

Tilly's argument on European revolutions further enriches the lessons learned about the intertwined powers of capital, military power, and coercion in state making. In *European Revolutions* he argues that at the end of the fifteenth century, politics and economics took a new shape from which emerged "revolutionary situations." These are defined by the emergence of contenders who advance competing claims to control the state, a commitment to these claims by a significant part of the population, and the inability of the state to deal with them. Revolutions and power centralization form part of the same process that eventually creates the nation-state. Indeed, Tilly presents his analysis of the state as a crucial theme in a theory of revolution.

Tilly's definition of revolution may be questionable. Perhaps he sees revolutions where we should see mere revolts with no revolutionary consequence. Or perhaps the problem is that he broadens too much the scope of our understanding of "revolutions." This may result in what social scientists most fear: unwarranted concept stretching. Yet because Tilly's main purpose is precisely to get rid of "narrow" readings of revolution that have limited European revolutions to 1789 or 1917, his argument is refreshing and renovative in lieu of a theory of state formation in Latin America that has been by and large rather quiet about the revolutionary component of the state-formation process.

Since the wars of independence, the first widespread revolutionary wars experienced by Latin America, most of the process of state making in the New Word can be interpreted as a chain of revolutionary situations similar to the one described by Tilly. In some cases, we could even apply this argument to the late twentieth century, as in El Salvador. Even in the 1990s, Colombia comes close to a Tillean revolutionary situation, where the state cannot efficiently deal with contenders or effectively undermine the commitment of a sizable part of the population to the contender's claims. Such an argument touches upon a favorite of Latin American literature on the state, that is, the contested issue of political stability. At what point can we say that the state is finally consolidated? And does consolidation mean stability? The question of what makes some states more stable than others takes us to the heart of Tilly's combination of revolution and state making, because it poses the question of whether the process of state making in Latin America as a whole is at all finished.

In Europe, stability was achieved in different ways and at different times. Holland and Britain, both solid and consensual states, furnish cases in point. Both achieved stability, but the Dutch required more than two hundred years (from 1566 to 1833) to achieve a political system durable enough to avoid revolution, while the British accomplished this already during the seventeenth century. In France, stability was achieved through many failures, which included an important revolution. In Russia, a situation of revolutionary success in the early twentieth century in terms of state making turned into resounding failure. This may convey a telling message to weak Latin American states: early success at state making may not guarantee stability. Indeed, placed into a bigger, "huge processes" perspective, perhaps the revolutions of the nineteenth and twentieth centuries are still evolving into yet another form of nation-state. In light of Tilly's argument, a closer look at the wars of independence and a reconsideration of the chain of revolutionary situations that followed add another angle from which to rethink some of the main tenets of the Latin American literature on the state.

Toward a Theory of State Making in Latin America

> I am convinced that the enemies of the nation do take
> advantage of the confusion about this question of the
> state. And I keep asking myself what the hell is the state
> . . . because the motherland and the state are really not
> the same thing. The Patria is us, here in the *montonera*,
> the good Orientales. And the state is an artificial command, made out of paper, without a heart.
> *Aparicio Saravia*[33]

What in 1902 puzzled Aparicio Saravia, the last guerrilla commander who fiercely resisted power centralization in Uruguay, still stands today as a central issue in the theory and practice of state making.[34] As long as institutions cannot reconcile split political loyalties and divergent political cultures into a dominant project of power centralization, the state, as

Saravia put it, remains heartless. How does a central power become a "community" in the imagination and hearts of the people?

History surprises. Tilly tells us that when Europeans decided that the age of revolution was over, starting in 1989 an almost unstoppable wave swept Eastern and central Europe, knocking down one regime after another. Modern Latin America has also surprised many who thought that wars of resistance and revolutionary guerrilla warfare were an atavism. War patterns in twentieth-century Latin America have followed and reinforced a tradition of guerrilla warfare that finds its origins in the nineteenth-century processes of state making. The whole of Central America has experienced important guerrilla wars, Mexico produced Chiapas in the midst of the North American Free Trade Agreement (NAFTA), Peru's Sendero Luminoso is still a presence, pockets of resistance are still to be found in Bolivia and Ecuador, and Colombia in 1999 still resembles a typical nineteenth-century situation in which at least two parallel armies dispute control over the national territory.

Contrasts between the European and Latin American contexts of state building sharply define two broad, but different, patterns of war and conflict resolution, one for each side of the Atlantic. Within these patterns, one can identify variations that very much matter, as Tilly finds in the cases of France and Britain.

Armies and Guerrillas

In most of Latin America, the *guerra de guerrillas* prevailed as the most common type of resistance to power centralization. This type of warfare helped create different *patrias*, smaller but stubborn pockets of resistance that embodied local subcultures and clientele networks. Culturally and even ethnically, these different social pockets often shared little; politically, they competed with one another to seize control of a larger territory. Wars of resistance and the multiplication of pseudo-armies remained natural components of this type of conflict. The failures of state makers at seizing and controlling larger territories speak of frustrated state projects and the inability of guerrilla-type armies to conquer neighboring territories, or to effectively control them if conquered. No hegemonic power was able to rise and grow as a continental state project, and the Pan-American dreams of Simón Bolívar, if he was really serious about them, lived only on paper.

As professional armies emerged late in the process leading to power centralization, central governments used guerrilla-type war instead. Guerrilla wars, as elsewhere, were fought mainly in rural areas, but in many cases they also affected the major urban centers, with consequences for coalition formation. The predominance of guerrilla warfare alone, however, would not be a strong enough reason for states not to build professional armies and at times, rural guerrillas do became armylike and states succeed at transforming guerillas into army battalions. But still rural guerillas seldom became professional armies. When they did, they did so as part of armies commanded by urban-based officer corps. Unlike in the Old World, in Latin America army building was, at times, not even a priority in the agenda of state makers. Because of this crucial difference, the enforcement of property rights and taxation took different forms. One can argue that guerrilla warfare delayed the process of army building. Not that Europe did not have its share of guerrilla warfare, such as the *Vendee* or the Spanish *guerrilla* against both the French and subsequent central governments. Yet these were more the exceptions than the rule. War among recognizable armies with strong ties to a central power were more common in Europe, while on the other side of the Atlantic caudillos in command of undisciplined militia maintained fuzzy connections with the central power.

In Latin America, competing "armies" more often than not claimed to represent "the state." By 1904, Aparicio Saravia was still challenging the central power in Montevideo with a force that also called itself the "national army." In Colombia, even under the centralizing policies of the *regeneración* in the 1880s and 1890s, at least two "armies" claimed to embody the legitimate government. Most of South America falls into the situation of two parallel armies fighting during the first crucial stages of state building. In Argentina, local guerrilla forces in the provinces were able to ally with one another and form a parallel government and a military force strong enough to defy, and at times defeat, Buenos Aires. A distinctive feature of Argentina, however, was that the confrontations between these two organized contenders resulted in the early formation of a central army. By the 1870s, Argentina was able to break the pattern of guerrilla warfare that prevailed for a longer time in Uruguay and elsewhere.

One can conclude that professional armies did not easily prosper in Latin America. The European regiment, for example, an effective device for securing the control of armed forces to the state, played a shabby role in Latin America up until the twentieth century. Europe also tells us that professional mercenaries contribute enormously to make armies more professional. One can argue that those mercenaries who marched alongside nationals in European armies contributed in an indirect but important way to state making. Latin America, however, cannot compare. One would have to look too hard to find similar soldiery. Although toward the end of the nineteenth century one can detect a few soldiers of fortune in some Latin American armies, they remained exceptions, and their contribution to the armies in which they served, rather modest.[35]

War and Societal Discipline

Authority and societal discipline are necessary ingredients of state formation. For many years, students of Latin America interpreted these notions as a product of culture, that is, the manifestation of a sort of Iberian lassitude. As powerful as they might have been, however, inherited cultural views on discipline and authority do not suffice to explain the characteristics of discipline and authority that paralleled the making of the nation-state. War and its effects on institutions and society, for instance, contributed to legitimate new forms of authority and social discipline. I have suggested that within the pattern of guerrilla warfare that dominated the New World, lines of command and loyalties tying soldiers and governments took a more confusing form than in Europe; and that, given a different context of interstate competition, the monopolization of coercion and the control of the national territory—key preconditions for the consolidation of recognizable lines of authority and discipline—took other forms. My point is that emerging notions of social discipline directly relate to patterns of conflict as well as the construction of armies and their social impact.

Unlike Latin America, for many centuries in Europe the nobility and its armies provided a more disciplined and identifiable axis of state making. The nobility, who often fought against, or become allied through marriages with, neighboring peers, provided a recognizable source of authority identifiable with the state. While resisting the rise of the modern state, the nobility nonetheless left a heritage of social discipline that stressed sharper lines of command. This, to a great extent, was absorbed by the new order. For instance, and from a very different theoretical standpoint than Tilly, Perry Anderson has suggested that the rise of the absolutist state in Europe, and in turn the rise of the modern state, was new only to a point. Modernity basically inherited an analogous body of regulations, laws, and lines of control. Anderson traces western European notions of political behavior and respect for the judicial system to a heritage connected as far back as Roman law. Kings, noblemen, and their armies, therefore, represented identifiable forms of power recognizable by all.

One can argue that the rise of strong royal armies in Europe, and the weakness of the professional military during state building in Latin America, had lasting consequences for societal discipline and culture. Notions of military discipline, for instance, permeated European society to an extent unknown in Latin America. Let me go back again to the importance of European regiments and their disciplinary social influence. Nowhere in the Americas does one find anything comparable to the social and cultural impact that Prussian, Austrian, or French regiments enjoyed already by the mid–nineteenth century. In the most extreme of cases, Prussia, by the 1870s every single, fit man was a member of a regiment or had been so in his youth. There, and in France and Austria at least, young men looked upon their conscript years as a rite of passage, and, as Keegan argues, conscription became "an important cultural form of European life."[36] In Latin America, neither armies nor regiments played a comparable role. Regiments, when they existed, did not really act as centers of national indoctrination and did not develop comparable linkages to their localities. The draft itself remained poorly enforced. Belonging to a regiment may have added to one's national identity, but the percentage of those who enlisted was minimal. Even in the most militarized societies of Latin America, this was and still is the case. During the process of nation building, if people made a connection between state and army, it was very likely negative and not necessarily linked with the notion of *patria*, or statehood. Argentina, again, could be considered an exception. There, government looked up to the army as a possible means to make good Argentineans out of immigrants who poured into the country during the second and third decades of the twentieth century. Forced recruitment among immigrants, however, was never really enforced.

Of course, this is not to make an argument for military discipline. Rather, it is to offer a contrast between military institutions and military culture as factors that shaped social discipline on both sides of the Atlantic. If social discipline can somehow be associated to military discipline and army development, as I think the case can be made for Europe, then Latin America diverged sharply from this pattern. While the clientelistic caudillo was no doubt a strong source of authority, in the context of frequent guerrilla warfare and labor scarcity, his rule seldom contributed to social discipline, for the protection he could provide was short-lived and more often than not unstable.

One can conclude that lines of authority—governmental or military—remained confusing during the postindependence period. Long after the consolidation of the nation-state in the late nineteenth century, most governments, including Argentina, could enforce only a very limited number of social norms and regulations; the idea of a disciplinary state existed only on paper. Therefore, state makers strongly appealed to ideology, rhetoric, emblems, and symbolic behavior to encourage loyalty, establish discipline, and create identity. From this standpoint, it is not surprising, therefore, that like state makers during the nineteenth century, most literature on the Latin American state has emphasized ideology, culture, and the influence of founding fathers in creating the nation.

Shall we feel disappointed that Latin America was lacking in European notions of discipline and authority? Not necessarily. A certain amount of chaos may also benefit democracy. As many Creoles and mestizos found out during the protracted conflict of nation building, confusing lines of command and social authority opened windows of opportunity for those at the bottom of the social ladder. Those discriminated against on the basis of race, wealth, last name, or profession found that they were relatively better off after the wars of independence. During most of the nineteenth century and for most of the region, discipline and modernity à la Europe, as state makers like the Argentine Faustino Sarmiento lamented, remained a weak force behind state making.

Since Latin American armies and governments did not necessarily grow together, civil-military relations differed from those in Europe. In addition to the obvious contrasts between European monarchies and Latin American republics, civil-military relations responded to the different patterns of conflict described. Depending on the timing of army formation and the role it played in state making, civil-military relations varied within Latin America. Uruguay and Argentina speak to this notion. In Uruguay the central army was not a state maker, and therefore civilian predominance over the military was stronger. By the early twentieth century, the small republic had constructed a state managed by civilians who enjoyed a remarkable degree of independence from the military establishment. In Argentina the army formed earlier, and therefore took a much more active role in state building. Civilian control remained weaker, and thus the coalition of landholders and professional military that built the Argentine state did so under frequent military intervention. Among other things, therefore, the timing of army building was also key for the development of civil-military relations.

To the example of the River Plate cases one can add others from most of the continent. Civilians and officers related to one another and built alliances depending upon the strength of the antiarmy coalition within a given government and the power of pockets of resistance to power centralization. Political parties were often used as vehicles to subordinate the military within the ruling coalition (e.g., Uruguay, Colombia, or Chilé). Parties penetrated the army by recruiting officers and rank and file, therefore rendering the military establishment dependent on party politics. A similar story can be told about places in which the parties were also strong, while a different one emerges in countries with weaker party systems, such as Argentina or Paraguay.

As argued, for the most part state building in Latin America also took place in the absence of interstate conflict. The European scenario of wars among monarchs finds no parallel in Latin America. Geography—mountain chains, jungles, deserts, poor roads, treacherous rivers—and Indian resistance also impeded the type of wars that provoked the well-studied bloodbaths in the Old World. With the exception of the military campaigns that were launched as part of the wars of independence (San Martin, Bolívar) and the Paraguayan War (1865–70) that united Brazil, Argentina, and Uruguay against Paraguay, Latin America fought no wars similar to the ones described by Tilly or Mann. Civil war in Latin America was more frequent, war among nations more rare.

In states with these characteristics, not much else was available to centralize power except strategies of economic development that relied heavily on trade and, later in the century, on foreign loans. In most cases, the sluggish economic performance of the state did not respond exclusively to deteriorating terms of trade or the impact of external debt and defective markets. Guerrilla wars contributed much to poor performance and seldom generated capital. Domestic trade and taxation, important forces of state making in Europe and Asia, remained contentious issues, and property rights and taxes were scarcely enforced. Unresolved conflict remained a serious problem. Most states found it difficult to claim a definite victory over their enemies until late in the early twentieth century, and therefore state makers had to make important tax concession to the landed elite and traders, especially in regions of high rural mobilization. This applies also to Argentina, a country that experienced unusual growth and economic success after the 1870s.

The question of why a central system of taxation did not develop in most of Latin America takes us back to the discussion of revolution as part of state formation: governments often used tax exemptions to placate local rebellions The state did not tax loyal caudillos, and when caudillos collected taxes from the rural populations, they pocketed the revenues. In some countries, well into the twentieth century neither war heroes nor their loyal following paid taxes. Although in Europe similar arrangements took place between kings and sectors of the nobility, taxes were still levied upon the rural populations. In Latin America, local rural populations paid for protection to the local caudillo or enlisted as militia in their armies; none of these activities tied them to the central government. At least in the River Plate, and this also applies to most other regions, the primary goal of government in granting special favors to caudillo-generals was to keep them out of politics and to prevent local insurrections that the caudillo, supposedly, was able to control. In Argentina and Uruguay, but more in the latter than the former, ruling coalitions resorted to military pensions as a major tool to control guerrilla militia and, later, the central military. Pensions benefited not only generals but also their descendants, especially unmarried women. In both countries and most of the continent, large sectors of the population were exempted from property taxes, and an income tax was never enforced.

Taxation was weakened as well by the feeble heritage of colonial institutions, which defectively tied center and periphery. Unlike in India after British rule, the few tasks that colonial bureaucracies had managed to perform efficiently became by and large irrelevant after independence. A colonial tax system did exist, but it collapsed as the wars altered power relations between urban centers and the countryside. As J. P. Barran has put it for Uruguay, and T. Halperin Donghi for Argentina, the wars brought about an increasing ruralization of social and political life; land-holders became more powerful, and popular culture more provincial.

Ideas and State Making

To close this sketchy theory of state making for Latin America, I must come back to the role of ideas and how they participated in constructing the nation-state. The states that emerged both differed from and resembled the original state projects that inspired the writings of the founding fathers. In Tilly's and my own world of state making, ideas alone seem unable to fully explain nation building. Ideationalist approaches, aware of this shortcoming, have tried to introduce corrections by including intervening variables, of either structural or psychological nature. More often than not, the approach ends up placing a heavy emphasis on the biography of state makers. The interplay between ideology and biographies, however, offers too delicate a balance between psychological profiles and skills vis-à-vis circumstances and opportunity. Indeed, the approach seems unable to include the unintended consequences of state making. The importance of unintended consequences is apparent when one contrasts initial projects of state making with final outcomes.

While in some fundamental aspects the River Plate states of the early 1900s bore a resemblance to the original plans in the minds of the founding fathers, in many others they represented their negation. In Uruguay, the 1830 constitution called for the elimination of political parties; instead, war reinforced the role of the parties in policy making, and the state became the child of the parties. The founding fathers wished for a political system dominated by an enlightened elite cast upon the principles of modernizing liberalism. Instead, conflict granted rural-based, traditional caudillos a strong role in decision making. The fathers and ideologues of the constitution wanted to consolidate a conservative, urban-based government coalition that could rule the destinies of the country. Instead, conflict resolution, more than the popularity of liberal ideas, led to the victory of liberalism at the end.[37]

In Argentina, contrary to the original design of the first state makers, in the 1880s the Orden Conservador represented the influence of the outer provinces rather than the total supremacy of Buenos Aires.[38] What Halperin Donghi has called the "exceptionally liberal" and inspiring thoughts of the founding fathers is hard to recognize in the Orden. The unintended consequences of war and conflict contributed to a final product that drifted from the goals of the May Revolution, or the daring democratic reforms of the 1820s under Bernardino Rivadavia. Moreover, the democratic thinking that characterized the Generación del 28, as well as the democratic and liberal imagining that resurged in the 1850s after the fall of Rosas, are hard to identify in the final outcome. The Orden did reform the educational system, separated church and state, and cleared the frontier—all features of the modern state. But in this period, as Natalio Botana argues, the provincial political elites still exerted considerable influence. More than ever before, wealth became the dominant prerequisite to access governmental posts, and participation in the political system was highly undemocratic and closed.

Some of the expectations of the founding fathers, however, materialized in the nation-states that consolidated at the end of the century. In Uruguay, reminiscent of the 1830 constitution, the *estado-patria* dichotomy was finally resolved by imposing a state project that favored urban interests. As Saravia feared, and the original project contemplated, the army that emerged in 1904 developed strong ties with urban interests, and the unruly gaucho was finally subjugated. In Argentina, party rivalry, as desired, finally ceased in the 1870s, a decade that marked a fusion of Federales and Unitarios. As the Federales gave up, state makers claimed reconciliation in a new and more modern order in which, according to *La Prensa* in 1874, "we are all Federales, we are all supporters of nationhood."[39] And, as state makers in Buenos Aires had long expected, during the 1870s, prosperity and European immigration did transform Argentina, facilitating state expansion.[40]

CONCLUSIONS

For those familiar with Tilly's work and the Latin American record of state building, it may appear that this chapter's efforts to establish a dialogue between these two bodies of literature remain futile. Within a Tillean world of state making, it could be argued that, compared with Europe, perhaps Latin America, sad to say, did not fight enough wars. One can also add that because Latin America had no colonies, it did not have to fund war making on foreign soils, and war could not be used as an instrument to control foreign markets. What I have claimed, however, is that Latin America fought a different type of war, and that these wars were as intense and consequential for institution building as wars in Europe.

It could also be argued that since Latin America, or at least the River Plate, does not fully fit in any of the paths defined by Tilly, then the proposed dialogue is impossible. The objective of the dialogue, however, was not to find a complete fit. Rather, it was to enrich theories of state making in both, especially on the Latin American side. No one was expecting that Latin America would squarely fit into Tilly's modes. At least, I did not. Nonetheless, it did share much with a combination of Tilly's modes and found a needed mirror in the Tillean mode of state making and revolutions combined. This finding begs for a redefinition of categories of analysis and a variation of a theory whose major premises, I argue, do apply.

I found it useful, however, to look at Latin America through Tillean lenses. The contrasts pointed to questions not fully explored in the literature on the Latin American state and forced a revision of commonly assumed notions. For example, the poorly studied subject of the formation of the armed forces and the evolution of civil-military relations stand as two major priorities within the research agenda after this Tillean tour of Latin America. These topics strike right into the core not only of literature on state formation but also of democratic theory. Work done from similar perspectives on Europe has already suggested likewise.[41] Our Tillean tour also suggests that the relation between capital and coercion, in connection with the development of state bureaucracies, provides a promising avenue for future research.

NOTES

Several people who were patient enough to read and comment on earlier versions of this chapter should be thanked. The first is Charles Tilly, who patiently labored through this piece and suggested, in part, the title. I also appreciate the insightful comments of Miguel Centeno, Herman Schwartz, and Jonathan Rosenberg.

1. Charles Tilly, *Coercion, Capital, and European States, A.D. 990–1990* (Cambridge, Mass.: Blackwell, 1990); and Tilly, *European Revolutions, 1492–1992* (Oxford: Blackwell, 1993).

2. For a fuller elaboration on the advantages of this particular pair comparison, see the introduction of my *State Formation and Democracy in Latin America: 1810–1900* (Durham, N.C.: Duke University Press, 2000).

3. See, among others, Miguel Centeno, "Blood and Debt: War and Taxation in Nineteenth-Century Latin America," *American Journal of Sociology* 102 (1997): 1565–606; Paul Gootenberg, *Between Silver and Guano: Commercial Policy and the State in Post-Independence Peru* (Princeton, N.J.: Princeton University Press, 1989); Hector Lindo-Fuentes, *Weak Foundations: The Economy of El Salvador in the Nineteenth Century, 1821–1898* (Berkeley: University of California Press, 1989); Florencia E. Mallon, *Peasant and Nation: The Making of Postcolonial Mexico and Peru* (Berkeley: University of California Press, 1995); Vincent Peloso and Barbara Tenenbaum, eds., *Liberals, Politics, and Power: State Formation in Nineteenth-Century Latin America* (Athens: University of Georgia

Press, 1996). Analysis of the twentieth century has also contributed to bringing the state back in, for example, Ruth Berins Collier and David Collier, *Shaping the Political Arena* (Princeton, N.J.: Princeton University Press, 1991); or Merilee Grindle, *Challenging the State: Crisis and Innovation in Latin America and Africa* (New York: Cambridge University Press, 1996).

4. Divisions between older and newer literature are, of course, relative. Many authors who can be placed in the older literature can also find a place in the newer one. Either their work evolved from one to the other, or it contained elements of both in the first place.

5. As a fairly recent example, see most essays in Mark A. Burkholder and Lyman L. Johnson, eds., *Colonial Latin America* (New York: Oxford University Press, 1990).

6. Seymour M. Lipset, *Political Man* (New York: Anchor, 1960); Richard Morse, "The Heritage of Latin America," in Louis Hartz, ed., *The Founding of New Societies: Studies in the History of the United States, Latin America, South Africa, Canada, and Australia* (New York: Harcourt Brace Jovanovich, 1964); Claudio Veliz, *The Centralist Tradition of Latin America* (Princeton, N.J.: Princeton University Press, 1980); and Veliz, *The New World of the Gothic Fox: Culture and Economy in English and Spanish America* (Berkeley: University of California Press, 1994).

7. On Peru, see Mark Thurner, *From Two Republics to One Divided: Contradictions of Postcolonial Nationmaking in Andean Peru* (Durham, N.C.: Duke University Press, 1997). I argue likewise for Uruguay, Colombia, and Argentina in *State Formation and Democracy*.

8. The culturalist perspective has long been disputed, especially in its extreme versions. Culturalist arguments shared common tenets with a venerable tradition in American politics and history that, from Toqueville to Hartz and Lipset, has also claimed that ethos and political culture best explain nation building. Cultural arguments about Latin and North America, however, differed in a very important aspect. In the case of the former, culturalists empowered Spanish culture with an iron grip over the development of the modern state and the political system. In the case of the latter, culturalists ascribed a much more creative and innovative character to the political culture emerging in the new soil.

9. Stanley J. Stein and Barbara H. Stein, *The Colonial Heritage of Latin America: Essays on Economic Dependence in Perspective* (Oxford: Oxford University Press, 1970).

10. The variables that shaped the state from this perspective are familiar: the dependent structure of the economy, the repressive use of labor, the type of labor force, the delayed timing and character of the insertion of Latin American economies into the world market, the concentration of land property in a few hands, the agrarian nature of the export sector, and so on.

11. Lindo-Fuentes, *Weak Foundations*.

12. For example, Robert G. Williams, *States and Social Evolution: Coffee and the Rise of National Governments in Central America* (Chapel Hill: University of North Carolina Press, 1994). To a point, Williams is rescuing dependency and world-system arguments that stress the impact of the expansion of the export economy on political institutions.

13. Mallon's *Peasant and Nation*, for instance, uses class conflict in a neo-Marxist fashion to talk about state making, with a focus on subaltern projects. In this sense, Thurner's *From Two Republics* could be placed close to Mallon's.

14. Nora Hamilton, *The Limits of State Autonomy: Post-revolutionary Mexico* (Princeton, N.J.: Princeton University Press, 1982). See the review of the literature on the Mexican state offered by Knight in this volume.

15. Dietrich Rueschemeyer, Evelyne Huber Stephens, and John D. Stephens, *Capitalist Development and Democracy* (Chicago: University of Chicago Press, 1992); Evelyne Huber Stephens, "Capitalist Development and Democracy in South America," *Politics and Society* 17 (1989): 247–80; Evelyne Huber and Frank Safford, eds., *Agrarian Structures and Political Power: Landlords and Peasants in the Making of Latin America* (Pittsburgh: University of Pittsburgh Press, 1995). For a critique of this approach, see the chapter by Samuel Valenzuela in this volume.

16. See Centeno, "Blood and Debt."

17. Exceptions, of course, exist. Authors, such as Bulmer-Thomas, who have decisively leaned toward political economy have purposely refrained from using culture or ideology in their thinking about the state. Victor Bulmer-Thomas, *The Economic History of Latin America since Independence* (Cambridge: Cambridge University Press, 1994).

18. Milton Vanger, *Jose Batlle y Ordonez of Uruguay: The Creator of His Times, 1902–1907* (Waltham, Mass.: Brandeis University Press, 1980); Vanger, *The Model Country: Jose Batlle y Ordonez of Uruguay, 1907–1915* (Waltham, Mass.: Brandeis University Press, 1980).

19. Nicolas Shumway, *The Invention of Argentina* (Berkeley: University of California Press, 1991). Shumway apparently makes this argument when interpreting the ideology of the military dictatorship in power in Argentina during the 1970s and early 1980s.

20. Francois-Xavier Guerra, *Modernidad e independencias: Ensayos sobre las revoluciones hispánicas* (Madrid: Editorial MAPFRE, 1992).

21. See, for instance, recent work on state building covering the 1870–1910 period in the River Plate region. Very serious structuralist historians, like José Pedro Barran, have turned their attention to cognitive processes and *historias de vida*. José Pedro Barran, *Historia de la sensibilidad en el Uruguay*, 2 vols. (Montevideo: Banda Oriental, 1990–93); José Pedro Barran and Benjamin Nahum, *Historia rural del Uruguay moderno*, 7 vols. (Montevideo: Banda Oriental, 1967–73). In essays written with Gerardo Caetano, both argue that *la vida privada* of the common citizen becomes the fundamental key to understanding institutions and politics. Gerardo Caetano and J. P. Barran, eds., *Sensibilidad sensualidad, e historias de vida en la transición a la modernidad* (Montevideo: Fin de Siglo, 1997).

22. Rafael Perez Torres, "National Identities and Notions of Otherness" (paper presented at the workshop on Immigration and the Working Poor, Center for Chicano and Latino Studies, University of California, Santa Barbara, March 1997).

23. German Carrera Damas, *Una nación llamada Venezuela* (Caracas: Monte Avila Editores, 1984); Damas, *Venezuela: Proyecto Nacional y Poder Social*

(Barcelona: Grijalbo, 1984); Charles Bergquist, *Coffee and Conflict in Colombia: 1886–1904* (Durham, N.C.: Duke University Press, 1978); Berquist, *Labor in Latin America: Comparative Essays on Chile, Argentina, Venezuela and Colombia* (Stanford, Calif.: Stanford University Press, 1986); Alvaro Tirado Mejia, *El estado y la politica en el siglo XIX* (Bogotá: El Ancora Editores, 1981).

24. Some important historical research has in fact argued for the importance of the earlier period of independence. Yet, in the final analysis, most historians adhered to the more established wisdom. See John Lynch, *The Spanish American Revolutions: 1808–1826* (New York: Norton, 1986); and Lynch, *Argentine Dictator: Juan Manuel de Rosas, 1829–1852* (Oxford: Clarendon Press, 1981).

25. This is especially true of the view of Latin American state making put forward in Rueschemeyer, Huber Stephens, and Stephens, *Capitalist Development and Democracy*.

26. Tilly, *Coercion, Capital, and European States*, 30; Tilly, *European Revolutions*, 31–32.

27. Michael Mann, *The Sources of Political Power*, vol. 1, *A History of Power from the Beginning to AD 1760* (Cambridge: Cambridge University Press, 1986).

28. Ibid., 28.

29. Tilly, *Coercion, Capital, and European States*, 51–66.

30. Indeed, as Schwartz has shown for Argentina, in the second half of the nineteenth century, landowners managed to transfer on to the state the absolute responsibility of the ongoing foreign debt. Herman Schwartz, *In the Dominions of Debt* (Ithaca, N.Y.: Cornell University Press, 1989).

31. Dependence on custom duties, of course, made governments extremely sensitive to disruptions in the prices of exports and imports. If customs were too high, the government could succumb to plain smuggling; if tariffs were too low, income plummeted.

32. This applies to the River Plate and to most other regions; El Salvador, for instance, seems to have been an extreme case. According to Lindo-Fuentes (*Weak Foundations*), during the nineteenth century, the state was able to collect only an extremely minimal revenue.

33. From the correspondence of Aparicio Saravia, letter to Nepomuceno Saavia, Los Duraznos Camp, September 11, 1902, Archivo Central de Las Fuerzas Armadas, Montevideo, Uruguay.

34. I use the term *state* as Collier and Collier do, that is, to designate the bureaucratic and legal institutions of the public sector and the incumbents of these institutions (Collier and Collier, *Shaping the Political Arena*, 789). This encompasses the government in the sense of the head of state and the immediate political leadership that surrounds the head of state, plus the public bureaucracy, the legislature, and the central army.

35. In Argentina and Uruguay, a number of immigrants were forced to serve in the militia under this or that general. The historical record shows both armies and guerrillas abducting, kidnapping, and forcing immigrants (and Creoles) to serve. But most of these foreigners could hardly be called professional mercenaries.

36. John Keegan, *A History of Warfare* (New York: Vintage, 1994), 20–21.

37. For an expansion on this point, see my essay "The Authoritarian Roots of

Liberalism: Uruguay, 1810–1845," in Peloso and Tenenbaum, *Liberals, Politics, and Power.*

38. The so-called Orden Conservador was born when Julio A. Roca (1880–86) succeeded Nicolás Avellaneda as president of the new Argentine Federation.

39. David Rock and Fernando López-Alves, "State Building and Political Systems in Late Nineteenth Century Argentina and Uruguay," *Past & Present,* forthcoming.

40. In 1880–81, Sir Horace Rumbold observed that "something of the yankee spirit of business is rapidly descending upon Argentine society . . . directing the energies of its politicians to more lucrative occupations than the party intrigues or barrack conspiracies." Rock and López-Alves, "State Building and Political Systems," 26

41. For a comparative analysis of army building and democracy in Europe, see Brian Downing, *The Military Revolution and Political Change: Origins of Democracy and Autocracy in Early Modern Europe* (Princeton, N.J.: Princeton University Press, 1992). See also my *Democracy and State Formation.*

Chapter Six

THE MODERN MEXICAN STATE:
THEORY AND PRACTICE

Alan Knight

CONCERTED EFFORTS to apply social theory to Latin American cases are surprisingly rare, especially in the field of history. When historians of Latin America deign to use theory, they tend to do so in a somewhat casual, ready-made way, sometimes, it seems, guided by passing fashion rather than practical utility. Dependency and structural Marxism have had their moments; today, subaltern studies is in vogue.[1] Political scientists, of course, have been more thorough and assiduous, canvassing a range of theories before plumping for whatever seems most suitable, fashionable, or conducive to getting tenure (e.g., rational actor models). Meanwhile, the grand synthesizers—those who eschew case studies in favor of ambitious cross-national, cross-temporal historical analyses (the only analyses that can really test general theories)—have rarely incorporated Latin America into their work: Mann, Giddens, Hall, Geertz, Tilly, Skocpol, and Barrington Moore say next to nothing about the continent (in which respect, of course, they follow in the footsteps of Marx, Weber, and Durkheim).[2] James Scott mentions it in passing; Benedict Anderson ventures one (interesting) chapter; Eric Wolf stands as a scintillating exception. Of the currently fashionable sources of historiographical inspiration, Foucault rejected grand theory anyway; E. P. Thomson was distinctly focused (some have said parochial) in his approach; while the subaltern logic of Ranajit Guha carries a strong parochial (if not ethnocentric) thrust.[3]

In short, with the possible exception of dependency, Latin America has neither produced an endogenous body of grand theory nor attracted much attention from grand theorists rooted elsewhere.[4] This book, in seeking to unite what is so often put asunder, is therefore performing a useful service; indeed, it may be that—shifting to a more topical metaphor—it has found a profitable market niche. For, given this relative neglect, one might expect the bright light of theory to illuminate some neglected corners of Latin American history, while that history, in turn, might help corroborate, qualify, or refute the grand theories that seek to straddle the globe.

The case I shall investigate—the Mexican state—is no doubt too narrow to offer serious corroboration, qualification, or refutation. Grand theory, by virtue of being grand, can live with exceptions, especially those that, like Mexico, are wont to vaunt their exceptionalism. But all countries and cases are exceptional;[5] hence any (negative) dissonance or (positive) congruence must give pause for thought. Therefore, if we encounter grand theory that "works" in the Mexican case, it is not only Mexicanists but also grand theorists who benefit; and, indeed, if we throw out grand theory that fails, we have at least helped clear the cluttered decks.

Given the richness and diversity of its history, Mexico offers plenty of grist to the mill of grand theory: early state formation; imperialism (pre-Columbian and Spanish); acculturation, ethnicity, and (proto-)nationalism; the articulation of modes of production; peasant (petty commodity?) production; revolution; dependency and "dependent development"; patrimonialism, populism, (bureaucratic) authoritarianism, hegemony, and democratization.[6] Each would repay further investigation, according to the rough terms of reference of this book. I avoided an obvious candidate—"revolution"—on the grounds, first, that I had written about it before and, second, that I was skeptical concerning its utility as an organizing concept for fruitful comparative analysis.[7] Some phenomena, I think, are too rare ("great revolutions") or sui generis (revolutionary causality) to permit meaningful comparisons. They are, in Eric Wolf's term, "just-so" stories, entirely amenable to narrative treatment or to individual analysis but resistant to broad cross-national, cross-temporal comparison.[8] Other explanations are different: they are more numerous and subject to certain patterned regularities: for example, industrialization (indeed, economic history may be a particularly appropriate field of serious comparative study)[9] and, the focus of this chapter, the state.

THEORIZING THE MEXICAN STATE

The state is the oldest problem in political theory; hence there is no shortage of theoretical texts. In addition, it is probably the oldest topic in Mexican "historiography," from the stelae of the Classic Maya to the equally monumental and didactic *Crónicas de la presidencia* of recent years. Hence the empirical data are overwhelming. Unfortunately, these two great torrents of literature have rarely mingled: promising titles—*Estado y lucha política en el México actual, El estado y los partidos políticos en México, Evolución del estado mexicano*[10]—tend to be empirical, even narrative, in style; highly Mexicanocentric in focus; and, to the extent that they engage with "theory," sweeping, assertive, and nonspecific. Hence concepts and categories proliferate: the Mexican state is, according to time and taste, bourgeois, exceptional, populist, patrimonial, Bonapartist, Caesarist, authoritarian, all-powerful, legitimate, "massified," and so on. All or none of these categories may be useful; however, it is often difficult to judge, since the categorization tends to be vague, unsubstantiated by either adequate empirical data or relevant theoretical citations.

This failing, of course, reflects a real difficulty. If we are to blend theory and data, we need to operate in two rather different mental universes: the rarefied world of theory, which recognizes no compelling frontiers; and the messy world of empirical (even archival) "facts"—a world of infinite complexity and, for the twentieth century at least, mind-boggling volume. Theory demands divergent thinking, empirical research convergent. The first results in "lumping," the second in splitting. We may, as fallible scholars, find ourselves distinctly out of sorts if we try to live at both levels (like tropical lowlanders who commute to the cold highlands, or highlanders who descend to the miasmal tropics). Certainly there is a constant tension between the empirical urge to split and the theoretical need to lump: the splitter (the historian) will constantly see exceptions to the general rule; the lumper (the theorist) will lose patience with a pernickety empiricism. Neither is necessarily "right": the most minute empiricist regularly "lumps," and the most high-flying theorist usually needs some intermittent contact with the empirical earth below.[11] It is a question, therefore, of balance: of framing the mass of empirical data, according to useful theory; and of selecting and refining theory in light of the empircal data, all within a spirit, one hopes, of Baconian skepticism.

What might such an approach tell us about the Mexican state, which has been the subject of such extensive comment? Theory is useful, I think, by way of providing organizing concepts; more specifically, it offers ways of organizing and analyzing data that may not be obvious, commonsensical, or straightforward.[12] A great many histories of Mexico (or anywhere else, for that matter) take the state for granted: roughly, it denotes the central government, the political apparatus—be it monarchical, imperial, democratic, totalitarian, or whatever. In the case of postrevolutionary Mexico, "the state" is often reduced pretty much to the federal executive, to the presidency, even—in anthropocentric style—to the president in Los Pinos himself.[13] "The state" is therefore a straightforward description; it denotes a political actor, the main player in Mexico's twentieth-century drama. To the extent that the identification is often personal or personalist (the president and his camarilla), further specification is hardly necessary, since people are definable individuals, the dramatis personae of the play.[14] However, theory—like science—reminds us that such commonsense approaches are fallible; it encourages us to look beyond people and appearances, to deeper structures and rationales. That is, it goes beyond description to focus on function: how things work and to what ends.[15]

However, one must beware of the ontological bases of such inquiry: some state theories, it seems to me, address state functions and goals in an appropriately objective (and "etic") fashion; that is, they try to explain the underlying rationale of *actual* states, in the real world. We might call this the *Aristotelian approach*. Other theories introduce a normative element: they are also—perhaps more—concerned with how states *ought* be. Such an approach, which we might term *Platonic*, has a long history; it is apparent, for example, in the organic/statist tradition, which exerts influence in Latin America;[16] some have imputed a normative/Platonic rationale to Marxism (i.e., to Marxist "critique" as opposed to Marxist "science"), though I do not consider this a relevant criticism.[17] My concern, as will become apparent, is with "objective," "Aristotelian" theory, not Platonic prescription. Like Hume, I think that a deep ditch should be dug between "is" and "ought," and that, for investigative purposes, we should stay on the "is" ("etic," "objective") side of this analytic divide.[18]

Thus, the various theories of the state, which might be usefully applied to the Mexican case, are concerned with state *functions*. Weber's state is conceived as an authority exercising a monopoly of violence over a given territorial area; and enjoying a measure of legitimacy (traditional, charismatic, or rational-legal).[19] Such a view is compatible with (but does not require) a liberal model of the state as a neutral arena, within which pluralist interests jockey for advantage.[20] The Weberian monopoly-of-violence criterion—being something of a lowest common denominator—is also compatible with (but obviously does not require) Marxist theories of the state, of which there is a bewildering variety.[21] Such (Marxist) theories may be usefully arrayed along a continuum that ranges from, at one extreme, the "agent" state (the state as the "committee for managing the common affairs of the whole bourgeoisie") to, at the other extreme, the relatively (very) autonomous state, with goals and interests distinct from the immediate interests of the bourgeoisie—or any other class.[22] Clearly, if this separation between state and ruling class becomes too great, if "relative" becomes "complete" autonomy, then the "Marxist" character of such a theory becomes questionable.

Indeed, the further in the direction of "relative autonomy" the state travels and the less it serves as a clear "agent" of class interests, the more it becomes amenable to rival theories, for which class and relations of production are at best secondary. From the Marxist perspective, "relative autonomy" is both a recognition of empirical reality (straightforward "agent" states being rather rarer than rigorous Marxists might have wished)[23] and also a refinement of theory: the state's "relative autonomy" is seen to reinforce long-term class interests at the expense of short-term; the state assumes a (relatively) autonomous role—as mediator, paterfamilias, social engineer, economic planner—thus benefiting the long-term survival and prosperity of the dominant class.[24] The state becomes responsible for externalities that individual capitalists (or feudal seigneurs) may be incapable of controlling. These externalities are various; hence, in part, the bewildering variety of "refined" Marxist theories of the state: the Gramscian tradition sees the state forging hegemony, avoiding a risky reliance on simple coercion; "structuralists" (e.g., Mandel, Poulantzas) incorporate this interpretation—of "the state . . . as a mediating body [serving] to preserve and enhance capitalist interests"—into a broader analysis that encompasses the state's economic-regulatory (as well as political-legitimating) role.[25]

While this may help toward an understanding of the complexity of the state, ancient and modern,[26] it carries some risks. First, like any functional thesis, it can degenerate into circular, unfalsifiable argument: whatever the state does is in the long-term interests of the dominant class. On this basis, historians have (I think wrongly) considered Cárdenas a deft manipulator of popular groups, hence an effective servant of bourgeois interests.[27] Ultimately, such an approach dismisses all social reforms or concessions to popular demands as farsighted stratagems designed to shore up the status quo: "things have to change in order that they stay the same."[28] Apart from being unfalsifiable—as well as often historically wrong—this approach implies a remarkable state omniscience, coupled with a no less remarkable popular gullibility.[29]

Second—and this may or may not be a source of concern—structuralist theory progressively parts company with Marx, certainly the confident and unequivocal Marx of the *Communist Manifesto*.[30] For, as we move along the continuum away from the "agent" state and toward the (very) autonomous state, we eventually enter different theoretical terrain: one in which class interests have become remote from state action (save—the ultimate disclaimer—"in the last instance"), and quite different rationales and causalities come to predominate (in every other instance).

At some point, therefore, we fall off the edge of the Marxist theoretical world and enter another universe. But there are various universes. If the state is "relatively autonomous" by virtue of juggling and reflecting conflicting sectional interests—without playing a decisive role itself—we find ourselves in a loosely liberal universe, populated by "night watchmen" states. If (more likely) we enter a universe where (very) autonomous states acquire independent interests, goals, and loyalties that are unrelated to class, we may detect a variety of alternative rationales. One

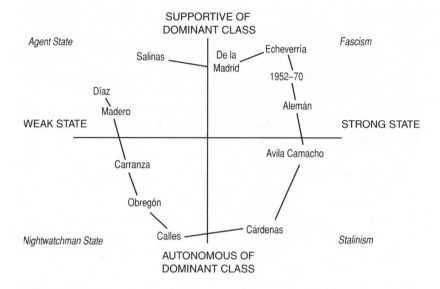

Figure 1.

fashionable version stresses the international environment: that Darwinian jungle of states which, by pressure of natural selection, forces states to compete, struggle, and develop (indeed, which may be responsible for the creation of a good many—"secondary"—states in the first place).[31] Thus, the old Prussian *primat der aussenpolitik* becomes a—the?—decisive factor, forging the state and shaping its character. Recent theorists, committed to "bringing the state back in," seem to be attracted to this—what we might call the Prussian—model,[32] as are some theorists of revolution, such as Skocpol, for whom great power rivalry bulks larger in their explanatory system than domestic social conflict.[33] Skocpol's thesis does not work for the Mexican Revolution, however;[34] and the relevance of the Prussian model for Mexican state building is both limited and ambiguous. Given its location ("so far from God and so near the United States"), Mexico could not realistically enter a regional arms race; indeed, Mexican military spending—both Porfirian and postrevolutionary—has been low, by Latin American standards.[35] The louring presence of the United States certainly alarmed Mexican statesmen and conditioned Mexican state building. Nationalist mobilization (e.g., March 1938) was one possible outcome; but the structural consequence of Mexico's geopolitical location was, more usually, conservative and capital-friendly. It deterred radical démarches and helped impose certain "limits to state autonomy," in the 1930s and again in the 1970s.[36] In particular, the existence of a long, porous border made exchange controls impossible and

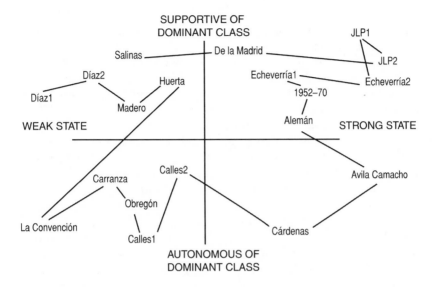

Figure 2.

facilitated capital flight, thus placing a powerful weapon in the hands of Mexican capitalists, which they successfully deployed in opposition to hostile administrations like Echeverría's.[37] Geopolitical logic thus made for a *less* autonomous, distinctly *un*-Prussian, state even if, politically, it favored incumbents, most egregiously with the Prinosaurian practice of "patriotic fraud."[38]

A more promising variant of this approach is put forward by Charles Tilly, for whom (modern, European) states emerge as a result of complex "protection rackets," whereby states offer societies guarantees against threats both at home and abroad: the former emanating, for example, from hostile social groups (including classes), the latter from aggressive rival states in the international arena.[39] Tilly's protection racket state—the state as mafia writ large—is a specific version of McNeill's yet grander theory of human "macroparasitism," whereby states and their associated elites are seen as feeding off their host societies, gratifying their particularist interests, providing few reciprocal benefits but, at the very least, abstaining from eating their host to death.[40] Again, though the model emerges from a wide sweep of history, its application to twentieth-century states (including Mexico's) seems plausible: it represents, after all, an organic counterpart of the rational-choice model of rent seeking (the states as a rent-seeking agency, exploiting a monopoly position). In the Mexican case, the *external* protection racket is, as I have already said, somewhat implausible; at best, only die-hard PRIístas believe—or believed—that the Partido Revolucionario Institucional (PRI) alone stands between Mexico and U.S. domination. *Domestic* protection is another matter. Though it may seem to resemble rational state agency—the state protecting the interests of the dominant class against subordinate resistance—the emphasis is rather different: it implies a relatively autonomous state, committed to its own survival and profit, selling protection to the highest bidder, even generating threats in pursuit of payoffs. This is not a rational "agent" state in thrall to the dominant class; if, in practice, it is the dominant class that pays for and gets protection, this merely reflects the logic of resources; like the Chicago gangster who, when asked why he robbed banks, replied, "because that's where the money is," so the mafioso state, like the Mafia itself, is bound to "protect" the rich because they are the ones with the money to buy protection.[41] But the relationship is necessarily arbitrary, discretionary, to a degree personalized. Protection is not transparent taxation. Furthermore, it requires some recurrent "threats": of popular insurgence from below or state aggression from above. It not hard to find warm assent to the notion that the PRIísta state constitutes a parasitic body, a political mafia—in Hansen's provocative phrase, "cosa nuestra."[42] Nor is it difficult to find historical examples of mafia-style protection, of discretionary "aggression" against private interests (e.g., expropriations), or of official support for popular mobilization (e.g., strikes and land seizures), which, from this theoretical standpoint, represent not so much high-minded populism as hardheaded "protection."[43]

Given the several overlaps and conceptual kinships that appear, it is possible to present a very rough schema which embodies several of the modal types, organized around two axes: (1) an east-west axis that corresponds, respectively, to a strong, relatively autonomous, usually bureaucratic, state at one extreme and a weak, puny state, lacking extensive power or autonomy at the other; and (2) a north-south axis denoting, respectively, a state serving dominant class interests and a state relatively emancipated from such interests, that is, one that is *either* neutral *or*—though this is unlikely—acting in the interests of subordinate classes. (Inasmuch as the state's relationship to the dominant class is crucial, class relationships are crucial too, and they certainly cannot be inferred from or reduced to state agency. In other words, class constitutes a key independent variable. I develop this point later, albeit briefly).

In terms of this schema, depicted in Figures 1 and 2, each quadrant is occupied by a recognizable ideal type: a relatively modest "agent state," closely controlled by dominant class interests, in the northwest quadrant; a liberal night watchman (or similarly weak, neutral state) in the southwest; a powerful reformist, revolutionary, or (possibly) "organic-statist" state in the southeast;[44] and a "stucturalist"/relatively autonomous state—deploying its autonomous power in the *broad* interest of the dominant class—in the northeast. To add some further refinements: a Leninist/Stalinist ("state socialist/state capitalist") regime would be due east, on the outer margins of the map, reflecting the fact that the state autonomy had, in this case, eclipsed the class order or re-created a new hierarchy under state auspices;[45] fascist regimes would be located in the northeast quadrant, "traditional" clerical/conservative regimes (such as Díaz's) in the northwest, and "bureaucratic-authoritarian" regimes somewhere in between.[46] Locations are, of course, fluid; regimes rarely remain in one place for long periods; movement may depend on external shocks or internal struggles among regime factions.[47] Certain movements seem logical, even predictable. Modern states have often tracked from west to east, acquiring additional autonomous, bureaucratic powers;[48] however, assumptions of unilinearity are clearly risky and highly vulnerable to historical reversals, whether individual or collective.[49] Revolutions are classic (individual) reversals: successful revolutions typically drag states briefly and dramatically into the southwest quadrant (the home of weak states, lacking clear class alignment), then—as Skocpol emphasizes—propel them rapidly to the east, in the direction of bureaucracy, autonomy, and ambitious social engineering.[50] A "great" revolution may even be defined in such terms: a sharp southwesterly movement (Tilly's phase of "multiple sovereignty"), followed by a more gradual trek due east, in the case of socialist revolutions (those that expropriate the bourgeoisie), or to the northeast, in the case of "bourgeois" revolutions that eventually achieve a stable union of state and bourgeoisie.[51] This last trajectory was, I argue, the path taken by the Mexican state after 1940.

When the "successful" revolutionary state enters the northeast quadrant, it finds itself in mixed company. For here—in the home of the relatively autonomous "structuralist" state—we encounter the epistemological problems mentioned earlier. The state appears to be strong, autonomous, and even interventionist; it may boast a big army and a swollen payroll (Marx's "enormous bureaucracy, well-gallooned and well-fed").[52] But, despite this ostensible autonomy, it remains in some sense the servant of the dominant class, whose long-term interests it guarantees, even at the expense of short-term sacrifices. The relative autonomy of such states is notoriously hard to gauge, since, by virtue of protecting dominant class interests, they align with the strong and tend to use state power against the weak (i.e., against subalterns). Given this bias, they do not usually put their ostensible autonomy to the acid test: that of bullying strong elites, rather than weak subalterns. However, there are revealing exceptions: Hitler's cavalier treatment of German big business or Pinochet's shakedown of Chilean private enterprise.[53] Conversely, the vaunted autonomy of the Mexican state looked somewhat superficial when, after years of "extended coincidence of interest" between government and the private sector, Echeverría briefly broke ranks and tried—but failed—to impose his will on the private sector in the early 1970s.[54]

This chapter seeks to locate the Mexican state—in its successive guises—within this simple schema. However, three additional clarifications are required: these concern (1) the character of the dominant class, (2) legitimacy, and (3) the definition and disaggregation of "the state." The first two can be dealt with briefly, the third is more complicated.

First, as already mentioned, the question of class alignments is important. It would be difficult to relate a given state to "the dominant class" if no such class existed. The north-south axis of the schema therefore carries implications about class relations as well as the state. The point is particularly significant in that the Mexican state is the product of a major social revolution, in which class antagonisms played a central role. Lack of space precludes any detailed analysis of the revolution's class origins and outcome, but the story can be briefly summarized—and, indeed, needs to be, since class and state are intimately connected through the long *trayectoría* of the Mexican Revolution. Porfirian Mexico came close to being a society run by landlords for the benefit of landlords.[55] Law, taxation, tariffs, political power, and social control all served the landlord interest.[56] If "oligarchic" Latin America is seen, *grosso modo*, as a society possessing a clear dominant class—landed oligarchs—then Mexico is a particularly good example of this type.[57] The revolution of 1910–20 did not destroy the landed class, but it decisively weakened that class and set in train a process of official reform and—no less important—unofficial social change, both of which further undermined landlord dominance.[58] The period 1920–40 is therefore ambiguous, or transitional: noteworthy less for the overweening power of the infant revolutionary state than for the progressive senescence of the Porfirian landed oligarchy. If the revolutionary state was "relatively autonomous," its autonomy derived as much from oligarchic decline as from state aggrandizement.[59] Meanwhile, the relationship of state to society was necessarily uncertain and ambiguous (as compared with the old class certitudes of the Porfiriato). Some "revolutionaries" sought détente with—even membership in—a reconstituted oligarchy. Some (e.g., Calles) favored liberal reform, culminating in a progressive, capitalist, perhaps Jacobin, republic. Some—Cárdenas, Múgica, Tejeda, Lombardo Toledano—sought to go further, espousing varieties of "socialism." As the Mexican state marched into the southeast quadrant of my schema, its final destination was uncertain: the first group favored a brisk about-face, leading to renewed oligarchic rule (an unlikely outcome, especially since the debacle of the Huerta regime in 1913–14); the second, conforming to the broad guidelines of bourgeois revolution, preferred a more circuitous route, which would take the state through relative autonomy toward a fresh alliance with a new (bourgeois, industrial) dominant class;[60] the third hoped to linger longer in the southeastern quadrant of state autonomy, disembarrassed of a dominant class, whether landed/oligarchic or bourgeois/industrial, promoting the *rectoría* of the state and some sort of socially just class equilibrium.[61] This third group were not Leninists, still less Stalinists, but they are as close as any major Mexican leaders have got to these distant "eastern" outriders. However, the third group lost, while the second group won. Their victory did not, however, usher in transparent bourgeois democracy; rather, the political carapace of Mexican industrial capitalism after the 1940s was a form of "inclusionary authoritarianism," of which more later.[62]

Such a class analysis may seem crude, and, certainly, it requires further refinement. As I note later, Mexico's regional variation produced contrasting outcomes over space as well as time: "dominant classes" in, say, Yucatán and Sonora were distinct. Dominant classes also display sectoral variations: some might choose to differentiate between, say, Porfirian and postrevolutionary landowners in *sectoral* rather than *class* terms.[63] In conclusion, I shall also suggest that the period since 1982 has seen a realignment of Mexican capitalism, with small and medium-sized national business giving ground to large, transnational capital. Important though these distinctions are, however, they are not crucial to the broad argument presented here, which concerns the state and its relationship to dominant classes (or, if you prefer, dominant sectors within classes).

A second clarification: this schema does not embody legitimacy, "the axial principle of the polity," in Bell's words, and a concept much in vogue in discussions of the modern Mexican state.[64] The schema seeks to depict state autonomy—the capacity of the state to achieve what Mann calls despotic power over society.[65] But despotic power does not necessarily imply legitimacy (even though some despotic regimes may have enjoyed real measures of legitimacy: e.g., Nazi Germany and Stalin's Soviet Union). Conversely, some weak states—states with limited will or capacity to dominate society "despotically"—have enjoyed undoubted legitimacy: Hapsburg New Spain, for example. If three-dimensional graphics were possible, a notional legitimacy axis could be added to the schema. However, it would be difficult, and probably illusory, to attempt such a measurement, even if it were technically possible. For—as I shall suggest—the legitimacy of the Mexican state remains something of a mystery. Like a good many social scientific concepts, it defies precise measurement and can only be evaluated, with any confidence, in extreme conditions, for which survey data are superfluous. We can make some reasonably safe comparative statements either cross-nationally (e.g., the Swedish state is more legitimate than the Zairean) or, sometimes, cross-temporally (e.g., the Porfirian regime was less legitimate in 1910 than it had been in 1890 or than the "revolutionary regime" would be in 1960). Such statements can—unusually—be backed by a wealth of "impressionistic" evidence. But precisely because the cases are extreme and unusual, the conclusions are fairly trivial. More interesting, but more difficult, would be "close" comparisons between, say, the contemporary democratic regimes of Chile, Argentina, and Brazil; or between the Mexican state in 1930 and 1940, or 1970 and 1990. But plotting such shifts in legitimacy is almost impossible; we lack appropriate survey data (even if such data were to be conclusive, which I doubt); and we cannot confidently infer attitudes and relationships either from political behavior or (as James Scott has reminded us) from public declarations.[66] Even the survival of a regime in the relative absence of overt coercion is not conclusive proof of legitimacy: compliance and consent are different commodities; and, as the 1910 revolution revealed, illegitimate regimes can maintain an image of "legitimacy"—based, for example, on popular memory of old repression, slick public relations, the "dull compulsion of economic relations," and, perhaps, the "naturalization" of state power, that is, the belief that there is no real alternative.[67] Thus, plotting the trajectory of a state's legitimacy is notoriously difficult: witness the frequency with which Mexico has, allegedly, experienced major ("legitimation"?) crises, from the 1960s down to the 1990s.[68] Yet the regime survives, not unchanging or unchallenged, but still in being.

"Legitimacy" also raises the problem of definition, which in turn obliges us to disaggregate.[69] Whose legitimacy is at issue? Regimes—even "simple," "traditional" regimes—are composites. Early modern monarchies—including that of New Spain—comprised crown, church, and orders/estates. Though it would be appropriate to distinguish institutionally between church and state, it would be misleadingly formalistic to ignore the church when considering "the state," since clerics governed, dispensed justice, and exerted a powerful ideological influence in daily (secular) life. Precisely for these reasons the power-hungry Bourbon state sought to clip clerical (especially Jesuit) wings; and, in doing so, it set the agenda for the liberal and Jacobin anticlericals of republican Mexico. By the time of the revolution, the church was firmly excluded from government, and, indeed, the state sought to build a secular legitimacy at the expense of clerical power—political and ideological. (Note that we can readily *discern* attempts to *build* legitimacy; it is evaluating the *success* of these efforts that remains tricky.) If, however, the "two swords" had now given way to one—for the secular state would brook no rival in its exercise of power—this did not make the secular state a simple monolith. On the contrary, the revolutionary state was a shifting mélange of interests, embracing president and central executive; a central legislature (which enjoyed a real independence in the 1920s);[70] a fractious military (only gradually tamed during the 1920s and 1930s) and a plethora of durable paramilitary organizations (*defensas sociales, guardias blancas*); powerful regional caudillos and their camarillas, who contested for provincial power and office, while keeping a wary eye on the center; local caciques, the "linkmen" between state and people, usually—though not invariably—holders of official posts, but whose power derived less from formal office than from the informal realities of caciquismo; and the burgeoning mass organizations—*sindicatos*, peasant leagues, *ejidos*, political parties—which sharply distinguished revolutionary from Porfirian politics, and which provided much of the raw material of state, caudillo, and cacique power.[71]

Where, within this shifting mélange, was the state? To reduce the state to the central executive would be arbitrary and, especially for the pre-1940 period, anachronistic; for the powers of the presidency were still in the making (witness the ouster of Ortiz Rubio).[72] Even after 1940, as presidentialism was consolidated, the powers of the president were less sure and sweeping than often supposed: presidents faced defeats and humiliations (Echeverria with his abortive tax reform, López Portillo with his doglike defense of the peso);[73] successful presidents were, perhaps, those who exercised power with restraint, who did not test the limits of presidential autonomy to the limit (e.g., Ruiz Cortines or López Mateos). If, in general, the power of the presidency has tended to increase (Cárdenas's defeat of Calles, the *jefe máximo*, was clearly a landmark), the relative weight of other components of the state has fluctuated. The military dominated politics in the 1920s, then went into rapid decline; recently, however, there have been clear signs of a resurgence of military influence, linked to Chiapas, the challenge of the Ejército Popular Revolucionario (EPR), and drug trafficking.[74] Throughout the long sweep of postrevolutionary history, however, paramilitary forces have remained important, particularly in rural areas. Sometimes, these forces occupied official niches: the *defensas sociales* of the 1920s, the armed *agraristas* of the 1930s. Though they did not behave with the punctilious rectitude of the Prussian guards,[75] they served at the orders of recognizable state incumbents, including powerful governors like Cedillo and Tejeda.[76] Some paramilitary groups lacked any such official status; they were private *pistoleros*, hacienda *guardias blancas*. But before we cast such undesirables into the outer limbo of "unofficial" darkness, far from the Weberian paradise of "legitimate violence," we should recall that they, too, often served official interests: Gonzalo N. Santos, a masterly exponent of Mexican politics, ensconced for decades at the heart of the Mexican state, had a busy team of *pistoleros*, as did many lesser caciques who enjoyed formal political office (e.g., as *diputados* or *presidentes municipales*).[77] And, in more general "functional" terms, such paramilitaries played a role in the enforcement of the state's will. Who ordered the *halcones* to attack demonstrators in Mexico City on Corpus Christi in 1971? Who shot Manuel Buendía, not to mention José Francisco Ruiz Massieu?[78] By their very nature, such events remain murky. But to ignore them, and to assume that their perpetrators have no links to the state (broadly defined), is like arguing that the clandestine activities of the CIA have no relationship to the U.S. government.[79] Either way—whether political violence reflects covert state coercion on the one hand or thoroughly freelance repression on the other—the state's supposed monopoly of legitimate violence is seriously compromised: for in the first instance the violence is clearly illegitimate, and in the second it rudely infringes the state's monopoly.

The question of mass organizations, though somewhat more transparent, is also tricky. The relationship of the official party to the state is an old conundrum.[80] What is clear is that the two have coexisted in close symbiosis. For most of the period, selection as a PRI candidate—for mayor, governor, congressman, president—was tantamount to election; hence, political conflicts centered around PRI "elections" (in the 1930s these were quite boisterous; later, they were centralized and state-managed; but the potential for internal conflict remained).[81] As party discipline solidified during the 1950s, patronage was distributed among the corporate sectors of the party, which embraced unions (the CTM), peasants (the CNC), and so-called "popular organizations" (CNOP). The PRI was not the sole party, but it was the *partido del estado*; it supplied the great bulk of state incumbents, at all levels, and it enjoyed privileged access to state resources—for electoral expenses, media subsidies, and pork-barrel public works. Even in today's more "transparent" politics, these advantages remain, reinforced by a host of state and parastatal agencies and programs (COPLAMAR, INFONAVIT, CONASUPO, Pronasol, Procampo).[82] State and party therefore remain incestuously intertwined; the legitimacy of the state became inseparable from the legitimacy of the party. (In this respect, Mexico stands somewhere between classic "pluralist" democracies—where the transient unpopularity of incumbents does not usually compromise the legitimacy of the state—and the one-party regimes of Eastern Europe, where state and party fused, and the two stood and fell together. Hence a pertinent question is whether the eventual fall of the PRI will resemble a pluralist change of party—which leaves the state intact—or will, instead, involve an Eastern European scenario, of simultaneous party and state collapse/transformation).

At any rate, any discussion of the Mexican state must take into account its mass base: a base that, while it might derive in part from a diffuse, incalculable "legitimacy," depends a great deal more—I would argue—on specific rewards and sanctions, dispensed by a mighty engine of state patronage, which reaches beyond political camarillas to local communities. This argument is not usually amenable to quantitative proof. Cartoons may speak louder than questionnaires. But, in the recent case of Pronasol, correlations between state patronage and electoral payoffs are clear.[83] Such a form of politicking is eminently durable and fungible. It does not fade with time—as memories of the revolution do.[84] It can be recurrently revived and repackaged. Though it demands state resources, and is therefore affected by fiscal cycles, it can acquire additional clout precisely in times of austerity, when, even if patronage declines, need is greatest; hence a little patronage goes a long way. It can work in cities as well as villages, in "modern" as well as "traditional" societies. It helps explain the survival—despite recurrent reports of his demise—of that classic Mexican figure, the cacique.[85] For, here too it would be naively formalistic to make a rigorous distinction between state and party, between formal officeholders and informal power brokers, between elected officials, bureaucrats, and caciques. They go together, forming complementary pillars of the Mexican "Great Arch," analogous to Britain's eighteenth-century "Old Corruption."[86]

Over time, it is generally asserted, central (executive, presidential) power grew at the expense of local, provincial, caudillo power. *Grosso modo*, that is clearly true. In the 1920s, the fragile government of Obregón had to defer to provincial political interests (indeed, the government was *built* on a series of center-periphery political pacts); it needed its local linkmen—like Gabriel Barrios in the Sierra de Puebla—who could mesh national and local political elites, and their mass respective followings.[87] Regional caudillos bulked large in national politics throughout the 1920s and 1930s: Osornio in Querétaro; Tejeda in Veracruz; Zuno in Jalisco; Cedillo in San Luis. Over time, it is true, power shifted toward the "center." Caudillo insurrection proved increasingly quixotic, even suicidal (compare Cedillo's valor in 1938 and Almazán's discretion in 1940). The decline of armed challenges should not, however, be taken as proof of the decline of provincial political power. Smart caudillos changed their style: as violence receded—and as the revolutionary generation became older, richer, fatter, sicker—so they espoused a more pacific, civilian, entrepreneurial brand of politics. The "new" provincial caudillos were exemplified by political fixers like Portes Gil in Tamaulipas or political entrepreneurs like Abelardo Rodríguez in Sonora, both of whom rose, briefly, to the presidency. The change was typified by the switch from Cedillo to Santos in San Luis; or by the generational mutations in the Figueroa family of Guerrero.[88] Even where the names remained—and durable Porfirian oligarchs survived[89]—they did so by virtue of adjusting to the new system, one in which an increasingly civilian, centralized, "massified" regime prevailed. But the absence of violent challenges should not lead us to an exaggerated evaluation of central state power. The revolutionary state was certainly consolidated, and smart caudillos learned to work with it, even within it (as Cárdenas realized but Tejeda, apparently, did not). But the state, too, made concessions. Provincial caudillos like Portes Gil enjoyed a wealth of local power and patronage, and could successfully juggle regional and national interests to their own advantage.[90] Powerful caudillos—albeit clever, calculating civilian caudillos—like Yocupicio could defy a powerful president like Cárdenas.[91] Coalitions of state governors could exert a clear influence on the presidential succession.[92]

During the postwar era, as a new generation took power, committed to a new(ish) project of industrialization, the centralization of political power no doubt accelerated, and the balance of forces between the central executive and provincial political interests tipped further in favor of the former.[93] Even during the heyday of the Pax PRIísta, however, provincial interests such as the Atlacomulco group remained powerful; if the authority of the central government went apparently unchallenged, this partly reflected the fact that the policies of the central government were acceptable to—and probably influenced by—provincial interests. Provincial business may have been excluded from the corporate institutions of the PRI; but, since those institutions were not exactly reliable channels of representation, the exclusion may not have rankled. Conversely, business interests (notably but not exclusively the Monterrey Group) had ways of making their views heard and respected. At the local, municipal level, too, the period after 1940 seems to have resulted in a political recovery by— we could loosely call it—the provincial bourgeoisie: in the Huasteca, Hidalgo, los Altos de Jalisco, and elsewhere.[94] The stable, centralized rule of the PRI, during its not-so-long heyday,[95] thus rested on a series of tacit deals and trade-offs; this ostensibly bulky, Bonapartist state, survived and prospered in large measure because it incorporated a range of interests— especially vested, propertied, interests—and because it did not choose to deploy its executive power in opposition to those interests. Business, in particular, got a good deal: low taxes, high tariffs, subsidies, credits, and public works (e.g., irrigation); the orthodox pro-business "bankers' alliance," Maxfield argues, had a lockhold on economic policy from the 1950s through the 1970s.[96] Mexican big business, it seems, enjoyed a closer and cozier relationship with Mexico's "revolutionary" regime than its Brazilian counterpart did with the Brazilian state; for an acute critic like Roger Bartra, Mexico came to possess "the most highly perfected bourgeois state machinery in Latin America."[97] While intrabourgeois, sectoral differences no doubt counted, these were secondary to the "mutually beneficial partnership," the "extended coincidence of interest," which united the state and the bourgeoisie as a whole during the heyday of the PRI.[98] The latter provided a capacious umbrella under which a variety of elites—entrepreneurial, syndical, bureaucratic—could huddle in cozy and comfortable collusion. The state enjoyed a degree of autonomy—it was not a mere agent of the bourgeoisie—but it used its autonomy sparingly, conservatively, and with due regard for capitalist interests: dispensing modest doses of social reform, emitting a constant stream of "legitimizing" rhetoric.[99] On those few occasions when the state flexed its Bonapartist muscles to the potential detriment of vested interests, it met with scant success: profit sharing failed; tax reform was compromised away; and, of course, Madrazo's political *apertura* soon closed.[100]

Meanwhile, the role of mass organizations atrophied. I do not subscribe to the view that the new mass organizations of the 1920s and 1930s were mere instruments of elite manipulation: this, as I have said, is a gross exaggeration of the power of the infant revolutionary state. *Sindicatos*, peasant leagues, and political parties (of which there were eight thousand during the 1920s) were to a real degree independent of the central government, and they embodied a measure of popular power. However, they also served the interests of provincial caudillos and local caciques who, in a context of continued sociopolitical flux, could champion popular cases from motives that were self-interested as well as sincere.[101] Class struggles—which were intense during the period—were bound up with the center-periphery struggle. In Yucatán, Oaxaca, and Chiapas, landlords still represented the closest thing to a "dominant class," and landlord power was linked to an autonomist project, directed against a federal government that was seen as distant, alien, threatening, and radical. Hence the proconsular expeditions of the years 1910–20 and the episodes of landlord reaction in the southeast, which were finally quelled by the 1930s.[102] In the center-west, where the revolutionary state faced its most violent challenge—the Cristiada—religious struggle also carried sociopolitical implications: while the Cristeros were not the simpleminded shock troops of reaction which they were labeled, they did conspire in a broadly regionalist, autonomist, and conservative resistance to "the revolution," which was, understandably, seen as alien, atheistic, and intrusively authoritarian.[103] Both forms of resistance—the secular landlord reaction of the southeast and the clerical opposition of the center-west—were part defeated, part co-opted. Their outright defiance of the revolutionary state failed: the Cristeros surrendered, the landlords of Chiapas and Yucatán shed their latifundia and relinquished coercive labor systems.[104] But the respective provincial elites survived, on new and different terms. They learned to coexist with the state and even to colonize its agencies, thus securing political access (direct and indirect) as well as economic benefits. Yucatán's henequen planters were no longer a "Divine Caste," but they retained—or recovered—a major role in henequen production, albeit within a context of close government regulation.[105] Throughout rural Mexico, local elites were able to colonize federal agencies like the SARH, DICONSA, and CONASUPO.[106]

A similar transformation affected mass revolutionary organizations. Independent challenges to the regime were seen to fail: witness the debacle of Tejeda's *agraristas*.[107] Like their caudillo and cacique masters, the revolutionary rank and file—*agraristas, ejidatarios*, trade unionists, party members—settled for compromise and compliance. They had received some tangible benefits during the years of reform—especially during the mid-1930s[108]—and, while these did not lead them into docile subservience, it did create subtle (and some not-so-subtle) forms of control, which curtailed popular militancy. The *ejido* was a contingent (hence revocable) land grant; *ejidatarios* needed credit; trade unionists depended on the CTM and the Juntas de Conciliacion y Arbitraje if they were to protect themselves, especially during the hard, inflationary 1940s. But did this barrage of pacts, deals, and partial surrenders imply a durable popular legitimacy? Did popular hearts beat faster every time the president commemorated the anniversary of the revolution? Did the vast array of revolutionary speeches, slogans, myths, and anniversaries display and reinforce an ideological hegemony, the basis of Mexico's strong state and enviable political stability?[109]

Should we ditch Marx and Weber and turn to Clifford Geertz as a theoretical guide to Mexican state formation?[110] I have my doubts. During the heyday of revolutionary reformism and popular mobilization—roughly, 1910 to 1940—such affective allegiances were certainly constructed, not least through the medium of popular caciques and caudillos: Tejeda and Cárdenas, Primo Tapia and Erasto Urbina.[111] The struggles they led, which were, in some measure, crowned with success, established a form of revolutionary legitimacy; but this was a *focused* legitimacy that linked specific social groups, via their struggles, to specific leaders, programs, and organizations. Cárdenas was unusual by virtue of mobilizing widely, knitting a host of causes into a loose, transient Cardenista coalition;[112] most mobilizing-and-legitimizing leaders, in contrast, operated at the level of the state (Tejeda) or the community/region (Tapia). Meanwhile, precisely because such struggles were bitter, often violent, zero-sum games, there were losers as well as winners—not to mention bemused spectators, anxious to avoid the crossfire. The great *reparto* in the Laguna (1936) gratified the insurgent *agraristas* but dispossessed the landowners ("the revolution giveth and the revolution taketh away," as one victim, General Eulogio Ortiz, put it, in so many words).[113] Similarly, every local inroad of the CTM alarmed the Monterrey Group or the conservative interests linked to Yocupicio in Sonora; every advance of "socialist education" horrified Catholics in Jalisco and the Bajío. A basic political mechanics prevailed: revolutionary "conquests" won adherents to the cause but also provoked equal and opposite reactions; and since, unlike Stalin, Mexico's revolutionaries did not usually liquidate their class enemies, the latter lived to fight another day—or, at the very least, lived to deny the state the deep and pervasive "revolutionary" legitimacy it sought.

The turbulent politics of 1938–40—a time of rumored coups, fears of civil war, marching *Sinarquistas*, and, in culmination, a dirty and contentious presidential election—illustrated the weakness of revolutionary hegemony.[114] Pockets of affective allegiance (e.g., the Laguna) were offset by rival pockets of profound hostility (León, Monterrey); and both, one suspects, were outnumbered by broad swathes of relative indifference, of uncommitted opinion, or grudging compliance. After 1940, I further suspect, the two antagonistic camps gradually shrank: as reform lost momentum, the popular constituency lost faith or looked elsewhere (to Lombardismo, the Communist Party, or to antistate leftist groups, which alleged that the state had betrayed the revolution); while the Right came to terms with a more moderate, pro-business, regime that conciliated the church, befriended the United States, and espoused cold war politics. The extremes shrank; the broad center expanded; the ruling party (PRM/PRI) became less an agent of genuine reform than a front for assorted political and economic interests that conducted their political battles (Laswell's who gets what, when, how)[115] in more discreet, even surreptitious, fashion. Smoke-filled rooms, fixed elections, and sporadic (often orchestrated) mobilizations replaced the overt, rambunctious, and polarized politics of the 1930s.[116] Strong affective allegiances weakened or (take the case of the Laguna *ejidatarios*) were channeled into independent dissidence. For some, the myths and promises of the revolution counted—and perhaps still count—but the "revolutionary" state progressively relinquished its claim to be their true repository and representative;[117] hence, perhaps, Mexico's schizoid political culture, which combined optimistic faith in the revolution with hard-bitten suspicion of the "revolutionary" state's officials.[118]

Though the official party could count on a measure of popular support, the most impressive popular movements of the post-1940 period came from outside its ranks: Sinarquismo, Henriquismo, Navismo; the *ferrocarrileros*, electricians, and students. The legitimacy of the regime, at best a "thin" legitimacy,[119] depended on its daunting monopoly of national power, its vast reservoir of patronage, and its calculating combination of sporadic reform and surgical repression. These were more than adequate means to maintain a stable political system, especially during a period (c. 1954–68) when, for both exogenous and endogenous reasons, brisk economic growth and low inflation combined. It was in these years, rather than in the turbulent 1930s, that a kind of bland populism—the PRI wrapped in the tricolor, promising all things to all men and women—came to prevail.

The fact that growth was sustained and living standards rose helped maintain this "thin" legitimacy—the legitimacy born of quasi-prescription, of the perception that "there is no alternative." A negative demonstration effect probably helped: a glance at the rest of Latin America yielded few attractive alternatives. The Cuban Revolution scared Mexicans more than it inspired them; conservatives found reassurance in Mexico's "perfect dictatorship."[120] The Left, meanwhile, took comfort from Mexico's civilian, mildly nationalist regime, which contrasted with Central American Sultanism or South American bureaucratic authoritarianism.[121] But I doubt that the impressive stability of the political system denoted strong, pervasive, affective allegiance to the revolution, still less to a regime that, while claiming a revolutionary birth, seemed increasingly dedicated to denying its paternity. To the old revolutionary/nationalist/Lombardista Left (a faction whose ideological contortions did not exactly inspire confidence),[122] the regime was at best a pale imitation of its Cardenista predecessor. To the old Right—clerical and/or entrepreneurial—the regime, though tolerable, was distasteful and worryingly prone to occasional fits of reformist delirium: with Echeverría's *reparto* in 1976 or López Portillo's bank nationalization in 1982. Measures such as these, which reminded leftists with long memories of the regime's reformist and nationalist past, may have renewed popular support among the old "revolutionary" constituencies; but, at the same time, they alarmed the Right and provoked political and economic reactions: capital flight, press criticism, bourgeois defections to the Partido Acción Nacional (PAN), all of which proved effective restraints on state autonomy.[123]

A roughly similar pattern—years of broadly conservative government punctuated by sporadic popular insurgencies and calculated concessions—seems to characterize certain states and regions: caciques came and went in cycles (cycles that, incidentally, did not follow any clear national pattern); movements of civic opposition achieved short-term results but failed to change the system as a whole.[124] Indeed, at the local level, state autonomy would seem to be *least* apparent, the domination of the local bourgeoisie most crude and "unmediated." Since about 1940, local caciques and elites have usually lacked the will or the capacity to promote genuine reform and redistribution, and hence the latter have tended to derive from federal initiatives: from rural education through *indigenismo* (INI) to CONASUPO and Pronasol. Such programs may be resisted or captured by local caciques and elites, but they cannot be initiated. In gross theoretical terms, the federal government displays greater autonomy of dominant class interests; hence, if survey data are to be believed, it has maintained—at least until recently—a somewhat cleaner image.[125]

But the difference is relative and has probably declined in recent years. The notion of a relatively autonomous (central) state, sagely governing in the broader interests of capital, dispensing measured doses of soporific reform to a population still hooked on the myth of the revolution, is grossly misleading. It overestimates the wisdom of the state and the gullibility of the population. It is true that the post-1950 (and, a fortiori, the post-1970) state was endowed with extensive powers.[126] It has a well-muscled, Bonapartist look to it. But it does not follow that the growth of state powers and agencies was accompanied by purposive coordination of those powers and agencies; on the contrary, as with other (semi-)authoritarian states, the image of a decisive, determined Leviathan is at odds with reality. The Mexican state could certainly thrash around and agitate the waters, as it did in 1976 and 1982. But it does not seem that this was very purposive or effective thrashing about. (Compare, say, the Ruiz Cortines and Echeverría *sexenios*: which proved more successful in the pursuit of its goals?) Indeed, by virtue of its sheer size, the regime risked becoming muscle-bound; it incorporated into its vast bulk so many conflicting interests that decisive, coordinated action proved difficult. State factions pulled in different directions like rival pectorals, expending vast quantities of energy, canceling each other out, but getting bigger in the process.[127] Sheer size did not bring relative autonomy; rather, it internalized social conflicts in the entrails of the state/party, causing—if we extend the corporeal metaphor—chronic dyspepsia.

Size also increased the scale of patronage (and corruption). This was highly functional to the regime's survival and reproduction, though not to its efficiency or executive capacity.[128] There was no political salvation outside the PRI (at least until very recently). The state became a massive engine of job creation; like the British Empire, it served as a system of "outdoor relief for the middle classes" who, while they were not *creations* of the revolutionary state, were, by the 1960s, major beneficiaries.[129] Hence the paradox of a regime that actively fostered the middle-class, while facing middle-class critiques and electoral opposition.[130] And the bigger the state, the greater its capacity for parasitism, for acquiring autonomous interests and goals geared *not* to the greatness of state and nation ("Prussian" autonomy: a concept of limited relevance for Mexico) but rather to the enrichment of state incumbents and their camarillas (i.e., patrimonial/parasitic autonomy).[131] The incidence of corruption no doubt varied, tending to coincide with periods of economic boom: with Alemán in the 1940s, López Portillo during the oil boom of the late 1970s, and Salinas during the neoliberal euphoria of the early 1990s.

During these periods, the quantum of corruption—certainly of perceived corruption—sharply increased, testing the tolerance of citizens, especially when boom gave way to bust (in 1982 and 1994–95). In such times, even thin legitimacy wore thinner; the state's reliance on coercion and clientelism could be seen through the faded fabric, and it was not a pretty sight. The state could no longer pose as a populist paterfamilias, governing for the collective good of the nation; nor, necessarily, could it be seen as the sage and farsighted facilitator of capital accumulation. Particular, personal, and patrimonial interests appeared to predominate, in the shape of Swiss bank accounts and newfound family fortunes. State autonomy, it seemed, served neither national nor class interests but rather those of a narrow parasitic elite: Old Corruption, Mexican-style.[132]

Such perceptions bred disillusionment and fomented crisis. Crises—even "legitimation crises"?—may not, of course, prove terminal. The Mexican system has weathered successive crises. The end of Cardenismo (1938–40) was a critical conjuncture, out of which a new, stable system emerged. The reaction to the excesses of Alemanismo—notably Henriquismo—prompted a modest political cleanup and a successful commitment to *desarrollo estabilizador*. The 1976 crisis was submerged in a tide of oil, credit, and spending. That of 1982 led to a new neoliberal project that, it would seem, proposed a fairly radical solution to Mexico's impasse: a robust commitment to free-market economics; a heterodox prices-and-incomes policy; a calculating tolerance of opposition parties (especially the PAN); and a crafty reformulation of traditional pork-barrel politics under the guise of Solidarity.[133] In the short term this project was strikingly successful: the economy was liberalized and, despite the political shocks of 1994, the PRI won the presidential election handily and not too dirtily. In the process, it could be argued, the state began to recast its sources of legitimacy. While Solidarity—and rural electoral politics in general—represented reinvented traditions, and the Pact of Economic Solidarity reflected the old, asymmetrical alliance of state and organized labor, economic liberalization, in contrast, was a genuinely new initiative, while tolerance of political opposition went further than ever before. President Salinas, meanwhile, outlined a new rationale for the state—lean, fit, efficient, and "modern"—and a new future for Mexico: prosperous, capitalist, competitive, technocratic, and *primermundista*.[134] Old atavisms—anticlericalism, anti-Americanism—would be buried. Old icons—the *ejido*, Cananea—would be toppled. Old myths—the *niños heroes*, Magonismo, Cárdenas—would be punctured. The legitimacy of the state would be grounded on technocratic competence, economic growth, and membership in the First World.[135]

Such a project implied a new set of social pacts, a new distribution of winners and losers. Mexico's *ejidatarios*—and grain farmers in general—

would have to fend for themselves. Employees in the state sector would face layoffs and a curtailment of perks.[136] Even medium industry—already at a serious disadvantage vis-à-vis the big conglomerates[137]—would be exposed to stiff foreign competition. Not only the ideological shibboleths of the revolution but also, and more important, the economic shelters of the import-substituting industrialization (ISI) project would be razed. Inasmuch as the doctrine of "social liberalism" justified an odd combination of neoliberal economics and paternalist social policy, Salinas could briefly enjoy the best of both worlds: a neoliberal appeal to the burgeoning bourgeoisie and middle class, and a traditional appeal to the urban and rural poor. Old and new legitimacies coexisted in uneasy but, for a time, successful symbiosis. The state was slimmed, its budget was cut, its proliferating presence reduced. Some observers—naive, disingenuous, or mercenary—saw a necessary correlation between economic liberalization and political democratization.[138] The state would cut back on rent seeking and parasitism and approximate more to the role of a honest, neutral night watchman: in terms of my diagram, it would march resolutely in a southwesterly direction.

Apart from seducing several foreign observers, this strategy was domestically successful in the short term.[139] Since, as I have argued, the old revolutionary shibboleths had lost much of their force, the opportunity cost of their disposal was tolerable.[140] For decades, leftists had lamented the decline and betrayal of *ejido*: why shed crocodile tears over a musty corpse? La Quina, jailed in the first great public relations stunt of the Salinas administration, was hardly a model martyr for the Left. More generally, with socialism and even Keynesianism in retreat, the Left lacked a counterproject, save that of "the revolution," a tired battle cry whose troops had dwindled and whose true and tested leaders were few.[141] And the historic counterproject of the Right—the PAN—had been in large measure appropriated by the PRI. In breaking the social pact that had loosely underpinned the ISI project, Salinas followed continental (or global) trends, to which no appealing alternative existed. Paradoxically, the administration that promised a liberal, pluralist state, in fact was one of the most active, innovative, even authoritarian:[142] the executive rode roughshod over the PRI, its corporate sectors, and provincial cadres (especially in states where PAN victories were allowed or contrived). If the PAN was tolerated, even discreetly encouraged, the PRD got short shrift. By slimming the state, Salinas achieved, as he said he would, a greater degree of state flexibility, perhaps autonomy.[143] Size and autonomy again failed to correlate (positively). The state also broke existing political pacts (albeit pacts that had been wearing thin for years, if not decades). Given the nature of the emerging political economy, ditching *ejidatorios* and trade unionists was a price worth paying, if business and the urban middle class could be won over.[144] And business, which had been luke-warm about De la Madrid in 1982, certainly welcomed Salinas's achievement of the presidency in 1988.[145] But the economic logic of neoliberalism went further: small and medium-sized domestic business, one of the chief beneficiaries of ISI, now became vulnerable; while privatization policies benefited a burgeoning financial and plutocratic elite, linked to international capital, to the PRI, and to the president himself.[146]

Had the economic boom continued beyond December 1994,[147] the project might have gelled, Chiapas, Colosio, and Ruiz Massieu notwithstanding. But the "mistakes of December," themselves the product, one suspects, of the overweening PRIísta hubris of late 1994, ended the boom, heralded a new bout of austerity, ruptured the incipient social pacts of Stalinism, and undercut whatever legitimacy the neoliberal state may have attained. Technocratic competence was shown to be grotesquely fallible, First World status a sad delusion. Millions of the middle class joined the roll call of casualties, while some (not all) of the new plutocracy went to the wall.

None of this ensures the demise of the PRI or of the distinctive state that it still commands [chapter edited prior to recent elections]. Previous crises have been weathered; and, although I suspect this is the deepest since the genesis of the system, survival should not be ruled out.[148] The economic die has been cast; in terms of training, temperament, and "path dependence," it is hard to see Zedillo reneging on neoliberalism. But neoliberalism does not mandate a liberal night watchman state; hence, a range of political options remain open.[149] As a result, Mexico-watchers find themselves reprising old debates and hypotheses.[150] Standing back from the wreckage, adopting a long-term perspective, can we discern patterns or directions? My diagrammatic trajectory of state formation reveals a neat circular motion: starting from its Porfirian ("agent-state") location in the northwest quadrant, the Mexican state has shifted in an anticlockwise direction through the southwest (revolutionary disintegration), the southeast (statist reform), to the northeast—that contentious sector where an apparently strong state broadly serves dominant class interests. (Regional patterns, though variable, would show a roughly similar trend: however, in that the autonomy of regional political actors would seem to have been pretty limited, and their representation of provincial bourgeoisies pretty faithful, the regional trajectory since 1940 would curve into the northwestern ["agent-state"] quadrant earlier and more completely.)

The neoliberal project, I have suggested, bade farewell to the old statist social pact and, more riskily, perhaps, turned its back on sections of private business. Did Mexico's economic opening therefore represent a bold,

Bonapartist challenge to strong vested interests—a classic example of the autonomous state flexing its muscles and determining the course of socio-economic change, *cueste lo que cueste*, as Victoriano Huerta liked to say? There may be a modicum of truth in this; certainly Salinista technocracy did not lack for confidence or chutzpah, and it implemented its policies with insouciant disregard for public opinion and lobbies alike.[151] But two qualifications are needed. First, if we define capitalism broadly and structurally, it could be argued that the neoliberal project aligned itself with the emergent winners (big, financial, multinational capital) at the expense of the anticipated losers: small and medium-sized domestic capital, which had been under threat since the 1970s.[152] In this sense, neoliberalism did not so much remake society as reflect and accelerate existing trends, of a global character.[153]

Second, whatever the causal relationship, a final paradox lurks in this conclusion (if it is valid). The neoliberal project implies a break with the past and with past social pacts. Even if driven—at the outset—by autonomous state initiative, its eventual destination is a tight dependence of state and society on international capital. As the December 1994 crisis revealed, Mexico's people and their leaders are now highly vulnerable to market swings, volatile capital flows, and the investment decisions of transnational corporations and pension funds.[154] If there is a "dominant class" in Mexico today, it is that often anonymous, tentacular "dominant class" whose interests now straddle the globe, defying strict definition or regulation. There are Mexicans—like Slim or Azcárraga—who arguably belong to that class; but the logic of their action is global rather than Mexican. To the extent—a considerable extent—that the Mexican state has served and continues to serve their interests, its relative autonomy has shrunk (in which respect, of course, it is not alone in the world).[155] Like other states, therefore, that of the PRI has relinquished autonomy and assumed a role more closely corresponding to that of an agent; it has, in other words, shifted toward the northwest quadrant, its direction determined in part by state initiative, in part by powerful trends in the global economy.

If this argument is broadly correct, the story ends roughly where it started. As the twentieth century ticks to its conclusion, the Mexican state finds it has come full circle: from Porfirian "agency," through revolutionary disintegration, to (significantly) autonomous reformism (1910 to c. 1940); through (weak) relatively autonomous support for national capital to neoliberal agency on behalf of multinational capital.[156] The story is, of course, a good deal more complicated. There have been lesser vicissitudes along the way (see Figure 2). And this formulation captures only part of the story: namely, the "strength" of the state and its relation to class forces. Analytically distinct, though bound up with this anticlockwise advance, are the themes mentioned earlier: we find a state that, for all its stability, has failed to establish either a clear Weberian monopoly of violence or an enduring legitimacy based on strong affective allegiances.[157] The Weberian monopoly has been compromised by recurrent illegitimate violence; legitimacy has been undercut by strenuous opposition before 1940 and by pervasive indifference after 1940. These two staples of state theory are not, in the Mexican case, analytic abracadabras. On the other hand, forms of clientelism and patronage have been crucial, by way of circulating and rewarding elites, securing expedient popular support, and projecting an image of immutability: *asi se gobierna, señores* (and no way else).[158] At best, this implies a "thin," *faute-de-mieux* legitimacy.[159] Since roughly 1940, state and business have usually maintained a close identity of interest; departures from this norm (1976, 1982) have reflected less the confident deliberations of a farsighted Bonapartist state than the erratic decision making of a factionalized regime prone to sexenial crisis.

Indeed, the relative autonomy claimed by the state manifested itself less by any bold assault on vested interests (though there were elements of this in Salinismo) than by assiduous rent seeking on the part of state elites. The "Bonapartist" state, "well-gallooned and well-fed," appeared in increasingly parasitic form, especially during times of economic boom: the 1940s, the late 1970s, the early 1990s. Drug trafficking has greatly compounded this endemic problem. Of course, given the sheer scale of this political enterprise, it has involved genuine reformers as well as self-seeking opportunists, populists as well as parasites. Indeed, this combination helped maintain the state: by periodically offsetting parasitic extraction with bouts of populist reform, the state has been seen to deliver *some* of the goods, to live up at least partially to its public transcript. Solidarity— "neopopulist solutions to neoliberal problems"[160]—was the last, best example of this syndrome. It now seems a spent force. Meanwhile, almost daily, fresh reports of egregious parasitism seem to break: drug running, money laundering, foreign bank accounts, perversions of the course of justice. What I have referred to as "hardball" politics (violent, dirty, and exploitative) has expanded its scope at the expense of "softball" (clean, decorous, and disinterested).[161] The state's relative autonomy involves not so much conciliatory mediation, constructive reform, or the rational furtherance of capital accumulation as an ancient patrimonialism wedded to a rapacious capitalism. This hardly seems a strategy for survival into the twenty-first century.

This guarded conclusion, of course, relates only to Mexico: it is a conclusion based on the application of various theories of the state to the Mexican case. Not surprisingly, perhaps, several theories (or approaches, emphases, perspectives) display some utility; none offers an infallible the-oretical passe-partout. The strictly defined "agent" state, faithfully enact-ing the will of the dominant class, is an elusive beast: dominant classes are not easily pinned down (especially for the pre-1940 period), and the state rarely enacts any single discernible "will." At best, we find ourselves not-ing the greater or lesser dependence of the state vis-à-vis "dominant classes" or, perhaps better, vis-à-vis the demands of political economy more broadly conceived.[162] Here, we reprise old debates concerning the structural dependence of the state upon capitalism, and the tense relation-ship—or trade-off—between political legitimation and capital accumula-tion; debates that, though old, seem to have acquired fresh relevance in the age of neoliberal reform.[163]

If the "agent" state proves elusive, the "relatively autonomous" state appears to be the norm. The problem is to determine the degree and char-acter of "autonomy" (a problem that involves looking not just at the state but also at the socioeconomic context within it which operates; "auton-omy" involves two different sets of variables). "Prussian" autonomy—autonomy predicated on geopolitical rivalry—is of little use by way of explaining Mexican state formation and character. The notion of state autonomy dedicated to the long-term interests of capital—the state as economic regulator or political mediator—makes more sense (it might be particularly relevant for the period c. 1940–70); but it runs the risk of an excessive "logic-of-capital" functionalism, whereby every state initiative, however unwelcome to the private sector, serves the long-term interests of capital ("in the last analysis"). Ultimately, such an argument is irrefut-able, and therefore vapid. Tilly's heretical alternative—relative autonomy dedicated to the self-interest of the state and its incumbents (crudely, the state as protection racket)—offers a useful alternative, which has the merit of falsifiability. Official peculation and rent seeking can be investi-gated (with some risk and difficulty, perhaps); the investigator does not fall into a bottomless functionalist pit.

It follows, therefore, that several perspectives offer enlightenment. They can provoke inquiry, provide "organizing concepts," and suggest cross-national parallels. From the historian's point of view (a notoriously narrow and empirical one, perhaps), this is what theory is for. Con-versely, historians do not set out to falsify theory, nor, as I said at the outset, can one case (Mexico) refute theory. The notion of "Prussian" autonomy might work—as a "heuristic device"—in other contexts (such as Prussia). Only an accumulation of individual "refutations" (i.e., dem-onstrations of a theory's irrelevance or wrongheadedness in numerous cases) can call a grand theory into disrepute. At best, the Mexican case suggests a few tentative pointers, some positive, some negative.

CONCLUSIONS

Finally, there is the question of the provenance of theory. The state theories I have considered are primarily of European origin. The grand theorists of the state—Marx, Weber, Gramsci—were Europeans. The secondary figures whom I have mentioned—Poulantzas, Skocpol, Tilly—are, if you prefer, "Western."[164] Certainly, I have cited no preeminent Latin American state theorist (the omission may reflect myopia on my part, of course). Does this matter? I do not think so. If, indeed, it is a question of myopia, and I have neglected Latin American grand theorists who—by virtue of being Latin American?—enjoy a superior grasp of relevant state theory, then one might expect their superiority to become evident in the marketplace of ideas. The latter, like most markets, may be skewed, but it is capable of admitting new ideas that display a demonstrable comparative advantage. Furthermore, I would strongly question any ethnically inflected theorization. That is, if we make the rash assumption that Latin America is somehow quintessentially and radically "different," hence amenable only to a distinctive "Latin American" analysis (one that is uncontaminated by "European" theory), then we impoverish our research, promote intellectual sectarianism, and, of course, fly in the face of history. For Latin America has been bound up with "European" and "Western" thought, as both consumer and contributor, for centuries. The lack of a Latin American "grand theory of the state" may be a pity, but it is of no great consequence. Europe, after all, did not invent dependency theory, but plenty of Europeans seized upon it with alacrity. It is not the provenance, but the utility, of theories that matters.

In the 1920s, the Mexican philosopher-activist José Vasconcelos embarked on a crusade to bolster Mexican nationhood, exalting the "cosmic race" and stressing nationalist values, whether in art or gastronomy. At one point, he came close to advocating a distinctively Mexican science: "If all nations then build theories to justify their policies or to strengthen their deeds, let us develop in Mexico our own theories."[165] But even the woolly-headed Vasconcelos paused before going down the road that leads to Stalinist genetics. "Or at least," he qualified himself, "let us be certain that we choose among the foreign theories of thought those that stimulate our growth instead of those that restrain it." The qualification is, of course, crucial. Vasconcelos was thinking primarily in socioeconomic terms; but if it is intellectual "growth"—or debate, reflection and, perhaps, "advance"—that we seek, then it would be a great mistake to introduce positive discrimination, or to pursue the chimera of a distinctively Latin American (or European, or Chinese) social theory. There should be no parochial patriotism in the realm of ideas.

NOTES

1. Florencia E. Mallon, "The Promise and Dilemma of Subaltern Studies: Perspectives from Latin American History," *American Historical Review* 99 (1994): 1491–515.

2. Michael Mann, *The Sources of Social Power*, vol. 1 (Cambridge: Cambridge University Press, 1986); Anthony Giddens, *The Nation-State and Violence* (Cambridge: Polity Press, 1985); John A. Hall, *Powers and Liberties: The Causes and Consequences of the Rise of the West* (London: Penguin, 1992); Clifford Geertz, *The Interpretation of Cultures* (New York: Basic Books, 1973); Charles Tilly, *Coercion, Capital and European States, A.D. 990–1992* (Cambridge, Mass.: Blackwell, 1992); Theda Skocpol, *States and Social Revolutions* (Cambridge: Cambridge University Press, 1979); Barrington Moore Jr., *Social Origins of Dictatorship and Democracy* (Boston: Beacon, 1966). Note, however, the recent interesting attempt to apply Barrington Moore to Latin America: Evelyne Huber and Frank Safford, eds., *Agrarian Structure and Political Power: Landlord and Peasant in the Making of Latin America* (Pittsburgh: University of Pittsburgh Press, 1995).

3. James Scott, *Domination and the Arts of Resistance: Hidden Transcripts* (New Haven, Conn.: Yale University Press, 1990); Benedict Anderson, *Imagined Communities: Reflections on the Origin and Spread of Nationalism* (London: Verso, 1983), chap. 4 ; Eric Wolf, *Europe and the People without History* (Berkeley: University of California Press, 1982); Mark Philp, "Michel Foucault," in Quentin Skinner, ed., *The Return of Grand Theory in the Human Sciences* (Cambridge: Canto, 1991), 67–68. My comment concerning Guha derives, perhaps unfairly, from a public lecture and subsequent discussion at Oxford University in 1993, at which Guha proposed and defended the proposition that only subaltern Indians could properly study subaltern Indians. I do not know how general this belief is among practitioners of subaltern studies; if it were strictly applied, there certainly would be a lot fewer of them.

4. For a roster of recent "grand theorists," see Quentin Skinner, "Introduction," in Skinner, *The Return of Grand Theory*, 3–20.

5. Alan Knight, "The Peculiarities of Mexican History: Mexico Compared to Latin America, 1821–1992," *Journal of Latin American Studies* 24 (supplement 1992): 99.

6. A somewhat arbitrary list: G. D. Jones and R. R. Kautz, *The Transition to Statehood in the New World* (Cambridge: Cambridge University Press, 1981); Wolf, *Europe and the People without History*, chap. 5; Florencia E. Mallon, *Peasant and Nation: The Making of Postcolonial Mexico and Peru* (Berkeley: University of California Press, 1995); Enrique Semo, *The History of Capitalism in Mexico* (Austin: University of Texas Press, 1990); Gary Gereffi and Peter B. Evans, "Transnational Corporations, Dependent Development, and State Policy in the Semi-periphery: A Comparison of Brazil and Mexico," *Latin American Research Review* 16 (1981): 31–64; Gilbert M. Joseph and Daniel Nugent, eds., *Everyday Forms of State Formation. Revolution and the*

Negotiation of Rule in Modern Mexico (Durham, N.C.: Duke University Press, 1994).

7. Alan Knight, "The Mexican Revolution: Bourgeois? Nationalist? Or Just a 'Great Rebellion'?" *Bulletin of Latin American Research* 4 no. 2 (1985): 1–37.

8. Eric Wolf, "Introduction," in Norman Miller and Roderick Aya, eds., *National Liberation: Revolution in the Third World* (New York: Free Press, 1971), 12.

9. An observation made with the strictures of Stephen Haber in mind (CLAR panel, "Trends and Transformations in Mexican History," AHA Conference, New York, January 1997, publication forthcoming).

10. Mario Huacuja R. and José Woldenberg, *Estado y lucha política en el México actual* (Mexico City: El Caballito, 1983); Pablo González Casanova, *El estado y los partidos políticos en México* (Mexico City: Era, 1981); Germán Pérez Fernández del Castillo, ed., *Evolución del estado mexicano*, 3 vols. (Mexico City: El Caballito, 1986).

11. Unless the theorists are Barry Hindess and Paul Q. Hirst, *Pre-capitalist Modes of Production* (London: Routledge, 1975), 311–12.

12. In which it resembles science: Lewis Wolpert, *The Unnatural Nature of Science* (London: Faber, 1992), xi–xii, 2, 11.

13. Enrique Semo, *Historia Mexicana* (Mexico City: Ediciones Era, 1978) 157–59. For a general warning against "making the state seem anthropomorphic, as if it were motivated by the will of a single leader," see Joel S. Migdal, *Strong Societies and Weak States: State-Society Relations and State Capabilities in the Third World* (Princeton, N.J.: Princeton University Press, 1988), 20.

14. Some theory appears to encourage a focus on state *personnel*: Barbara Geddes, *Politician's Dilemma* (Berkeley: University of California Press, 1994), 1; Stephen D. Krasner, "Approaches to the State: Alternative Conceptions and Historical Dynamics," *Comparative Politics* 16 (1984): 224, 227, 231.

15. Cf. Wolpert, *The Unnatural Nature of Science*, 12, 16–17.

16. Alfred Stepan, *The State and Society: Peru in Comparative Perspective* (Princeton, N.J.: Princeton University Press, 1978), 26–45. Organic theories and images of the state are, of course, as old as antiquity: Alexander Passerin D'Entreves, *The Notion of the State* (Oxford: Oxford University Press, 1967), 17–18.

17. Alvin W. Gouldner, *The Two Marxisms* (London: Macmillan, 1980), 32ff. Similar criticisms have been made of Machiavelli (D'Entreves, *The Notion of the State*, 39–40) and could be made of Weber. R. M. MacIver, *The Modern State* (Oxford: Oxford University Press, 1964), generalizes that "in this study we are in the perilous region where ideals may shape not only the future of actualities [*sic*] but [also] our present conception of them" (4).

18. David Hume, *A Treatise of Human Nature* (1739; Oxford: Clarendon, 1978), 469.

19. Migdal, *Strong Societies*, 18–19; David Held, and Joel Krieger, "Theories of the State: Some Competing Claims," in Stephen Bornstein, David Held, and Joel Krieger, eds., *The State in Capitalist Europe* (Boston: Allen and Unwin, 1984), 5–8. For an intelligent application of a broadly Weberian perspective to Latin American state building, see Laurence Whitehead, "State Organization in Latin America since 1930," in Leslie Bethell, ed., *The Cambridge History of Latin*

America, vol. 6/2 (Cambridge: Cambridge University Press, 1994), 3–98 (note p. 6); and for a Latin American critique of this perspective, see Atilio Broron, *State, Capitalism and Democracy in Latin America* (Boulder, Colo.: Lynne Rienner, 1995), 131–32.

20. Stepan, *State and Society*, 7–17; Fred Block, *Revising State Theory* (Philadelphia: Temple University Press, 1987), 4–5; and for a defense of pluralism, Gabiel A. Almond, "The Return to the State," *American Political Science Review* (1988): 859–67.

21. "The Marxist theory of the state remains a muddle": Block, *Revising State Theory*, 51. The variety—or muddle—may stem from the fact that Marx "died before he was able to begin a full-scale systematic treatment of the state" (Stepan, *State and Society*, 18; cf. Bob Jessop, *State Theory* [Cambridge: Polity Press, 1990], 25); hence the lack of an authoritative canon. Clyde W. Barrow, *Critical Theories of the State* (Madison: University of Wisconsin Press, 1993), chaps. 1–2, offers a useful guide; and Jessop, *State Theory*, chap. 3, a dense defense.

22. The quote, of course, is from the *Communist Manifesto* (Stepan, *State and Society*, 20). The bibliography is extensive: on the famous Miliband-Poulantzas debate, which revolves around (very roughly) agency versus autonomy, and its theoretical fallout, see Barrow, *Critical Theories*, 24–30, 57–58, 77ff.; and Jessop, *State Theory*, 29–30.

23. "Most scholars working on these issues, no matter what their theoretical and ideological commitments, (now) believe that governments can and often do act independently of underlying socioeconomic forces." Geddes, *Politician's Dilemma*, 2.

24. This may apply to feudal as well as capitalist formations; hence the pathbreaking analysis of Perry Anderson *Lineages of the Absolutist State* (London: New Left Books, 1974).

25. Barrow, *Critical Theories*, 51ff.; Block, *Revising State Theory*, 13, 53–54.

26. Apart from Anderson (*Lineages of the Absolutist State*), which deals with early modern absolutist states within a Marxist framework, see also S. H. Rigby, *English Society in the Late Middle Ages* (Basingstoke: Macmillan, 1995).

27. Arturo Anguiano, *El estado y la política obrera del Cardenismo* (Mexico City: Ediciones Era, 1975). I argue against a capitalist-functionalist interpretation of Cardenismo in "Cardenismo: Juggernaut or Jalopy?" *Journal of Latin American Studies* 26 (1994): 73–107.

28. This phrase—from Lampedusa's *The Leopard*—has become something of a cliché in Mexicanists' discourse; however, it is usually (and often usefully) cited in the context of PRIísta political reformism, especially since 1977. It cannot be generalized to *all* reform (political, social, economic) in *all* postrevolutionary periods. Unfalsifiable circularity is not confined to Mexico, of course: Block (*Revising State Theory*, 40), refers to "an inverted functionalism where all social institutions fit the logic of capitalist accumulation"; note also Dietrich Rueschemeyer and Peter B. Evans, "The State and Economic Transformation: Toward an Analysis of the Conditions Underlying Effective Intervention," in Peter B. Evans, Dietrich Rueschemeyer, and Theda Skocpol, eds., *Bringing the State Back In* (Cambridge: Cambridge University Press, 1985), 67.

29. An interesting test case (only marginally relevant to Mexico) arises from

the current dismantling of welfare states, which have often been cited as classic examples of capitalist functionalism; yet dismantling has not (yet) resulted in a series of legitimation crises: Barrow, *Critical Theories*, 122–23.

30. Block (*Revising State Theory*, 53–55) notes the problem and argues that Marx anticipated a "relative autonomy" argument; unfortunately, he did so in *The Eighteenth Brumaire*—a text that is as confusing as it is coruscating.

31. Robert Carneiro, "A Theory of the Origins of the State," *Science* 169 (1970): 733–38.

32. Theda Skocpol, "Bringing the State Back In: Current Research," in Evans, Rueschemeyer, and Skopcol, *Bringing the State Back In*, 7–8. Mann, *Sources of Social Power*, and the same author's "The Autonomous Power of the State: Its Origins, Mechanisms and Results," in *States, Wars, and Capitalism* (Oxford: Blackwell, 1988), 1–31, display a similar "Weberian-Hintzean" perspective (the term is Skopcol's, "Bringing the State Back In," 9). For a trenchant critique of this approach, see Paul Cammack, "Review Article: Bringing the State Back In," *British Journal of Politics* 19 (1989): 261–90, which makes—among others—the valid point that the plea to "bring the state back in" is of limited relevance to studies of Latin America, the rest of the Third World, or even Europe (not to mention the Second World); it embodies, in other words, an ethnocentric concern, emanating from and reflecting post-1950 North American social science. It is also ironic that the plea was made just as the role of the state was shrinking around the world: Boron, *State, Capitalism and Democracy*, 126–7; Albert Fishlow, "The Latin American State," *Journal of Economic Perspectives* 4, no. 3 (1990): 61.

33. Skocpol, *States and Social Revolutions*.

34. Alan Knight, "Social Revolution: A Latin American Perspective," *Bulletin of Latin American Research* 9, no. 2 (1990): 175–202.

35. Dan A. Cothran, *Political Stability and Democracy in Mexico: The "Perfect Dictatorship"?* (Westport, Conn.: Praeger, 1994), 37, 147.

36. Nora Hamilton, *The Limits of State Autonomy: Post-revolutionary Mexico* (Princeton, N.J.: Princeton University Press 1982); Julie A. Erfani, *The Paradox of the Mexican State* (Boulder, Colo.: Lynne Rienner, 1995), 113–14.

37. Sylvia Maxfield, *Governing Capital: International Finance and Mexican Politics* (Ithaca, N.Y.: Cornell University Press, 1990), 71, 75, 120, 145.

38. That is to say, incumbents (i.e., PRIístas) could justify their incumbency on the grounds of *la patrie en danger*, even to the extent of fixing elections. NAFTA has strengthened U.S. government support for the incumbent regime, even if it has made the regime somewhat more senstive to U.S. scrutiny.

39. Charles Tilly, "War and State Making as Organized Crime," in Evans, Rueschemeyer, and Skopcol, *Bringing the State Back In*, 169–91.

40. William McNeill, *Plagues and Peoples* (Garden City, N.Y.: Anchor-Doubleday, 1976).

41. Notions of "the-state-as-mafia," though rarely systematic, can be found scattered through the literature. "In its early development the state is likely to have a thoroughly parasitic and predatory character," Rueschemeyer and Evans observe ("The State and Economic Transformation," 61); but it is not clear why "later" states should behave so differently. For older intimations of the idea, note

that the early Marx conceived of the state as "extraneous and parasitic" (Jessop, *State Theory*, 26); while Saint Augustine drew the mafia parallel explicitly: "When justice is absent, what else are kingdoms than large gangs of robbers? And what else indeed are such gangs than rudimentary kingdoms?": D'Entreves, *The Notion of the State*, 22.

42. Roger D. Hansen, *The Politics of Mexican Development* (Baltimore: Johns Hopkins University Press, 1973). I have noted warm assent on occasions when this analogy has been made in student and academic circles in Mexico.

43. Ernest Gruening, *Mexico and Its Heritage* (London: Stanley Paul, 1928), 365–75, gives graphic examples of syndical "protection" in the 1920s. Foreign companies regularly complained of similar practices in the following decade. Echeverría used comparable techniques in his battle with *Excelsior* in the 1970s: Daniel Levy and Gabriel Szekely, *Mexico: Paradoxes of Stability and Change* (Boulder, Colo.: Westview, 1983), 94–99. Frans J. Schryer, *Ethnicity and Class Conflict in Rural Mexico* (Princeton, N.J.: Princeton University Press, 1990), chap. 15, describes "a decade of contrived land invasions" in the Huasteca.

44. Stepan, *State and Society*, 26–7.

45. Geddes, *Politician's Dilemma*, 5.

46. This arrangement would seem compatible with Linz's well-known distinction between authoritarianism and totalitarianism: Stepan, *State and Society*, 43–45. On "bureaucratic authoritarianism," see David Collier, ed., *The New Authoritarianism in Latin America* (Princeton, N.J.: Princeton University Press, 1979).

47. Skocpol, "Bringing the State Back In," 14.

48. "Relative autonomy" and "late capitalism" are often assumed to correlate: C. B. MacPherson, "Do We Need a Theory of the State?" *Archives Européennes de Sociologie* 18 (1977): 234–35. A similar tendency toward greater state capacity and resources is also discerned, mutatis mutandis, in Latin America: Whitehead, "State Organization in Latin America."

49. MacPherson, "Do We Need a Theory of the State?" written twenty years ago, employs these arguments in favor of a relative autonomy–late capitalist correlation (237–42): there are "apparently endemic wage and price controls," coupled with "a growing restiveness within the labor force over its subordination to organization and technology (wildcat strikes and shop-steward militancy)"; "the whole personnel of the public sector . . . owe their relative job security and relatively high wages to the state"; and "the relative autonomy of the state will increase as the state gets more deeply involved in the management of the economy, the stabilization of markets, and the subsidization of production and prices." *Autre temps, autres moeurs!*

50. Skocpol, *States and Social Revolutions*. "Successful" is a key qualifier: some revolutions never proceed beyond the (southwestern) phase of disaggregation (e.g., Taiping?); some achieve only partial or transient postrevolutionary stability (e.g., Bolivia). One of the problems with Skopcol's thesis—that successful revolutions are, above all, state-building phenomena—is that the "great," successful revolutions on which she concentrates (France, Russia, China) necessarily embody durable state building *by virtue of being "great" and successful*; the argument contains a circularity.

51. Knight, "Social Revolution."

52. Karl Marx, *The Eighteenth Brumaire of Louis Bonaparte* (Moscow: Progress Publishers, 1977), 104, 110.

53. Block, *Revising State Theory*, 88–89; Tim Mason, "The Primacy of the Political," in S. J. Woolf, ed., *The Nature of Fascism* (London: Weidenfeld and Nicolson, 1968), 165–95; Alfred Stepan, "State Power and the Strength of Civil Society in the Southern Cone of Latin America," in Evans, Rueschemeyer, and Skopcol, *Bringing the State Back In*, 320–24.

54. Erfani, *Paradox of the Mexican State*, 108, 111; Maxfield, *Governing Capital*, 88–89, 120–21; Carlos Arriola, "Los grupos empresariales frente al Estado, 1973–86," *Foro Internacional* 16 (1976): 449–95; Samuel Schmidt, *The Deterioration of the Mexican Presidency: The Years of Luis Echeverría* (Tucson: University of Arizona Press, 1991), chap. 4.

55. Alan Knight, *The Mexican Revolution*, 2 vols. (Cambridge: Cambridge University Press 1986), vol. 1, chaps. 2–3.

56. Ibid., 92–115. Porfirian landlords often directly—"instrumentally"—controlled the state: for example, most state governors were landlords; some, like Creel and Terrazas in Chihuahua, Escandón in Morelos, or Torres in Sonora, were classic oligarchic/*latifundista* figures. Lower in the political hierarchy—with the *jefes políticos*, for example—landlord power tended to be more indirect and "structural." Between them, Miliband and Poulantzas would not find it difficult to justify describing the Porfiriato as a landlord state. Whether those landlords were capitalists (ergo, whether this was a *capitalist* state) is a different question, to which a brief and simple answer is impossible.

57. Some supposedly landlord/oligarchic states in fact embodied a distinct division of labor: in Argentina, for example, the economically dominant pampas landlords did not directly control politics, which were the preserve of a different, specialized "caudillo" elite: Poulantzas, rather than Milliband, may prove the better guide: see Tulio Halperín Donghi, "The Buenos Aires Landed Class and the Shape of Argentine Politics," in Huber and Safford, *Agrarian Structure*, 39–66, which is confirmed by Roy Hora, doctoral research in progress, Oxford University. In Porfirian Mexico, the division of labor was less marked, "instrumentality" more clear-cut.

58. Alan Knight, "Land and Society in Revolutionary Mexico: The Destruction of the Great Haciendas," *Mexican Studies/Estudios Mexicanos* 7, no. 1 (1991): 73–104.

59. Knight, "The Mexican Revolution," 5.

60. A class which, incidentally, the state did not create, as sometimes asserted, but whose history stretches back into the nineteenth century, notably to the industrial and commercial boom of the 1890s.

61. Arnaldo Córdova, *La ideología de la revolución mexicana* (Mexico City: Ediciones Era, 1973).

62. Levy and Szekely, *Mexico*, 113–18.

63. Along the lines of Juan Felipe Leal, "El estado y el bloque en poder en México, 1867–1914," *Historia Mexicana* 23 (1973–74), 700–721.

64. Quoted in Philip Abrams, "The Difficulty of Studying the State," *Journal of Historical Sociology* 1, no. 1 (1988): 68.

65. Mann, "The Autonomous Power of the State," 1, 5; and Mann, *Sources of Social Power*, 169–70, 477. However, the latter, (pp. 8–9), introduces yet another fourfold typology of power (intensive/extensive, authoritative/diffused). Is despotic a subcategory of authoritative? We are told (p. 515) that despotic power is a variant of "Parsons's 'distributive power,'" which (flipping back to 6–9) seems to sit outside Mann's fourfold typology. No doubt the confusion is in the eye of the beholder.

66. Scott, *Domination and the Arts of Resistance*.

67. Ibid., 66, 75. At the risk of reopening a can of semantic worms, it could be said that this corresponds roughly to Mann's "diffused power": *Sources of Social Power*, 8.

68. Specifically in 1976, 1982, 1988, and 1994. "Crisis" literature includes Raymon F. Vernon, *The Dilemma of Mexico's Development* (Cambridge, Mass.: Harvard University Press, 1966); Judith Adler Hellman, *Mexico in Crisis* (London: Holmes and Meier, 1978); Miguel Basañez, *El pulso de los sexenios: 20 años de crisis en México* (Mexico City: Siglo XXI, 1992).

69. Erfani (*Paradox of the Mexican State*, p. 120) argues the need to disaggregate the modern (1970s) Mexican state; a similar argument is made, in general terms, by Joel Migdal, Atul Kohli, and Vivienne Shue, "Introduction," in *State Power and Social Forces* (Cambridge: Cambridge University Press, 1994), 3.

70. Jeffrey Weldon, doctoral dissertation in progress, UCSD.

71. Joseph and Nugent (*Everyday Forms of State Formation*) offer case studies and arguments that illustrate the range and complexity of revolutionary politics, while avoiding both populist romanticism and elitist "statolatry."

72. Joel S. Migdal ("The State in Society," in Migdal, Kohli, and Shue, *State Power*, 14) seeks to demystify the "aura of invincibility" that attaches to state leaders and, I think rightly, criticizes Mann for his excessive focus on the "higher levels" of the "state elite."

73. Dale Story, *Industry, the State, and Public Policy in Mexico* (Austin: University of Texas Press, 1986), 132, 160–62; Maxfield, *Governing Capital*, 131. Gereffi and Evans ("Transnational Corporations," 52) argue that the international pressures exerted on Echeverría illustrate that "the band of acceptable policy is exceedingly narrow and that the penalties for stepping outside it are strict and swift"; twenty-five years later, the argument would, presumably, be even stronger.

74. Miguel Angel Centeno, *Democracy within Reason: Technocratic Revolution in Mexico* (University Park: Pennsylvania State University Press, 1994), 49–50.

75. *Did* the Prussian guards behave with punctilious rectitude?

76. Dudley Ankerson, "Saturnino Cedillo: A traditional Caudillo in San Luis Potosí," and Heather Fowler-Salamini, "Revolutionary Caudillos in the 1920s: Francisco Mújica and Adalberto Tejeda," both in David Brading, ed., *Caudillo and Peasant in the Mexican Revolution* (Cambridge: Cambridge University Press, 1980), 148–59, 183–90.

77. Claudio Lomnitz-Adler, *Salidas del laberinto* (Mexico City: Joaquín Mortiz, 1995), 256, 262, 267; Víctor Raúl Martínez Vázquez, "Despojo y manipulación campesina . . .," in Roger Bartra et al., *Caciquismo y poder político en el*

México rural (Mexico City: Siglo XXI, 1980) 150–54. Many more examples could be given, of course.

78. Note also Centeno, *Democracy within Reason*, 227.

79. Geddes (*Politician's Dilemma*, 1) defines the state in terms of "regimes, governments, specific administative agencies, and *even individuals who act on behalf of goverments*" (my emphasis); Mano Negra, Gonzalo N. Santos's prize *pistolero*, was, therefore, a state agent as much as any Prussian *Beamte*.

80. Victoria Rodríguez and Peter Ward, "Disentangling the PRI from the Government in Mexico," *Mexican Studies/Estudios Mexicanos* 10, no. 1 (1994): 163–86. I would agree with Peter Smith, *Labyrinths of Power* (Princeton, N.J.: Princeton University Press, 1979), 57, when he states that "it would be incorrect . . . to assert that the party runs the government in Mexico, and the reverse is probably closer to the truth."

81. Colin Clarke, "Opposition to the PRI 'Hegemony' in Oaxaca, 1968–94," in Rob Aitken et al., eds., *Dismantling the Mexican State?* (Basingstoke: Macmillan, 1996), 269, 283–88.

82. Analyses of these bureaucratic acronyms can become somewhat abstract and elitist; a valuable study, avoiding these pitfalls and stressing the *interaction* of state and popular agency, is Jonathan Fox, *The Politics of Food in Mexico* (Ithaca, N.Y.: Cornell University Press, 1992).

83. Juan Molinar Horcasitas and Jeffrey Weldon, "Electoral Determinants and Consequences of National Solidarity," in Wayne Cornelius, Ann Craig, and Jonathan Fox, eds., *Transforming State-Society Relations in Mexico: The National Solidarity Strategy* (La Jolla, Calif.: Center for US-Mexican Studies, UCSD, 1994), 123–41.

84. Linda S. Stevenson and Mitchell A. Seligson, "Fading Memories of the Revolution: Is Stability Eroding in Mexico?" in Roderic Ai Camp, ed., *Polling for Democracy* (Wilmington, Del.: Scholarly Resources, 1996), 59–80.

85. Alan Knight, "México bronco, México manso: Una reflexión sobre la cultura cívica mexicana," *Política y Gobierno* 3, no. 1 (1996): 15–19.

86. E. P. Thomson, "The Peculiarities of the English," in *The Poverty of Theory and Other Essays* (London: Merlin Press, 1978), 48–49.

87. Keith Brewster, "Caciquismo in Rural Mexico during the 1920s: The Case of Gabriel Barrios," *Journal of Latin American Studies* 28 (1996): 105–28.

88. Romana Falcón, "Saturnino Cedillo: El último gran cacique militar," and Enrique Márquez, "Gonzalo N. Santos o la naturaleza del 'tanteómetro político,'" both in Carlos Martínez Assad, ed., *Estadistas, caciques y caudillos* (Mexico City: UNAM, 1988), 363–84, 385–94; Ian Jacobs, "Rancheros of Guerrero: The Figueroa family and the Revolution," in Brading, *Caudillo and Peasant*, 76–91.

89. Mark Wasserman, *Persistent Oligarchs: Elites and Politics in Chihuahua, Mexico, 1910–40* (Durham, N.C.: Duke University Press, 1993).

90. Arturo Alvarado Mendoza, *El portesgilismo en Tamaulipas* (Mexico City: El Colegio de Mexico, 1992), 323–25.

91. Adrian Bantjes, "Politics, Class and Culture in Postrevolutionary Mexico: Cardenismo and Sonora" (Ph.D. diss., University of Texas at Austin, 1991).

92. Luis González, *Historia de la revolución mexicana, periodo 1934–40: Los días del Presidente Cárdenas* (Mexico City: El Colegio de Mexico, 1981), 227.

93. Culminating, perhaps, in the Salinas presidency, the "zenith of presidential power": Centeno, *Democracy within Reason*, 94–96. If central government power is measured in budgetary terms (a fairly crude device), the trajectory would reveal steady but moderate growth from the revolution through the 1950s and 1960s and a rapid acceleration thereafter; federal government spending represented 6 to 7 percent of GNP through the 1920s and early 1930s, rising to 9–10 percent during the later 1930s and 1940s; in 1961 it stood at 14 percent, in 1971 at 30 percent, and in 1981 nearly 50 percent: ibid., 82–83; and James W. Wilkie, *The Mexican Revolution: Federal Expenditure and Social Change since 1910* (Berkeley: University of California Press, 1970), 7.

94. Frans J. Schryer, *The Rancheros of Pisaflores* (Toronto: University of Toronto Press, 1980); Tomás Martínez Saldaña and Leticia Gándara, *Política y sociedad en México: El caso de los Altos de Jalisco* (Mexico City: Instituto Nacional de Atropología e Historia, 1976). I shall go on to suggest that, at the local/regional level, state autonomy was weaker, "bourgeois" rule more crude and unmediated, an argument that, it seems, is not confined to Mexico: Block, *Revising State Theory*, 191 n. 28.

95. It is worth recalling that the "heyday" of the PRI, strictly defined to embrace stable, inflation-free growth, rising living standards, a weak electoral opposition, and smooth sexennial successions, really stretches only from 1954 to 1968, or a little beyond. It is a conjunctural as much as a structural phenomenon. Another way of putting it: for most of its life (1929–54, 1968–97), the PNR/PRM/PRI has lived with political and economic challenges, some of them serious.

96. Maxfield, *Governing Capital*, 9, 85, 87, which gives, for example, 1970–71 figures of tax relative to GNP, which reveal how undertaxed Mexico was: Mexico, 8 percent; Peru, 15 percent; Venezuela, 21 percent; West Germany, 38 percent.

97. Gereffi and Evans, "Transnational Corporations," 47; Roger Bartra, *Agrarian Structure and Political Power in Mexico* (Baltimore: Johns Hopkins University Press, 1993), 129.

98. Centeno, *Democracy within Reason*, 69; Erfani, *Paradox of the Mexican State*, 93.

99. Bartra, *Agrarian Structure*, 130. Again, I should stress that the undoubted prevalence of "legitimizing" rhetoric does *not* denote actual legitimacy; indeed, the two may negatively correlate.

100. Erfani, *Paradox of the Mexican State*, 94–95, 108, 111, 114; Susan Kaufman Purcell, *The Mexican Profit-Sharing Decision* (Berkeley: University of California Press, 1975); Luis Medina, *Hacia el nuevo estado: México, 1920–93* (Mexico City: FCE, 1994), 208–11.

101. Compare Fowler-Salamini, "Revolutionary Caudillos"; Gilbert M. Joseph, "Caciquismo and the Revolution: Carrillo Puerto in Yucatán"; and Raymond Buve, "State Governors and Peasant Mobilization in Tlaxcala," all in Brading, *Caudillo and Peasant*, 169–92, 193–221, 222–44.

102. Knight, *Mexican Revolution*, 2, 240–51.

103. Jean Meyer, *The Cristero Rebellion* (Cambridge: Cambridge University Press, 1976). Meyer views the Cristiada as a quintessentially religious movement and is reluctant to discern ulterior motives; Jennie Purnell (work-in-progress) argues convincingly that the Cristeros—like the southern secessionists of Oaxaca or Chiapas—sought to defend provincial society, including its hierarchies and vested interests, against external threat; religion was both an end in itself *and* a facade for secular concerns.

104. It is often (wrongly) stated that the revolution "passed Chiapas by"; for a good analysis of reform in 1930s Chiapas, see Jan Rus, "The 'Comunidad Revolucionaria Institucional': The Subversion of Native Government in Highland Chiapas, 1936–68," in Joseph and Nugent, *Everyday Forms of State Formation*, 272–80.

105. Jeffery Brannon and Eric N. Baklanoff, *Agrarian Reform and Public Enterprise in Mexico* (Tuscaloosa: University of Alabama Press, 1987), 53–54, 58, 68–72, 94.

106. Martínez Vázquez, "Despojo y manipulación campesina," 165, 181, 184–85; Fox, *Politics of Food*, 168–69, 181; although Fox makes clear that federal initiatives also offered campesinos opportunities to press their interests and secure economic benefts and/or political leverage.

107. Heather Fowler-Salamini, *Agrarian Radicalism in Veracruz, 1920–38* (Lincoln: University of Nebraska Press, 1978).

108. Like the heyday of the PRI, the heyday of Cardenista reform was brief: having ousted Calles, Cárdenas had about two years, 1936–37, during which political and economic conditions favored—or allowed—radical reform; by 1938 economic recession, the resurgence of the Right, and the repercussions of the oil expropriation were conspiring to rein in reform: see Hamilton, *Limits of State Autonomy*.

109. Ilene V. O'Malley, *The Myth of the Revolution* (New York: Greenwood, 1986).

110. Geertz being touted—on the basis of his analysis of nineteenth-century Balinese court ritual—as a theorist of state ceremonialism, indeed, of "the state as a normative order": Krasner, "Approaches to the State," 232–33.

111. Paul Friedrich, *Agrarian Revolt in a Mexican Village* (Chicago: University of Chicago Press, 1977); Rus, "The 'Comunidad Revolucionaria Institucional,'" 274–80.

112. Knight, "Cardenismo: Juggernaut or Jalopy?"

113. González, *Los días del Presidente Cárdenas*, 103.

114. Alan Knight, "México y Estados Unidos, 1938–40: Rumor y realidad," *Secuencia*, January–April 1996, 129–54.

115. Harold Laswell, *Politics: Who Gets What, When, How* (Cleveland: World, 1958).

116. Note, for example, Echeverría's "secret personal working relationship" with Eugenio Garza Sada, head of the Monterrey Group (Erfani, *Paradox of the Mexican State*, 111); and Echeverría was—to quote an earlier president (López Mateos)—on the "left within the Constitution."

117. Rob Aitken, "Neoliberalism and Identity: Redefining State and Society in

Mexico," in Aitken et al., *Dismantling the Mexican State*? 28–32, offers a good example: the steelworkers of Ciudad Lázaro Cárdenas who, while they "valued the ideology of the Revolution" and even "supported the ideology of the State," "were critical of its (the State's) practice" and shared "a common perception that the State, or rather the elite in control of the State, had betrayed the rights expressed in the ideals of the Revolution and hijacked it for their own purposes." In Scott's terms, the elite were hoisted by the petard of their public transcript. Local studies of this kind offer, in my view, much better insights into "legitimacy" (or its absence) than aggregate survey data.

118. Gabriel A. Almond and Sidney Verba, *The Civic Culture: Political Attitudes and Democracy in Five Nations* (Boston: Little Brown, 1965), which, despite its methodological failings, captured (schizoid) elements of Mexican "political culture," which subsequent commentators have corroborated: Knight, "México bronco."

119. Scott, *Domination and the Arts of Resistance*, 72.

120. Rafael Segovia, *La politización del niño mexicano* (Mexico City: El Colegio de México, 1975), 104–5; Vargas Llosa's famous description, now academically endorsed: Cothran, *Political Stability and Democracy in Mexico*.

121. Mexico's progressive face was often turned outward; the regime displayed a more consistent leftism in its foreign policy than its domestic policy; hence its qualified support for Cuba, Allende, and the Sandinistas, its critiques of the Vietnam War and Zionism, its flirtations with *tercermundismo*—all of which were rapidly revised in the later 1980s and 1990s.

122. Hence the quip: "who goes to bed with the State, wakes up next to Lombardo": Barry Carr, *Marxism and Communism in Twentieth-Century Mexico* (Lincoln: University of Nebraska Press, 1992), 303.

123. Bartra, *Agrarian Structure*, 144–47; Schmidt, *The Deterioration of the Mexican Presidency*, 100–102; Maxfield, *Governing Capital*, chap. 6.

124. Jeffrey W. Rubin, "Popular Mobilization and the Myth of State Corporatism," in Joe Foweraker and Ann L. Craig, eds., *Popular Movements and Political Change in Mexico* (Boulder, Colo.: Lynne Rienner, 1990), 247–70; Schryer, *Ethnicity and Class Conflict*, pts. 3, 4.

125. Knight, "México bronco," 10–11, 22–23.

126. See note 94.

127. Judith A. Teichman, *Policymaking in Mexico: From Boom to Bust* (Boston: Allen and Unwin, 1988), chap. 7; Maxfield, *Governing Capital*, 133, 137; Erfani, *Paradox of the Mexican State*, 117–19, which, following Rosario Green, links mounting bureaucratic tensions and foreign debt to the state's reluctance to increase taxes; an argument that accords with Fishlow's proposition ("The Latin American State," 67) that, with regard to the continent's economic travails in the 1980s, "the real villain of the piece is fiscal inadequacy"—itself a sure sign of states lacking autonomous will or capacity.

128. We have, in other words, a trade-off between Mann's "authoritative" and "diffused" power: the first reflected in executive capacity, the second in regime durability and "penetration" of society (see note 65).

129. Smith, *Labyrinths of Power*, 58–59; under Echeverría alone, central government employees increased from 300,000 to 1.3 million: Merrilee Grindle,

Challenging the State: Crisis and Innovation in Latin America and Africa (Cambridge: Cambridge University Press, 1996), 51.

130. Did official solicitude for the middle class reflect (1) the inexorable logic of "development" or "modernization"? (2) calculating political payoffs? (3) class and cultural kinship? I know of no extended discussion of the problem. Compare, perhaps, how the Shah of Iran dug his own political grave by embarking on obsessive "modernization": Migdal, *Strong Societies*, 20.

131. On camarillas: Smith, *Labyrinths of Power*, 50–51ff.; Centeno, *Democracy within Reason*, 146–49, 159, 160–70; Roderic Camp, "*Camarillas* in Mexican Politics: The Case of the Salinas Cabinet," *Mexican Studies/Estudios Mexicanos* 6 no. 1 (1990): 85–107; Jorge Gil-Mendieta and Samuel Schmidt, "Las redes de poder en México," *Este País* 44 (November 1994): 2–18.

132. Thomson, "Peculiarities of the English," 48–49; on corruption, see Stephen D. Morris, *Corruption and Politics in Contemporary Mexico* (Tuscaloosa: University of Alabama Press, 1991).

133. It may be debated how "new" the neoliberal project was; there had been intimations of such a course back in the 1970s, even the late 1960s; and, as regards toleration of electoral opposition, the story goes back at least to 1977, if not 1958. There can be little doubt, however, that—in part because he presided over a fairly united, like-thinking administration—Salinas pressed ahead with much greater purpose and conviction than any of his predecessors.

134. Centeno, *Democracy within Reason*, 193; and, straight from the horse's mouth, Alicia Hernández Chávez, "Mexican Presidentialism: A Historical and Institutional Overview," *Mexican Studies/Estudios Mexicanos* 10, no. 1 (1994): 224–25.

135. Centeno, *Democracy within Reason*, chap. 7.

136. Grindle, *Challenging the State*, 83–86, 89–92, summarizes deregulation.

137. Maxfield, *Governing Capital*, 105.

138. M. Delal Baer, "Mexico's Second Revolution: Pathways to Liberalization," in Riordan Roett, ed., *Political and Economic Liberalization in Mexico* (Boulder, Colo.: Lynne Rienner, 1993), 51–68, a sub-Fukuyama "analysis" that, traducing Mexican and world history alike, confidently asserts that "the key elements of the PRI's modernizing coalition, the private sector and the middle class, are the constituents most politically sophisticated and committed to a democratic transition"—as in Italy in the 1920s, Germany in the 1930s, Brazil in the 1960s, Argentina and Chile in the 1970s, and so on.

139. Centeno, *Democracy within Reason*, 16.

140. Especially while the economy was growing: Grindle, *Challenging the State*, 86, 89–90.

141. The startling success of Cuauhtémoc Cárdenas in 1987–88 illustrated that the appeal of revolutionary nationalism, when delivered with some credibility, was far from spent; the problem was that credibility was often lacking; and even the neo-Cardenistas lacked a coherent and convincing alternative economic policy.

142. It therefore encapsulated Kahler's "orthodox paradox": "the use of the state to reduce and diminish the economic influence of politics": Centeno, *Democracy within Reason*, 34.

143. Ibid., 193; negative proof, perhaps, of Evans's argument that "expansion of the state's role is not synonymous with enhanced capacity": Peter B. Evans, "Transnational Linkages and the Economic Role of the State: An Analysis of Developing and Industrialized Nations in the Post–World War II Period," in Evans, Rueschemeyer, and Skocpol, Bringing the State Back In, 200. However, my tentative conclusion is that, even if neoliberal reform was associated with enhanced state capacity vis-à-vis important domestic constituencies, this outcome was possibly conjunctural rather than structural, and, more important, it implied a growing "dependency," or lack of autonomy, vis-à-vis international agents.

144. Grindle, Challenging the State, 58–59, 86. Kevin J. Middlebrook, The Paradox of Revolution: Labor, the State and Authoritarianism in Mexico (Baltimore: Johns Hopkins University Press, 1995), 293ff. Of course, Salinas still needed the CTM, if only to contain wage demands; however, that containing role was less crucial than in the past, and the CTM's capacity to deliver the vote had certainly dwindled.

145. Maxfield, Governing Capital, 136; Centeno, Democracy within Reason, 13.

146. Centeno, Democracy within Reason, 18; Rafael Rodríguez Castaneda, "El reporto de la riqueza en tiempos de Salinas de Gortari," Proceso, July 12, 1993, 6–9.

147. This counterfactual raises the tricky question of culpability: was the neoliberal model fundamentally flawed (i.e., a crash—or major "correction"—was eventually inevitable); or was it basically sound but blown off course by the "mistakes of December"? For a critical review of the "new economic model," see Victor Bulmer-Thomas, "Conclusions," in Victor Bulmer-Thomas, ed., The New Economic Model in Latin America and Its Impact on Income Distribution and Poverty (London: ILAS, 1996), 295–314.

148. "Survival" on what terms? The key question, in my view, is whether the PRI can lose a presidential election and peacefully surrender national power to an opposition party. Even then, cautious observers might wish to see how the new party-in-government comports itself—that is, whether it "PRI-ifies" itself, thus reproducing old elements of "the system," or, rather, consummates a decisive break with the past and institutionalizes transparent, pluralist politics within the framework of a Rechtsstaat.

149. Grindle, Challenging the State, 15.

150. Wayne A. Cornelius, Judith Gentlemen, and Peter H. Smith, eds., Mexico's Alternative Political Futures (San Diego: Center for US-Mexican Studies, 1989).

151. Centeno, Democracy within Reason, 219–22; Grindle, Challenging the State, 113–20.

152. Maxfield, Governing Capital, 102–6, 115.

153. Ibid., 116.

154. Erfani, Paradox of the Mexican State, 177.

155. Maybe "dependency" was consigned to the scrapheap of history a little prematurely; or, to put it differently, perhaps it paradoxically acquired theoretical cachet at a time (the 1960s) when its applicability was in fact declining; rather as

"the state" was (analytically) "brought back in" just when it was being shown the door by governments around the world.

156. Centeno (*Democracy within Reason*, 245) notes "the many parallels between the new elite in control of the Mexcan state and its *científico* predecessors."

157. Failings that are not, of course, confined to Mexico.

158. As Porfirio Díaz said of José Vicente Villada, governor of the State of Mexico: Ricardo Avila, " 'Así se gobierna, señores!': El gobierno de José Vicente Villada," in Jaime Rodríguez O., ed., *The Revolutionary Process in Mexico* (Los Angeles: UCLA, 1990), 15–32.

159. Scott, *Domination and the Arts of Resistance*, 72.

160. Denise Dresser, *Neopopulist Solutions to Neoliberal Problems* (San Diego: Center for US-Mexican Studies, 1991).

161. Knight, "México bronco."

162. To focus excessively on specific classes—usually the bourgeoisie—can lead to a crude reification, whereby "the bourgeoisie" is endowed with specific aims, goals, and interests. A broader "political-economy" approach identifies the systemic pressures and tendencies to which all classes—dominant classes included—are subject.

163. Not that the debate is proportional to the relevance. As with a good deal of social science, major paradigms (e.g., dependency, structural Marxism, "bringing the state back in," postmodernism) often seem to flourish when least relevant and to wilt when most needed.

164. As we move from "European" (which at least has some precision) to "Western" (which has very little), we come to see the futility of such labeling. If Skocpol and Tilly are "Western," what are Prebisch, Mariátegui, and Lombardo Toledano?

165. Mauricio Tenorio-Trillo, *Mexico at the World's Fairs: Crafting a Modern Nation* (Berkeley: University of California Press, 1996), 212.

Chapter Seven

SAMUEL HUNTINGTON AND THE
LATIN AMERICAN STATE

JORGE I. DOMÍNGUEZ

"THE MOST IMPORTANT political distinction among countries concerns not their form of government but their degree of government. The differences between democracy and dictatorship are less than the differences between those countries whose politics embodies consensus, community, legitimacy, organization, effectiveness, stability, and those countries whose politics is deficient in these qualities." So begins Samuel P. Huntington's *Political Order in Changing Societies,*[1] one of the most widely influential and insightful books on comparative politics ever written.[2] Its concern is normative as well as analytic. In a retrospective comment on his own writing, Huntington has noted, "I wrote [*Political Order*] because I thought political order was a good thing." Moreover, he added, his "purpose was to develop a general social science theory of why, how, and under what circumstances order could and could not be achieved."[3]

Huntington's concern with order, and his apparent downgrading of the significance of the distinction between democracy and dictatorship, easily earned him a reputation as a conservative; some used much harsher epithets.[4] Often lost in such crude labels was Huntington's equally clear understanding that the quality of order also mattered. Order was, for example, a prerequisite for liberty. "Men may, of course, have order without liberty, but they cannot have liberty without order. Authority has to exist before it can be limited."[5] He demonstrated his very substantial interest in liberty and democracy by publishing a book on the subject, *The Third Wave: Democratization in the Late Twentieth Century*, some two decades later.

The reputation for conservatism had one important effect, however. Among Latin Americanists, Huntington was read but, for the most part, not followed. At the time of the publication of *Political Order*, the subfield of the study of Latin American politics was about to be overrun by scholarship on international dependency. A great many scholars of Latin America at the time, moreover, were not enamored of the political order prevailing in their own countries and thus were not instinctively attracted to a book for which order was both an analytic starting point and a key political value. And, as we shall see, the book does not feature one single approach to the study of politics but several, thus making it difficult to emulate—and most Latin Americanists did not try.

And yet, exclusive attention to Huntington's normative concerns, albeit appropriate in the assessment of the work of any scholar, can get in the way of appreciating the eclectic range embodied in *Political Order*. This book resists easy ideological classification. Depending on the chapter and its passage, Samuel Huntington could be called a Marxist, a Leninist, a Fabian, a modernizationist, an institutionalist, or, as some might say today, "whatever."

In this work, I seek to assess several of Huntington's key ideas especially in the light of pertinent experiences from Latin America.[6] First, I argue that different segments of *Political Order* represent rather different intellectual approaches. Parts of the work are best read, indeed, as Marxist, Leninist, and Fabian, not as conservative tracts, though in each reading the concern for order endures. This "cafeteria" of academic approaches makes it difficult to emulate the book, to found a school of thought, or to develop a method for research according to its prescriptions. In the late 1960s and early 1970s, intellectual "open-mindedness" was not in vogue among Latin Americanists.[7] Huntington's eclecticism made for a much more interesting and insightful book but, among Latin Americanists, a less influential one. His approach in this book, therefore, enhanced its intrinsic intellectual interest and value, but it reduced the likelihood of its impact on this subfield.

Second, I argue that the conceptual core of the book is both innovative and problematic. Huntington sought to be an iconoclast, breaking in significant ways with prevailing scholarly opinion. His emphasis and focus on politics and on the institutions of the political system turned a new page for scholarship on comparative politics. Nevertheless, he remained recognizably within a "modernization" approach through his emphasis on process and his surprising relative inattention to the institutions "inside" the state. The conceptual apparatus of the work leads away from the state toward the study of political conflict, not to an understanding of the state itself. His residual "modernizationism" did not endear him to a Latin Americanist community seeking to flee that school of thought. And his relative inattention to the state made his work less helpful to scholars seeking to understand the rise of powerful and repressive bureaucratic-authoritarian regimes in the 1960s and 1970s.

Third, I conclude with an analysis of Huntington's principal intellectual contribution, namely, the study of political parties—a contribution from whose recognition most Latin Americanists would gain much.

Huntington argued that it was parties, not just the clever, not just slowly changing structures, and not political culture that can give both continuity and motion to politics, and he specified how and under what circumstances various outcomes occur. In this regard, his work surpassed the prevailing literature and itself has not yet been surpassed.

THREE FACES OF HUNTINGTON'S SCHOLARSHIP

Huntington as Marxist

"Military interventions are only one specific manifestation of a broader phenomenon . . .: the general politicization of social forces and institutions."[8] Huntington argues that military coups are principally instances of raw social conflict. For him, it is "fallacious to attempt to explain military intervention in politics primarily by reference to the internal structure of the military or the social background of the officers doing the intervening."[9] Instead, military coups and military rule are the product of changing social class coalitions.

In oligarchic praetorianism, he argues, the dominant social forces are the landlords, the upper clergy, and military officers. With the emergence of the middle class, however, a new coalition develops in which the middle class becomes the dominant actor; younger officers are the agents of this new class coalition. Huntington called these "breakthrough" coups. His examples of oligarchic and breakthrough cases are often drawn from the Latin American experience. For instance, he counts as breakthrough coups those in the cycle, begun in Chile in the mid-1920s, that continued in various countries until the eve of the cold war; his use of evidence is consistent with that of his Latin Americanist sources.[10]

Circumstances change with the rise of organized labor and its entry into politics, Huntington claims. To block the attempt to transform the structures of power, privilege, and society, the middle class calls on the armed forces to stage "veto" coups to overthrow labor-leaning governments or to prevent their consolidation of power. Huntington explains the difference in the effects of military coups as a function of a changed social structure: "The more backward a society is, the more progressive the role of its military; the more advanced a society becomes, the more conservative and reactionary becomes the role of its military." The change in the role and social effects of the military in Argentina from the late nineteenth century to the mid–twentieth century is his principal Latin American example.[11]

This approach to the study of military intervention stands in some contrast to Huntington's own prior work on the military. In *The Soldier and the State*, Huntington argued that the likelihood of stable or unstable civil-military relations hinges on relations of power, professionalism, and ideology.[12] Institutions and ideas help to shape and govern the pattern of civil-military relations. And yet, these concepts are absent from the comparable discussion in *Political Order*.

The Huntington of *The Soldier and the State* thus serves as the best critic of the Huntington of *Political Order*. In the latter book, Huntington's relative inattention to the role of institutions and ideas in his analysis of military coups left him somewhat unprepared to understand either the Peruvian military coup of 1968 and the "left-reformist" government that followed it or the right-wing bureaucratic-authoritarian coups that began in Brazil in 1964 and spread elsewhere in South America over the next decade. In Huntington's scheme, the "Peruvian experiment" begun in 1968 is difficult to explain because Peru's social structure already featured the class coalitions that are supposed to lead to veto coups. How, then, could a military government in Peru seek to change the social structure, overthrow a middle-class president and weaken middle-class power, and provide opportunities (albeit limited) for the participation of the urban poor?[13]

The Brazilian political regime established in 1964 had, to be sure, an important class character at its origin, but its establishment and development can be understood only through comparable attention to the important role of military socialization, professionalism, mission, and ideology—concepts relatively absent from the analysis of military coups in *Political Order*, though close to the heart of the argument in *The Soldier and the State*. Soon after the 1964 coup, the Brazilian military turned against many of its social class allies from the time of the coup. The new bureaucratic-authoritarian regime sought to establish its independence from Brazilian society and promulgate a set of rules and institutions derived substantially from preferences within the institution of the armed forces.[14]

The oddity, therefore, in Huntington's admittedly brief flirtation with intellectual Marxism is that, as an analyst of Latin America, he might have been more influential had he not changed his scholarly views. Nevertheless, Huntington's account of the pattern of Latin American military intervention was more complete and systematic than anything hitherto available. His scholarly discussion of coups in Latin America was superior to what Latin Americanists had been writing. Only subsequent to *Political Order*, and in dialogue with it, did other scholars improve on Huntington's analysis.[15]

Huntington as Leninist

"Revolutions produce little liberty, but they are history's most expeditious means of producing fraternity, equality, and identity." This is so,

Huntington continues, because "revolution . . . involves moral renewal"; indeed, "every revolution is a Puritan revolution" because of its commitment to ferret out corruption. As a result, "material deprivations, which would have been insufferable under the old regime, are proof of the strength of the new one. The less their food and material comfort the more people come to value the political and ideological accomplishments of the revolution for which they are sacrificing so much."[16] To be successful, however, a revolution must give birth to a revolutionary party.

Huntington celebrates the efficacy of the Leninist party as a means to construct political order and subordinate social forces—the very forces that could otherwise promote military coups. "Lenin and Mao were right when they stressed the primacy of a political organization independent of social forces and yet manipulating them to seek its ends."[17] Indeed, he notes, "The effectiveness of the Leninist model can also be seen comparatively in the two instances where it and alternative approaches were applied side by side to the same people with the same culture, with roughly the same level of economic development, and in adjoining territory: Korea and Vietnam." Huntington unequivocally asserts that the North in each case had achieved greater "real political stability . . . which led one to have confidence that when Ho and Kim passed from the scene neither country would suffer the political disruption and violence which followed the departure from office of Syngman Rhee and Ngo Dinh Diem."[18] On that forecast, Huntington was analytically correct and prescient.

With regard to Latin America, Huntington compares the Mexican and Bolivian revolutions to make the point that the first succeeded but the second one failed to create political order. First, Bolivia's revolution involved too little violence. Violence is the midwife of order in Huntington's analysis; only after a "nasty, brutish" period of Hobbesian violence do citizens long for order, and only violence can eliminate the contending claimants for power who otherwise become sources of future disorder. Second, Bolivia lacked in statesmanship; every president maneuvered to retain or to return to power. Mexico's firm rule of no presidential reelection, in contrast, stabilized and institutionalized revolutionary power, he argues. Third, the ruling party in Mexico succeeded in subordinating social forces; the Nationalist Revolutionary Movement in Bolivia did not. Finally, Bolivia was relatively free of antiforeign nationalism, while Mexico bristled in such feelings. Public support for revolutionary leaders can be mobilized more easily when it can be presented as a defense of the homeland.

Huntington's analysis of Bolivia is consistent with what Bolivianists have written.[19] His analysis of Mexico, however, does not fit his own argument very well, though his comparison between Mexico and Bolivia is apt and illuminating. Contrary to the gist of his argument, the Mexican Revolution did not produce a Leninist party. Mexico's ruling party was founded through a deal among military chieftains and other elites. It did not have party members in any meaningful sense for most of its history. It was never an exemplar of moral renewal, much less puritanism, and it never exalted the virtues of sacrifice.[20] Whatever the merits of Huntington's analysis of Leninism might be in Europe or East Asia, there is no clear correspondence between it and the one Latin American case (Mexico) that he discusses in greatest detail. Mexico's ruling party created political order by means other than those emphasized by Huntington in this study.

Huntington did not attempt to apply his analysis to revolution in Cuba, but, had he done so, it would have fit much better than it did for Mexico. The level of violence involved in the 1950s in Batista's overthrow was limited, but it rose much higher during the first half of the 1960s; relative to Cuba's population, the revolutionary government in the 1960s jailed more political prisoners and held them in prison longer than would any bureaucratic-authoritarian regime in Latin America. The creation of the new Cuban Communist Party was somewhat delayed, but by the mid-1960s this party had most of the attributes of ruling "vanguard" Leninist parties: it was small, selective, and mobilizational; commanded primacy over social forces; and brooked no opposition. In the 1960s, the Cuban revolutionary government certainly attempted moral renewal; it was strikingly and aggressively puritanical in its approach to homosexuals, for example. This revolutionary regime confronted the United States, was assertively nationalist, and exalted the virtue of sacrifice on behalf of the homeland and future generations.[21]

The legacy of the revolutionary 1960s and the role of the Leninist party are among the reasons that the Cuban political regime survived the collapse of the Soviet Union. Cuban leaders have also long been blessed with timely U.S. government actions that have helped them to rally patriotic Cubans to the leadership's side; these range from the 1961 invasion at Playa Girón (the Bay of Pigs) to the enactment of the Helms-Burton Act in 1996. You need not believe us, Cuban leaders have told their people, when we argue that the United States is ready to invade us (1961) or cares more about property rights than about your personal well-being (1996)—just look at the actions of its government! Huntington's variables, in short, explain well the consolidation and survival of Fidel Castro's government.

Huntington's faith in the Leninist party and his comparison of the two Koreas and the two Vietnams, cited earlier, also seemed to mark him as an anticulturalist. The point of the comparison, after all, was that culture did not lead to comparable institutions and comparable outcomes in the two Koreas and the two Vietnams; culture neither shaped their destinies nor prevented intracivilizational clashes. On the contrary, specific institutions reshaped the life of each half of the nation to bring about quite different results. From a reading of these passages in *Political Order*, one would not have forecast Huntington's reincarnation in the mid-1990s as the author of *The Clash of Civilizations*, in which culture on a grand scale is a key explanation of human behavior.[22]

Huntington as Fabian

"Revolutions are rare. Reform, perhaps, is even rarer. And neither is necessary. Countries may simply stagnate."[23] Notwithstanding such a gloomy initial assessment of the prospects for reform, Huntington provides a subtle account of the likelihood for and strategies of reform. In contrast to his structuralist and coalitionist analysis of military interventions and his paean to the Leninist party as an organization, Huntington's study of reform focuses, above all, on individuals who enact change, often through non-Leninist parties.

Although reform may be rare, would-be reformers can be found in quite different life circumstances. They could be Social Democrats or Christian Democrats; Huntington's Latin American examples include Venezuela's Rómulo Betancourt, Peru's Fernando Belaúnde, and Chile's Eduardo Frei Montalva. They could be military officers, among whom, however, he cites no Latin American. For most reformers, military or civilian, Huntington counsels a Fabian strategy, which he describes as "the foot-in-the-door approach of concealing his aims, separating the reforms from each other, and pushing for only one change at a time."[24]

Huntington identifies a problem for reformers that, he suggests, was common in Latin America. Reform in highly urbanized settings may be a catalyst for revolution. The city is the permanent source of opposition to the government. University students are likely to oppose the government, Huntington argues—any government. The same is true, albeit to a less dramatic extent, for other urban middle-class groups. In this fashion, Huntington accounts for problems in establishing political order in the 1960s in such countries as Colombia, Venezuela, and the Dominican Republic. Reform should not be undertaken, therefore, to pacify urban demands, for such an endeavor will fail and will waste politically valuable resources.

Huntington's strongest case on behalf of reform, therefore, bypasses urban settings and focuses on the countryside, where reform is a substitute for revolution and, therefore, is more likely to foster political order. Huntington claims that land reform is the most likely means to create and sustain political stability. Peasants who do not fear that they would be evicted from their lands or suffer ruinous taxation and prices are likely to remain loyal to the country's rulers. He celebrates the conservatizing results of land reform in Japan, Korea, Mexico, and Venezuela in the mid–twentieth century, and, indeed, his analytic point is impressive.

Huntington's general advocacy of land reform illustrates well why reform may be so rare. Land reform should appeal to conservatives who are the political heirs of Benjamin Disraeli, but often conservatives are the very landlords who may be dispossessed. The political and economic interests of such would-be reformers are at odds.

As applied to Latin America, Huntington proves prescient once again when he forecasts severe conflicts over land tenure in Guatemala and El Salvador. He foresees comparably severe conflicts in Peru and Brazil. It is not clear, however, which variables explain why this forecast was correct for the first two but less so for the latter two. Huntington does argue that land reform is more difficult in democratic regimes mainly because all reform requires a greater concentration of power than such regimes permit. In democratic parliaments, landlord forces can often stop or undermine a land reform program. "Latin American legislatures have also traditionally been the graveyards of land reform measures," Huntington wrote accurately.[25] This helps to explain the relative failure of land reform efforts in Brazil and Peru before the 1964 and 1968 coups (and in other countries) but makes it all the more intriguing why elites in El Salvador and Guatemala, which had concentrated power sufficient to carry out reform, failed to anticipate in timely fashion the severe conflict that would break out in their respective countries, in part over land tenure issues, and act according to Huntington's recommendations.

Huntington's analysis helps, indeed, to explain why reform has been rare in Latin America. And yet it is in part because of the way he defines reform that its rarity is highlighted. Huntington is interested in reform in this work only insofar as it consolidates or undermines political order. Reforms for other purposes—improving the quality of government services, reducing poverty, reorienting the direction of economic policy—are not pertinent to his book. These other kinds of reform did take place in several Latin American countries at various moments while Huntington was writing his book, or prior to it. In particular, he ignores important reform efforts that took place in Argentina and Chile under the Arturo Illia and Eduardo Frei presidencies.[26] Similarly, the economic reforms implemented in many countries in the 1990s, intended to improve the quality of economic performance, would not have been within the purview of Huntington's analysis; such reforms become pertinent in his analysis only when they are directly related to the consolidation of newly established democracies. For these reasons, Huntington's reforms are rare: he has defined the category so that examples are observable only infrequently.

Between Modernizationists and Institutionalists

In 1965, Huntington published an article, on the subject that would lead eventually to *Political Order*, which brought him instant notoriety because he broke with the prevailing scholarly consensus in studies of comparative politics. Huntington feels especially proud that he punctured the optimism that, in his view, was undermining comparative scholarship at the time.[27]

That scholarly consensus focused principally on behavior outside of the institutions of government. In the work represented best by Gabriel Almond, there was an attempt to specify the structures and functions of political processes. Almond, alone and in consecutive collaboration with James Coleman and G. Bingham Powell, also sought to understand the "input" and "output" capabilities of political systems, though there was much less attention to the processes within the black box of the state. "Political development" was the label given to the process of political change in countries outside Western Europe and North America.[28] A different scholarly tradition emphasized the importance of values, personality, and changes in them; Daniel Lerner and Lucian Pye were noteworthy exponents.[29] A third scholarly approach emphasized social processes and the complex and interrelated set of changes that they represented and brought about; Karl Deutsch was a main proponent.[30]

These and other scholars were aware of the difficulty of bringing about change, of the resistance to change, and of the setbacks on the path to change once it had begun. Nonetheless, in each of these writings there was a clear sense of movement toward something called "modernization" or "development." In 1965, Huntington broke with that assumption in the very title of his article "Political Development and Political Decay," whose main point was disarmingly simple: decay was conceptually just as possible as development, and empirically no less frequent.[31] This work launched a process of scholarly reexamination that would weaken the consensus in comparative politics that had come to be known as the modernization school. In *Political Order*, the words *political development* and *political decay* were for the most part quietly deleted, purged to avoid teleological temptations.[32]

And yet Huntington's argument in *Political Order* retained substantial components of the modernization approach. In the first chapter, the analysis builds on the relationship between "social mobilization," identified as Deutsch had done, on the one hand, and economic development, on the other. If social mobilization outruns the growth of the economy, the result is social frustration. Should it, in turn, grow more quickly than the opportunities for social mobility, then political participation will increase. Political instability will result if political participation spreads more quickly than political institutionalization. Only in these later stages of the analysis do political institutions come in, though they do so decisively.

Huntington's approach to institutions remained markedly processual, clearly responsive to the dominant perspectives of the modernization school. Just as students of society wrote about social mobilization and those of the economy about economic development, so he would focus on political institutionalization. This was an important and creative scholarly contribution at the time, but it also set a limit to his iconoclasm: he was interested in processes akin to those of the modernization school, often in the very terms framed by those scholars, even if he was much more skeptical than other scholars that these processes would generate institutionalization in most countries.

The first chapter of *Political Order* is a clarion call to study political institutions. Huntington identifies several concepts—adaptability, coherence, complexity, and autonomy—to assess the extent of institutionalization and writes at some length about them as a way to think about the problems of political order and disorder. He proposes operational measures for these concepts, but, surprisingly, for the most part they are not systematically employed in the rest of the book.

One reason may be that the concepts are more difficult to employ than it appears at first sight. Arguably, for example, an increase in an entity's complexity may well reduce its coherence. If so, the two concepts cannot both be part of one and the same process of institutionalization. Adaptability and autonomy, in turn, are not the exclusive property of an organization but are relational variables. Only in the relationship between an organization and something outside it can we tell whether the organization is adaptable and autonomous. The problem thus arises that adaptability and autonomy may include within each concept the behavior that they seek to explain. In order to know whether X is independent from Y, for instance, we need to know something about both X and Y; the concept of autonomy is not a sole property of X, nor can autonomy explain the relationship between X and Y.

Each of the four concepts, nonetheless, is analytically valuable. The ensemble of four focuses scholars on different aspects of a process of institutionalization, and some scholars have attempted to apply these ideas empirically.[33] The difficulty characteristically arises when one attempts to use them jointly and systematically as part of one and the same multifaceted concept.

Huntington does not merely drop after the first chapter the conceptual apparatus that he builds therein; he also drops attention to the institutions of the state. In subsequent chapters, he explores contrasting politico-cultural traditions, the role of leadership in reform of both traditional polities and other forms of regimes, the likelihood of military coups and revolutions, and the role of political parties. The institutions of the state are notable for their absence. To be sure, there is sporadic attention, to the bureaucracy but no sustained study. The armed forces are not analyzed in their own terms but only, as already noted, as potential politicized praetorian actors. Constitutional organs such as courts, legislatures, or the role of executives (as distinct from the role of individual leaders) are also discussed only in the context of commenting on other matters. Formal electoral procedures are not addressed in any depth. The word *state* does not appear in the index, nor is it employed as a concept. The word *government*, much more in vogue at time, appears often but it is not the object of Huntington's theorizing.

Political Order is a child of its times. As Almond, Pye, and Deutsch did in their own work in their own fashion, *Political Order*, too, emphasizes processes that poke at, provoke, envelop, threaten, bolster, weaken, or strengthen "the state" but without much looking inside the black box. Huntington's *Political Order* might be described as "closet modernizationism."

Its principal difference from the then prevailing scholarship, and its signal merit, was its sustained attention to the *political*, not just to processes that impinge on politics, and specifically to political leaders and political institutions. As I will note in a later section, its emphasis on political parties is innovative and in many ways pathbreaking. Its concern with the institutions of the political system, even if not necessarily those of the state, was a major advance over the sociologistic and economistic tenor of the scholarship then produced by political scientists. And his insistence on the need to study institutions would assist other scholars in years to come to give greater attention to the institutions of the state itself.[34]

The Surprisingly Missing Variables

Huntington first made his reputation as a student of the military; soon he would add the study of international security and defense to his scholarly laurels.[35] And yet international variables are virtually absent from *Political Order*, which includes only one brief discussion of the impact of war on state formation: "War was the great stimulus to state building."[36] Had Huntington in this book developed this theme, with which he was so familiar from his previous work, he might have come much closer to a theory of the state in *Political Order*. And he would have formulated a more complete theory of revolution.

As noted earlier, Huntington writes about the eventual utility of revolutionary war to consolidate political order in Mexico. He might have speculated on whether the wars of late-nineteenth-century South America contributed to the consolidation of states while the "long (interstate) peace" of twentieth-century Latin America permitted the armed forces to become politicized, depriving central state leaders and institutions of the means to build national cohesion, in contrast to the experiences in Europe. He might have wondered whether greater international threats to the survival of the state might have stimulated quicker improvements in literacy, in health care, or in the development of manufacturing, as well as military professionalism, as did occur in European countries subject to interstate war.

Nor does Huntington pay much attention to the impact of international variables in the areas of trade, finance, or direct foreign investment. He leaves that intellectual terrain unoccupied—fertile ground for the writings of the "dependency" school that were already under way.[37]

Had Huntington paid more attention to international factors, he might have had greater impact on Latin Americanist scholarship, whose focus was then turning sharply to privilege international variables as the key to explain the hemisphere's condition. And because Huntington would probably have emphasized the impact of international war more than the impact of the international economy for state building and its consequences, he would have provided a valuable, early, and sensible correction that might have helped to prevent the fall of much Latin Americanist scholarship into economistic international dependency arguments.

Political Order, moreover, is principally a work of comparison among countries at different moments in their histories, not a historically driven comparative work.[38] This is, of course, an important difference between Huntington, on the one hand, and Barrington Moore[39] or Alexander Gerschenkron,[40] on the other, for the latter two—writing at approximately the same time—formulated historically rooted explanations as the core of their analysis. This book and some of Huntington's others show, of course, stunning historical learning.[41] But in eschewing the formulation of historical explanations—in contrast to simply employing historical examples to make other points—Huntington also may have missed the opportunity to fashion a theory of government or a theory of the state. A historically grounded discussion of political institutionalization—more than a listing of abstract concepts—might have led him more directly to the black box of the state. *Political Order* shows the analytic power of comparisons in the hands of a master; it would have been even more masterful had it also featured more historical explanations.

HUNTINGTON'S LATIN AMERICANNESS

Huntington has never claimed to be an expert on Latin America; indeed, he has never presented himself as an expert on any one of the world's geographic regions. (Arguably, he is a leading "area studies" expert on the United States.)[42] And yet, as should already be evident, *Political Order* is significantly informed by research on Latin America, much more so than has often been the case for leading comparativists.

Huntington's study of Latin America contributed to several important features of *Political Order*. Latin America, and those who wrote about the region, celebrated the "twilight of the tyrants" in the late 1950s,[43] only to mourn the rise of new tyrannies in the 1960s. Latin America's political experience in the 1960s contributed to Huntington's general worry about the prospects for political order; in particular, the breakdown of Latin America's democratic regimes in those years led him to insist, as already noted, that there cannot be "liberty without order." Certainly the Latin American cases educated Huntington to understand the weakness of mediating institutions between state and society, the feeble differentiation in many instances between state and party, and the porousness of the state to many powerful forces in society and economy.

Latin America's experience also contributed greatly to Huntington's understanding of praetorianism, that is, the politicization of all social forces including, but not limited to, the military. Many of Huntington's examples are drawn from the region. He shows a keen understanding of both specific military coups and general aspects of the relations between the military and society more generally. Even his general underemphasis of the importance of military ideas, missions, professionalism, and institutions is quite faithful to his Latin Americanist sources.

Latin America figures prominently in Huntington's reasoning as an example of both the possibility and the difficulty of reform. Rómulo Betancourt and Eduardo Frei appear often as committed and effective political leaders, but so, too, do landlords and the legislatures they control as obstacles to reform, opposing even reforms that might make it more likely that order would endure. Five of Huntington's seven examples of countries where conservatives should most clearly have understood that land reform was in their own long-term interest are in Latin America (Bolivia, Brazil, El Salvador, Guatemala, and Peru). Of the next eleven countries for which the same generalization would apply, though with less urgency, all but two are Latin American.[44] Latin America made Huntington keenly aware of the significance of marked inequality for politics and the fate of peoples.

Closer attention to Latin America might have led Huntington, however, to think more about the institutions of the state itself, and specifically about the impact of bureaucracy. Such reflection might have helped him consider whether bureaucratic traditions were best understood as cultural legacies from the colonial past or as constructions and reconstructions in each country's history with the passing of time. Such work would have helped him as well when his interests turned toward greater attention to cultural factors in the years that followed.

Similarly, a closer dialogue with the Latin Americanist literature emerging at the same time as he was preparing his book would have alerted him to the significance and impact of international variables not just in the world of scholars but also in the experiences of the countries he sought to understand. In what ways did international factors weaken or strengthen the prospects for order? That question remained unasked; Latin Americanists would have asked it perhaps too often but were certainly right in raising it. (Huntington himself would return to this analytic concern with international explanations when he sought to understand the reemergence of democratic politics worldwide in the 1970s and 1980s.)[45]

THE FOCUS ON POLITICAL PARTIES

Political Order is, above all, a sustained comparative study of the role of political parties. It is a measure of Huntington's regrettable lack of influence on the study of Latin American politics that the dominant scholarly works of the 1970s and 1980s in this subfield paid so little attention to political parties.

Fernando Henrique Cardoso, as a working politician, would rediscover political parties, but his most famous work (written with Enzo Faletto) accords little analytic significance to parties.[46] Guillermo O'Donnell's rightly famous work on the emergence of bureaucratic authoritarianism focuses, above all, on structural economic variables. Political parties are subsumed under the vague catchall category called "populism," but they are not analyzed in their own terms in detail.[47] O'Donnell's subsequent pathbreaking work with Philippe Schmitter on transitions to democracy called attention to the skill of politicians, not to partisan organizations through which many of them would work.[48] In the 1980s and 1990s, a vast scholarly literature arose on social movements; much of it ignored political parties, and, to the extent that it did not, it saw parties as malignant forces that subvert or thwart the consolidation of civil society.[49]

Of course, there have always been scholars who have studied political parties in Latin America,[50] but their work never captured the imagination and attention of the profession as a whole, in contrast, for example, to work by other scholars on political parties in western Europe, North America, or India. One reason, no doubt, is the prevalence of authoritarian regimes in Latin America from the mid-1960s to the mid-1980s—precisely the years of the "takeoff" of Latin American studies in the United States. Parties could not function legally in many countries; many elections were fraudulent, and in a number of countries no elections were held at all. The subject was difficult to study, to say the least.

Chileanists, not surprisingly, have written the most about political parties (even when they have been writing more generally, not just about Chile). A distinguished intellectual trajectory connects, for example, Federico Gil, James Petras, Robert Kaufman, Timothy Scully, Arturo Valenzuela, and J. Samuel Valenzuela.[51] Venezuelanists are a close second, including such scholars as John Martz, Daniel Levine, and Michael Coppedge,[52] to mention in both instances individuals from different scholarly generations and points of view. A general comparative, intellectual argument about political parties in the region, comparable to, building on, modifying, or rebutting what Seymour Martin Lipset and Stein Rokkan did for the study of parties in western Europe, has yet to be written, however.[53] The intellectual ferment for such eventual work is being sown at long last thanks to the work of David and Ruth Collier and the fine collective work led by Scott Mainwaring and Timothy Scully.[54]

Huntington formulated an important assessment of the role of political parties and their impact on the prospects for social change. He discussed at some length the problems of what he called "the fragility of the no-party state." Such a political system is less likely to foster social change and more likely to be victim to repeated military coups. The long-term experience of Central American countries comes to mind. Political order, in contrast, is most likely where political parties are strong. I have already discussed Huntington's celebration of the efficacy of Leninist parties from the perspective of increasing the odds for political stability, and his favorable comments about the contributions of Mexico's Institutional Revolutionary Party to political order in that country. But his approval of the utility of political parties is much more extensive.

Huntington argues that one- and two-party systems are much less likely to suffer from military coups than are multiparty systems. In Latin America, the longest-lived actual or virtual one-party systems (Mexico and Cuba) have, indeed, been remarkably free from coups. Both of Latin America's historic two-party systems in Uruguay and Colombia have also been much less vulnerable to military coups than multiparty systems. I have argued elsewhere that the advantages that these party systems once had disappeared in the 1990s, but this contemporary observation does not detract from the historical value and accuracy of Huntington's analysis.[55]

Political parties make an especially valuable contribution to political order, Huntington argues, when they become the vehicle for a lawful and peaceful "green uprising," that is, the incorporation of the peasantry into the political system. He presents a comprehensive analysis of this problem worldwide. In the Latin American context, he cites the important contributions of Mexico's ruling party under President Lázaro Cárdenas and of Venezuela's Acción Democrática under Rómulo Betancourt. And he assesses the shortcomings of other Latin American parties that were unable to generate comparable results.

More generally, Huntington indicates that, especially at their foundational moments, one-party systems are quite effective at concentrating power, two-party systems compete to expand the suffrage and the connection of individuals to these parties, while multiparty systems distribute power and impede both the concentration and the expansion of political power, including the expansion of effective suffrage rights. For example, at the foundational moments for polyarchy in Uruguay and Argentina early in the twentieth century, and for Colombia in the mid–twentieth century, their respective two-party systems generated intense political mobilization. In contrast, until the 1960s a principal trait of the Chilean multiparty system had been the slow pace of the extension of effective citizen rights to many Chileans and the protection of the inherited partisan architecture from additional competition.

The discussion of the significance of political parties permeates the book. Parties ward off military interventions, are the agents of effective reform, are the key to understanding whether a revolution would give birth to a new political order, and are the best instrument for a society's achievement of its goals. The defeat of authoritarians is not just the product of "fortuna" and "virtù" but of politicians building and channeling effective support through parties. The enactment of reforms is not just the result of clever leaders, or the technically talented, but the outcome of prolonged processes of persuasion, disciplining, and commitment that parties can perform best. Revolutions often fail to accomplish their objectives; only parties can deliver on a promise of a revolutionary future. Democratic politics, as Huntington would argue at much greater length in a subsequent book, is unthinkable without parties.

Political Order builds up to its final chapter, which is devoted exclusively to the assessment of political parties. The book concludes with a short section on the organizational imperative, in which Huntington quotes both Lenin and Eduardo Frei on the importance of partisan organization in bringing about either concentrated power or representational gains, respectively: "In the modernizing world he controls the future who organizes its politics."[56]

In its analysis of the evolution, role, and effect of political parties, *Political Order* had no peer when it was published. Nor has it been overcome. Parties are the premier institutions of concern to Huntington in this work. He did not give us a theory of the state applicable to Latin America, but he produced a subtle, comprehensive analysis to enable us to understand a vital intermediary political institution between the state and society. That is the book's central intellectual achievement. Scholarship about Latin America would have been much better had the book's impact among Latin Americanists been greater.

NOTES

1. Samuel P. Huntington, *Political Order in Changing Societies* (New Haven, Conn.: Yale University Press, 1968), 1.

2. I believe that this assessment of the work's influence is not controversial. Nonetheless, I should state that Samuel Huntington chaired my dissertation committee and has long been a colleague and a friend. We have co-taught the Comparative Politics Field Seminar to Ph.D. students in the Harvard Department of Government and coauthored "Political Development," in Fred Greenstein and Nelson Polsby, eds., *Handbook of Political Science*, vol. 3 (Reading, Mass.: Addison-Wesley, 1975).

3. Samuel P. Huntington, *The Third Wave: Democratization in the Late Twentieth Century* (Norman: University of Oklahoma Press, 1991), xv.

4. For a short intellectual biography, see Robert D. Putnam, "Samuel P. Huntington: An Appreciation," *PS* (fall 1986): 837–45. A lifelong activist in the Democratic Party, Huntington even voted for George McGovern for president. In the 1968 presidential elections, he was one of Hubert Humphrey's chief academic advisers; in 1977, he worked on the National Security Council staff for President Jimmy Carter.

5. Huntington, *Political Order*, 7–8.

6. Earlier versions of this chapter were presented at the XX International Congress of the Latin American Studies Association, Guadalajara, April 17–19, 1997, and at a conference, "The Other Mirror: Comparative History and Latin America," held at Princeton University, February 20–21, 1998. I am grateful to the participants for many helpful comments. I am also grateful to Samuel Huntington and Thomas Ertman for their comments. I alone am responsible for mistakes in interpretation, analysis, or facts.

7. The *LASA Forum* has been publishing the reminiscences of past presidents of the Latin American Studies Association. In generally cautious language, they reveal the rise of intellectual intolerance in the association in the 1970s and early 1980s. See Henry A. Landsberger, "When a LASA President Was Only 66 Percent

'P.C.': Secrets from LASA's Past—Keys to the Future," *LASA Forum* 26, no. 4 (1996): 7–8, 22; Thomas Skidmore, "The LASA Presidency in the Early '70s," *LASA Forum* 27, no. 2 (1996): 10; and Jorge I. Domínguez, "Presidency in the Early 1980s," *LASA Forum* 27, no. 3 (1996): 11–12. See also Robert A. Packenham, *The Dependency Movement: Scholarship and Politics in Development Studies* (Cambridge, Mass.: Harvard University Press, 1992).

8. Huntington, *Political Order*, 194.

9. Ibid., 193.

10. Huntington relies on various sources but most heavily on Edwin Lieuwen, *Generals vs. Presidents* (New York: Praeger, 1964); John Johnson, *The Military and Society in Latin America* (Stanford, Calif.: Stanford University Press, 1964); and Martin C. Needler, "Political Development and Military Intervention in Latin America," *American Political Science Review* 60 (1966): 616–26.

11. Huntington, *Political Order*, 221.

12. Samuel P. Huntington, *The Soldier and the State: The Theory and Politics of Civil-Military Relations* (Cambridge, Mass.: Belknap Press of Harvard University Press, 1957), chap. 4.

13. See Abraham Lowenthal, ed., *The Peruvian Experiment* (Princeton, N.J.: Princeton University Press, 1975); Cynthia McClintock and Abraham Lowenthal, eds., *The Peruvian Experiment Reconsidered* (Princeton, N.J.: Princeton University Press, 1983); and Alfred Stepan, *The State and Society: Peru in Comparative Perspective* (Princeton, N.J.: Princeton University Press, 1978).

14. See Alfred Stepan, *The Military in Politics: Changing Patterns in Brazil* (Princeton, N.J.: Princeton University Press, 1971); and Stepan, ed., *Authoritarian Brazil* (New Haven, Conn.: Yale University Press, 1973).

15. See various essays in Abraham Lowenthal and J. Samuel Fitch, eds., *Armies and Politics in Latin America* (New York: Holmes and Meier, 1986).

16. Huntington, *Political Order*, 309, 311, 312.

17. Ibid., 338.

18. Ibid., 343.

19. See, for example, James Malloy, *Bolivia: The Uncompleted Revolution* (Pittsburgh: University of Pittsburgh Press, 1970); and Christopher N. Mitchell, *The Legacy of Populism in Bolivia: From the MNR to Military Rule* (New York: Praeger, 1977).

20. Mexico did have a brief period of commitment to socialist education in the 1930s, but it did not last long, and it stopped well short of the revolutionary sweep evident in other countries. For analyses of the history of Mexico's ruling party, some of which were available to Huntington as he wrote, see, among others, Frank Brandenburg, *The Making of Modern Mexico* (Englewood Cliffs, N.J.: Prentice-Hall, 1964); Nora Hamilton, *The Limits of State Autonomy: Postrevolutionary Mexico* (Princeton, N.J.: Princeton University Press, 1982); Kevin Middlebrook, *The Paradox of Revolution: Labor, the State, and Authoritarianism in Mexico* (Baltimore: Johns Hopkins University Press, 1995); Robert Scott, *Mexican Politics in Transition*, rev. ed. (Urbana: University of Illinois Press, 1964).

21. See Jorge I. Domínguez, *Cuba: Order and Revolution* (Cambridge, Mass.: Harvard University Press, 1978). For a comparison between Cuba and

Bolivia that is consistent with Huntington's analysis, see Jorge I. Domínguez and Christopher N. Mitchell, "The Roads Not Taken: Institutionalization and Political Parties in Cuba and Bolivia," *Comparative Politics* 9 (January 1977): 173–93.

22. Samuel P. Huntington, *The Clash of Civilizations and the Remaking of World Order* (New York: Simon and Schuster, 1996).

23. Huntington, *Political Order*, 344.

24. Ibid., 346.

25. Ibid., 389.

26. See, for instance, William Ascher, *Scheming for the Poor: The Politics of Redistribution in Latin America* (Cambridge, Mass.: Harvard University Press, 1984).

27. Personal communication, Samuel Huntington, January 1998.

28. Gabriel Almond and James S. Coleman, eds., *The Politics of Developing Areas* (Princeton, N.J.: Princeton University Press, 1960); and Gabriel Almond and G. Bingham Powell, *Comparative Politics: A Developmental Approach* (Boston: Little, Brown, 1966).

29. Daniel Lerner, *The Passing of Traditional Society* (Glencoe, Ill.: The Free Press, 1958); Lucian W. Pye, *Aspects of Political Development* (Boston: Little, Brown, 1966).

30. Deutsch's most famous formulation appeared as "Social Mobilization and Political Development," *American Political Science Review* 55 (1961).

31. Samuel P. Huntington, "Political Development and Political Decay," *World Politics* 17 (1965).

32. See Huntington's own explanation for the quiet deletions in "The Change to Change: Modernization, Development, and Politics," *Comparative Politics* 3 (1971): 304 n. 42.

33. I have employed Huntington's concepts repeatedly, though with the mixture of success and difficulty that these observations suggest. See two of my books, *Cuba: Order and Revolution*, and *Insurrection or Loyalty: The Breakdown of the Spanish American Empire* (Cambridge, Mass.: Harvard University Press, 1980). See also Domínguez and Mitchell, "The Roads Not Taken."

34. For a loud call that the time to pay attention to the state itself was overdue, see Peter B. Evans, Dietrich Rueschemeyer, and Theda Skocpol, eds., *Bringing the State Back In* (Cambridge: Cambridge University Press, 1985).

35. Samuel P. Huntington, *The Common Defense: Strategic Programs in National Politics* (New York: Columbia University Press, 1961).

36. Huntington, *Political Order*, 123.

37. Particularly influential in the United States was André Gunder Frank, *Capitalism and Underdevelopment in Latin America* (New York: Monthly Review Press, 1969).

38. This is especially noteworthy in the most self-consciously historical of the chapters, namely, chapter 2, entitled "Political Modernization: America versus Europe." Each of the two entities, "America" and "Europe," seems frozen in time.

39. Barrington Moore, *Social Origins of Dictatorship and Democracy* (Boston: Beacon, 1966).

40. Alexander Gerschenkron, *Economic Backwardness in Historical Perspective: A Book of Essays* (Cambridge, Mass.: Belknap Press of Harvard University Press, 1962).

41. Huntington, *The Soldier and the State*; Huntington, *American Politics: The Promise of Disharmony* (Cambridge, Mass.: Belknap Press of Harvard University Press, 1981).

42. See, most especially, his *American Politics: The Promise of Disharmony*.

43. Tad Szulc, *The Twilight of the Tyrants* (New York: Holt, 1959).

44. Huntington, *Political Order*, 382.

45. Huntington, *The Third Wave*, 85–100.

46. Fernando Henrique Cardoso and Enzo Faletto, *Dependency and Development in Latin America*, trans. Marjory M. Urquidi (Berkeley: University of California Press, 1979).

47. Guillermo O'Donnell, *Modernization and Bureaucratic-Authoritarianism: Studies in South American Politics* (Berkeley: Institute of International Studies, University of California, 1973).

48. Guillermo O'Donnell and Philippe Schmitter, *Tentative Conclusions about Uncertain Democracies: Transitions from Authoritarian Rule* (Baltimore: Johns Hopkins University Press, 1986).

49. Many of these writings are excellent, to be sure, which is one reason that I have collected many of them in Jorge I. Domínguez, *Social Movements in Latin America: The Experience of Peasants, Workers, Women, the Urban Poor, and the Middle Sectors* (New York: Garland, 1994). See also Jorge I. Domínguez, *The Roman Catholic Church in Latin America* (New York: Garland, 1994).

50. For fine journal articles published over the years, see Jorge I. Domínguez, ed., *Parties, Elections, and Political Participation in Latin America* (New York: Garland, 1994).

51. Federico G. Gil, *The Political System of Chile* (Boston: Houghton Mifflin, 1966); James Petras, *Politics and Social Forces in Chilean Development* (Berkeley: University of California Press, 1970); Robert R. Kaufman, "Corporatism, Clientelism, and Partisan Conflict: A Study of Seven Latin American Countries," in James M. Malloy, ed., *Authoritarianism and Corporatism in Latin America* (Pittsburgh: University of Pittsburgh Press, 1977); Timothy R. Scully, *Rethinking the Center: Party Politics in Nineteenth and Twentieth Century Chile* (Stanford, Calif.: Stanford University Press, 1992); Arturo Valenzuela, *The Breakdown of Democratic Regimes: Chile* (Baltimore: Johns Hopkins University Press, 1978); and J. Samuel Valenzuela's chapter in this volume and the citations therein.

52. John D. Martz, *Acción Democrática: Evolution of a Modern Political Party in Venezuela* (Princeton, N.J.: Princeton University Press, 1966); Daniel H. Levine, *Conflict and Political Change in Venezuela* (Princeton, N.J.: Princeton University Press, 1973); and Michael Coppedge, *Strong Parties and Lame Ducks: Presidential Partyarchy and Factionalism in Venezuela* (Stanford, Calif.: Stanford University Press, 1994).

53. See Seymour Martin Lipset and Stein Rokkan, "Cleavage Structures, Party Systems, and Voter Alignments: An Introduction," in Seymour Martin Lipset and Stein Rokkan, eds., *Party Systems and Voter Alignments: Cross National Perspectives* (Glencoe, Ill.: The Free Press, 1967). There have been some limited attempts.

The first, by Federico G. Gil, preceded the Lipset-Rokkan efforts by fifteen years; see Gil's "Responsible Parties in Latin America," *Journal of Politics* 15 (1953): 335–48. Two subsequent efforts were Douglas A. Chalmers, "Parties and Society in Latin America," *Studies in Comparative International Development* 7 (1972): 102–26; and Robert H. Dix, "Cleavage Structures and Party Systems in Latin America," *Comparative Politics* 22 (1989): 23–35.

54. David Collier and Ruth Berins Collier, *Shaping the Political Arena: Critical Junctures, the Labor Movement, and Regime Dynamics in Latin America* (Princeton, N.J.: Princeton University Press, 1991); and Scott Mainwaring and Timothy Scully, eds., *Building Democratic Institutions: Party Systems in Latin America* (Stanford, Calif.: Stanford University Press, 1995).

55. Jorge I. Domínguez and Jeanne Kinney Giraldo, "Parties, Institutions, and Market Reforms in Constructing Democracies," in Jorge I. Domínguez and Abraham F. Lowenthal, eds. *Constructing Democratic Governance: Latin America and the Caribbean in the 1990s* (Baltimore: Johns Hopkins University Press, 1996).

56. Huntington, *Political Order*, 461.

Chapter Eight

CLASS RELATIONS AND DEMOCRATIZATION

A REASSESSMENT OF BARRINGTON MOORE'S MODEL

J. Samuel Valenzuela

ARRINGTON MOORE'S *Social Origins of Dictatorship and Democracy* belongs to a long social science lineage that seeks to find societal-based explanations for political phenomena, and, within it, to a sublineage that focuses on class relations as providing the basic set of determining factors. Its emphasis on class in order to explain the formation of different kinds of regimes as nations modernize was therefore hardly novel when it was first published in 1996.[1] What made it break new ground at the time within the societal and class-relational view of politics was that both its Marxist (to which Moore's work has closer affinities) and its non-Marxist variants had long focused mainly on urban classes or on relations between segments of the upper class, while *Social Origins* emphasized primarily the dominant and subordinate classes engaged in agriculture, focusing secondarily on the nature of the links between landowners and the bourgeoisie.

This chapter takes a critical view of the class-relational model proposed by Moore to account for regime formation. On the one hand, his model is far too abstract. The effects of different classes and their relations on political development cannot be examined without focusing on concrete individuals whose actions were both enabled and constrained by a series of factors that were not necessarily related to their class positions, such as their organizational resources, the noneconomic interests they may have held, the institutional envelopes of the state and of the existing regime, the personal connections they may or may not have had with heads of state, armed forces, or bureaucracies, their correct or incorrect perceptions of what they should do to best preserve their essential interests, and so on. Such more specific factors determined whether class-related actors (i.e., individuals who were members of a certain class or who were involved in organizations that generally articulated and defended specific class interests) acted in similar or in different ways in shaping political change in their respective settings. On the other hand, Moore's model is far too restrictive. It takes an act of faith to present a model in which all interests that have a significant effect on the course of regime formation and change are class based. This simplification is perhaps not a fundamental flaw in a small number of countries where political cleavages did revolve largely around class divisions and where the timing of democratization was such that its political leaderships emerged in conjunction with class-linked organizations, all of this after the formation of solid national states—as in Sweden—but it shows important limitations whenever it confronts cases with a more complex set of cleavages, timings, or weaker states. Other collective identities and interests may have been important, the timing of change may have been such that political institutions were established with enduring consequences when certain class-based or non-class-based interests were better organized than others, means of doing politics that did not involve creating a democratic regime may have seemed more expedient, important power holders may have impressed the course of change with their vision and ambition in ways that had little apparent connection to societal forces, and so on.

This discussion draws from the history of democratization in nineteenth- and early-twentieth-century Chile to reveal the limitations of Moore's model. In so doing, it also takes issue with the currently most widely available interpretations of Chilean political and historical development, notably—in English—those found in the work of Brian Loveman, Maurice Zeitlin, and in the sections on Chile in Rueschemeyer, Huber Stephens, and Stephens's examination of the Moore thesis in a number of national cases.[2] These authors, all of whom find confirmation of Moore's basic notions in the Chilean experience, have drawn from—and contributed to—a very influential strand of Chilean political historiography that began to develop in the 1940s and 1950s. This historiography had argued that the nation's large landowners were an antidemocratic force, and hence its views were readily compatible with those developed by Moore in the mid-1960s; as a result, I will assimilate this historiography to the "Moorian" interpretation of Chilean history even though it predates Moore's opus.[3] Key elements in this literature do not stand up to the scrutiny of more careful research. It is contradicted by the fact that two basic stepping-stones in the development of Chilean democracy, namely, the extension of suffrage to all literate males in 1874 and the institution of procedures to ensure the secrecy of the vote in 1890, were championed by Conservative Party leader Manuel José Irarrázabal and his colleagues.[4] This party has invariably been presented in the literature on the Chilean case as the main force that stood for large landholding interests. While this is questionable, it is true that key party leaders were landowners, and one of the important social and electoral bases of the party was the rural area of the Chilean Central Valley just north and south of Santiago, where large estates dominated the countryside. Irarrázabal himself was one of the nation's wealthiest landowners. He was also the descendant of a family of the highest ranking nobility during the colonial or monarchical period that ended with independence from Spain in 1818.[5] This has led analysts to link the Conservative Party to a Chilean "aristocracy."

Moore did not provide a clear justification for the cases he chose for his analysis.[6] He argued simply that small nations were not worth considering because "the decisive causes of their politics lie outside their own boundaries."[7] But if the world's small nations were exceptions to the proposition that political regimes were the product of the constellation of class forces, this meant that for most countries in the world the class determinants did not explain regime formation. One of the cases Moore analyzed, namely, India, stood out from the others given the fact that it was under colonial rule, and therefore its institutions were significantly shaped by the metropolitan power, that is, by exogenous influences. Moore was perfectly aware that in this case political factors took precedence over class and socioeconomic structure. He noted that the latter would have pushed India into a nondemocratic route, but British colonial administration had the effect of "preventing the fateful coalition of a strong landed elite and weak bourgeoisie that . . . has been the social origin of rightist authoritarian regimes."[8] Nonetheless, if a country is neither a colony nor a protectorate of another one, Moore's thesis should apply to it regardless of its size. In those cases where regimes were formed under conditions of formal political independence, even though the national class fabric may have included foreign investors and interests, as was often the case, Moore's class constellation argument should take precedence over others if it is a valid one.

Moore's argument also should have referred only to processes of regime formation that were completed before the beginning of World War II. In this sense, again, India should not have been included in his discussion. The Allied victory over Nazism and fascism gave much greater currency to democratic forms of government among the forces all over the world that Moore saw as predisposed to rightist authoritarianism.

Given the fact that most Latin American countries have been independent since the early nineteenth century, they provide an excellent terrain for examining Moore's thesis. In fact, it is difficult to understand why Moore did not even consider examining any Latin American experiences in his analysis. Belonging to the Western cultural space, with leaders imbued in—and contributing further to—the new doctrines of representative government and separation of powers that had originated in Europe and the United States, Latin American nations were among the first to experiment with electoral institutions and presidentialist variants (except—most durably—in Brazil) of democratic constitutionalism.

Within Latin America, the Chilean case is the most important one for an assessment of the Moore thesis given that it provides, as I will show here, the clearest refutation of it. As I will note briefly in the conclusion to this chapter, the historical record of other cases can be seen as apparently confirming Moore's model, or they can lead to inconclusive results. Chile also furnishes one of the clearest examples in Latin America of the step-by-step construction of a democratic framework during the period that coincides with the first wave of democratization out of nineteenth-century oligarchic regimes. Chilean republican constitutions, the most important one of which was enacted in 1833, established the separation of powers typical of liberal democracies, including an independent judiciary and a relatively strong bicameral congress (given its controls over the purse, the deployment of armed forces, and the right to censure ministers and presidents). The military was clearly subordinated to constitutional governments beginning in the 1830s. A lively and critical press can already be found in the 1840s, and more durably after repressive measures in the middle to late 1850s. The freedoms of association for political and social purposes followed a similar pattern and were guaranteed in a constitutional amendment enacted in 1874—also through Conservative Party influence. However, as occurred in the United States, among many other countries, the right of workers to unionize legally was challenged until the 1930s, even though unions did develop from the latter part of the nineteenth century, and artisanal and miners' organizations of various kinds can easily be traced back to the 1840s. The use of civil over canon law for all but church governance, the freedom of religion, state-run education and confessional pluralism in private education, municipal rather than church control over cemeteries, a civil registry (including civil marriages and their annulment)—all measures resisted by the church— were in place long before the formal separation between church and state in 1925. Elections were held regularly every two or at most three years since the 1820s to fill presidential, congressional, and municipal offices, although electoral procedures made it very difficult for opponents of the government to defeat the officially favored lists of candidates until the changes introduced in 1890.

Despite the risk of repeating what is well known, this chapter presents the fundamental aspects of Moore's model, as well as criticisms and additions to it. It then presents and discusses the interpretation of Chilean political history that has been used to confirm Moore's thesis, showing that its historiography is flawed. Subsequently, it considers whether the Chilean rural sector could possibly be assimilated, despite the superficial indications to the contrary, to Moore's pro-democratic class constellation. After rejecting this possibility, the chapter sketches elements of an alternative view of democratization, drawn from a different theoretical lineage, that leads to focusing on factors that are missing from Moore's approach. Concluding comments return to the uniqueness of the Chilean experience by setting it in a comparative framework.

MOORE'S BASIC MODEL

After his long exploration of the rise of democracies or dictatorships in eight nations (England, France, the United States, China, Japan, India, Germany, and Russia, although no specific chapters were devoted to the latter two), Moore concluded that democracies were more likely to develop, as in England or in the northern United States, where landowners practiced "commercial," or fully market-driven, agriculture. In these settings landowners became very much like the urban bourgeoisie in their entrepreneurial ways, hiring as much labor as they needed to produce efficiently; and even if landed interests initially may have been stronger than bourgeois ones until economic development reversed this tendency, the dominant class nonetheless bore the stamp of bourgeois hegemony as there was no significant difference between the two segments. By contrast, dictatorships usually emerged where landowners practiced a "labor-repressive" form of agriculture that relied on coercive mechanisms—such as slavery, serfdom, feudal dues and obligations, or other abusive labor, land rental, and/or produce marketing arrangements—and where landowners were able to remain the leading segment of the dominant class, subordinating a weaker bourgeoisie to them and insisting on retaining the socioeconomic arrangements from which they benefited. Whether the result was a fascist or a communist dictatorship depended largely on the relative strengths of the bourgeoisies and of the rebellious impulses of the peasants who were involved: the success of fascism stemmed from stronger dominant groups and a more passive peasantry, and of communism from the opposite mix. The eventual rise of democracies where agriculture was characterized by labor repression, as in France, required a successful "bourgeois revolution" or, as in the United States, victory in a civil war that accomplished the same basic task of transforming the agricultural world in the South. Hence, in Moore's succinct summary, for a democratic regime to emerge, "the political hegemony of the landed upper class had to be broken or transformed. The [field laborer or the] peasant had to be turned into a [wage earner or a] farmer producing for the market instead of for his own consumption and that of the overlord. In this process the landed upper-classes either became an important part of the capitalist and democratic tide, as in England, or, if they came to oppose it, they were swept aside in the convulsions of revolution or civil war. In a word the landed upper-classes either helped to make the bourgeois revolution or were destroyed by it."[9]

Moore's work stimulated a considerable following among scholars who sought to clarify some of his definitions of important terms, democracy included, as well as to confirm and refine his arguments. The result has been the development of a long list of observations to the basic model, some of which are closer to the literature of an alternative lineage that focuses on the significance of state institutional and political-organizational variables in explaining the formation or collapse of regimes. Thus, Theda Skocpol has noted the significance of the autonomy of the state and of its crisis in detonating revolutions, bourgeois or otherwise, and Ross, Skocpol, Smith, and Vichniac have summarized research pointing to the importance of examining the influence of geopolitical factors or of institutional and organizational features such as parliaments, electoral laws, and political parties that may affect the course of political change.[10] Curiously, Moore himself presented and discussed casually many of these elements in the lengthy historical accounts of his cases, such as when he noted the significance of the monarch's lack of a standing army for the development of democracy in England.[11] And yet he did not make an effort to draw them into his overall explanatory model, thereby remaining within the class-relational approach and opening the way for others to note their omission.[12]

Other analysts have criticized aspects of Moore's model itself. Thus, Rueschemeyer, Huber Stephens, and Stephens have questioned the characterization of the bourgeoisie as a basically pro-democratic force. They note that the bourgeoisie may have contributed in some cases to establishing "parliamentary government" (or, in Huber's more precise terms, given the Eurocentric bias of the previous formulation, it may have supported "representative and responsible government"), but they add that it was almost always opposed to "the final extensions of suffrage to the working class."[13] Rueschemeyer, Huber Stephens, and Stephens also reproach Moore for neglecting the role of the working class, which in their view was the crucial actor in the final creation of democracies precisely because it pressured in favor of inclusion by demanding universal male suffrage. This latter point is stated forcefully by Geoff Eley as well.[14] It is most clearly evident in northern Europe and Australia, but alternative explanations are needed to account for cases in which workers were enfranchised before the rise of the labor movement.[15] Other authors such as Andrews and Chapman acknowledge that workers may have been important actors, but they point out that in some cases the middle class also played a role in the formation of democracies that must not be underestimated.[16] This view echoes that of the earlier generation of political modernization writings, although its reasoning is different from that of the earlier authors, who focused on the middle class's education and supposedly tolerant political culture as the decisive elements making it a democratizing force. All these observations are presented as additions to Moore's model that do not alter its basic contentions. In particular, followers of Moore's vision accept the basic notion that "labor-repressive" landowners who controlled large and economically significant tracts of land were a consistently antidemocratic force everywhere, and this is taken both as the basic proof of the value of Moore's class-relational model and as the fundamental starting point for all further specifications of it.

Despite the importance of the "labor-repressive" notion in Moore's conception, he has been criticized for a lack of clarity in the use of this term. In his most forceful statement, he explained that its difference with "commercial" agriculture lay in the fact that the former relied on "political" and the latter on "market" forces to extract a surplus from peasants, a distinction that Skocpol rightly rejected (because markets also contain political determinants) and that Rueschemeyer, Huber Stephens, and Stephens found "too rigid."[17] It is therefore impossible to assess Moore's model without developing a more precise conception of this crucial category.

"Commercial" agriculture requires market-oriented production, while the "labor-repressive" mode is compatible with situations in which it is destined mainly for lord and peasant self-consumption. However, this is not the essential difference between the two. "Labor repressive" agriculture may also be market-driven in the sense that it may produce to satisfy consumer or agro-industrial demand, as was the case with slave plantation agriculture in the Americas. Similarly, in both forms of agriculture there may or may not be important limitations (such as entails) on the free sale of land. Hence, the core difference between them lies in their labor use regimes. "Commercial" agriculture refers to situations in which labor is free to move and is hired for a wage at the prevailing labor market rate, which may be affected by poor law or welfare provisions, minimum wage and labor laws, protectionism, tax relief, subsidies, and/or employer as well as worker combinations, although Moore does not really discuss these elements.

By contrast, and trying to keep as close as possible to Moore's uses of the term, "labor-repressive" agriculture should be viewed as encompassing, first, those situations in which landlords relied on laborers who were prevented from moving in search of new opportunities, either in agriculture or in other areas of the economy, and in which their remuneration (in money, in kind, or calculated as the cost of supporting laborers as individuals or with their families) was clearly below what they would obtain elsewhere if they were able to move, taking advantage of a free labor market. The impediments to laborers' mobility could stem from their court-enforceable status obliging them to work the land, as in the case of slaves or serfs, from state repression against laborers in order to favor landowners, or from state-tolerated but landowner-organized repression. Unless there was a clear pattern of abuse and trickery behind them, cases in which landowners could pressure laborers to remain on the fields to fulfill labor contract provisions whose written or unwritten terms the latter had freely agreed to for reasonably limited periods of time should not be viewed as instances of labor repression. As noted by Bauer, the debt peonage found in some areas of Latin America such as northern-coastal Peru was of this kind: the debts originated in relatively large cash advances given to laborers in the highlands for agreeing to contracts calling on them to do seasonal work in coastal plantations.[18] Such practices could be classed, therefore, as part of the rather wide variety of institutional forms through which the labor markets of "commercial" agriculture were organized. And, second, "labor-repressive" agriculture should include those situations in which landlords or agricultural merchants could extract a surplus from peasant producers by virtue of the latter's obligation to give them part of what they produced, to pay them various dues or tributes in money or labor, to process the grain they harvested only in their mills, and/or to sell produce only through their offices or establishments. Such obligations could stem from the strongly entrenched customary norms of caste or castelike societies, with rigid status and privilege distinctions, and, again, they could be enforceable by the courts. They could also be the product of systematic repression by the state or by the landowners or landowner-merchants even in the absence of any ascriptive or legally sanctioned status differences. In the first situations of labor repression, landlords or their agents organize production; in the second, peasants do.

If this clarification captures well what Moore had in mind, its problem is that it turns the notion that "labor-repressive" landowners were an antidemocratic force into an obvious point. After all, they relied on producers who were denied the most basic rights of citizens in a democracy, namely, the freedom of movement, equality before the law, and/or protection from abusive practices in what amounted to racketeering. Insofar as democratization necessarily implied denying landowners or landowner-merchants the possibility of abusing their subordinates, a privilege they enjoyed given their superior status or their ability to benefit from force, they could be expected to oppose it.[19] Democratization was not in their interest.[20]

Perhaps because of the truistic quality of this point, Moore's followers have tended to expand greatly the meaning of the "labor-repressive" category. They have taken a cue from Moore's own example, given his many passing references not to "labor-repressive" landowners as being the antidemocratic force but simply to ones who are "strong" (relative to the bourgeoisie) for one reason or another. This slippage occurs notably in Moore's discussion of the Prussian landlords.[21] By the nineteenth century they did not resort to "labor-repressive" practices in the strict sense of the term, that is, relying on the feudal strictures of the past; they were devoted, rather, to a capitalist form of agriculture, and by the end of the century the great majority of East German landlords were in fact of bourgeois origin.[22] The effects of this extension of the Moorian conception can be seen in the work of Allub, who, writing on Argentina, implied that all powerful landholding classes in peripheral capitalism were antidemocratic, given the texture of the relationship they had with their subordinates.[23] Allub noted that Argentine landowners developed "commercial" agriculture but were still able to subordinate the bourgeoisie to their interests, not vice versa, and remained a pro-authoritarian force.[24] Rueschemeyer, Huber Stephens, and Stephens have proposed a more specific expansion of Moore's category of antidemocratic landowners by defining it as "landlords dependent on a large supply of cheap labor."[25] This conception may have the virtue of overcoming the rigidity some reproach in Moore's distinction between the two forms of agriculture, but it does not have the virtue of clarity either. What is the difference between landowners who are "dependent" on cheap labor and those who can be said, rather, to take advantage of low wages as any capitalist would? If there is a large supply of labor, its price presumably will be cheap, but how cheap does it have to be to turn landowners into an antidemocratic force? Because this formulation can imply the existence of a free labor market, albeit one in which there is an excess supply of labor, it effectively turns Moore's distinction into a continuum in which the distinguishing feature between "commercial" and "labor-repressive" agriculture becomes the amount landowners are willing to pay labor. Some cutoff point would therefore have to be given in order to indicate when the quantitative measure becomes a qualitative distinction. Or is it the case that all landowners engaged in labor-intensive production while benefiting from a lax labor market are antidemocratic? Although this is a dubious proposition, it is indeed what has been implied in this literature. Both the strict and the expanded conceptions of "labor-repressive" landowners have informed the Moorian interpretation of Chilean history, as can be seen from the following summary.

CLASSES AND THE FORMATION OF THE CHILEAN POLITICAL REGIME: THE MOORIAN INTERPRETATION

The general image that springs from this interpretation is that Chile since the early nineteenth century was controlled politically by a dominant class composed mainly of large "aristocratic" landowners. They formed the social bases of support for authoritarian political groups after independence from Spain, by backing first the so-called *pelucones* group and, after the mid-1850s, the Conservative Party. Their estates extended sometimes into the tens of thousands of hectares and were devoted to an inefficient, labor-intensive agriculture exploiting a poverty-stricken rural population. Labor relations were supposedly "feudal" insofar as the subordination of peasants to the landed proprietors was much like that of the serfs of medieval and early modern Europe. The principal agricultural laborer of the large estate was the *inquilino*, or service tenant. In exchange for year-round work, the *inquilino* received a minimal cash payment, a ration of food (usually bread and beans) for each day he worked, and a series of benefits consisting generally of a modest ranch, an acre or so for his family to cultivate for its own sustenance, and access to pasturelands for two to four large animals. This labor practice is assumed to have derived from the grants of labor (encomiendas) given by the crown to leading Spanish settlers during the colonial period.[26] As such, the institution was the "last link in the chain of slavery."[27] Even well into the twentieth century, the subordination of the *inquilinos* and their families to their "masters" is described as total.[28]

An emerging mining, financial, and industrial bourgeoisie associated with the Liberal Party and in part with the Radical Party is supposed to have gained strength in the midcentury. It tried but failed to wrest power from the landowning class in two civil wars. Having forged an alliance with a growing middle class, this group then sought to expand suffrage, resulting in the elimination of the income requirements (variously presented in this literature as occurring in 1874, 1884, 1885, or 1888).[29] However, the electoral process remained subject to abuse by those in power and by local notables. The change did nothing, in particular, to alter the political supremacy of the landed class because—in what is one of the most durable simplicities in the analysis of Chilean politics—the rural dependents of the haciendas were coerced into voting for the candidates favored by the landowners, many of whom were landowners themselves. Because the boundaries of Chilean electoral districts gave disproportionate weight to the rural areas, this literature notes that the landholding class was able to retain positions of power in the legislature and national government such that it could prevent any legal reforms unfavorable to its interests. Eventually a new and weaker bourgeoisie merged with the landowning oligarchy through marriage ties and cross-investments, thereby absorbing the landed group's values and outlooks, turning its back on the democratic aspirations it had previously championed. Thus, Chile never had a "bourgeois revolution."[30]

The democratic struggle was then taken up, according to these authors, by a middle class composed of professionals, white-collar public and private employees, and medium to small businessmen, as well as by some popular organizations. They were linked mainly to the Radical Party, as well as to some progressive segments of the Liberal Party. They succeeded in putting a temporary end to oligarchic government with the 1920 election of Arturo Alessandri, a then populist "middle-class" Liberal. However, the oligarchy made it impossible for him to carry out any meaningful reforms. Labor laws were enacted in 1924 under military pressure, and a social security system was created, but these changes did not extend to the countryside and did not alter the basic inequalities in the nation's social and political conditions.

Given these frustrations, the rights of workers and peasants were supposedly taken up subsequently by the emerging parties of the Left, both Socialist and Communist. While these parties succeeded in claiming the presidency in an alliance with the middle class represented by the Radical Party under the Popular Front coalition in 1938, fundamental changes still did not occur given the strength of the landed interests in Congress and even their influence through some members of the Radical Party itself. Analysts insist that landowners continued to control peasants, forcing them to cast ballots for candidates they selected aided by a supposed lack of secrecy of the vote. Only in 1958 did changes in electoral procedures introduce an effective secret ballot, thereby freeing, for the first time ever, the peasantry to vote as it wished. The changes also stimulated electoral participation by both men and women—the latter having been enfranchised in 1949. This led to a dramatic decline in electoral support for the Right in the 1960s and opened an era of reforms that included unionization of farmworkers and agrarian reform. It was only then that Chile had or came close to having a democracy. However, these and other gains proved to be short-lived as the leftist government of Salvador Allende that was elected in 1970 was destroyed by the military coup of 1973, which was supported by the then fully fused landed and bourgeois families.

While this interpretation contains some elements of truth, as does any caricature, it is not tenable given more careful historical research.

INACCURACIES OF THE MOORIAN-COMPATIBLE INTERPRETATION OF CHILEAN HISTORY

There are four basic problems with this interpretation. The first refers to the dating of the inception of Chilean democracy. Given the fact that elections and constitutional government were long-standing characteristics of the Chilean political system, this literature emphasizes that the effects of landowner hegemony in the society were such that the nation did not really have a democracy until popular pressures, peasant unionization, changes in electoral laws, and a process of agrarian reform broke this hegemony in the 1960s and early 1970s. Hence, Moore's analysis is apparently confirmed in this literature simply by denying that Chile had a democratic regime before those changes. The second difficulty refers to the assessment of the characteristics and actions of the Conservative Party. Invariably presenting this party as attached to landed interests, this literature argues that it was a reactionary and fundamentally pro-authoritarian force. The third inaccuracy is reflected in the assessment of the rural vote as one that was always coerced and controlled. And the fourth pertains to the characteristics of the rural labor regime and to the place of landowners within the Chilean upper class. Each of these points will be examined separately in what follows.

The Inception of Chilean Democracy

A basic preliminary issue in examining the origins of political regimes is the determination of when they begin, whatever their imperfections, in the case or cases that are being analyzed. This sets the stage for focusing on the forces and circumstances that intervened in their formation. It is necessary to distinguish the founding moments from subsequent extensions or deepening of their characteristics. Any discussion of the origins of a regime should obviously focus on the first, more important moment of its installation. Moore himself was thinking only of the very basic elements of a democratic regime in his analysis, otherwise he would not have stopped his discussion of France with the Revolution or of the United States with the Civil War.

When democracies originated after a sharp break with the past due to the collapse of an authoritarian regime, the issue of determining the difference between their inception and their subsequent deepening is usually settled from the outset. But when democratization occurred through a succession of reforms, resulting in the creation of a regime that retained the constitutional framework and many of the institutional practices of the past, as occurred in Chile and in most other cases of first-wave democratization, then the matter of when the regime was basically set in place is more difficult to settle.

There is no space here for a full discussion of the difficulties raised by the identification of the point at which a process of democratization through reforms generates what can be classed as a democratic rather than an authoritarian regime. Suffice it to say that it is a point at which a critical, qualitative change in the nature of the political regime occurs, after which political leaders should realize that their careers are in the last analysis dependent on winning elections instead of on courting official favor from those who already have state power—as occurs in any authoritarian setting, whatever its specific features. It therefore represents a transformation that politicians and contemporary observers should perceive clearly as having redefined the nature of the political game. Its fundamental mechanism in determining who holds power becomes the preferences made by voters when choosing between candidates who emerge from freely organized political groups or parties in elections their leaders accept as not being stacked irremediably against them. Naturally, the electorate should be broad enough to permit groups or parties that seek to represent all significant political sensibilities in the population to enter the electoral arena and compete effectively in it. In the history of most processes of first-wave democratization, this condition was reflected primarily in the rise of parties seeking to represent working-class interests by fielding candidates in elections, among other activities. Moreover, the exercise of authority by elected governments should not be second to that of nonelected figures such as monarchs, high civil servants, judges, or military officers, neither in general terms nor in specific policy domains.[31] In order to evaluate the Moorian interpretation of Chilean history, the question becomes, then, when did this kind of qualitative transformation occur?

Among the works offering the Moorian interpretation of Chile, only Rueschemeyer, Huber Stephens, and Stephens work with an explicit definition of democracy. They argue that—in addition to cabinets that must be responsible to parliaments or elected presidents, to the subordination of the military to civilian rule, to the respect for the outcomes of nonfraudulent and nonnotable controlled elections, and to the necessary freedoms—a democracy is attained only when all male adults (except foreign residents, even long-term and legal ones) are allowed to vote (whether or not they exercise this right).[32] This means that although about 73 percent of all men over twenty-one years of age were already entitled to vote in Chile by 1932 given advances in literacy, Chile did not have a democracy until the constitutional amendment granting illiterates the vote was adopted in 1970![33] Rueschemeyer, Huber Stephens, and Stephens insist that this measure was adopted under labor pressure, probably because 1970 was the year Salvador Allende's Popular Unity government took office. This assertion permits them to confirm their point that labor was a key actor everywhere in generating full democracy, although the Chilean labor movement and parties of the Left did not contribute any more than other forces at the time to enfranchising illiterates.[34] In fact, at no time after 1874 did labor and leftist leaders mount any campaigns to press for the elimination of the literacy requirement. They did not view it as necessary. By the early twentieth century the main leader of the Socialist Workers' Party (soon to be the Communist Party) was convinced a majority of the electorate should be voting for his party given its class position.[35] Moreover, and most important, the constitutional reform giving illiterates the vote in 1970 was not seen as a fundamental change in the nature of the Chilean political regime by any contemporaneous politicians or observers.[36] With good reason: the illiteracy rate was down to less than 10 percent by then. Permitting women to vote in Switzerland certainly represented a much more important deepening of democracy at about the same time, although Rueschemeyer, Huber Stephens, and Stephens dismiss this decision as irrelevant in creating a "full democracy."

This perception of a fundamental change that, to repeat, is essential in determining when a democracy begins, occurred instead in the wake of the 1890 electoral law and the 1891 civil war, as the government was finally prevented from being able to use its ample arsenal of electoral intervention tools to favor official candidates. The new electoral system was first tested in the legislative elections of 1894. It resulted for the first time ever in Chilean electoral history in first- and second-place victories by opponents of the government. Subsequently, the main parties of the time obtained roughly the same percentages of the vote in legislative elections until the realignment of the party system in 1925–32, despite changes in the party coalitions in the government.[37]

The fundamental alteration created by the 1890 electoral procedures was indeed noticed at the time. For example, Julio Zegers, a Liberal leader who lamented the change because he was never able to regain a congressional seat, indicated that "the true cause of the difference between the old and the new governments lies in the fact that the [previous] system of official intervention [in the elections], inspired in lofty political purposes, favored the election of honest, dignified and patriotic citizens, whereas the free elections of our days, tarnished by the market for votes, are unscrupulous in their designations."[38] The testimony of the head of the Democratic Party, the most important one from an electoral point of view linked then to the labor movement, also confirms the point that the change was widely perceived at the time, while providing an understandably different evaluation: "Given the electoral frauds, only in 1894 was the party able to elect its first deputy and various municipal councilors, and from that date on its representatives in the communes and in parliament have been increasing constantly."[39] Similarly, an analyst of Chilean politics writing in 1920 noted that the secret vote was a "great conquest" when introduced thirty years previously.[40]

Hence, despite its deficiencies, mainly its incomplete suffrage due to the absence of gender equality in voting rights, Chilean politics began its experience with the rudiments of a democratic regime with the 1894 elections. Consequently, the focus of the analysis of the forces that intervened at the origins of Chilean democracy should be placed in the latter part of the nineteenth century.

This conclusion is certainly at odds with the assessment of Rueschemeyer, Huber Stephens, and Stephens that the Chilean regime was, at best, a "competitive oligarchy" before the 1920s.[41] They back up this characterization with an allusion to the role played by committees of the largest municipal taxpayers (rural notables, by implication) in the electoral process, which supposedly allowed them to manipulate the results of elections by controlling the extent of voter participation. As an example of this capacity, these authors contend that when "effective" popular participation threatened to "escape" the oligarchy's "control" in 1912, the taxpayer committees "decided to greatly reduce participation through the process of registration. The number of registered voters dropped from 598,000 in 1912 to 185,000 in 1915."[42] If this was what actually happened, it would indeed be a sufficient reason to look for a later date in which to place the inception of a basically democratic regime in Chile. However, it is not true that the largest taxpayers on municipal treasury lists could, or did, slash the number of electoral registrations.

Opponents of the government first resorted to using the largest taxpayers on municipal treasury lists to generate committees in charge of administering electoral procedures through the 1874 electoral law.[43] The purpose of this initiative was to eliminate the biased and highly partisan influence of the pro-government authorities that administered them. Following mechanisms set in the 1884 electoral law, the committees were elected by assemblies of the thirty to almost sixty (depending on the size of an electoral district's population) largest urban and rural municipal taxpayers with proportional representation, assuming, as apparently occurred in fact according to a contemporary observer, that this would ensure that they would include men of different partisan positions.[44] The electoral laws from 1884 on stipulated very strictly the manner in which committee members were to exercise their duties, establishing fines or imprisonment for noncompliance. The committees had no power to slash the electoral registries or to deny registration to those who solicited it without basing themselves on the law. Negative decisions could be appealed by prospective voters in the courts.

The sharp drop in voter registrations for the 1915 elections can be explained quite simply. During the nineteenth century, voters had to register during a two-week period in November before each electoral year. Following the initiative of Senator Irarrázabal, a Conservative, legislators in 1890 decided to make the registry "permanent" until a new law declared it invalid. As a consequence, by 1912 the electoral rolls included the names of many voters who had died. The result, after much discussion, was a new electoral law approved by Congress and the president in 1914 (not by the largest municipal taxpayers!) that canceled all registrations and forced citizens to reregister. Naturally, this led to a reduction in the number of registrants that went far beyond the elimination of the deceased from the rolls, because many voters did not bother to reregister or were unaware that they had to do so. The decline in the numbers of registered voters cannot be attributed, therefore, to the political machinations of an economic oligarchy acting through the committees formed out of municipal taxpayer lists to run the nuts and bolts of the electoral system.

The electoral effects of the reduced number of voters were the opposite of what Rueschemeyer, Huber Stephens, and Stephens imply. The liberal parties—which were led by upper-class individuals—were the biggest losers of votes as a proportion of the total between 1912 and 1915. By contrast, the parties associated with working-class and middle-class groups, namely, the Democratic and Radical Parties, at the same time scored important increases in their proportions of the electorate, while the Conservative share remained about the same.[45] Registrations of voters for the Democratic, Radical, and Conservative Parties suffered proportionally less because their voters tended to be better connected to social organizations. Moreover, if the taxpayer committees had acted in ways that altered the electoral results, contemporary observers, especially those of the Left, would have denounced them. However, there is no record of such denunciations in, for instance, the four-volume collection of labor and leftist leader Luis E. Recabarren's letters and articles covering the full extent of his political career, in which he refers on numerous occasions to elections and to his own electoral campaigns.[46]

In sum, the operation of the taxpayers' committees as a mechanism for voter registrations is not sufficient cause to classify the Chilean system after 1890 as a "competitive oligarchy." The inception of an incomplete suffrage democracy in Chile may be set at the time of the 1894 elections, and the analysis of the forces leading to it must therefore be situated in the middle to late nineteenth century. A complete suffrage democracy can be said to have originated with the extension of suffrage to women in 1949. Enfranchisement of illiterates was not an important change insofar as voting rolls were basically open to anyone who learned how to sign his or her name.

The Democratizing Influence of the Conservative Party

The fact that Conservative Party legislators, who supposedly represented the landowning "aristocracy," were the prime movers of the 1874 and 1890 reforms against the wishes of Liberal presidents certainly does not fit the image that is painted of these political forces in the Moorian interpretation of Chile. Naturally, the Conservatives can be viewed as seeking, in 1874, to enfranchise "their" rural dependents in order to have them vote for their favored candidates, and, true enough, the occupational distribution of the individuals who registered to vote in 1878 does show an enormous increase in the number who were classified as working in agriculture.[47] But if prior to democratization the political system was an autocracy controlled by the large landowners, as noted in the Moorian literature, then why would the Conservatives have any political need to eliminate the income specifications to vote in order to enfranchise their rural dependents? Moreover, if the Conservatives' intent was to force their rural dependents to vote for their favored candidates, why did they make such an effort to convince, successfully, the legislators in 1890 to ensure the secrecy of the vote by introducing the secret chamber at the polling places and by obliging voters to place their ballots in officially provided envelopes?[48] These questions point to elements that cannot be reconciled with the Moorian interpretation of Chile's political history. In addition, the fact that the main leader of the Conservative Party, Manuel José Irarrázabal, and some of his Conservative colleagues in Congress were landowners in a peripheral capitalist national society contradicts the extended version of Moore's model presented by Allub.[49] Assuming that the personal class position of actors makes them representatives of their class interests, such Conservative figures were nonetheless in favor of pivotal changes promoting democratization.

The Conservative Party was also the first to advocate women's suffrage in Chile. A key party leader spoke publicly in its favor in 1865, and the party presented the first women's suffrage bill in 1917.[50] The party was also more sensitive to social issues than were other major forces at the time. It was the first to sponsor social legislation, beginning with a law on popular housing in 1906, and it presented the first comprehensive set of labor and social laws in 1919—including provisions regarding the formation of unions that anticipated some of the main features of the Wagner

Act adopted in the United States a decade and a half later. In sum, with respect to both democratic reforms and social legislation, Conservatives took more progressive positions than most Liberals and even Radicals.

Were Rural Voters Coerced?

Despite the important vote the Conservative Party obtained in cities, especially in Santiago, one of the areas where it consistently obtained a larger than average proportion of electoral support was in the rural Central Valley, where conspicuous Conservative landowners had their properties. This has contributed to the image of the party as rurally based. Nonetheless, the Liberal Party also drew important support from the rural Central Valley, even if its electorate did fluctuate more from one election to the next. Liberals also had an important electorate in southern agricultural areas such as Malleco and Cautín Provinces, and Radicals obtained significant numbers of rural votes in the south as well.[51] The fact that the rural populations of these areas voted for these parties has stimulated the already mentioned notion that peasants were forced to vote for the candidates chosen by landowners.

This assumption has been especially significant in connection with the Conservative Party, given the image of Liberals and Radicals as urban-based parties and the regularity of electoral support for Conservatives in the most characteristic and richest agricultural section of the country. It is buttressed by the many reports of electoral agents who vaunted their success in electing their candidates by transporting rural voters to the polls, resorting to economic "incentives"—described by their opponents as vote buying—and using various strategies that were supposed to provide confirmation that such voters did what was expected of them in the secret chamber.[52] Naturally, in the agents' view the results were explained by their efforts, a point that justified their own emoluments. Similarly, losing candidates, mainly those of the Left, focused on the agents' role in mobilizing rural voters to explain and justify their own lack of success in obtaining more electoral support from the rural populace. Hence, both the political agents and their opponents created, each suiting his own purpose, an image of passive rural voters who did not express their own preferences at the polls but simply followed orders or instructions. Given such a coincidence of views regularly repeated by opposing sides, this bit of Chilean political folklore has been accepted as a fundamental truth in basically all analysis of the nation's politics, from observers to social scientists.

However, could it not be the case that voters in rural areas willingly supported the candidates who received important majorities in rural districts? The notion that peasant voter choices were the product of trickery or coercion stems from the unstated assumption that their natural inclination would be to vote following their supposed class interest, that is, for the left. But many lower-class voters, even unionized industrial workers, do not express their preferences at the voting booth in this manner. There is the possibility of a deferential vote: if in England, why not in Chile?[53] This kind of voting probably benefited landowners of all persuasions. All rural workers were free to move, and those remaining in the countryside could be expected to have seen greater benefits than disadvantages in their situation, and to have had a more favorable evaluation of their superiors. Otherwise they probably would have joined the massive migration from rural to urban areas that transformed Chile from an overwhelmingly rural country in 1875 to a majority urban one by 1930, and that reduced the rural population to about a fifth of the total by 1970.

In addition, where, as in Chile, political identities were formed on the basis of factors other than class, class voting was less important. The Conservative Party stood for a defense of Catholic values in Chilean society. Because the rural populations of the Central Valley lived in the most densely Catholic part of Chile, and (in particular) because Conservative landowners built chapels, sponsored schools run by religious orders, celebrated religious holidays and patron saint days, and so on, it is more than likely, given the mobility of the rural workforce, that their stable dependents also were committed Catholics.[54] This would explain why the Conservative rural vote was more consistent than that of the other parties. Is it not understandable that peasants in the densely Catholic areas would vote willingly for candidates of the Conservative Party, as did most devoted Catholics in other parts of Chile before 1930?[55] Social networks built around religion reinforced this process by creating stronger than normal ties among the rural inhabitants.

The common practice of offering voters certain "incentives," mentioned as a significant tool in the coercive arsenal, does not alter this analysis. In fact, vote buying indicated that voters were indeed not coerced as much as enticed. It cannot be argued that all voters who lined up to receive a compensation voted the way they did only because they were paid, although this has been assumed in the literature under discussion here.[56] In fact, that was probably less likely than the following three additional possibilities. First, the payment only made the difference between actually voting and deciding to abstain; hence, the money compensated for the costs associated with going to the polls, which were often quite distant, or simply gave the voter a needed incentive to vote. Second, voters, at least the poorer ones, may have lined up to collect money from candidates for whom they would have voted willingly in any case, payment or no payment. And third, voters may have taken the money but voted, nonetheless, for another candidate. The latter possibility must have been common enough at the turn of the century to prompt a contemporary observer to note that "there are voters who sell themselves to one or another [candidate], and to whoever is willing to pay, without it being clear, in the end, for what party they actually voted."[57] This comment certainly does not fit the image of vote buying as part of a widespread system of voter coercion; it does implicitly reaffirm the fact that the voting procedures, following the 1890 electoral law, permitted the secrecy of the vote.

Were Landed Interests "Hegemonic" and Based on "Labor-Repressive" Practices?

It would be a gross simplification to claim that Chile had a distinct class of landowners at the top of its social pyramid at any point in the nineteenth century. The nation's economy always drew its most important capital accumulations from mining exports. During the period that authors most frequently identify with the unrivaled hegemony of landowners, namely, the 1830s to the early 1860s, the value of mining exports was in fact an average of about three times larger than that of agriculture.[58] Consequently, Villalobos states an obvious conclusion in asserting that the overwhelming majority of the largest fortunes in Chile by the 1870s were derived from a "bourgeois" origin, namely, from mining, commerce, industry, and finance.[59] He also notes that the fusion of landholding and "bourgeois" families began very early on and was a continuous process, and that by the War of the Pacific (1879) it was "very advanced if not complete."[60] The richest families invested as well in land or acquired it through marriages. Moreover, the most prominent landholders, given their other, more profitable ventures, were not dependent on the income they received from the land, and they held it for uses other than agriculture. It could be used as a hedge against inflation, a significant feature of the Chilean economy since the 1870s. It served as the easiest way to obtain credit for other investments, because most credit in the nineteenth century was in the form of mortgages over fixed assets. It was a means to control access to mineral deposits that could be found eventually. Such deposits could be exploited by anybody who found and maintained a continuous operation to extract them. Land titles did not grant automatic claims to minerals under the soil following Chilean legislation legated from the colony, thereby making access to possible mineral resources a matter of crucial importance. Land could also be held to control access to water and to forests, elements used not only for agricultural purposes but also for mineral enterprises. The importance of water, forests, and possible mineral resources explains to a great extent why the large estates held so much land in hills and mountains that had little, if no, agricultural use themselves—acreage that made the estates so large.

Land was also used to plant vineyards to produce quality wines that added to a family's prestige in Chile and abroad, and for recreational purposes as upper-class families spent summers in the countryside but resided the rest of the year in Santiago. Agricultural production on the estates, aside from that of the labor service tenants, was usually turned over to an administrator, while certain sections could also be rented out. Hence, the large estates were in many cases not viewed by their owners primarily as agricultural enterprises.

Because the owners of most large estates did not derive their income primarily from agriculture, it cannot be asserted that their economic position was dependent on extracting a surplus from service tenants or from the rural workers who were hired when needed. However, a main concern for owners was that their landholdings not be money losers, and this meant that cash payments to the workforce were best kept to a minimum. With their large surface, and as long as agricultural land values and rural property taxes remained as low as they did until the 1950s, it was easy and much more rational to pay, at least in part, for labor services in land.[61] Such land benefits (*regalías*) not only were a feature of the compensation given to the *inquilino* (who was, for this reason, more a renter than an agricultural worker) but also were common practice to pay for the services of everyone else in the enterprise, from the accountant and company store manager to the administrator. For example, Bengoa indicates that a Central Valley estate in 1910 gave the administrator, the effective head of the enterprise given the absentee owner or owners, a little over seven acres of irrigated land for growing vegetables, a little less than two acres to cultivate wheat, the right to graze ten animals, and twenty pesos per day.[62]

This meant that there was agriculture of very different intensities in the large rural estates. With the exception of vines and a few other specialty crops such as ornamental plants, usually tended by trained personnel, the most extensive and least productive use of the land generally was tilling it for the direct benefit of the estate owner or owners. The large estates used low technology, given the lack of interest of owners in investing in their rural operations when higher profits could be drawn elsewhere. Labor for such areas was provided at times of harvest by hired hands and more permanently during the year by the *inquilino*, who often hired someone else to fulfill the labor service he exchanged for the land he used.[63] The *inquilino* had better things to do than to work for the estate: he and his immediate family were best off devoting energies to the intensive cultivation of their plot, to raising animals, and to selling the excess on the town market, if not the estate warehouse.[64] The *inquilino* was at the top of the dependent rural population hierarchy, and the advantages of this position (a doubtful one from the point of view of an efficient agricultural enterprise) dictated the fact that so many *inquilinos* remained on the estates. Bauer notes that the use of labor service tenants continued much longer in Chile than elsewhere, because neither estate owners nor *inquilinos* had much interest in abolishing it. The market pressures that began in the 1950s were the ones that eventually did away with this form of labor.[65] The more efficiency was essential in order to succeed with an agricultural enterprise, the less resort there was to the *inquilino* as a source of labor. Hence, it is hard to maintain that a labor arrangement that gave *inquilinos* greater advantages than those they would have had as paid agricultural workers or as industrial workers corresponded to a "labor-repressive" form of agriculture. The *inquilinos* were connected to a broader national labor market for unskilled or semiskilled workers, but they chose to stay on the farms. Bengoa notes that *inquilinos* who were, circa 1920, literally next to Santiago's expanding outer streets remained on the farm even though they earned slightly less than industrial workers in monetary terms. He calculates the *inquilinos'* compensation at 3.6 pesos per day, including nonmonetary payments, while an industrial worker at the time earned 4.5 pesos. But the quality of life and security of the *inquilino* were preferable to those of the urban worker, who could become unemployed.[66]

All of these points undermine the appropriateness of viewing the Chilean case from the perspective of the previously mentioned literature, and therefore cast doubt on the adequacy of seeing a confirmation of Moore's antidemocratic class constellation in this case. But perhaps Moore's analysis can be applied in the opposite way, that is, by noting that the Chilean case contains a confirmation of his pro-democratic class constellation.

MOORE'S PRO-DEMOCRATIC CLASS CONSTELLATION IN CHILE?

This scenario is in many ways more plausible than the previous one. If the richest families in the country drew their main income from mining, banking, and commerce ever since the eighteenth century, the fact that they also owned the largest rural estates did not make them a typical landowning class. The rural estates complemented their patrimony, furnished them a political base in the provinces, and served recreational and other purposes. It made little economic sense for them to invest heavily in agriculture, which explains the slow adoption of new technology to produce staple crops. Such a context points to a central conclusion in Moore's terms: the Chilean bourgeoisie and its interests were the dominant—not the weaker—element in the nation's upper class, and this is, of course, a key component of Moore's pro-democratic class constellation. To it must be added that "lord" and "peasant" relations can hardly be described, as noted earlier, in the strict or expanded senses of the term as "labor-repressive." With the potential mobility of its laborers (including the *inquilinos*), the existence of a national labor market in which they could participate, and the fact that large landowners did not "depend" on low-wage labor for their prominent position in the Chilean economy because it was derived from other investments, the nation's agriculture, despite its peculiarities, was closer to Moore's "commercial" type.

Moreover, Chile never had a strong aristocratic component in its social structure as did the European and Asian cases Moore discusses. The colonial aristocracy (in the literal sense of individuals with hereditary titles of nobility associated with entailed dominions) was extremely small. It had grown to only twenty-seven families (or twenty, judging from the repetition of certain patronymics) by the end of the eighteenth century.[67] The legal framework of Spain's American colonies was designed to maximize the power of the central state, not to facilitate the development of local or regional powers under nobles of various grades. The crown was suspicious of American-born notables, whatever their titular pretensions, and nobility did not guarantee a role in the colonial state because the main officials were, exceptions aside, of peninsular background. Titles of nobility were sought by prominent eighteenth-century families, many of them new to the country, as a means to enhance their social status, but it was not easy to have them recognized unless proof could be shown of a direct lineage to Spanish nobility, nor to obtain much respect from the colonial authorities after receiving them. An indication of this state of affairs was the fact that the richest of Chilean nobles, a count, had to request in writing in a long, drawn-out process that the authorities address him as "Señoría."[68] The small group of nobles on the eve of independence was also composed largely of new blood. Only five of them descended from the 164 Spanish settlers who had received Indian labor and land from the crown before 1655.[69] The essential source of the nobility's fortunes was commerce, not their landed estates.[70] Bauer's assessment, against that of McBride, is that the entails had very little impact on Chilean rural society and that their final abolition was an event of minor significance.[71] By the early decades of independence, most families of noble background, having lost their titles with the advent of the republic, were eager to disentail their estates so that they could have access to mortgage credit.

Colonial Chile also did not develop the elaborate relations of dominion and vassalage that emerged in medieval Europe, and the principle *"nulle terre sans seigneur"* was never applied. Hence, the many references in Chilean historiography to "seignorial relations" established in the rural world by the "aristocracy" of landowners overseeing a subject peasantry constitute inappropriate images. Chilean *inquilinos* did not have to pay homage to any lords, were never bound to the land as were central European serfs until the nineteenth century, nor did they have to pay or fulfill any of the multiple dues, corvées, strictures, and obligations associated with the French seigneury.[72] Although French peasants had been free of serfdom for centuries and hence could move, by the eighteenth century virtually every plot of land was still connected to the rights of a lord, often recently ennobled from having bought his title and its rights. Sometimes peasants were obligated to several of them, given the bits and pieces where they labored as employees, renters, sharecroppers, or even proprietors. Tocqueville captured the latter's predicament, revealing the fundamental inequalities of status of the ancien régime, when he referred to a prototypical peasant who manages, after years of savings, to buy his own piece of land:

> to acquire it, he had to pay a right, not to the government, but to other proprietors in the area who were just as removed from public affairs and just as powerless as he. Once he finally possesses the land, he sinks his heart as well as his grain in it. This little piece of land belongs to him. . . . And yet, the same neighbors show up to remove him from his field to make him work elsewhere without pay. If he wants to defend his seedlings against the animals they hunt, they are there to prevent him from doing so. The same people wait for him to demand a toll when he goes across the river. He confronts them again when he goes to market, as they sell him a right to sell his own produce. And when, after returning home, he wants to consume what remains of his own wheat, this wheat that grew under his eyes and by his own hands, he cannot do it unless he first sends it to be ground in the mill and cooked in the ovens of these same people."[73]

The "proprietors," "neighbors," and "people" in this passage were, of course, lords.

The Chilean small proprietors, sharecroppers, *inquilinos*, or hired laborers never faced such a situation. The encomiendas were a forced labor system, but as noted by Góngora this institution had largely been abandoned by the early eighteenth century given the cost of maintaining not only the laborer himself but also his family.[74] Góngora adds that the institution of the *inquilino* did not stem from the encomienda, but that it emerged from land rental arrangements that had become common in the eighteenth century. At that point *inquilinos* paid a canon in kind or in money, and it was only later, as markets for agriculture expanded, that this payment was substituted for labor service.[75] Given this origin, the service tenantry was derived from an arrangement that was basically market-driven rather than one that contained forcible impositions on individuals who occupied a formally defined inferior social status. The use of slaves in Chilean agriculture was not widespread before abolition in the wake of independence from Spain.

The fact that Chile also had a substantial segment of small to medium-sized rural properties (i.e., economically viable family holdings) within its main agricultural area (from Copiapó to Chillán) contributes another important element to a Moorian pro-democratic constellation.[76] This group was more significant in the nineteenth century than in the twentieth, as small properties became smaller and smaller given the effects of inheritance laws. Unlike the large proprietors, small to medium landholding families' did not have enough assets to prevent the division of the land either by having a family member buy others out, by having only one person inherit the land while other siblings received other family assets, or by co-owning estates that were large enough for all. The existence of this segment in rural society, to which can be added those who rented agricultural properties, meant that Chile had a significant population of independent peasants who were important suppliers to city markets.[77] As a result, they did relate to urban social and economic life, and, in the nineteenth century many would have been enrolled in the National Guard and, for this reason, would have been part of the electorate of the time.

This alternative way of interpreting the Chilean class equation leads, once more, to the question of why the mentioned authors earlier thought the country needed a "bourgeois revolution." However, although this interpretation is probably more plausible than the former one, it is also insufficient as an explanation for democratization of the country's political institutions during the course of the nineteenth century. I will explain why after a brief digression.

The central difficulty with using a class-based structuralism to explain political change is that it assumes that the only truly significant political divisions stem from class positions. In certain circumstances a link between class position and political attitudes—which may be deduced by the analyst without even ascertaining the actors' opinions—may well hold true barring individual idiosyncrasies. This will most likely be the case when the issues at hand relate to the very survival or viability of privileged class positions occupied by social and political actors. However, in the absence of such fundamental issues, the actors' views cannot be predicted with any accuracy simply on the basis of them an objective class-structural placement. Their attitudes may be determined by a wide variety of other factors, not the least of which are the allegiances and commitments they may have given them an identification with, or membership in, a broad array of other social categories or groups. Such other, non-class-related identities may even prevent the formation of organizations to preserve class interests as the need for these arises. It all depends on the depth of the feelings and allegiances generated by other cleavages. Similarly, such other divisions may provide the motivation for actors to attempt to forge democratic institutions.

The Moorian interpretation of Chile has unduly assumed that the Conservative Party stood for landowner interests, and that it took antidemocratic positions. But if the large rural property owners in Chile did no depend on labor repression for their survival as a class, and if there was no significant challenge to landowner interests (in part given the cross-sectoral nature of the upper class's assets), then there was no need for landowners to coalesce politically into a landowners' party. Other political issues could push them in different directions. And indeed landowners could be found in all major non-working-class parties of the time.

The differences between political actors in these various parties cannot be explained, consequently, by remaining within the framework of a class-based analysis. Nor can such an analysis explain the motivations of the Conservative Party leaders in seeking democratic reforms, or their concern for the living conditions of the popular segments of society; these stemmed from the Conservatives' religious convictions. The Conservative Party emerged, beginning in the late 1850s, from a secular-religious conflict in Chilean society and politics. Conservatives defended the application of a Catholic outlook on all important aspects of society as well as national legislation. Given that the secularizing and anticlerical forces in the other major parties controlled the government, and that the antidemocratic electoral procedures, as well as the lack of basic freedoms to organize political and social groups, hampered the ability of Conservatives to gain positions of power and to spread their message, they struggled for over three decades to secure the necessary political reforms that would ensure democratic rights. This process culminated in the electoral reform of 1890.

Given that the Conservative Party was essentially one of Catholic defense, it would perhaps have been better for the party's historical image if it had called itself the "Catholic Party," or even the "Center Party," as did the party of Catholic defense that emerged in Germany.[78] Like the Zentrum, Chilean Conservatives had a cross-class base of support that was well organized in the cities and the rural areas. Their pro-democratic positions made them adopt similar views to those of Belgian liberal Catholicism.[79] Their receptivity to the development of new trends in social Christian thought helps to explain their sensitivity to social issues. On most socioeconomic issues, unlike the Liberals, the Conservatives took centrist positions, although the irony is that, given their respective labels, analysts have made the opposite assumption. Opponents of the Conservatives often chided them for their lack of "progressivism," but this referred to their positions regarding the religious and educational issues that divided them. In short, the literature discussed here neglects consideration of political cleavages other than class, and this becomes a significant limitation when analyzing political development in cases where other cleavages—such as the secular-religious conflict that had a major impact on Chilean party politics—were important.

ELEMENTS OF AN ALTERNATIVE INSTITUTIONAL-ORGANIZATIONAL APPROACH TO DEMOCRATIZATION

The alternative perspective delineated here takes as its starting point a focus on the motives, views, ideologies, organizations, resources, and social bases of support of the actors who carry out regime changes. It also focuses on the institutional envelopes that both enable and constrain their actions, thereby affecting their political capabilities, and on the intended and unintended consequences of their initiatives for the development of the process of change. It postulates that democratic political change resulted from "critical historical moments in which the balance of political forces tilts in favor of élites and social forces of often very different ideologies, who press for democratic institutions in the expectation that they will be advantageous for consolidating or increasing their power, safeguarding their interests, and/or resolving in the least costly manner a political crisis."[80] This perspective remains closer to the sequence of historical events than the class and social-structural one favored by Moore. While it does not assume that all political agents act either overtly, surreptitiously, or in an unintended manner only to secure class interests, it also captures the influence of socioeconomic and class factors insofar as some political actors may be pursuing or defending interests that pertain to them. In the institutional-organizational perspective, references to the actions of "classes" or of other large categories of the population constitute an inadequate abstraction for the specific analysis of regime change.

Analysts who examine political change with the social-structural approach contend that it allows them to grasp in the most parsimonious way possible the essential set of factors that determine such change. Even if the effects of the structural variables may not be evident at a certain moment in time, they assert that these will become manifest in the long term. Other more immediately determining elements, such as the capacity of some political groups to organize themselves to press for their interests more expeditiously and with better timing than their opponents, are understood by such analysts to be largely epiphenomenal. Nonetheless, as was the case with Moore's own presentation of the cases he analyzed, historical accounts written from a class-based perspective are peppered with references to more immediate political, organizational, and institutional variables. By making such factors a center of the analysis, it should be possible to develop general propositions that can facilitate the analysis of regime change. What follows illustrates the directions that this kind of exploration may take in reference to processes of first-wave democratization that occur endogenously, that is, in the absence of an imposition of political change through foreign influences.

At the onset of such processes it is always possible to identify tensions and conflicts that emerged given the capacity of the state to penetrate society, injuring collective or individual interests in it, and the authoritarian nature of the regime. The latter permitted rulers to take what social forces perceived to be arbitrary decisions that were contrary to their values and/or interests, given the absence of any institutional means to hold the elite accountable for its actions. Because the development of this conflict was predicated on the prior consolidation of a strong state that could enforce power holder dictates, such consolidation was a prerequisite (but not a sufficient condition) for endogenous processes of democratization. When facing a weaker state, social and political actors affected by the decisions of the authoritarian power holders could choose to ignore them. They could also launch a rebellion and either impose their will on rulers, overthrow them, or secede to form a new nation-state. While such situations could evolve toward democratic outcomes, this was the case only if they first generated a stronger state.

The tensions and conflicts created by the capacity of an authoritarian state to penetrate society were also deeper and more frequent when social and economic actors had acquired—given their status and/or market positions—the capacity to command important resources, including the ability to organize collective action, independently of the state. Hence democratization was also favored by the formation of a strong civil society. When facing their opponents in it, authoritarian rulers were unable, or were unsure of being able, to suffocate them with repressive measures alone. The authoritarian power holders also became dependent on the resources the private economy could generate. The combination of the strength of the authoritarian state and the strength of civil society increased the chances that the clash between the two would result in a standoff. Democratization offered a resolution to this stalemate and its resulting political instability and uncertainty by redefining the manner in which rulers exercised authority, limiting it but at the same time making it more secure and binding, instilling electoral procedures to access it, and making it permeable to the influence of organized society.

The frequency and depth of conflicts between state and society, as well as the standoff between the two, increased with economic development, creating the push for democratization that emerged in the nineteenth century. For this reason analysts have long noted an association between development and democracy.[81] Democratization was also facilitated by the diffusion all over the world, especially in the Western cultural space (i.e., in Europe, the Americas, and the English colonies of settlement), beginning in the late seventeenth and eighteenth centuries, of democratic constitutional blueprints for the organization of government. Political actors in most national settings did not have to invent such models, even if they created specific variants of them. The notion that government could be organized on a different basis provided a powerful stimulus to the actions of opponents to authoritarian rulers, as can be seen readily in the nineteenth-century histories of the Western world. In Hispanic America, republican democratic constitutions became a standard model of reference for all political actors after the break with Spain, even if they did not always live up to their provisions or ideals. While Brazil remained under Bragança rule even after independence from Portugal, following the spirit of the times after the defeat of Napoleon it became a constitutional monarchy with an elected parliament (albeit with less than democratic electoral procedures, as most everywhere else). Consequently, the Iberic New World followed an unusual political evolution when compared with England, Sweden, or other European cases where democracy emerged on a step-by-step basis. In Latin America, certain aspects of democracy were adopted in principle and, with some peculiarities, in fact, before they were well established in most of the old continent. This was particularly the case with elections and suffrage rights, which tended to antecede in practice the institutions to guarantee political rights of expression and organization in what is a reversal of the "normal," that is, European, pattern.

The political actors who emerged to press for democratization were associated with a wide variety of interests from one case to another, including of course class interests. The variations in terms of who these actors were and how they were organized affected the kinds of democracies that were formed, their overall stability, the characteristics of their party systems, and the shape of their social interest organizations. Economic development increased the capacity of all actors, not only those related to economic interests, to pressure the state. While the religious-secular divide was instrumental in generating democratizing actors in Chile, in other cases regional elites, linguistic minorities, working-class groups, peasant societies, business associations, and so on, may have been significant. Different groups may as well have championed different aspects of the construction of democratic institutions, a matter that varied from case to case. Such variations produced long-lasting consequences. For instance, taking only those settings that had some kind of electoral mechanism before the onset of democracies, a central difference between them had to do with whether income requirements and/or class-weighted votes for male suffrage were dropped before or after the inception of their respective labor movements. When such movements emerged before this change in suffrage procedures, as in northern Europe, the labor movement took a central role in pressing for the extension of suffrage; as a result, party organizations related to it emerged more vigorously than in those settings, as in France, Switzerland, and most of the Americas—North and South—where such a vote was a given through the actions of other forces before the labor movement arose. Strong social democratic parties were in this sense the product of a unique coincidence in the timing of suffrage extension and labor movement.

For complex reasons, including cultural ones, some national settings seemed more predisposed to developing stronger civil societies given the ease with which organizations emerged within them. This had to do in part with the kinds of social conflicts that divided the population. Some such cleavages involved individuals who were predisposed to engage in collective action given the density of their sociability and, therefore, the strength of peer pressures within it, as well as the clarity of their sense of injury from the actions of others. If a national society, even if it was relatively poor in comparison to others at the time, was cleaved into divisions that provided the grounds for a relatively easy activation of collective organization, then it was more likely to have the kind of civil society that was associated with early pressures for democratization than a richer one that did not happen to be cleaved in the same manner. Religious divisions often formed the basis for such collectivities. The rich organizational life related to the secular-religious divide in Chile is a case in point. Similarly, labor movement formation provided this kind of social basis for politically significant collective organization.

And yet, even given easily formed organizations, not all of them would press for democratization when facing an authoritarian state. For instance, if the segments of civil society that were most easily formed into powerful organizations generated pressures to secede from the national state rather than to reform the regime, democratization usually encountered much greater difficulties. The same was the case in societies in which a large segment was composed of a subordinate and suppressed ethnic, linguistic, religious, and/or racial group, as in Bolivia or Guatemala. In each instance, the study of democratization requires an examination of how the politically significant organizations were constituted, the kinds of political orientations they developed, and how close they were to authoritarian power holders. These circumstances generated variations in the views and political insertion of their leaders. For instance, unlike what Rueschemeyer, Huber Stephens, and Stephens assert as one of their central premises, it cannot be said that labor leaders everywhere had pro-democratic attitudes.[82] In some settings, as in Chile and France, where workers had the same rights of citizenship as the middle and upper classes but the building of unions was particularly difficult, important segments of the labor movement developed a highly ambiguous attitude toward democracy, condemning it as a tool of the bourgeoisie.[83]

While it always took pressure from political and social actors who were outside the inner circles of power, and therefore regime opponents or potential regime opponents, to institute the process of change by reacting negatively to state initiatives, this does not mean that all processes of democratization were actually led by such actors. Power holders seeking to preempt or forestall a political crisis after they sensed the pressures exerted upon them could, eventually, initiate democratizing reform themselves, although they did not necessarily see it as the beginning of a process leading to full democratization. Even political and social leaders who were generally ill disposed to democratic procedures could come to the conclusion that this kind of reform was the best resolution for the difficulties at hand, calculating correctly or incorrectly that it would prevent a worse outcome from their point of view. And, vice versa, those who professed democratic convictions could often turn out to be antidemocratic in their actions, if not their pronouncements, if and when power fell into their hands. Although concrete issues relating to the consequences of state policies may have been the trigger for processes of change, the actors pursuing it must reach the conviction that the object of their actions should be a redefinition of how authority is exercised, not simply a redress of their grievances. In some cases, democratization occurred even in the absence of such a conviction, given pressures on the new power holders from other powerful actors—possibly even those who were formerly associated with the authoritarian regime—or perhaps given an agreement among the actors of different interests and outlooks who nonetheless formed a coalition against the authoritarian rulers. Democratization offers them an opportunity to settle their own differences peacefully.

The personal characteristics and qualities of individual leaders do matter in determining the course of change. Thus, Chile's President Bulnes, a general, chose in 1851 to back up the election of his successor by personally leading the government's armed forces against the insurgency led by General Cruz, the defeated candidate, although the latter was a relative and comrade-in-arms. Had Bulnes remained on the sidelines, it is highly likely that Cruz would have won the civil war, and the principle that presidents had to be renewed through elections, the outcome of which all parties must respect, would have been severely weakened—as occurred at the time in most other Hispanic American countries. Similarly, how different French history would have been had Louis XVI put aside his rigid conception of the place in society and politics of the three orders after he grudgingly convened the Estates-General, and had he allowed the assembly as a whole, with the Third Estate's majority, to evolve into the parliament of a constitutional monarchy. France had a dull king, one who was incapable of grasping the significance of the events of the day.

In addition to being initiated by the tension created by state authoritarianism and its capacity to penetrate society, endogenous processes of democratization may be triggered as well by a significant crisis of organization and/or authority within the state apparatus itself. A diffident or slothful monarch; a head of state who is viewed as being corrupt or inept by the armed forces; a bureaucracy that functions in a discombobulated way and is unable to control frontiers, dispense justice, collect taxes, or facilitate economic development; a conflict between different branches of the state (such as the courts or legislatures versus the monarch, or officials supervising electoral processes versus the president and his cabinet)—all such situations can be potent circumstances for leadership to emerge within the apparatus of the state itself to press for new definitions of the regime, in the process forging alliances and enemies among state officials, as well as with various social forces. The greater the demands placed on state performance given modernization, a tenuous geopolitical position, or an unexpected crisis of one sort or another, the greater the chances that such internal state tensions will emerge. Even strong authoritarian states, that is, those whose offices and functions penetrate society and are essential for the proper regulation of its affairs and markets, may experience such a crisis. The authoritarian nature of the regime generally prevents the necessary flexibility to deal with the crisis through institutional procedures.

Political action does not occur in a vacuum of state and regime institutional definitions no matter how authoritarian the regime. Whatever differences existed, for instance, between the political attitudes of English and French landowning nobles could well have been more the result of the institutions of the respective monarchies as they evolved after Louis XIV's success and Charles I's failure rather than simply the product of class relations between landowners, urban bourgeoisies, and peasants. By 1789 the French monarch continued to be the center of a state with very weak formal institutions that offered virtually no protection from arbitrary power. The king could ignore the advice of the *parlements*, insisting that they register his decrees, and his lettre de cachet sufficed to condemn anyone to a dungeon until further order. The English Crown had been forced to relinquish such powers beginning in the thirteenth century, and although the limitations, on royal authority had to be reasserted by opponents with the force of arms on several occasions, and both the power of Parliament and the formalization of the rule of law through the courts were later developments, by the turn of the eighteenth century these were firmly in place. The study of democratization requires a careful examination of these institutional features and legacies, which they provided powerful parameters to the actions of the participants in processes of political change. The French ancien régime had an elaborate court life, but its formal political-institutional structure provided virtually no elements on which to build democratization. By contrast, the more elaborate set of precedents, settlements, and understandings that served as underpinnings to the English monarchical regime remained as a guide to the actors' views of what was and was not possible even in periods of upheaval. Actors fell back on them in order to legitimate their conduct even as they altered fundamental aspects of the monarchical regime, turning it eventually, in the course of the nineteenth century, into a democratic constitutional monarchy even if complete and equal suffrage rights were not finally in place until 1928. Many institutional constructs associated with democracies could, and did, emerge well in advance of the actual inception of democratic regimes.

The Chilean Constitution of 1833 provides a significant illustration of the importance of institutional definitions for the possibility of democratic change through reform. Despite the fact that the executive's interference in elections permitted presidents to forge large pro-government majorities in the legislature, senators and deputies were elected for fixed terms of office and therefore could become opponents of the government while their mandates lasted. It was this feature that permitted Conservatives, Radicals, and some Liberals, all in opposition to the president of the moment even though virtually nothing else united them, to adopt the suffrage bill of 1874. The pressure to change the electoral rules resulted from the fact that the Conservatives moved to the opposition after benefiting, given their prior coalition with the incumbent president, from official interference on their behalf in the congressional elections of 1872. Knowing that they could no longer count on the executive's help for the next election, Conservatives tried to change the rules of the electoral game to prevent the executive from composing anti-Conservative congressional majorities though electoral interference. The reform therefore resulted from an elementary calculation of political survival, but it was made possible given the prior institutional definitions: members of Congress were secure in their seats until the next election, and they could form a majority to bend presidential wishes. Such an alliance would not have been able to carry out the same change given a constitutional arrangement permitting the head of state, as in Brazil and many other monarchical regimes at the time, to dissolve the legislature at will, calling new elections.

Authoritarian regimes force opponents to organize themselves to pressure power holders in different ways. In some cases these are compatible with democracies, as when the regimes operate with electoral processes, though vitiated, and legislatures, though controlled and/or impotent. In such circumstances, democratization is easier and usually longer lasting. Civil and political society anticipate it. However, in other authoritarian situations opponents have no choice but to resort to means, such as insurrections and coups d'état, that are destabilizing to any form of political order. Latin American countries during the nineteenth century, notably in Peru and Uruguay, provide many examples of changes of government through these means. When this is the case, it may be difficult for all opponents of newly democratized regimes to abandon the well-learned styles of doing politics of the past, as well as the resources to do so. The ensuing democratic instability, with frequent authoritarian reversals, may well follow from the retention of such mechanisms for political pressure and change by powerful actors, not from any particular features of the class structure. They may even flow more from the ambitions and resentments of key figures than from any other clearly definable reason. It is hard to discover, for instance, any great policy differences between Manuel Oribe and Fructuoso Rivera in Uruguay, although thousands died in the battles that their enmity created.[84] The nation's two main parties can be traced back to it.[85] Leaders who specialize in having links with the military to exert their power do not develop the same degree of commitment as do others to respecting the results of elections. Insurrections continue the political battle that has not been won through electoral means. A lasting and veritable democratization is extremely difficult in such circumstances until state power holders are able to impose a thorough defeat on those who resort to such means of doing politics, as occurred in Uruguay in 1904.

In sum, while working with the assumption that regime change—democratization in this discussion—cannot be understood without focusing directly on the motives and actions of political and social actors, this perspective tries to elucidate the background conditions that will set them on a course to initiate such a change. It does not neglect the social bases of politics, but it also focuses on state-society relations, institutional definitions, sequences of events, the characteristics of organizations, and critical moments in which the quality of leaders can make a difference. As such, this perspective approaches the study of regime change from a viewpoint that is conceptually more supple and sensitive to the surprises of history.

CONCLUSIONS

Using the history of the Chilean process of democratization, this chapter has challenged the adequacy of examining this process through Moore's class-relational model. The main advocates of democratization were motivated by their hope to prevent greater secularization of Chilean institutions, not by their class positions. Moreover, key leaders among them were themselves landowners, and one of their party's main social bases was among large landowners and their dependents in the richest agricultural area of the country. In short, the very actors who should have been antidemocratic were, on the contrary, the most determined advocates of democratic change.

However, as noted in the detailed description of the Chilean rural world, the nation's landowners did not rely for their income and positions—unlike what has been implied in the literature—on "labor repression" in the strict sense of this term. The Chilean case does not disprove, therefore, what I referred to above as an obvious point, namely, that if class relations are heavily woven with norms and practices that contradict the basic human and democratic rights of peasants or agricultural workers, as occurs in the strict sense of Moore's "labor repression," then there is a high probability that landowners will indeed be an antidemocratic force. The advent of democracy will not permit such landowners to continue their modus operandi, and it is likely that they will organize in order to challenge those who would advocate it. Instead, the Chilean case does show that the expanded version of the notion of labor repression, that is, the one that stresses that all large landowners are antidemocratic, or that all landowners employing cheap labor are antidemocratic, is incorrect. Conservative landowners in Chile certainly owned huge estates, and they did have what was for them a cheap labor force given the widespread use of labor tenancy arrangements.

In this specific sense the Chilean case is quite unique given the clarity with which it permits a refutation of Moore's thesis. Examining other Latin American settings from Moore's point of view (and using only the expanded notion of labor repression) does not generate such a striking disparity between the model and the historical evidence. Beginning with the arguably democratic cases, Uruguay can be understood to have had "commercial agriculture," for which reason the rise of its democracy at the beginning of the twentieth century does generally fit Moore's model, without necessarily being explained by it. Costa Rican democracy can be attributed to the country's land tenure pattern, an unusual one in Central America given the predominance of family farms. Argentina is a curious case given that it can be used to confirm Moore in two senses. The focus is either on the fact that it developed democracy after 1912 (which can be attributed to market-driven agriculture) or on the fact that its democracy broke down in 1930, generating a long-lasting authoritarian regime (which can be linked to the large size of rural properties and the strength of the agricultural interests).[86] The analysis of Moore's thesis is very

difficult and inconclusive in Colombia given the enormous regional disparities in land tenure patterns and types of agriculture, as well as the
endemic weakness of the central state.[87] Turning to the situations in
which democracies did not really develop or consisted of only brief episodes before the mid-1930s (Mexico, Brazil, Venezuela, Paraguay, and
the Andean countries), all had large rural estates and great inequities.[88]
Brazilian, southern Mexican, and highland Peruvian landowners may
also be seen as employing labor-repressive practices in the strict sense of
the term during much of the nineteenth and even the early twentieth century. Central American countries other than Costa Rica either fall into the
same pattern of large landownership (and even labor repression in the
strict sense in some areas) or should not be considered at all in this analysis given the fact that their political processes were excessively determined
by foreign interests.[89]

Similarly, European cases also do not provide the same kind of clear
refutations of Moore's model as does Chile. Anomalies can be found at
regional, intracountry levels. (For instance, Galician land tenure patterns
were unusually equitable in Spain, and yet this region was one of the
strongest bastions of support for Franco's forces.) The French nobility
was indeed largely antidemocratic given its use of labor repression in the
strict sense of the term during the ancien régime, and during the nineteenth century—after losing much of its land and privileges—its most
characteristic elements were at best recalcitrant supporters of democratic
arrangements at certain moments, when not open conspirators against
the republics that embodied them. Other Latin European nineteenth-century landowners, particularly noble ones, took similarly negative positions as their French counterparts toward the advance of democracy.
Moore's own discussion of the German case placed its characteristic Prussian landowners in the antidemocratic category, while the English had
"commercial agriculture." The smaller northern European cases all had
small, rural property owners and/or market-driven agriculture as well.

Does this mean that the Chilean experience should be dismissed as a
unique and peculiar exception, but that the Moore thesis should be retained—with not only the strict but also the expanded version of the notion of labor repression—given that other settings do not seemingly contradict it? Or does this mean that the inapplicability of the Moore thesis
to Chile should lead to questioning whether it does indeed work in other
settings in the expanded sense? I take this latter position, for two reasons.
First, the Chilean case refutes the Moore thesis all too thoroughly. Again,
how can the leading figures pressing for democratization be precisely the
ones that the Moore model predicts should be opposed to it? And how
can the course of democratization in this case be understood without examining the influence of factors other than class, that is, religion, politi-

cal-institutional strictures, actors' conceptions regarding what makes government legitimate, and so on? Second, the fact that large landowners, in some cases from noble families, took antidemocratic positions and views in other cases may very well stem from factors that have nothing to do with class relations. The Chilean case shows that this model, in its expanded version, is incorrect. Hence, there is good reason to assume that the model does not work elsewhere in these terms and that the antidemocratic postures of landowners in those other cases are, in fact, a coincidence with respect to the model. In other words, such antidemocratic postures and actions may be due to other factors, even though landowners fit the profile that, according to the expanded version of labor repression, should make them into an antidemocratic force. Hence, the examination of the Chilean case, permits questioning, for instance, whether class relations really had anything to do with the attitudes of Prussian landowners toward democratization. In his own specific discussion of the German case, Moore associates the Prussian landed nobility and its antidemocratic posture to its links with the imperial bureaucracy and military rather than to its labor practices or the extent of its dominions.[90]

Although in other cases it may be much more difficult to prove the existence of such close connections between landowners and authoritarian officeholders in governments, legislatures, bureaucracies, or armed forces—after all, except for the latter, most of them tended to be lawyers—this link or association may prove to be an adequate explanation for the antidemocratic reactions of landowners when it became a factor in the course of democratization. Large landowners were an important factor in local economies, and in many cases authoritarian state policies could be expected to cater to their interests. Hence, when such states came under pressure to democratize, it would not be particularly surprising to find landowners taking pro-regime positions because the coming political change could conceivably affect their interests, and this even after all feudal vestiges and forced labor systems had been eliminated. However, this support for the authoritarian status quo can also be found among other capitalists, well-placed professionals, and other groups for the same reasons. This kind of reaction is not exclusive to landowners and is context-dependent. The opposite situation, the one that can be observed in Chile, proves the point. When a clear-cut clash divided political actors in such a way that those who had an important social base among landowners could sense, correctly or incorrectly, that they could derive certain advantages over their opponents from democratization, they had no difficulty in advocating it. Chilean landowners linked to the Conservative Party drew the same conclusion that their English Tory counterparts had already drawn. Large rural properties and a more or less benevolent presence in the social fabric of rural life could be political assets in the era of expanded suffrage politics.

Similarly, landowners in other settings may well have taken antidemocratic positions for reasons that had, strictly speaking, nothing to do as well with their class despite not having close connections with authoritarian power holders. While their Catholicism motivated the democratizing initiatives of Chilean Conservatives who were committed republicans given their support for the nation's independence from Spain, the opposite was true of their counterparts in Latin Europe. In their experience, democratization was spurred by secular and pro-republican forces, and such forces were anti-Catholic. The process of Italian unification that accompanied democratization in that country was directed necessarily against the temporal domains of the Pope, who became a "prisoner of the Vatican." The Vatican prohibited Catholic participation in Italian elections until 1903. These events forged the attitudes of Latin European nobles and landowners (some of them ex-landowners given the expropriation of their dominions), and prevented them, exceptions aside, from supporting democratic change. Instead, they yearned for the restoration of Catholic monarchies and aligned themselves with defeated dynastic alternatives and pretenders. Such contextual and political factors took precedence over their class positions in explaining their attitudes, as can readily be revealed by examining their respective cases from an institutional and organizational perspective.

NOTES

My gratitude to Erika Maza Valenzuela for comments and suggestions that have improved this text. My appreciation to Alan Knight, Miguel Angel Centeno, Tulio Halperín-Donghi, and Fernando López-Alves for their insightful reactions to its earlier versions.

1. Barrington Moore, *Social Origins of Dictatorship and Democracy: Lord and Peasant in the Making of the Modern World* (Boston: Beacon, 1966).

2. Brian Loveman, *Struggle in the Countryside: Politics and Rural Labor in Chile, 1919–1973* (Bloomington: Indiana University Press, 1976); Maurice Zeitlin, *The Civil Wars in Chile (or the Bourgeois Revolutions That Never Were)* (Princeton, N.J.: Princeton University Press, 1984); Dietrich Rueschemeyer, Evelyne Huber Stephens, and John D. Stephens, *Capitalist Development and Democracy* (Oxford: Polity Press, 1992).

3. The following is only a brief listing of books that develop this historiographical interpretation: Ricardo Donoso, *Desarrollo político y social de Chile desde la Constitución de 1833* (Santiago: Imprenta Universitaria, 1942); Hernán Ramírez Necochea, *La guerra civil de 1891: Antecedentes económicos* (Santiago:

Editorial Austral, 1951); Marcelo Segall, *Desarrollo del capitalismo en Chile: Cinco ensayos dialécticos* (Santiago: n.p., 1953); Julio César Jobet, *Ensayo crítico del desarrollo económico-social de Chile* (Santiago: Editorial Universitaria, 1955); Julio Heise González, *150 años de evolución institucional* (Santiago: Editorial Andrés Bello, 1960). Earlier works that inspired it will be mentioned later.

4. The importance of the 1874 electoral reforms was first established in a paper I wrote as a student at Columbia University in 1971. It was published in expanded form as J. Samuel Valenzuela, *Democratización vía reforma: La expansión del sufragio en Chile* (Buenos Aires: IDES, 1985). The significance of the electoral law of 1890 is contained in J. Samuel Valenzuela, "La ley electoral de 1890 y la democratización del régimen político chileno," *Estudios Públicos* 71 (1998), 265–96.

5. Irarrázabal descended from Spanish-Basque nobility of Guipúzcoa, the only family in Chile of true peninsular noble origins. See Julio Retamal Favereau, Carlos Celis Atria, and Juan Guillermo Muñoz Correa, *Familias Fundadoras de Chile, 1540–1600* (Santiago: Zig-Zag, 1992), 329–47.

6. For a discussion of the importance of the choice of cases and of procedures to do so, see J. Samuel Valenzuela, "Macro Comparisons without the Pitfalls: A Protocol for Comparative Research," in Scott Mainwaring and Arturo Valenzuela, eds., *Politics, Society, and Democracy: Latin America: Essays in Honor of Juan Linz* (Boulder, Colo.: Westview, 1998), 237–66.

7. Moore, *Social Origins of Dictatorship and Democracy*, xiii.

8. Ibid., 431. While Moore therefore argues that India confirms his analysis, he fails to see the contradiction of appealing to a political factor in order to do so.

9. Ibid., 429–30.

10. Theda Skocpol, *States and Social Revolutions: A Comparative Analysis of France, Russia, and China* (New York: Cambridge University Press, 1979); George Ross, Theda Skocpol, Tony Smith, and Judith Eisenberg Vichniac, "Barrington Moore's *Social Origins* and Beyond: Historical Social Analysis since the 1960s," in Theda Skocpol et al., eds., *Democracy, Revolution, and History* (Ithaca, N.Y.: Cornell University Press, 1998), 1–21. See also Theda Skocpol, "A Critical Review of Barrington Moore's *Social Origins of Dictatorship and Democracy*," in Theda Skocpol, *Social Revolutions in the Modern World* (New York: Cambridge University Press, 1994), an article first published in 1973.

11. Moore, *Social Origins of Dictatorship and Democracy*, 32.

12. For example, Skocpol, "A Critical Review," 38.

13. Rueschemeyer, Huber Stephens, and Stephens, *Capitalist Development and Democracy*, 141; Evelyne Huber, "Introduction," in Evelyne Huber and Frank Safford, eds., *Agrarian Structure and Political Power: Landlord and Peasant in the Making of Latin America* (Pittsburgh: University of Pittsburgh Press, 1995), 7.

14. Geoff Eley, "The Social Construction of Democracy in Germany," in George Reid Andrews and Herrick Chapman, eds. *The Social Construction of Democracy, 1870–1990* (New York: New York University Press, 1995), 107.

15. This occurred in France, the United States, Switzerland, Colombia, Argentina, and Chile, among other cases, although Rueschemeyer, Huber Stephens, and Stephens deny that this was the case in Chile (*Capitalist Development and De-*

mocracy, 305). In offering explanations for the Swiss case, these authors indicate that the bourgeoisie proved to be, exceptionally, a fully pro-democratic force favoring inclusion (86). This fact is inconsistent with their own analysis, but not with Moore's.

16. George Reid Andrews and Herrick Chapman, "The Social Construction of Democracy, 1870–1990: An Introduction," in Andrews and Chapman, *The Social Construction of Democracy*, 18–19.

17. Moore, *Social Origins of Dictatorship and Democracy*, 434; Skocpol, "A Critical Review," 36; Rueschemeyer, Huber Stephens, and Stephens, *Capitalist Development and Democracy*, 288.

18. Arnold Bauer, "Rural Workers in Spanish America: Problems of Peonage and Oppression," *Hispanic American Historical Review* 59 (1979): 38–39.

19. Careful research in some cases may find that such landowners may have contributed, exceptionally, to democratization through the unintended consequences of their actions, sometimes in pursuing other more pressing goals. They may also have supported heads of state or political leaders who, in the end, may have acted in ways that went contrary to their interests. The support of conservative and slave-owing landowners in Brazil for a monarchy that, in the end, abolished slavery can be viewed as a case in point.

20. In discussing slavery, Moore is aware of the fact that this point is very obvious. For instance, he notes that the victory of the North in the American Civil War was a "political victory for freedom," adding that this "seems obvious enough to require no extensive discussion" (*Social Origins of Dictatorship and Democracy*, 153).

21. See ibid., 435–38.

22. For a characterization of agriculture in large East German estates as "capitalist," see David Blackbourn, "The Discreet Charm of the Bourgeoisie: Reappraising German History in the Nineteenth Century," in David Blackbourn and Geoff Eley, *The Peculiarities of German History: Bourgeois Society and Politics in Nineteenth-Century Germany* (Oxford: Oxford University Press, 1984), 181. Blackbourn notes that, by 1859, "57% of the Prussian *Rittergüter* were already in non-noble hands. By the 1880s bourgeois estate owners possessed two thirds of the total number of estates even in the eastern provinces of Prussia" (182).

23. Leopoldo Allub, "Orígenes del autoritarismo en Argentina," in Leopoldo Allub, ed., *Orígenes del autoritarismo en América Latina* (Mexico City: Editorial Katún, 1983), 49–193.

24. Ibid., 10, and chap. 3.

25. See, for example, Rueschemeyer, Huber Stephens, and Stephens, *Capitalist Development and Democracy*, 288.

26. The assumed historical link between encomienda and *inquilinaje* was first presented as fact by Claudio Gay in the final two volumes on Chilean agriculture, published in 1862 and 1865, of his *Historia Física y Política de Chile*, reprinted as Claudio Gay, *Agricultura Chilena* (Santiago: ICIRA, 1973) the supposed origins of *inquilinaje* appear in vol. 1, 181–83.

27. Ibid., 182.

28. The master-slave image to describe the relationship between landowners and *inquilinos* was popularized by George McCutchen McBride, *Chile: Land and*

Society (New York: Octagon Books, 1971), first published in 1936. McBride's elaborate caricature of the *inquilino* fixed the vision of this institution for several generations of writers. See, in particular, Loveman, *Struggle in the Countryside,* who follows and amplifies McBride's depiction, especially 34–35.

29. The correct date is 1874; see Valenzuela, *Democratización vía reforma.* The constitutional article requiring income and property to vote was not dropped until 1888, but it had already been bypassed by a provision in the 1874 electoral law stating that knowing how to read and write was sufficient proof of income. This was an easy assumption to make, given that the requisite income levels were deliberately set well within the reach of the lowest paid categories of the workforce. Literacy was not required of all voters until 1861. The elimination of the proof of income requirements led to a tripling of the numbers of registrants, from 49,047 in 1873 to 148,737 in 1878; Valenzuela, *Democratización vía reforma,* 118. This latter figure represented about a third of the adult male population. For political reasons, voter registration declined during the mid-1880s, recovering subsequently. While the numbers of voters remained relatively small, broader segments of the population did become politicized and involved in elections. On this point see J. Samuel Valenzuela, "Building Aspects of Democracy before Democracy: Electoral Practices in Nineteenth-Century Chile," in Eduardo Posada-Carbó, ed., *Elections before Democracy: The History of Elections in Europe and Latin America* (London: Macmillan, 1996), 240–48.

30. This image has been popularized, in particular, by Zeitlin's *The Civil Wars in Chile,* a work peppered with historical inaccuracies. Its arguments are similar to those in Luis Vitale, *Interpretación marxista de la historia de Chile. Ascenso y declinación de la burguesía minera: De Pérez a Balmaceda (1861–1891)* (Frankfurt: Verlag Jugend und Politik, 1975).

31. For discussion of the minimal features of democratic regimes along these lines, see Valenzuela, *Democratización vía reforma,* 28–35. The notion that for a democracy to exist the suffrage has to be broad enough for there to be a "complete party system" (31), means that some regimes may be considered democracies despite not having full suffrage rights; I labeled these "incomplete suffrage democracies." For a discussion of tutelary powers and reserved domains of policy that undermine democratic authority, see J. Samuel Valenzuela, "Democratic Consolidation in Post-transitional Settings: Notion, Process and Facilitating Conditions," in Scott Mainwaring, Guillermo O'Donnell, and J. Samuel Valenzuela, *Issues in Democratic Consolidation: The New South American Democracies in Comparative Perspective* (Notre Dame, Ind.: Notre Dame University Press, 1992), 62–66.

32. Rueschemeyer, Huber Stephens, and Stephens, *Capitalist Development and Democracy,* 303–4. The disregard of voting rights for women does seem awkward in a construct that is so strict in setting the terms for male participation in the electorate. Elsewhere, these authors indicate that unionization rights are part of the essential elements of a democracy (288), although this notion is not repeated in the explicit definition contained on pages 303–4.

33. Ibid., 184 and elsewhere. The 73 percent figure is taken from Erika Maza Valenzuela, "Catolicismo, anticlericalismo y extensión del sufragio a la mujer en

Chile," *Estudios Públicos* 58 (fall 1995): 175, table 1. Estimates of the potential size of the electorate in other sources are misleading because they use official literacy figures that include the population that is under voting age. Those under age twenty-one constituted about half the Chilean population, and given both the lack of universal coverage of primary education and the importance of adult literacy efforts by all kinds of associations, a larger than expected proportion of illiterates before the late 1930s were minors. Maza Valenzuela estimates the literacy rate by deducting all underage cohorts.

34. The 1970 amendment to the constitution permitting illiterates to vote (and lowering the voting age to eighteen) was supported by all parties when it was discussed in Congress in 1969. It was finally approved in January 1970. This was before Allende became a candidate for the presidential race held in September. Enabling legislation for illiterates to vote was enacted in 1971, but this was merely a technical change in the law needed to comply with the new constitutional amendment.

35. See, among other letters and articles in which he made the same argument over the years, Luis Emilio Recabarren's article of May 14, 1920, in Ximena Cruzat and Eduardo Deves, eds., *Recabarren: Escritos de prensa,* vol. 4, *1919–1924* (Santiago: Terranova Editores, 1987), 128. Recabarren's assessment of the large numbers of voters who were, or could be, linked to labor organizations was shared by observers opposed to the Left. For instance, Alejandro Silva de la Fuente, "Voto secreto o voto público," *Revista Chilena,* year IV, no. XXXI (May–September 1920): 440, noted that the secret vote had to be retained in order to prevent unions and labor federations from pressuring workers into voting for their preferred candidates.

36. Rueschemeyer, Huber Stephens, and Stephens (*Capitalist Development and Democracy*) acknowledge as much on page 305, although on page 184 they describe the 1970 reforms as a "breakthrough to full democracy," a point that is consistent with their argument.

37. On the 1925–32 realignment, which benefited the Left, see J. Samuel Valenzuela, "The Origins and Transformations of the Chilean Party System," in Fernando J. Devoto and Torcuato S. Di Tella, eds., *Political Culture, Social Movements and Democratic Transitions in South America in the XXth Century* (Milano: Feltrinelli Editore, 1997), 70–73.

38. Cited by Mario Góngora, *Ensayo sobre la noción de Estado en Chile en los siglos XIX y XX* (Santiago: Ediciones La Ciudad, 1981), 31.

39. *Convención extraordinaria del Partido Demócrata* (Santiago: Imprenta y Encuadernación "La Universal," 1922), xii.

40. Silva de la Fuente, "Voto secreto o voto público," 439.

41. Rueschemeyer, Huber Stevens, and Stevens, *Capitalist Development and Democracy,* 306.

42. Ibid. See also Evelyne Huber and John Stephens, "Conclusion: Agrarian Structure and Political Power in Comparative Perspective," in Huber and Safford, *Agrarian Structure and Political Power,* 190.

43. The assumption in Arturo Valenzuela, *Political Brokers in Chile: Local Government in a Centralized Polity* (Durham, N.C.: Duke University Press, 1977), 214, that such committees were created between 1912 and 1915 in order

to control the expansion of popular participation, is incorrect. Rueschemeyer, Huber Stevens, and Stevens base themselves in part on this source.

44. See Jermán Hidalgo Revilla, *Estudio crítico comparativo de la lei de elecciones de 1884* (Santiago: Imprenta de la Librería Americana, 1885), 9, 34.

45. The vote for various Liberal parties (including the National Party) declined from 54 to 42.4 percent while the Democratic share went from 4.8 to 7.9 percent and that of the Radicals from 16.6 to 21.2 percent. The Conservative vote remained the same at about 21 percent, while a new Socialist Workers' Party obtained 0.4 percent. See Ricardo Cruz Coke, *Geografía electoral de Chile* (Santiago: Editorial del Pacífico, 1952), 53.

46. See Cruzat and Deves, *Recabarren*. In 1925 a permanent electoral registry office was organized by the central state, and civil servants and notary publics substituted the largest contributors to municipal treasuries in the registration of voters. The individuals in charge of the voting tables on election day and of the initial count of votes were henceforth chosen by lot by the electoral registry officials and the notaries. However, the 1925 law stipulated that the drawing had to be conducted among individuals who were preferably proprietors, professionals, or those who paid income tax (Article 34 of Law 14.279 of 1925). Again, the notion was that such individuals had to have higher education than the average voter in order to man the voting tables and count the votes initially. As far as I know, this change in procedure was not seen at the time as anything but a technical one; it is more than likely that many of the same approximately six thousand individuals in charge of vote reception and vote counting before this change continued their same duties after it.

47. While basing himself on figures in Valenzuela, *Democratización vía reforma*, 118, this is the argument presented by Arnold Bauer, "Chilean Rural Society and Politics in Comparative Perspective," in Cristóbal Kay and Patricio Silva, eds., *Development and Social Change in the Chilean Countryside: From the Pre-Land Reform Period to the Democratic Transition* (Amsterdam: CEDLA, 1992), as well as in his "Landlord and Campesino in the Chilean Road to Democracy," in Huber and Safford, *Agrarian Structure and Political Power*. The questionable aspect of this interpretation is that it continues to identify Conservatives only with landowner interests, a point to be addressed later. If the number of registered voters who were employed in agriculture increased greatly after 1874, this was because the population was largely rural, and because it had the greatest difficulty before the law changed in *proving* that it met the income requirements despite their low levels.

48. From the very first electoral laws, Chilean legislation called for a "secret" vote, but the actual voting procedures did not guarantee it until 1890. It is impossible to understand why Rueschemeyer, Huber Stephens, and Stephens (*Capitalist Development and Democracy*, 305 and elsewhere) insist that Chile did not have an effective "secret ballot" until 1958, while they argue that Argentina had it after the application of the 1912 Saenz-Peña law. In fact, Chile's voting procedures on the day of the election anticipated *in a stricter* way those adopted in Argentina with this law by over two decades! If these procedures did not generate a secret ballot in Chile, how could the less stringent version adopted in Argentina have done so? The difference that made the protection of secrecy stricter in Chile was

that voters in Argentina had to sign the exterior of the envelope in which they put their ballot before dropping it into the ballot box. Illiterates had to mark the envelopes with a cross, or with their thumbprint if their identity was questioned. With such procedures an Argentine electoral agent could verify, if need be, the way in which his charges had voted by looking at the signatures or marks on the envelopes when opening the votes to count them. Argentine polling places also did not have a record of voter signatures because the names of all adult men were copied from military draft records, and election day officials were not given the originals of those lists. By contrast, in Chile, a voter had to sign the voting table's list of voters, which formed part of its official acts, and the signature was compared for identification purposes with the one on the voter registry, which was made available to voting day officials. The envelopes were not supposed to have any marks other than the official one. As a result of these differences, it was easier to supplant voters in Argentina than in Chile. For a reference to the signature, cross, or thumbprint required of Argentine voters on the envelopes, see Carlos Malamud Rikles, *Partidos políticos y elecciones en la Argentina: La Liga del Sur (1908–1916)* (Madrid: UNED, 1997), 202. Moreover, although illiterates could vote in Argentina, no provision was made for them to be able to choose among the ballots of the different candidates, whose names were all printed in letters or required the ability to write them in. Hence, the openness of the Argentine system to voter choice by illiterates was highly questionable. I thank Carlos Malamud for his further clarification of the Argentine voting system in a private communication of February 5, 1999.

49. Allub, "Orígenes del autoritarismo en Argentina."

50. See Maza Valenzuela, "Catolicismo, anticlericalismo," 137–95.

51. See Cruz Coke, *Georgrafía electoral de Chile*, chap. 5, for a description of the areas of strength of Chilean parties.

52. For a balanced presentation of this aspect of voter mobilization, see Federico Gil, *The Political System of Chile* (Boston: Houghton Mifflin, 1966), 223–24.

53. On the notion of "deference," see Walter Bagehot, *The English Constitution* (1867; London: Fontana Press, 1993), 248–52. On deference among English urban workers, see Robert T. McKenzie and Allan Silver, *Angles in Marble* (London: Heinemann, 1968); and among English rural workers, see Howard Newby, *The Deferential Worker: A Study of Farm Workers in East Anglia* (Madison: University of Wisconsin Press, 1979).

54. José Bengoa, *Historia social de la agricultura chilena*, vol. 2, *Haciendas y campesinos* (Santiago: Ediciones SUR, 1990), 90–95, describes the social setting of large haciendas owned by committed Catholics. He notes that owners created schools for boys and girls, mutual aid societies, pension schemes, and cooperatives for the workforce. See also pages 36–37.

55. Francisco Undurraga, a Conservative landowner, provides an illustration of the importance of the Catholic vote in rural areas as he describes how he campaigned for a deputy seat in 1900 by passing out leaflets during Sunday mass. Francisco R. Undurraga V., *Recuerdos de 80 años (1855–1943)* (Santiago: Imprenta El Imparcial, 1943), 146–47.

56. Gil (*The Political System of Chile*, 224) does not make this facile assumption.

57. Juan Bautista González R., *Revisión de la lei electoral; o sea observaciones sobre algunos artículos de la Lei de Elecciones de 20 de agosto de 1890 con la reforma de 18 febrero de 1896* (Santiago: Imprenta y Encuadernación Aurora, 1900), 20.

58. Calculated from República de Chile, *Estadística comercial correspondiente al año de 1875* (Valparaíso: Imprenta del Universo de G. Helfman, 1876), 570, 573. The precise factor is 3.09, and refers to the years 1844 to 1861.

59. Sergio Villalobos, *Origen y ascenso de la burguesía chilena* (Santiago: Editorial Universitaria, 1987), 58.

60. Ibid., 110.

61. Bengoa (*Historia social de la agricultura chilena*, 37–38) refers to the low profits derived from the land and therefore the interest of owners to run an enterprise with the lowest possible monetary costs.

62. Ibid., 94.

63. In one very detailed study of an agricultural valley just north of Santiago, the authors found that 90 percent of the *inquilinos* hired someone else to do the work they were supposed to do for the hacienda; half of these individuals were not related to the *inquilino*. Rafael Baraona, Ximena Aranda, Roberto Santana, *Valle de Putaendo: Estudio de estructura agraria* (Santiago: Instituto de Geografía de la Universidad de Chile, 1961), 235. The authors concluded that the *inquilinaje* hides a "rental of land paid for in money," and that for this reason the *inquilino* had no interest in seeing agricultural wages rise (237).

64. The Santiago food market, the largest in the country, was supplied almost entirely by small producers, many of whom were in fact working on lands owned by the large landowners, as either *inquilinos* or *medieros* (sharecroppers). See Bengoa, *Historia social de la agricultura chilena*, 38.

65. Bauer, "Chilean Rural Society," 22–30.

66. Bengoa, *Historia Social de la agricultura chilena*, 64–65.

67. See Arnold Bauer, *Chilean Rural Society from the Spanish Conquest to 1930* (Cambridge: Cambridge University Press, 1975), 17.

68. See Villalobos, *Origen y ascenso de la burguesía chilena*, 37, which refers to the *Conde de la Conquista*. Mateo de Toro Zambrano y Ureta acquired the title in 1770, soon after buying the huge estate of "La Compañía" that had belonged to the Jesuits. He claimed, incorrectly, to be a descendant of Juan de Toro, a sixteenth-century conqueror from Trujillo in Extremadura. See Retamal Favereau, Celis Atria, and Muñoz Correa, *Familias Fundadoras de Chile*, 622–37, for an account of the false genealogical claim.

69. Bauer, *Chilean Rural Society from the Spanish Conquest*, 17.

70. See Villalobos, *Origen y ascenso de la burguesía chilena*, 19–20, which summarizes research on this question.

71. McBride, *Chile*, 200; Bauer, *Chilean Rural Society from the Spanish Conquest*, 20–21.

72. For an elaborate account of the many facets of this institution and its remarkable resilience, see Roland E. Mousnier, *Les Institutions de France sous la monarchie absolue, 1598–1789*, vol. 1, *Société et etat* (Paris: Presses universitaires de France, 1974), chap. 11.

73. Alexis de Tocqueville, *L'Ancien régime et la révolution* (Paris: Editions Gallimard, 1967), 96.

74. Mario Góngora, *Origen de los "inquilinos" de Chile central* (Santiago: Editorial Universitaria, 1960), 68–71.

75. Ibid., esp. 72–73, 85, 98.

76. McBride discusses the independent small rural producer in *Chile*, chap. 8. He indicates that in central Chile in 1925 there were, in 1925, 8,888 farms of 21 to 50 hectares (a size that would be considered relatively large in most areas of western Europe), and 19,568 of between 5 and 20 hectares (235). These were all ample enough (depending on the soil and topography) to generate a marketable income for families.

77. McBride interviews one such producer on the train; ibid., 232–33.

78. Gabriela Mistral was well aware of this misnomer. See Eduardo Frei Montalva, *Memorias (1911–1934) y correspondencias con Gabriela Mistral y Jacques Maritain* (Santiago: Colección Espejo de Chile, 1989), 131.

79. For detailed treatment of the origins and characteristics of the Chilean Conservative Party, see J. Samuel Valenzuela and Erika Maza Valenzuela, "The Politics of Religion in a Catholic Country: Republican Democracy, Social Christianism, and the Conservative Party of Chile, 1856–1925," in Austin Evereigh, ed., *The Politics of Religion in Europe and Latin America*, forthcoming.

80. I draw this sentence from my *Democratización vía reforma*, 132.

81. For an early formulation of this relationship, see Seymour Martin Lipset, *Political Man: The Social Bases of Politics* (Garden City, N.Y.: Doubleday, 1960), chap. 2. It has been reaffirmed in cross-national statistical analysis since then. However, Lipset's arguments (and those of the numerous works that followed his), in order to explain this relationship, were very different from the one presented here, as they focused on the moderating influences of higher standards of living and education on political opinions. Lipset's discussion did not focus on the process of democratization but rather on the conditions that favored democratic stability and continuity.

82. Rueschemeyer, Huber Stevens, and Stevens, *Capitalist Development and Democracy*.

83. For an elaboration of these points, including the effects of the timing of democratization on the creation of working class, see J. Samuel Valenzuela, "Labour Movements and Political Systems: Some Variations," in Marino Regini, ed., *The Future of Labour Movements* (London: Sage, 1992), 51–101.

84. For a history of Uruguay during this period, see Ariosto D. González, "La República Oriental del Uruguay desde 1830 hasta nuestros días," in Ricardo Levene, ed., *Historia de América*, vol. 9: *América contemporánea* (Buenos Aires: Editorial Jackson, 1943). This author notes that the conflict between Oribe and Rivera was fueled by "passions of predominance, by envy, by intrigues, by narrow personal interests" (196).

85. See Fernando López-Alves, "Wars and the Formation of Political Parties in Uruguay, 1810–1861," in Eduardo Posada-Carbó, ed., *Wars, Parties and Nationalism: Essays on the Politics and Society of Nineteenth-Century Latin America* (London: ILAS, 1995), 5–26.

86. The first type of confirmation is favored by Rueschemeyer, Huber Stevens, and Stevens, *Capitalist Development and Democracy*, and the second by Allub, "Orígenes del autoritarismo en Argentina."

87. See Frank Safford, "Agrarian Systems and the State: The Case of Colombia," in Huber and Safford, *Agrarian Structure and Political Power*, for an elaboration of this notion.

88. John Coatsworth ("Los orígenes sociales del autoritarismo en México," in Allub, *Orígenes del autoritarismo en América Latina*, 197–218) confirms Moore's thesis in the Mexican case following an analysis that could be repeated with some variations in the other countries. Coatsworth notes that after the initial dislocations produced by independence, the authoritarian nature of the state was the product of the reassertion of a powerful landed class in association with a weak bourgeoisie. The main difference with Moore's authoritarian cases, namely, Japan and Germany, was the role of foreign investors. This reinforced authoritarianism because the state had to guarantee political stability in order to attract such capital, an essential ingredient to produce the Latin American version of state-led modernization. See especially pages 210, 215.

89. For an analysis of Central American cases in the light of Moore's model, see Lowell Gudmundson, "Lord and Peasant in the Making of Modern Central America," in Huber and Safford, *Agrarian Structure and Political Power*, 151–81.

90. See Moore, *Social Origins of Dictatorship and Democracy*, 435–38.

PART III

LIVING AND BELONGING

Chapter Nine

THE DISCIPLINARY SOCIETY IN LATIN AMERICA

MIGUEL ANGEL CENTENO

T HE ASSOCIATION of modernity with discipline is pervasive (with differing degrees of explicitness) in the work of many of the classic writers on the revolutions that brought about capitalism and democracy. Modernity is viewed as "an increasing objectification and disciplining of subjectivity, an ever-intensifying ordering of the soul."[1] In the classic perspective, to be modern means to maximize and optimize resources, to economize and impose rational constraints on desires, to develop a "managed" life. This in turn depends on the objectification of individuals, requiring political, economic, and social discipline. Modernity implies the disciplining of political passions into rational interests, piratical pillage into competitive accumulation, particularistic patronage into civil norms.

While any unidimensional definition of what it means to be modern will be obviously unsatisfactory, the concept of discipline captures many of the social and psychological changes that accompanied the "Great Transformation" in the West and that arguably still represent the central issue of much of contemporary social science. Even more important than any conceptual clarity which the term *discipline* may have is the critical symbolic role it has played in the classic writings on the rise of the modern world. Discipline is a theme that reoccurs throughout the classic literature on social change. Whether it be Marx railing against the factory floor, Weber fearfully predicting the rise of bureaucratic concerns, Simmel's pessimistic view of the marketization of relations, Elias's civilizing process, the Frankfurt school's alarm over the coming hegemony of instrumental reason, or Foucault's "carcereal" society, modernity is judged to involve a series of constraints, be they institutionalized or internalized. Modernity, whatever its other characteristics, is perceived to involve an expansion of economic and political possibilities at least partly driven by greater control over the physical world and the development of socialized self-discipline.

More contemporary writings have not ignored this concept, nor have they arguably moved away from definitions of modernity that embrace it. The now decade-old "transitology" literature often addresses the need to improve market and democratic discipline.[2] There is the concern, for example, with transforming the work habits of whole generations of Eastern Europeans trained to "pretend to work."[3] The language of the so-called Washington consensus is crammed with notions of fiscal and economic discipline.[4] The appeal of authoritarian regimes able to impose the required "tough love" of a transition often accompanies fears that democratic regimes would be too undisciplined to say no. Robert Putnam's rediscovery of the central importance of civil community often appears to have little to do with democracy per se and more with administrative efficiency and social control—civil communities simply help make the proverbial trains run on time.[5] James Scott offers illuminating examples of high modernism and its infatuation with discipline. While he does not often use the term, what links Brasilia, collectivization, or scientific agronomy but an attempt to impose discipline on an unregularized nature and population?[6] Outside of academia, the notion of discipline has enjoyed a new boom whether it is in calls for "stricter standards" in education, uniforms in the classroom, or the enforcement of better public manners.

The persistence of discipline as a concept is particularly interesting because the founding texts either are fairly limited in scope or have been seriously criticized for historical fallacies. Weber's treatise is less than ten pages long, and while full of the insights and erudition we associate with him, it lacks the conceptual clarity and empirical vigor of other works. Foucault's contribution is even more flawed. Richard Hamilton's critique thoroughly demonstrates the limitations of the Foucauldian "method" and the acceptance far too often granted his often enigmatic statements.[7] Elias's notion of "civilizing process," if more historically accurate, lacks the conceptual rigor usually required of such theoretical concepts. Yet whatever one may think of the validity of the concept (much less the advisability of formulating public policy around it), discipline is an undeniable trope of the literature on what used to be called modernization. In the end the concept may prove useless or worse for our understanding of historical change, but discipline is too central to the development of social science to be ignored.

This is of particular importance in the case of Latin America. Perceived disciplinary failures are a central theme in the Black Legend to which several other authors in this volume have referred.[8] The presupposed relative underdevelopment of a disciplinary society in Latin America has been used to certify that continent as somehow "premodern"—not having quite made it through the cultural transition required by both industrial capitalism and competitive democracy. The implication is that Latin America lacks what we may call "disciplinary capital"—the capacity to coordinate or exert concerted effort in the satisfaction of a particular goal. Such a perspective is often accompanied by the denial of a possible "responsible" democracy in the continent, requiring the continuation of tutorial regimes.

Such views persist in popular images of *mañana*, corruption, and administrative laxity, but they also have their equivalents in the academic literature. The view that "development is a state of mind" and that Latin Americans are "wrongheaded" has a variety of exponents, including Claudio Veliz, Richard Morse, the early Howard Wiarda, and Lawrence Harrison.[9] Certainly parts of modernization theory could also be read in this light. Parsonian pattern variables, the search for an entrepreneurial elite, and the disdain of traditionalism all share an undercurrent of discipline. More recently, David Landes has attempted to resuscitate similar cultural explanations for societal success or failure.[10] Celebrations of the East Asian "miracle" (prior to late 1997) often cited the supposed discipline of these societies and how these habits have contributed to the region's economic development. "Iberian" lassitude could not hope to compete with "Confucian" devotion. Combined with cultural critiques of continental *mentalités*, comparisons of the two regions at times implied that the differences in their economic performances had much to do with a Latin American deficit of moral discipline.

The call for discipline has also been a mainstay of bureaucratic-authoritarian regimes and their technocratic successors. At the heart of recent neoliberal policies is the assertion that the global market both encourages and requires discipline—in this case the sacrifice of wages by employees, and, at times, the sacrifice of immediate profits by employers. Nor has the left lacked advocates of cultural transformations, such as Che Guevara's fascination with the "new socialist man." Be it the peasantry or the bourgeoisie, critical actors in the process of development are judged to lack a necessary drive, fortitude, or rigor.

Rather than castigating the region for this supposed failure, this chapter asks a set of interrelated questions: How has discipline been defined in classic works on the "Great Transformation"? What are its institutional bases? How can we begin measuring discipline for comparative purposes? Finally, what can the Latin American experience tell us about the validity and usefulness of the concept, and what can this notion tell us about Latin America?

Defining Discipline

Despite the central importance that discipline plays in much of classic social analysis, it does not offer a coherent definition of what is meant by the concept.[11] The meaning and implications of the phenomenon are elaborately discussed, but the content of the concept needs to be teased out or deduced.

First, discipline obviously implies obedience. For Weber, discipline involves the "exact execution of the received order, in which all personal criticism is unconditionally suspended and the actor is unswervingly and exclusively set for carrying out the command."[12] This obedience must be uniform—based on "habitual routinized drill" rather than "heroic ecstasy" or "personal devotion." For Foucault, the new form of obedience is also characterized by an automatic response that essentially skips the stage of understanding.[13]

The development of such obedience requires the creation of a society of surveillance. Anthony Giddens has elevated the pervasiveness of surveillance to one of the four defining characteristics of modernity and refers to it as perhaps the most important function of the modern nation-state.[14] This new form of power is simultaneously "individualizing and totalizing." It is individualizing in that at its core is the ability to monitor, and correct individual conduct. It is totalizing in that it is impossible to escape, and it is involved in all aspects of life. Through the normalization of behavior—the explicit definition of what is to be expected—the identification of deviant individuals becomes easier. Modern discipline seeks to break down a social collective into its individual components and then reorganize these into a more efficient unity.

The goal of that obedience has also been transformed. This involves the transition of the coercive into the therapeutic. Authority's interest is no longer just the punishment of bad behavior but also the active encouragement of the good. It involves the replacement of what has to be done (through the threat of coercion) by what should be done (through the promise of optimality). Beginning in the eighteenth century, "the traditional mandate of government shifted from the passive duty of preserving justice to the active, dynamic task of fostering the productive energies of society and providing the appropriate institutional framework for it."[15] The nature of crime becomes very different under these circumstances. It is no longer solely restricted to a "positive" act—an active transgression. Nonobservance or subpar performance is also criminal. Punishment is meted out not only for disobedience but also for nonconformity or even nonoptimal behavior.

What is perhaps most important about modern discipline is not only its omnipresence but also the manner in which it is enforced. No matter the critical role played by surveillance, the modern version of discipline relies more on the self than on some external other. In contemporary society "the prison gates can be opened, because society has become one enormous prison."[16] It is the elevation of a social superego to dominance that accounts for the particular organized behavior of industrial society, and it is that which characterizes its distance from other forms of life. Impulse has been moved "behind the scenes," and the policeman has been internalized.[17] This process is what John O'Neill is referring to when he calls Weber "an archeologist of the power man [sic] exerts over himself."[18] Foucault equally emphasizes this notion of self-control. For example, discipline is intended to create "a body manipulated by authority, rather than imbued with animal spirits."[19] Elias sees it as a "moderation of spontaneous emotions," which arises from the increasing interdependency of modern life that in turn depends on every individual "regulating his behavior with the utmost exactitude in accordance with the necessities of this network."[20] As it reduces the significance or control of "passions," discipline allows for the much more productive control of dispassionate "interests."[21]

Central to this development is the rise of a *spirit* of discipline. For Foucault, this involves the development of academic disciplines and philosophical *epistemes* through which contemporary knowledge about the world is organized and legitimated. Not only is knowledge a source of power, but power is expressed through the domination of particular ways of interacting with the world. Thus, the hegemony of a positivist method in the social sciences (and subsequently in public policy) cannot help but create a more ordered and restrained analysis of the world. James Scott notes that it is in the very nature of high-modernist policy science to force reality to fit into preordained models. For Elias, civilization was inherently a form of self-consciousness expressed through conduct and behavior. Weber's contribution focuses on the creation of a "spirit of capitalism": an ethos in which the duty of the individual is to increase his capital. This new spirit imposes a discipline of saving and accumulation on what had previously been mere brigandage or conspicuous consumption. The importance of a new ideology of capitalism has been hotly debated, but the rise of a new social culture of constraint is largely accepted.[22]

Precisely because of the apparent disappearance of coercion, modern discipline appears as a liberating reform. Discipline is the other side of the coin of legal rights and citizenship obligations; the generalization of discipline makes the universalization of citizenship possible. The Reformation and the Enlightenment, as well as the rise of capitalism, impose a new set of constraints while simultaneously destroying traditional fetters. In fact, the development of a disciplined society requires the elimination of *formal* hierarchical social orders. All social classes must be brought into the new web of constraint.[23] Viewed another way, political rights can be safely granted when compliance is already guaranteed. Because new forms of discipline are not so explicitly associated with individual power holders, they become much more an assumed part of the natural order. The truly disciplinary society can be relied upon to operate "with quasi-natural effect, i.e., removed from historical and political conscious-ness."[24] Through this normalization, discipline becomes depoliticized—one is not obeying anyone but himself.

Discipline is thus defined by the following special properties: (1) auto-matic obedience that is (2) maintained by omnipresent surveillance, (3) monitored by internal psychological mechanisms, (4) requiring positive acts and not mere restraint, (5) justified by a hegemonic belief system, (6) and encompassing privileges of equality accompanying responsibility.

Where does discipline come from? As both Weber and Foucault make clear, it is taught. They emphasize the creation of what Goffman has called "total institutions," which perform the role that Foucault assigns to his (apparently fictional) version of Bentham's Panopticon: to "induce in the inmate a state of conscious and permanent visibility that assures the automatic functioning of power."[25] These institutions possess the key ar-chitectural and organizational qualities required of them to become peda-gogical machines. I have concentrated on the four institutions that in the classic literature are most associated with the rise of disciplinary moder-nity: prisons, armies, factories, and schools.[26]

Prisons are perhaps the most famous example of such institutions be-cause they were the subject of arguably Foucault's most read (and most readable) book. According to Foucault, the shift in penology that oc-curred in the late eighteenth and early nineteenth centuries is more than a mere quantitative shift in degrees of punishment or torture. What changes is the "target" of punishment—the spirit for the body. The point is to replace constant surveillance or pain with an internal process of control—to teach rather than to punish. This involves a training of the body, the normalization of deviance through its scientific analysis, and the rendering of individuals to the constant knowledge of central authorities.

The military is another classic institutional breeder of discipline. Weber saw the origin of modern forms of discipline in ancient Greek war; for him, military discipline gives birth to all discipline.[27] Greek hoplites and Roman legionnaires gained supremacy over more "heroic" rivals. It was discipline and not gunpowder that initiated the transformation of warfare.[28] Weber sees in the transition in military organization in the Napoleonic era a parallel to the advance from private capitalism to public finance.[29] Foucault similarly recognizes the critical role played by the mil-itary in the development of modern discipline: "By the late 18th Century, the soldier has become something that can be made; out of a formless clay, an inapt body, the machine required can be constructed; posture is gradually corrected; . . . one has got rid of the peasant and given him the air of a soldier."[30] In the last decade, "bellicist" treatments of the origins of the state (e.g., McNeill, Tilly, Mann) have confirmed the central role played by military mobilization in the development of modern administrative and political institutions.[31]

As we have learned from the now classic works of Thompson and Pollard (among others), factories are another set of sites for disciplining a population into new forms of timed control. Factory work is the ultimate expression of the new discipline because it involves silence, hierarchy, and obedience. Factory discipline was used to maintain control over labor but also was seen as a way of "improving the moral habits of the laboring poor, to make them orderly, punctual, responsible, and temperate."[32]

There is also a long tradition of recognizing the important role played by schools in inculcating discipline. Foucault clearly emphasizes the role played by primary and secondary schools. By the eighteenth century, the school had become a "machine for learning."[33] For him, the prototypical example of institutionalized discipline is the examination that seeks to differentiate between individuals while applying judgment with subsequent rewards and penalties. The examination, for Foucault, is the ultimate superimposition of power and knowledge relations. The constant measurement allows for ranking of individuals according to the degree to which they have "learnt" their discipline. And it is arguable that the modern school teaches little else. For John Meyer, for example, schools serve to teach a generic institutional order. Their main purpose is to teach children obedience, compliance with rules, and acceptance of schedules.[34] According to Bowles and Gintis, schools serve to teach a more specific capitalist ethos and to prepare different sectors of the population for their "assigned" role in the economy.[35]

THE UNRULY SOCIETY?

How useful is this concept for understanding Latin America? Is it a valid and useful notion, or does it merely reflect the darker visions of members of the Frankfurt school or what Hamilton calls Foucault's "paranoid style"? Much of the problem with the concept of discipline is the inherent difficulty in arriving at some common measure that allows for comparative analysis. Several major difficulties immediately suggest themselves. First, such measures reflect subjective judgments on whether social phenomena indicate the presence of discipline. Second, there is the obvious problem of observer bias or inescapable subjectivity, which would make any type of comparison difficult, if not impossible. There is also the difficulty of discretionary use of examples, which could be selectively employed to illustrate any variety of theoretical positions. Perhaps most worrisome is the choice of behavioral arena. Should one focus on public or private behavior? Should we look for discipline inside the home or outside? Public behavior may fail to reflect the discipline or domination imposed by gender or patriarchal roles within the home. We might also ask which is more important, a disciplined elite or a disciplined mass? Is it sufficient to have a disciplined bourgeoisie, or must one also create a disciplined proletariat? The selection of measures of discipline would likely reflect the interest or biases of the observer. Much of what might be judged disciplined behavior may simply be that which is congruent with a set of preordained social goals and/or values. The term *discipline* is too easily used to mean permitted or accepted behavior rather than reflecting the more specific attributes discussed earlier.

Even when comparing discrete units working for constrained goals, judgments of "disciplinary capital" are often nothing but post facto attempts to disguise incomprehension of the causal order of events. Facing a situation in which neither success nor failure can be explained by the available information, there is the often easy temptation to blame (or credit) an essentialist quality. Thus, for example, successful athletic teams that do not appear to possess extraordinary talent are said to win because of their discipline. East Asian miracles defy postcolonial constraints because of their "Confucian" discipline. Similarly, those that lose despite their skills are judged to lack the same qualities. Discipline has become such a value-laden term that it has often served as a thin disguise for racist comments about a particular population. Derogatory comments about the work habits of subaltern races and ethnic groups are an almost universal phenomenon. Similarly, selected groups are judged to possess superlative discipline that solely accounts for their rise, and model minorities serve to show less disciplined ones the errors of their ways. Other than producing bad social analysis, this would be an innocuous practice except for the fact that it carries strong evaluative connotations and that these judgments often "inform" policy decisions.

Precisely because of such dangers, it is worthwhile to attempt to measure discipline rigorously; such a pervasive concept must be reflected in some social action. There is much to be said for the empirical value of anecdotal observation. For example, simple observation of traffic patterns would probably provide rankings of social discipline that would be fairly consistent among a number of observers. In Caracas, drivers do not stop at red lights; in Zurich, pedestrians stop for them even on carless Sundays. One could also compare the martial style of militaries. Certainly the Prussian military pomposity is quite different from the more casual style of Mexican or Venezuelan soldiers. One may also suggest connections between cultural habits and the presence of a "disciplinary ethos." There are, for example, differences in sport preferences (e.g., free-flowing soccer versus regimented U.S. football) or personal health (the continuing Latin American bafflement with the North American exercise mania).

Unfortunately, attempts to impose quantitative rigor on the concept (as required by American academic *disciplines*) do not get us very far. I have tried to locate data that would contribute to a somewhat more systematic empirical "disciplinary index," which would permit some acceptable level of rigor in comparative analysis and also would enable systemic study of the relationship between discipline and development. I gathered data on such plausible candidates for measuring social discipline as savings rates, corruption, violent crime, and strike activity.[36] Some very rough patterns do emerge, for example, in the comparison between East Asia and Latin America, and between individual countries (e.g., Chile seems to have the closest pattern to the "dragons"). Yet there was considerable variance within the continent and no clear pattern between regions. Despite high savings rates, East Asian societies often scored worse on corruption (and we have now seen the depths of this in several cases), while Chile reported higher crime rates than other Latin American countries.

This preliminary exercise demonstrates the inherent ambiguity of a principle of discipline. The wide variance found across measures within single countries makes it difficult to accept a unitary notion of "social discipline." Some countries are corrupt, but they save. Others are fairly crime free, but the labor movement is strong. If nothing else, this should make us doubt any cultural determinist notion of a "pure" disciplinary society.

Problems with the data also serve to highlight problems with decontextualizing analyses of discipline. Let us take the example of savings rates, which, on the surface, would appear a reasonable measure of frugality. But, at least in the case of Latin America, elite savings may rarely be reflected in domestic data. Secret but bountiful bank accounts in New York or Zurich may be the product of a lifetime of disciplined, if distrustful, saving. Crime figures are equally dangerous because they may also hide significant social practices. Crimes in shantytowns are likely to be underreported. In this way, the Latin American figures may underestimate the amount of social chaos. More important, however, crime in and of itself may not be an indication of indisicipline, but just the opposite. The apparent collapse of monopoly over the means of violence in areas controlled by *narcotraficantes* in Colombia, for example, can be seen as failures of social discipline. But drug lords are also expressions of the creation of complex multinational enterprises working with a set of rules that may be just as constraining as their more formal equivalents. Similarly, strike activity may be read as a sign of undisciplined workers or as an indication of organized discipline by labor in its fight with capital.

Given all these difficulties, there appears little support for any attempts to establish quantitative regional or cultural measures of some essentialist quality that we could define as discipline. The dispersion and unreliability of such measures would frustrate any attempts at causal inference and would highlight the possibility of confusing cause and effect. Indices of discipline may simply be measuring the results of institutional practices having little to do with the kinds of social and psychological developments described earlier. While the argument for a link between the manifestations of modernity and discipline may be superficially persuasive, the relationship appears to be at most one of correlation rather than causation. In part because he disdained such mainstream concerns, in part because his method made it impossible, Foucault failed to establish a clear line of causality: Does discipline bring on modernity or vice versa? Weber is somewhat clearer. Certainly his work on bureaucracies would indicate that they are both a functional response to organizational needs *and* stimulants of development. His early work on the Protestant Ethic of course suggests the primacy of a new worldview sharing many of the characteristics of Foucauldian discipline. Later work on the rise of capitalism carefully avoids any monocasuality, but again it would appear that the rise of particular institutional forms precedes modern phenomena such as the state or complex markets. Elias is perhaps the clearest because he appears to see discipline as the consequence of the increasing complexity of relations required by the modern world.

A similar ambiguity plagues more recent work. Despite the apparent rigor of his method, Putnam is at a loss to explain why some regions behave differently from others. There are correlations with numerous possible variables, and there is a clear pattern of historical continuity, but the origins of a functional government in the end recede into the mists of the fourteenth century. The reader has to take much of the argument as given if he or she is to accept the critical role played by civic communities. In the case of James Scott, while the concept of high modernism is a wonderfully rich heuristic device, the relationship between the ideology described and the outcomes is more inferred than proven. High modernism, much like discipline, may capture apparently related aspects of social phenomena but not play a significant role in their developments.

There is little support for any attempt to link such a concept to dependent measures of "modernity" or development. One possible conclusion from the absence of clear quantitative evidence is that, indeed, Latin America is "underdisciplinized," that the bases of institutional modernity have not flourished in the continent—in short, that Latin America is not "modern." On a variety of levels, this is patently absurd unless we choose to purposefully define modernity as something so European or North American that no other locale might qualify. In fact the very apparent "indiscipline" of Latin America (at least in anecdotal accounts) would exist in considerable contrast to the many obvious manifestations of "modernity" we find throughout the continent. We also must be careful with assigning a causal primacy to a set of behaviors associated with "modernity." If we compare our various measures with an index of human development (as good a measure of modernity as we are likely to get), we find that there is no clear correlation with the variety of disciplinary indices. Conversely, societies not considered "modern" would score quite high on any disciplinary index. The Incas of Peru, for example, perhaps represent the zenith of disciplined governance, yet were they "modern"? The Latin American experience would suggest that modernity as measured by any possible index is not necessarily associated with the incorporation of a social discipline. Much as was discussed about economic development in an earlier generation, we can say that discipline exists in pockets that do not extend to a much wider society.

Even if we do not accept a causal relationship between discipline and modernity, we may wish to retain the former notion as a descriptive, if not an explanatory, one. Even here, however, the Latin American example highlights several erroneous assumptions.

First, much of the literature on discipline presumes a high level of social *inclusion*: disciplinary society requires the prior existence or the parallel development of a notion of a single society. That is, for Foucauldian discipline to function it has to be all-inclusive. Gone with the notion of kingly sovereignty is the assumption of aristocratic exemption or the passivity or marginality of lower orders. All are subject to the totalization of discipline through the ubiquity of key institutions. Thus, if Foucault emphasizes discipline as the "darker side" of democratization, one might also emphasize a basic form of equality as the "lighter side" of a carcereal society. In the society-as-prison metaphor, internal walls have collapsed only to be rebuilt in the periphery. But in Latin America those walls remain, preventing precisely the normalization of discipline that Foucault emphasizes. Nowhere is this more evident than if we look at relative levels of inequality. It is important to remember that the rise of "disciplinary society" is closely correlated with the at least formal flattening of social relations. It should not come as a surprise that those countries with the highest levels of discipline as exemplified in our admittedly imperfect measures are also those with the lowest levels of inequality. The performance of Costa Rica, and of Cuba in some of the indicators discussed above, would tend to support such an interpretation. (Chile's inequality, however, would challenge that link.) The study of the relationship between discipline and development in Latin America may be best served by beginning with the issue of equality rather than punishment.

The Latin American experience challenges a second major assumption that "modern" discipline has evolved beyond *coercion*. The critical image here is of a more sophisticated and developed form of control that gradually has abandoned explicit, public violence. Even the most casual observer of Latin American political life can remark that the forms of control have not developed toward less explicit forms of violence. The symbol of authority in Latin America is not necessarily an internal Freudian policeman but a riot policeman with dogs. The trust in the population that is so assumed in much of Foucault and Weber has not developed on the continent. Paradoxically, political regimes in Latin America may be more explicitly repressive because the population has been less "well trained." Such a view would turn much of the "Iberian" critique on its head; the culture of the continent is not inherently more authoritarian, but just the opposite. It is precisely for this reason that more extensive dictatorial measures would need to be implemented. When faced with opposition, regimes have also not retreated from the use of "traditional" forms of coercion. The gallows and the public display of torture have not disappeared from the continent. The differences in the form of coercion radically alter the expectations of discipline.

The Latin American experience also demonstrates the weakness of an assumed *depoliticization* of discipline. Foucault errs in assuming a depersonalization of power that normalizes hierarchical relations. New forms of discipline have been anything but normalized or depoliticized on the continent. In economic terms, the imposition of efficiency, for example, has not been sheared of its class implications. Hierarchy and power in Latin America remain unhidden from view. The schoolhouse and the army represent the state, the factory the capitalist. The imposition of new orders has not been naturalized or neutralized but remains under public contention. If nothing else, the Latin American cases would make us question the extent to which the depoliticization did occur—that is, to what extent was the disciplinary project one without a subject? If this were the case, then the key question would be how specific interests were able to universalize their claims. Conversely, we may ask why it is that Latin American society has not allowed the obfuscation of interests.

Finally, the classic notion of discipline assumes the *institutionalization* of power relations. Education takes place in formal schools; production occurs in bureaucratic organizations; punishment is controlled, supervised, and purposeful; and violence is monopolized by the state through an army. Foucault can assume that power is hidden, inclusive, and noncoercive because he assumes that it takes an institutional form. Yet in Latin America those institutional manifestations of authority associated with discipline have not gelled in the same form as in Europe and North America. The state has not possessed the capacity to tax its population enough to construct more formal systems of governance. In their place, coercion has a clear and violent face. As was the case with equality, note that there does exist a correlation between some of the measures of "discipline" as described earlier and institutional development. Chileans and Cubans are not necessarily more disciplined, but their lives are constrained within a very different set of institutional practices than those of Peruvians or Dominicans.

SEARCHING FOR INSTITUTIONS

Does the classic discussion of discipline have anything to teach Latin America? Yes, although not through the analysis of discipline itself but by way of the study of the specific institutional developments associated with it. The best way to respond to the Black Legend of cultural stereotyping is to offer historically grounded alternative accounts. For example, if we are dissatisfied with explanations of corruption that emphasize the presence or absence of a "professional ethos" in a particular national culture, we may wish to explore the development of institutional constraints on corruption or the development of a specific administrative esprit de corps. Rather than castigating a supposedly piratical (in the Weberian sense) bourgeoisie, we might analyze the institutional incentives available to encourage domestic consumption or investment.[37] This requires that we move away from a search for disciplinary values or normative conducts and concentrate more on institutions that are associated with instilling specific behaviors.

What do we know about the institutions considered most important for the development of discipline? What information we do have suggests that Latin America's pattern of institutional development was radically different from Europe's. But what is also noteworthy is the dearth of deep historical analysis and especially intracontinental comparative efforts.

A wonderful book edited by Ricardo Salvatore and Carlos Aguirre has explored the rise of the penitentiary in Latin America, a subject largely neglected until now.[38] The rule of gallows and the torture chamber à la Foucault lasted much longer on the American continent than in Europe. Prison reform in Latin America was also arguably used much more explicitly as a way of controlling the poor—jails were not considered as forms of reforming society as a whole. Penitentiaries were not naturalized as they were in Europe—they represent a specific form of authority directed at a specific social actor. In general, the penitentiary never assumed as important a role in the prison system in Latin America as in Europe or the United States. Much as we will see in the other cases, only a small percentage of criminals were subjected to this new form of control. Based on contemporary data, Latin American countries as a whole appear to place a relatively smaller part of their population under these forms of control than do European countries when we consider a generally higher crime rate.[39] What might Foucault's concern with these concrete panopticons teach Latin Americanists? Certainly, if nothing else, to pay much more attention to crime and its control. With some notable exceptions, we know little of this form of social disobedience and the manner in which society controls it.[40] Such analysis not only would provide a much needed addition to the literature on state formation but also would give us insights into the definition of deviance and its historical evolution. Finally, given the dramatic surge in violent street crime in almost every Latin American city over the past two decades, such a history might provide the necessary contextualization of the current crisis.

Regarding the second disciplinary institution, Latin America has not involved large numbers of its population in the armed forces, despite its reputation for military activity. In a current project, I have been exploring the extent to which the "bellicist" accounts of state development apply to Latin America.[41] Few of the standard relationships seem to hold. First, states do not often make war. There is a great deal of violence on the continent, and it is often associated with political causes, but societies are not militarized as was the case in western Europe. When wars did occur, they did not impose fiscal discipline, and the state was unable to expand its extractive capacities. Nor did war create coalescing nationalisms, a classic form of disciplinary ideology. The most significant break in the assumed universal pattern is the very low level of participation in the armed forces. Latin American militaries are tiny in comparison to their European counterparts, and thus very small segments of the population have been exposed to the military disciplinary martinet. While there is a very rich literature on the military in political life in Latin America,[42] we know remarkably little about the armed forces as a social institution. The relationships between the military and regime types, their links with the United States, and their role in various civil wars are relatively well studied. Aside from a few isolated dissertations and papers, however, we know little about the sociology of conscription and its relationship to citizenship or social behavior. Given the centrality of its social role in Europe and the United States, treating the military purely as a unitary political actor without larger considerations of its contribution seems counterproductive for Latin American studies.

While factories in Latin America may have engaged in some of the same disciplinary functions of the nineteenth-century equivalents, these did not extensively include later developments such as Fordism and Taylorism. Factories also arose at a much later time, with subsequent important differences in labor's response.[43] It would appear, for example, that popular resistance to an "industrial discipline" usually emphasized class dynamics rather than the cultural and social assault documented by historians of eighteenth- and nineteenth-century Europe. Luddism does not appear to have been very significant in Latin America. Rather than factories enforcing a discipline that served the interests of some amorphous pattern, the studies we have emphasize how they came to generate perhaps the most significant assaults on the social order. The factories did not necessarily turn their workers into machines, but they were the home of some of the most radical actors on the Latin American political stage. While we do possess a considerable literature on Latin American labor, we have less information on factories themselves.[44] As in the case of the military, we know a great deal about labor's political role and its function within the various economic regimes experienced by the continent. What we know much less of is how factories transformed laborers, how they generated new cultural forms of opposition, and how they may have served in the creation of "modern" disciplined men and women.

As with the other institutions considered the carriers of modern discipline, Latin American schools have not received the scholarly attention they deserve or that granted their western European and North American counterparts.[45] This may be changing. Elsie Rockwell's work in rural Tlaxcala indicates that, at least in Mexico, schools did serve as classrooms for modern discipline.[46] The response of the population, however, was not as passive as the Foucauldian account would lead the reader to believe. Schools remained contested zones. Moreover, as in the case of the military, much smaller percentages of the population were exposed to this education for the continent as a whole. As in the case of manufacturing, there is also the danger of confusing discipline with development. The important point is that institutions that have been identified as critical for the progress of disciplinary societies appear to be less developed in Latin America and, more important, less inclusive.) Finally, schools can rival factories as centers of subversion and revolt. Not only universities but also secondary schools have provided the leaders, ideologies, heroes, martyrs, and organizational bases of a significant number of Latin American revolutions. It would be hard to imagine them as the tools of a disciplinary order.

This brief survey suggests some lessons about the role of institutions in Latin American studies. As discussed in the introduction to this volume and in various chapters, our field has generally ignored key organizations and social phenomena that have received much more attention in Europe and the United States. Often this has to do with management of scarce resources. When the military is bombing the presidential palace, it is natural to first ask why it does so rather than analyze its role in the construction of social patterns. When illiteracy is rampant, it makes little sense to speak of mass socialization via schools. Nevertheless, the shortage of work on these institutions is emblematic of a neglect of the "middle ground" that has characterized Latin American studies. We sorely need solid institutional histories not because they would provide a possibly different view of discipline but because we lack many of the fundamental bases for an understanding of Latin American society as a whole. How people learn, work, and fight remain significant empirical mysteries.

But we do know enough to say that many of these institutions played a more limited role in the creation of contemporary Latin America than was the case in other regions. What does this tell us about the continent? How has the different role played by total institutions shaped its experience with "modernity"? The point is not to ask once again why Latin America is missing some aspect of developed societies but to begin defining how Latin America developed in this different manner. We might ponder, for example, the relationship between crime and the state or the manner in which nationalist rituals were taught under these different circumstances. The answers to these questions would enlighten Latin American studies and also suggest ways to improve standard, universalized accounts.

Returning to discipline, we also need to ask whether it is so necessary to modernity as the classics supposed. One of the strongest and more widely held assumptions about the requisites for modernity is the need to make behaviors and attitudes, standard and uniform. The complexity of modern life requires, in this view, a surrender of individuality—a trope found in practically every classical account. The Latin American experience suggests that at least some of the outward forms of this discipline (i.e., institutional life) need not be replicated. It might also suggest, however, that the disciplinary function takes place somewhere else on the continent. If public institutions are the schools of discipline for Europe and North America, the family and the household may fulfill a similar role in Latin America. Future work might well consider the extent to which discipline in Latin America may be gendered or socialized in childhood. The apparent difficulty with grounding the concept of discipline in the experience of the continent should lead us not to dismiss it but to begin shifting the kinds of questions that it calls to mind.

CONCLUSIONS

How can the experiences of Latin America and the notion of a disciplinary society inform each other? Certainly the very preliminary evidence discussed here would indicate that the concept is an amorphous one. Measuring a phenomenon as supposedly pervasive and central to a major historical transformation is exceedingly difficult. Cross-societal comparisons are even more so. This exercise also should make us appreciate the very great heterogeneity within the continent. If nothing else, it should make us doubt simplistic accusations of a missing cultural nexus. As we can see from the data provided, explanations of association would no doubt favor institutional developments instead of essentialist qualities.

Despite the obvious caution with which we might wish to treat the concept, there is also enough of a pattern within Latin America to indicate that "social discipline" may capture (much like a statistical factor analysis) an underlying set of social structures. I suggest that both the ambiguity and the apparent fit with some stereotypical impressions of these societies require that we devote much greater attention to the institutional sources of social discipline. That is, what we may learn from the classic emphasis on discipline is not so much a new metatheory with which to explain Latin American exceptionalism but a new research agenda. It is noteworthy that while certain segments of Latin American life (e.g., trade, the church) have received considerable attention, those institutions associated with discipline and its development have been relatively underanalyzed. Their relationship with other social phenomena may have been studied (e.g., civil-military relations), but the social impact of the institutions themselves (e.g., what the army teaches recruits) remains largely unstudied. One of the more useful fruits of the process of "importing" theoretical concepts from other areas is to point out the relative dearth of analyses in particular social sectors or phenomena.

If classical theory can learn some caution from the different pattern witnessed in Latin America, those of us who study the region may also feel freer to engage in theoretical plagiarism and to borrow theoretical concepts that are outside of our area studies tradition.

NOTES

With many thanks to Bruce Western, Fernando López Alves, Patricio Silva, and Deborah Kaple for their helpful suggestions.

1. Robert van Krieken, "The Organization of the Soul: Elias and Foucault on Discipline and the Self," *Archives Euopéennes de Sociologie* 31 (1990): 353.

2. It also would be worthwhile to analyze the relationship between fascist ideology and a fascination with discipline.

3. See Michael Burawoy and P. Krotov, "The Soviet Transition from Socialism to Capitalism: Worker Control and Economic Bargaining in the Wood Industry," *American Sociological Review* 57 (1992): 16–38.

4. John Williamson, ed., *The Political Economy of Policy Reform* (Washington, D.C.: Institute for International Economics, 1994).

5. Robert Putnam, *Making Democracy Work: Civic Traditions in Modern Italy* (Princeton, N.J.: Princeton University Press, 1992). Philip Gorski has argued that a "disciplinary revolution" is the 17th–18th century was required for the construction of states. See "The Protestant Ethic Revisited: Disciplinary Revolution and State Formation in Holland and Prussia," *American Journal of Sociology*, 99 (1993): 265–316.

6. James Scott, *Seeing Like a State* (New Haven, Conn.: Yale University Press, 1997).

7. Richard Hamilton, *The Social Misconstruction of Reality* (New Haven, Conn.: Yale University Press, 1996), chap. 6.

8. It is important to note that Latin Americans have been active participants in the castigation of the continent for lack of discipline, for example, Domingo Sarmiento's "Civilización y barbarie."

9. Claudio Veliz, *The Centralist Tradition of Latin America* (Princeton, N.J.: Princeton University Press, 1980); Richard Morse, "The Heritage of Latin America," in Louis Hartz, ed., *The Founding of New Societies: Studies in the History of the United States, Latin America, South Africa, Canada, and Australia* (New York: Harcourt Brace Jovanovich, 1964); Howard J. Wiarda, ed., *Politics and Social Change in Latin America* (Amherst: University of Massachusetts Press, 1974); Lawrence Harrison, *Underdevelopment Is a State of Mind: The Latin American Case* (Lanham, Md.: Center for International Affairs, Harvard University, and University Press of America, 1985).

10. David Landes, *The Wealth and Poverty of Nations* (New York: Norton, 1998).

11. The term originates in the Latin *disciplina* (teaching, learning) and, relatedly, *discipulus* (pupil). It first appears in its modern form in the thirteenth century, implying punishment, instruction, training (especially of mental faculties or moral character), the control gained by enforcing obedience, or the orderly or prescribed conduct or pattern of behavior, and, finally (and perhaps most important) self-control.

12. Max Weber, *Economy and Society* (Berkeley: University of California Press, 1978), 1149.

13. Michel Foucault, *Discipline and Punish*, 2d. ed. (New York: Vintage, 1995), 166.

14. Anthony Giddens, *The Consequences of Modernity* (Cambridge: Polity, 1991), 56

15. Marc Raeff, "The Well-Ordered Police State and the Development of Modernity in Seventeenth Century Europe: An Attempt at a Comparative Approach," *American Historical Review* 80 (December 1991): 1226.

16. Stefan Breuer, "Foucault and Beyond: Towards a Theory of the Disciplinary Society," *International Social Science Journal* 120 (May 1989): 237.

17. Van Krieken, "The Organization of the Soul."

18. John O'Neill, "The Disciplinary Society: From Weber to Foucault," *British Journal of Sociology* 37, no. 1 (1986): 43.

19. Foulcault, *Discipline and Punish*, 155.

20. Norbert Elias, *The Civilizing Process* (Cambridge: Blackwell, 1994), 446–48.

21. Albert Hirschman, *The Passions and the Interests* (Princeton, N.J.: Princeton University Press, 1978).

22. Nicholas Ambercrombie, Stephen Hill, and Bryan Turner, *The Dominant Ideology Thesis* (London: Allen and Unwin, 1980), chap. 4.

23. Elias, *The Civilizing Process*, 459, 509.

24. O'Neill, "The Disciplinary Society," 50.

25. Foulcault, *Discipline and Punish*, 201.

26. Other possible candidates would obviously include medicine and health services in general or (following Scott) professions such as architecture or agronomy. A fascinating question is why political parties in Latin America have tended to have such relatively weak institutional bases and why there have been no significant Leninist parties in the continent.

27. Weber, *Economy and Society*, 1155.

28. Ibid., 1152.

29. Ibid., 1155.

30. Foucault, *Discipline and Punish*, 135.

31. As Hamilton emphasizes, a key problem for such a view is to explain why the particular form of discipline associated with the military did not produce an "earlier" form of modernity.

32. O'Neill, "The Disciplinary Society," 47.

33. Foucault, *Discipline and Punish*, 138, 165.

34. John Meyer and W. Richard Scott, with the assistance of Brian Rowan and Terrance E. Deal, *Organizational Environments: Ritual and Rationality* (Beverly Hills, Calif.: Sage, 1983).

35. Samuel Bowles and Herbert Gentis, *Schooling in Capitalist America: Education and the Contradictions of Economic Life* (New York: Basic Books, 1976).

36. For savings, IMF, *World Economic Outlook* (Washington, D.C.: IMF, 1996), and Manuel Agostin, "Savings and Investment in Latin America," *UNCTAD Review* (1995); for corruption, Transparency International, Corruption Index based on surveys of international business executives; for crime, Bureau of Justice Statistics, Special Report, International Crime Rates, May 1988; strikes from B. R. Mitchell, *International Historical Statistics: The Americas* (New York: Stockton Press, 1993).

37. The perfect example here is Stephen Haber's *How Latin America Fell behind: Essays in the Economic Histories of Brazil and Mexico, 1800–1914* (Stanford, Calif.: Stanford University Press, 1997).

38. Ricardo Salvatore and Carlos Aquirre, eds.,*The Birth of the Penitentiary in Latin America* (Austin: University of Texas Press, 1996).

39. UN *Compendium of Social Statistics and Indicators*, 1988, table 34; Marc Mauer, "Americans behind Bars: The International Use of Incarceration, 1992–1993."

40. Outstanding examples would include Thomas Holloway, *Policing Rio de Janeiro: Repression and Resistance in a Nineteenth-Century City* (Stanford, Calif.: Stanford University Press, 1993); and Paul Vanderwood, *Disorder and Progress: Bandits, Police, and Mexican Development* (Lincoln: University of Nebraska Press, 1981).

41. *Blood and Debt: War & Statemaking in Latin America* (University Park: Pennsylvania State University Press, forthcoming). See also the chapter by Fernando López-Alves in this volume.

42. A list of authors would include Alfred Stepan, Robert Potash, Frederick Nunn, David Ronfeldt, and Christon Archer.

43. An interesting question in this regard is the extent to which slave plantations served a similar functional purpose as factories in the eighteenth and early nineteenth centuries.

44. Daniel James and John French, eds., *The Gendered Worlds of Latin American Women Workers: From Household and Factory to the Union Hall and Ballot Box* (Durham, N.C.: Duke University Press, 1997). Previous efforts included Daniel James, *Resistance and Integration: Peronism and the Argentine Working Class, 1946–1976* (New York: Cambridge University Press, 1988); María Patricia Fernández-Kelly, *For We Are Sold, I and My People* (Albany: State University of New York Press, 1983); Peter Winn, *Weavers of Revolution: The Yarur Workers and Chile's Road to Socialism* (New York: Oxford University Press, 1986).

45. As in the other cases, there are obvious exceptions with the work of John Hodge and Mary Kay Vaughan being the most obvious. Traditionally, however, it has been too easy to dismiss public education as merely another arm of a capitalist state (à la Ivan Illich) without analyzing the actual socialization processes involved.

46. Elsie Rockwell, "Schools of the Revolution: Enacting and Contesting State Forms in Tlaxcala, 1910–1930," in Gilbert Joseph and Daniel Nugent, eds., *Everyday Forms of State Formation* (Durham, N.C.: Duke University Press, 1994).

Chapter Ten

MICHEL DE CERTEAU AND LATIN AMERICA

ROBERT M. LEVINE

THIS CHAPTER examines the contributions of the historian and cultural anthropologist Michel de Certeau (1925–86), asking how his theoretical approach might be applied to the study of Latin America. Although de Certeau illustrated his analysis mostly with examples drawn from France, his ideas have been widely discussed throughout the world, including in Latin America. A poststructuralist like Jacques Derrida, Paul de Man, and J. Hillis Miller, de Certeau explored the ways that cultural texts and systems are influenced by the process of language. He was an exponent of discourse theory, asking to examine culture; the ways people talk themselves into doing things, including violent acts; and resistance.[1]

In all linguistic creations, the poststructuralists argued, there was something more than what was conveyed by written texts. De Certeau addressed this issue by examining cultural stresses and the subtle ways in which ordinary people resist systems from within. For this reason, his insights, like those of James C. Scott, are very applicable to the region.[2] Unlike Scott, who uses fieldwork as the basis for his analysis, de Certeau is abstract and highly theoretical. Still, de Certeau, more than any of the other poststructuralists, read history deeply and engaged in dialogue with grassroots activists.[3] "History," de Certeau wrote, "is entirely shaped by the system within which it is developed."[4]

Michel de Certeau, born in May 1925 into the postwar French generation traumatized by the calamitous experience of World War I, was a brilliant but withdrawn and personally austere youth. The new outbreak of fighting in 1939 and the subsequent invasion and occupation of his country by Nazi forces interjected new anxieties into his life. When World War II ended, he entered a Jesuit seminary, and he was ordained in 1950. He was a nonconformist, however, even as an adolescent, when he objected to the political passivity of the Roman Catholic clergy, and, according to one biographer, he considered some of the actions of the French church in collaborating with the Pétain regime to have been sinful.[5] As a Jesuit, he chose a path as an academic and editor. After earning a graduate degree in early modern religious history, he became a professor; he also served as associate director of the Society of Jesus' journal *Christus* and as a member of the editorial board of the Jesuit monthly, *Études*.

In the mid-1960s he traveled and taught in Latin America. When he returned to France, he confronted a personal crisis of identity and direction. Professionally he struggled to enlarge his scholarship to encompass history, ethnography, linguistics, theology, and psychoanalysis. He suffered a grave injury in an automobile accident in August 1967 (in which his mother died, and he lost sight in one eye). Finally, he became caught up in the heady events of May 1968. He objected to the elite's lack of social consciousness and its materialist desires. He joined the faculty of the Department of Cultural Anthropology at the University of Paris-VII (Jussieu). Yet, although he had become caught up in the emotional energy of Latin American liberation theology, he refused to take on a student from Latin America who had come to Paris hoping to have him direct his dissertation. He withdrew inside himself, marked by the events of his generation and declining to take a militant role. It was during this period of freewheeling discourse that he became convinced of the critical importance of speech and language. Speech, he wrote, "is what grants entry into the concert of voices where partial, contradictory, or inchoate truths confront, contradict, and complete one another; it gives nourishment to every member of the social body."[6] De Certeau's rhetorical devices transcended their classical grounding in French linguistics and emerged as a multifaceted new way of posing arguments about the culture of mankind. He created an intermediate zone between literary theory and criticism on one hand and history and the social sciences on the other. In the words of John Beverley and James Saunders, he sought "a space that goes beyond the disciplines, that subjects them, that is 'transgressive' in some sense."[7] De Certeau's analysis about what he termed the "death of speech" is useful in the analysis of Latin American cultural history. Luís Madureira, for example, uses this theme in his analysis of Mário de Andrade's authorship of the Brazilian classic *Macunaíma* (1926), recalling Andrade's own agitation a decade and a half later over his empty feeling in rereading his melancholic final chapters, a "silencing" of narrative and narrator.[8]

Influenced by ideas as far-ranging as Freud's *Civilization and Its Discontents* and the writings of nineteenth-century anarcho-syndicalists, and engaged in conversations with many of the impressive array of French intellectuals in his generation, from Pierre Bourdieu to Michel Foucault, de Certeau emerged during the 1970s as a central figure in French cultural studies. This field had emerged in the late 1950s and early 1960s in the work of British academics Richard Hoggett, Raymond Williams, and E. P. Thompson, who were employed in universities and adult education centers and wrote about British class structures and beliefs. All of them, in one way or another, called for a reassessment of the term *culture*, seeing it as an aggregate of individual experiences, a shifting mass of signs rather than a single entity, or, in the words of José Joaquín Brunner, as "a 'cultured' vision of culture."[9] In the transition from the British school to studies more influenced by French structuralism, the empirical traditional waned. That generation set the ground rules for social history within a soft-Marxist cultural paradigm. Cultural studies passed through at least three phases: a broadly written, narrative "culturalism" during the 1960s; structuralism in the 1970s, with its more formal approach to explicit models of the past; and, ultimately, poststructuralism, sometimes called "cultural materialism."

De Certeau's post-1968 writings fall into the poststructuralist school. Contemporary Europeans, especially the French, tended to be structuralists, working with polysystems theory rooted in structuralism and emphasizing language. Elsewhere, however, especially in Canada, Australia, and the United States—as well as in India and Latin America—scholars broadened their agendas to include multiculturalism and linguistic pluralism. Cultural studies in these places turned to sociology, ethnography, and history, emphasizing questions of hegemonic relations in text production in terms of relations between colonized and colonizer. Randal Johnson, for example, addresses this theme in his article "Tupy or Not Tupy: Cannibalism and Nationalism in Contemporary Brazilian Literature," speaking of the intellectual "cannibals" of the modernist movement: "Imitation and influence in the traditional sense of the word are no longer possible. The *antropófagos* (cannibals) do not want to copy European culture, but rather to devour it, taking advantage of its positive aspects, rejecting the negative and creating an original national culture that would be a source of artistic expression rather than a receptacle for forms of cultural expression elaborated elsewhere."[10]

De Certeau published three books on culture and language: *La Prise de parole* (1968; translated as *The Capture of Speech*); *La Culture au pluriel* (1974; *Culture in the Plural*), and *L'Invention de quotidien* (1980, new edition 1990; *The Practice of Everyday Life*). Some of the ideas in *Everyday Life*, the study with the greatest impact among scholars, including the dyad of "strategy" and "tactic," and his work on the linguistics of enunciation, appeared in the final chapters of *Culture in the Plural*. As Tom Conley observes, de Certeau addressed "how to sift through the specious truths we have inherited in the name of culture." He was an activist, and he hoped that his ideas would be translated into deed. His earlier writings dealt with theory; his later essays and books instructed how ordinary people can obtain agency through practices that pluralize communication. His writings "engage ways of changing the world."[11]

During the early 1980s, de Certeau taught several courses in the history department of Mexico's Universidad Iberoamericana. More of his books were translated into Spanish than English.[12] The journal of his host university, *História y Gráfia*, remains heavily influenced by de Certeau, or, in the words of Claudio Lomnitz, "De-Certeau-ism." De Certeau is appreciated in scholarly circles in Latin America, which for the most part are more theoretical and less empirical than traditional scholarship in the United States. Because de Certeau's writings anticipated these new categories of topics among scholars in postcolonial Latin America, his writings are of particular interest. Inspired by Foucault, de Certeau argued that writing, or textualization, depends as much on the collective expectations of readers as upon the collective sense of historians about what they produce. Historians, he contended in his essay "The Historiographical Operation," construct a "social place" that determines who is admitted to their "club," what are the written (and unwritten) rules of belonging to that "club," and what is acceptable and what is not. Fellowships, prizes, who gets published and who does not—all are dependent on "insider" status.[13]

His prescriptions for activist scholarship in political and cultural issues offer useful approaches to the study of Latin America. Foremost were his observations about strategies for studying popular religion, his writings on historical methodology, and his approach to what he termed "ethnic economies."[14] During his mid-1960s visits to Brazil, Chile, Ecuador, and later Mexico, de Certeau found himself thrust into the heady (and dangerous) world of the liberation theologists. From the first, he struggled with the question of violence versus nonviolence. He wrestled with the contradictory role of the Roman Catholic Church in the region, the only institution, he argued, with the capacity to mobilize the people, indeed, to furnish the manpower to protest social injustice, yet, on the other hand, an institution faced with shrinking powers and widespread defections to what he called "nationalist movements" such as Brazilian Umbanda, one of many dynamic forms of religious syncretism wholly independent of the Latin American Roman Catholic Church and in most ways antithetical to it.

De Certeau was particularly enraged by the 1966 assassination of Father Camilo Torres by the Colombian army and by the murder of activist priests during the next decade by various authoritarian regimes in the region. These acts, he wrote in his essay "The Guerrilla Martyr," become a new Christian discourse in the political arena. He quotes the Bolivian Father José Prats from Teoponte in 1970: "It matters little if they accuse me of being a guerrilla or a communist because, in a world in which three-quarters of the inhabitants are dying of hunger, what is the difference if they kill a simple person like myself?"[15] Father Prats's message, he comments, crystallizes many of the effects of the discourse between violence and nonviolence. Christians who are politically aware, he wrote, are married to the "excommunicated figures" of the guerrilla and the communist. He admires them deeply: "Monks and Christian martyrs continue to go into guerrilla struggles in the mountains, just as they used to take refuge in the deserts of Egypt." He lauds Father Domingo Lain, who became the head of the Colombian guerrilla insurgency in 1970, recalling Lain's words: "Now begins my true priestly consecration, which requires total self-sacrifice so that people will be able to live." De Certeau extols the martyrs for their willingness to leave behind personal comfort and "the professional security that in Western Europe so often serves as exits from the disillusionment engendered by an outdated ideology of 'vocation.'" Their martyrdom has been valuable, he argues: "The spirituality ushered in by [their] deaths has created a space for hope; it has given credence to the revolution that was fading away; it has mystical force at the very moment when it is losing its immediately political influence."[16] "New paths are being charted," he wrote; "these nascent credibilities attest to what is most fragile, but also most moving and fundamental, in all social life."[17]

De Certeau and his fellow "new cultural historians" claimed that everything must be opened to continual questioning, that the writing of history shapes interpretation, and that the relationship of historians to the truth must be reexamined.[18] In the words of Mark Poster, cultural history demands that historians confront the representational power of writing. As long as historians sidestep the question of their own role in "producing" knowledge, all of their work, "old" or "new," is rejected by the challengers.[19] De Certeau (and Jacques Derrida, Roland Barthes, François Furet, Jean Baudrillard, Roger Chartier, and others) argued for new directions and methodologies; new themes for examination (consumerism, daily life, flows of imposition and constraint, feminist and anticolonialist discourse, and so on). Modernity, they argue, is coming to an end, and something new is emerging. Ambivalence must be reintroduced to the relation between past and present. Introducing a new rhetorical lexicon, they sought to tear apart standard definitions, preferring to analyze things fluidly, along the lines of Mikhail Bakhtin's definition of Carnival as "a conception of a liberating zone in which oppressive social norms are riotously overthrown."[20]

More than anything else, de Certeau's point of view derived from linguistic studies, particularly Wittgenstein's model of ordinary language and what de Certeau refers to as the "speech act." This happens when speakers make use of language in ways fitting personal needs. To understand a text, he argued—in a manner similar to that of the linguist J. L. Austin—required a grasp not only of what the speaker said but also of what he meant. De Certeau applied this approach to his study of culture, and therefore to the practice of everyday life. Individual action, he claimed, is never totally reducible to the structures in which it occurs. De Certeau challenged more traditional historical approaches, claiming that they tend to isolate and immobilize their object of study. He points to the rise of quantitative history as indicative of historians' doubts about the stability of language, what he calls its "polysemy." But this simply displaces the problem of interpretation. Quantifiers, he argues, "reduce the active side of consumption to the appearance of passivity."[21] Quantifying social historians, Mark Poster says, "enact a more forceful intrusion into the archives than did their political historian counterparts a generation ago."[22]

De Certeau influenced the evolution of a historiographical approach known as *spatial history*. As practiced by cultural geographers, social anthropologists, literary critics, and others, spatial history focuses on modes of reality as revealed especially in places of public assembly—from amusement parks to international expositions to museums and shopping malls. Foucault called them as a class "heterotypes," part of the larger landscape of urban spaces and "natural" landscapes that we inhabit.[23] De Certeau closely studied the connection between space, "tactics," and "strategy," and his observations go beyond the issue of resistance and individual behavior. De Certeau called into question Bordieu's conception of "habitus," arguing that this model retrojects culture back into psychology. Without question, his intellectual probings into space and human behavior gave new impetus to the debate over to what extent freedom of will remains possible.[24]

One of de Certeau's most emphatic instructions is that culture must be understood not as an exclusivist monument celebrating human mastery of nature but as a collective range of manners and doing.[25] Culture too often is limited to the formal arts and letters of the elite. Rather, de Certeau saw cultures in the plural, as ways, practices, styles, modes, fashions, and behaviors that, taken together, form the context in which people interact within society. Pluralization of culture—beginning with the act of birth and the first conscious moments of every person—is resisted by the imposition of unilateral languages of culture. In this regard, de Certeau was an anarchist, fighting tooth and nail against the pressures to conform and to remain silent. Official regulations deny people the richness of their own creative discourses.

As his point of departure, de Certeau devoted much of his analysis to resistance in everyday life to structures of domination. Ordinary people trespass on public spaces, since the nineteenth century using them as places for consumption, the defining activity of modern life. In 1851 the first great world exhibition was held in London, the prototype of all world's fairs and the source of modern patterns of consumption in the industrial nations, as well as the first widespread use of advertising to encourage consumption among ordinary citizens. This concept did not originate with de Certeau: Karl Marx was the first major social theorist to argue that capital created a world in its own image, one that "glorified profit, greed, competition, and exploitation."[26] But de Certeau has taken this concept in new directions, exploring commodity semiotics in a search for those moments when dominant strategies fail and resistance rises. To de Certeau, all consumer tactics automatically occur at the margin of society.

De Certeau instructed his readers to identify and to reject language used by oppressive political regimes. This language is not only ideological; it is integrated into everyday life by being given socioeconomic function, by being made into a commodity. When the Brazilian military dictatorship in the late 1960s wished to intimidate the population, it placed striking messages, designed by the same advertising agencies that promoted laundry detergent and colas, on billboards throughout urban areas; the billboards depicted an empty hand and the statement "Without Documents You Do Not Exist." "The market," de Certeau wrote, "can only hope to produce oblivion among its consumers"—although, ironically, what the military regime was saying is that citizens who do not conform by duly registering and subjecting themselves to its scrutiny themselves will be relegated to oblivion. For de Certeau, violence implied a growing distortion between what a discourse says and what a society does with it. Language is an "organized place that allows things to happen." It silences speech. "A literature of perversion follows a literature of defection," he said. Language in a totalitarian society, he argues, "excommunicates groups and individuals who are marginalized, forced into defending themselves as exiles, and dedicated to discovering themselves within the repressed."[27]

De Certeau would have been infuriated by the language used by the military regimes in Argentina, Chile, Uruguay, Bolivia, Paraguay, the Dominican Republic, Nicaragua, Brazil, and every other place in the hemisphere under dictatorship. Consider the proclamation of the Brazilian women's March of the Family for God and Liberty, organized by a nun, Sister Ana de Lourdes, against the presidential administration of João Goulart in March 1964, weeks before the overthrow of that government by a right-wing civilian-military coup that ushered in twenty-four years of dictatorship:

> This nation which God gave us, immense and marvelous as it is, faces extreme danger. We have allowed men of limitless ambition, without Christian faith or scruples, to bring our people misery, destroying our economy, disturbing our social peace, and to create hate and despair. They have infiltrated our Nation, our Government Administration, our Armed Forces and even our Churches

> with servants of totalitarianism, foreign to us and all consuming. . . . Mother of God preserve us from the fate and suffering of the martyred women of Cuba, Poland, Hungary and other enslaved Nations![28]

Or the historical justification given in the aftermath of the repressive military government by one of its supporters:

> We Brazilians know that teamwork is more effective than individual effort. Teams . . . prepare us for dialogue and increase our capacity for efficiency. The social order is best served by liberty, justice, love, truth, and solidarity. Man in his process of self-improvement deals with other men. Thus responsibilities are not simply individual, but social as well. Social order results from the perfect interrelationship of necessities and freedom, the middle ground for which is responsibility. . . . To subordinate our own freedoms to the common good is the maximum norm of the exercise of liberty in the social order.[29]

An emotional and sensitive observer, de Certeau would have lashed out in anger at these statements, labeling them examples of "sick languages, . . . objectively servile, . . . the trash left in the wake of power."[30] Wherever *more* jargons are made available to analyze cultural malaise, the *less* is spoken or even done to remedy the condition, he argued.[31] Dominant elites manipulate "culture in the singular," staged cultural goods. They manipulate, inverting reality in Orwellian ways to form language that is frozen (*gelé*) by being turned into what de Certeau described as the "outrageous, cancerous symptom of a society divided between the technocratization of economic progress and the folklorization of civic expression . . . an inner dysfunction: the fact that the appropriation of productive power by privileged organisms has as a corollary a political disappropriation and regression of the country."[32]

It would be interesting to speculate, however, how de Certeau might have analyzed the use of language in left-wing authoritarian regimes, such as Sandinista Nicaragua and Castro's Cuba. Although he taught in Mexico, he never wrote about the post-Cárdenas governments of corruption and authoritarian impunity hiding behind the banner of the Mexican Revolution, which had sunk into a caricature of its legitimate revolutionary promise. He reserved his wrath, however, for the Chilean military police, the opponents of clerical progressivism, the armed forces of the Right—and their supporters in the Vietnam-era United States military command.

Ordinary people, naked before the abusive power of the state and the pressures of consumerism, nonetheless have the capacity to strike back, he contended. De Certeau made the ordinary man a hero, writing that he is a silent master of everyday experience because he does not interpret or translate his experience as do "experts" in history, sociology, or anthropology; rather, he creates his own text (or poem) as he goes along. Unreadability and invisibility are the key to what makes the everyday the everyday. The hero is a *flaneur*, a subject of "walkabout sensibility," in that act exercising resistance and producing urban space to his own taste. Even in hostile environments, the *flaneur* still strolls. De Certeau believed that history writing, like all writing, constructs the reality it purports to represent. The historian is mistaken, he posits, in believing that the everyday can be summarized by an inventory of things, what Braudel called "a weighing of the world," or perhaps what Clifford Geertz calls "thick description." Rather, the very weakness of ordinary man's lot, de Certeau asserts, is his strength.[33] De Certeau, then, understood popular culture as "a way of operating," of "making do." What he asked us to do is to examine lives carefully, to see how they are lived and "how sites are constructed in the interstices of the vast socio-economic systems."[34] Ultimately, he favors struggle and disobedience to resist the "secret violence of virtuous feelings," risking confrontations with the sources of power.

De Certeau hated modern patterns of consumption and sought evidence of occurrences of resistance in which ordinary people undermined the imposed relations of power. De Certeau is constantly aware of the pressures created by the dominant cultural economy for its products to be consumed (i.e., socially recognized). His conjecture rests on the idea that ordinary people extract ways of resisting from the products and goods that they acquire each day as consumers—items as mundane as newspapers, television programs, and groceries. They cannot escape the dominant cultural economy, but they can adapt it to their own ends. Discipline, he asserts, is constantly deflected and resisted by those who are caught in its "nets," and their "dispersed, tactical, and makeshift creativity" constitutes an "antidiscipline" that Foucault's analysis overlooks.[35]

De Certeau called this *la perruque* (the wig), an act in which the employee does things for him- or herself while ostensibly working for the boss: writing a love letter on the job, for example, or using the company's tools to make something to take home. These acts persist despite measures taken to repress them. On a larger scale, there was the example of resistance on the part of the indigenous peoples of the New World who subverted the dominant Spanish colonial system by eluding norms of exchange and behavior.

He praised students and intellectuals living under government repression who subvert required texts by poaching, resisting by posing different interpretations from the official ones. Many scholars have been taken by this notion, since it gives license to bold leaps of the imagination. Henry Jenkins, for example, uses de Certeau's notion of "textual poaching" to demonstrate how the canonical texts of *Star Trek* are revised and re-envisioned by Trekkies.[36] Folk literature, to de Certeau, was also a form of resistance, considering the fact that the unfortunate often come out on top in tales and legends, as they do in Brazilian Carnival and its rituals of social and status inversion. Power relations are present at all levels, de Certeau contends, and as such they can be manipulated in self-defense even at the bottom of the social ladder. Blunt and pointed in his own use of language, he esteems the underdog. "Manuel, a vagabond peasant in the slums of Mexico City," he wrote, "was already designating a cultural revolution when, thinking he was a piece of shit, he barely dared. . . . He dreamed to 'find the appropriate words' to 'sing the poetry of life,' to 'express the lowest passions in the most beautiful way.'"[37]

Social history, the dominant field of study of Latin America since the 1960s, took as its rallying point the belief by its practitioners that earlier political-intellectual historiography was too narrative, too elitist, and too unconcerned with history "from the bottom up." Even though the new social historians saw their approach as a radical departure from traditional history, during the 1980s both groups of historians found themselves under attack, this time from the new cultural historians, faulting both groups for failing to understand the role of agency. The accusers, including de Certeau, claimed that both traditional and revisionist schools of historians sought to attain the truth about the "real" in history, and therefore took for granted that texts were "transparent mediations between the past and the present." Historians, he argued, must search for self-understanding; without such acknowledgment, there would be no professional ethics, no realization of the aims of inquiry. He would have esteemed Pierre Nora's multivolume foray into French social and cultural history, translated into English as *Realms of Memory*.[38] This collective effort reflects on the symbols of France's historical self-understanding. It analyzes sites and events; religious persecution; and issues of time and place, of local and regional cleavages, and of human generations. The books illustrate exactly de Certeau's quest for a history of symbolism, treating the past not in terms of events but through the ways in which it is remembered and forgotten.[39]

De Certeau's most enduring contribution to the study of Latin America comes in his application of his ideas about language and power to contemporary struggles for social justice. He loved Latin America, so much so that sometimes his enthusiasms ran away with themselves. He wrote carelessly about the names of places he was describing. He located "Crato, Juazeiro, Itapetim, etc." in "the Pernambuco," in which they are not, bestowing, in the process, on the northeastern state a title applied during the nineteenth century by Englishmen to Argentina. He was so enthusiastic about movements for social justice that his portraits of local activists, especially when they were clergymen, border on the hagiographic. He extolled the "great deeds of Frei Damião, the charismatic hero of the region, . . . constantly qualified by the successive accounts of the celestial punishments visited upon his enemies."[40] His abstract categories blend with the real. He wrote about the stratifying partition of socioeconomic space, organized by the immemorial struggle between "the powerful" and "the poor," and the field of constant victories by the rich and the police. There no truth is said, he argues, except in whispers and among peasants: *Agora a gente sabe, mas não pode dizer alto* (Now people know what is going on but they can't talk about it out loud). He concluded: "In this space, the strong always win and words always deceive experience in accord with that of a Maghrebian syndicalist in Billancourt [a Renault factory outside of Paris]:[41] 'They always fuck us over.'" He offered ways to evaluate the impact of the "popular religions" sweeping Latin America, stressing language. Evangelical Protestantism and other religions spread by missionaries prior to 1970, he noted, came from outside and acted as a means to close the door on revolution by opening another onto personal salvation. The collapse of democratic political systems, further, creates an affinity for popular religious expression that is vast but ostensibly immobile. To study and to understand these new religious impulses, he suggests, work must be done at the local level after first taking stock of the *economic* analysis of intolerable situations. This must be done at the local level, he argues, and steps must be taken to understand the religious language used in popular religion, often stratified and complex. Popular religion also uses the language of folktales and popular memory. In each country, he wrote, "is also born a reserve that is more suspicious with regard to protests belonging to other Latin American nations, *a fortiori* with regard to generalities on the division between the elite and the masses." Nationalism appears in religious form "that announces to everybody what still has a political efficacy for no one."

For religious cadres that have fallen back on popular religion out of expediency, de Certeau lashes out in anger. Priests in Brazil, Chile, and elsewhere, under the dictatorial regimes in their countries in the 1970s, abandoned, at the moment of danger and decision, the militants whom they initially encouraged.[42] Their "prudent" alignments with the regimes in power, moreover, were failures, because they brought no additional power to act. Rather, such collaborationism by the hierarchy betrayed priests and humiliated their churches. As a French Jesuit, de Certeau was remembering the shameful experience of his church with the Vichy regime. This produced, he wrote, a growing disparity between the two terms that were initially associated with each other: *popular* and *religion*. In his essays on popular religion, he suggests that it is not sufficient to disparage forms of religious expression as syncretism. Instead, drawing on his work on popular resistance, syncretism allows the masses to surreptitiously reappropriate dominant culture—the ruse of expressing oneself in the language of the *other*.

De Certeau spent most of his time in Brazil in the old, impoverished port city of Recife, the center of the long-decadent sugar export economy of the northeast. To understand the rich nature of messianic and popular religious movements in that region, he encouraged his contemporaries to study with particular care strategies of language use. Religion, he said, is a privileged site for strategies of language "that, with an invisible violence, is characterized by a redeployment or a practice of the received language right where no autonomous expression has yet been legitimated."[43] The rural "and even subproletarian" population of Recife's hinterland, the *sertão*, he argued, has developed a kind of cultural bilingualism, one that first takes account of how things are and then exploits this understanding by inventing "a different, egalitarian society in which the poor finally make good and the bodies of the sick are cured." Religious language, then, gives the weak the opportunity to transcend what cannot be observed to a vision of the extraordinary and the miraculous. De Certeau further speculated about the role of revolutionary ideals in inverting the order of forces kept in a sacred space. This goes to the heart of understanding the northeast's centuries-old history of millenarian and messianic cults and movements, the most ill-fated of which was the destruction in 1897 by government forces of the *sertão* religious community of Canudos and the massacre of almost all of its population.

De Certeau, however, believed that authoritarian government sows the seeds of its own eventual destruction. All the while the repressive order remained in power, "a thousand tactics began to infiltrate, in the camouflage of adhesion, the possibility for another ambition to reappropriate it."[44] But he wanted faster resolution, hinting that revolutionary violence was justified and that clerics sometimes needed to leave behind nonviolent methods to revolutionary action. "It is striking," he wrote, that Latin American bishops favor nonviolent methods in their conflicts with the ruling powers, citing examples ranging from Monsignor L. E. Proaño in Ecuador, a controversial radio priest, to Monsignor P. Casaldaliga in São Félix in Mato Grosso. In this case, however—the threatened expulsion of a Spanish-born priest because he had defended marginalized rural populations and small-scale expatriate farmers—the episcopate took his defense.[45] The same tendency holds in social struggles, he complained, citing the example of the stubborn twelve-year strike (beginning in 1962) in the Perús cement factory in São Paulo, in which the beleaguered striking workers received no meaningful support from persons or groups committed to just causes.

De Certeau clearly felt that Latin America's liberation theology movement was hindered in some ways by its continent-wide organization.

Since most of the movements engendered under the banner of nonviolent liberation were pointedly nonideological, he argued, they emphasized the analysis of techniques of action. This promotes actions that the local groups can control, limiting the possibility of objectives.[46] The goal, he advised, is to avoid a division of labor between theorists and those carrying out actions. Consciousness-raising, then, furnishes instruments for the analysis of reality. Knowledge is an action and is born of action. There must be a rupture, he argues, with expected forms of social behavior. Noncooperation—peasants refusing to pay a tax in Panama; Guarani Indians refusing to attend the schools assigned to them in Paraguay, the bishop of Crateus (in Brazil) and Riobamba (Ecuador) refusing to take part in government ceremonies—provokes reaction: a creative "tactic of *no*" that de Certeau believed was necessary to mobilize social groups and give their goals legitimacy by "displac[ing] the geography of legality by replacing it with a more fundamental reference." Whatever is credible, de Certeau concluded, gains authority; whatever is imposed has power. Action that denies legitimacy to those in power is an important weapon. Nonviolent strategies, then, become laboratories in which experiments are carried out to test the means that a group has to challenge or control the systems of power. And religious experience, he maintained, plays a "new and important role in this fallow field of political life."[47]

De Certeau's criticisms of historians' methodologies are shared by many others. After all, historians do tend to see what they want to see and to hear what they want to hear. "Sometimes I have to distinguish between what I am hearing, and what I wanted to hear," Erik Erickson admitted during a soul-searching debate with Robert Coles about interviewing techniques.[48] Library shelves on Castro's revolution are filled with books either demonizing the regime or blindly extolling its virtues. The very choice of topics for study is telling. We have seen a plethora of theses and books about slave resistance, popular insurrectionists, labor solidarity, the role of women, yet there are virtually no studies of the conservative mentality that dominates Latin American life, or corruption, or impunity—in short, of how Latin America really works. How many historians of Brazil's benighted labor unions, or of the Workers' Party (Partido Trabalhista) slant their findings by their deep-seated personal feelings of sympathy for their subjects?[49] Nor are leftist historians uniquely susceptible to projecting their biases onto their research: we have the example of Mary Wilhermine Williams's *Dom Pedro the Magnanimous*, a 1937 biography that refers to the Brazilian emperor as Christlike.[50] Latin American history textbooks published in the 1960s and 1970s reflected the American bias that gave high marks to countries with two-party systems—even when democracy there was limited (or even a sham) and favored political parties named "reformist," "democratic," or, in the Argentine case, "radical."

Another telling assertion of de Certeau's was his contention that there are limits to the extent to which actors are wholly dominated by or integrated into centralized systems of control. Even this, however, runs the risk of oversimplification. The tragedy that resulted when rural peasants trekked from their homes to Antônio Conselheiro's New Jerusalem at Canudos to await the coming of the millennium, only to be provoked by government troops and ultimately massacred, shows what centralized systems of control do when they are made aware of acts of popular resistance, however peaceful and innocuous. The savage repression that followed the coup against Chile's Salvador Allende (1973) is another example of the extent to which authoritarian and totalitarian governments can overpower overwhelmingly. The Mothers of the Plaza de Mayo in Buenos Aires, Argentina, embarrassed the military dictatorship by their courageous acts of civil disobedience, but their actions did nothing to bring back the lives of their children—even though becoming the focus of the international media helped, in fact, to bring down the military regime.

De Certeau's implicit assertion of the division between the everyday (located "down below") and the visible power structure that imposes itself from above seems a social division reminiscent of the Marxist Henri Lefebvre. Lefebvre, however, finds everyday people victims, forced into silence, and "manipulated in ways . . . damaging to their spaces and their daily life." De Certeau searches for what the ordinary man invents in his routine, but to what extent this liberates and raises the quality of life remains to be seen. His primary hypothesis is that behaving within imposed systems constitutes a form of resistance. Groups and individuals caught in the net of discipline do find refuge in tactics that draw on "dispersed, tactical, and makeshift creativity," but to what degree do these tactics produce meaningful relief for the oppressed?

A problem with theories about resistance, however, that find heroic behavior in the daily lives of ordinary people is not that individual acts of defiance and resistance lack praiseworthiness but that finding satisfaction in small daily acts of defiance and coping overlooks, for those dedicated to meaningful social change, the larger and bleaker picture. This includes the consequences of generations of exploitation, of the social acceptance of widening gaps between haves and have-nots, of the insidious legacy of what Robert Mangabeira Unger calls the institution of "wage repression," which has trapped salaried workers in Latin America for generations. Can it be that oppressive social systems look the other way at workers who use their employer's telephone because they do not have one at home, or at field hands who steal ears of corn or tubers of cassava, exactly because they understand the need for such acts as safety valves? If Brazilian elites accept the inversion of social roles at Carnival because they last only a few days, and because they are essentially harmless, so what if peasants learn to strike back at the landowning class by refusing to make eye contact or by stealing some firewood if the oppressive system survives intact? De Certeau, to be sure, best knew France, where workers were depoliticized. It is not so much that he was opposed to revolution as that he was looking for a praxis in a nonrevolutionary time. It would be fascinating to have De Certeau's observations about Latin America today, caught up in the dizzying process of free-market economics. Would he have foreseen the sharp decline of liberation theology, the silence of the Left, the success of forms of evangelical Protestantism devoid of social conscience, the decline of public universities, and the defection of world-class faculty—full retirement pensions in their pockets—starting new careers in "for-profit" private institutions formerly considered third-rate?

More than anything else, de Certeau's work pleads with us to study how society works. It is lamentable that so many studies of Latin American life emphasize the institutional. Civil society is examined on the basis of laws and constitutions, not on how people are affected by their application. Economists routinely ignore the underground (or "alternative") economy, even though experts blandly claim that half of Latin America's population depends fully or in part on the underground economy to survive. We study political parties and mobilization but say little about how corruption functions, or ascription, or family ties. Some social anthropologists like Roberto DaMatta examine social rituals (the *jeito*, for example, and *carnival*), but his scholarship is regularly attacked as "empirical" by more theory-minded critics, and his findings are often dismissed as being "journalistic."

It is curious that de Certeau, who devoted so much energy to studying the layered nuances of daily life, was gender blind. His subjects are male ("man" and "his" protest against domination) or gender neutral, but he fails to recognize the ways in which women resist.[51] After all, do not women hold unrecognized power in the family and in other spheres? Lionizing the underclass regardless of gender shrugs off the suffering. If the weak, as de Certeau claims, "continually turn to their own ends forces alien to them," then why do poverty and hardship in rural and urban Latin America increase? Is living in cardboard shacks under highway bridges an acceptable form of resistance? What is the point of acknowledging that the poor live "down below," below the thresholds at which visibility begins?

De Certeau asked that we never forget that tactical victories are fragile. The weak cannot keep what they win, but they are doomed to walk the earth in spaces appropriated by the dominant culture. There are, he argues, "polemological spaces" ("which perspicacious country people saw as a network of innumerable conflicts covered up with words") and utopian spaces ("in which a possibility, a definition miraculous in nature, was affirmed by religious stories"). Lucid discourse, he says, "turned up fake words and prohibitions on speaking in order to reveal an ubiquitous injustice, . . . that of history."[52] People make space habitable, like a rented apartment, but they must soon give it back and move on to other spaces. They must always be on the watch for opportunities that must be "seized on the wing." And perhaps his most useful lesson is his criticism of social theories, especially those deriving from Max Weber, that "visualize action in modern society only on the model of a calculation of self-interest."[53] In this way, de Certeau encourages us to study the Latin American underclass as foreigners in their own land, on their own terms, and as a useful way to understand the restraints placed upon by them by the "hegemonic structures of power."[54]

Carlos J. Alonso argued that the rhetoric of cultural discourse in Latin America is rendered more difficult because of a lingering radical ambiguity and ambivalence about the position of Latin American culture.[55] De Certeau's writings on Latin America help deal with this ambiguity through his use of practical words (struggle, commitment, ethic, practice, authority, power) to convey the feeling that desired fundamental change could and will happen in Latin America. He died in 1986, in the midst of the retreat of armed forces dictatorships in Latin America but before the global embrace of free-market economics and its de-emphasis on what its critics derided as "social engineering." Liberation theology in Latin America is seen today as passé, although the survival of peasant revolt in Chiapas and the faint stirrings of the Left in Brazil, mostly in the form of the militant Landless Movement but also in the rebirth of the chances for the Workers' Party, represent exactly the kind of popular resistance that de Certeau advocated. Just as speech had been "captured" in the events of 1968, from place to place in Latin America it rose to be heard and captured, if only to die down again. De Certeau's drive to elucidate social problems through the study of different languages of contestation remains a praiseworthy goal. De Certeau tells us to listen to speech, to music, to oral innuendos, to the "hybrid types of exchanges that go unseen or unnoticed in life in general."[56] Like France's government apparatus in 1968, the governments of Latin America seek to maintain "an obsolete, quasi-panoptic order of social control that reaches back well beyond the nineteenth century."[57] The distinction between the temporal and the spiritual as two jurisdictions remains structurally inscribed in both societies, "but now," he wrote in The Practice of Everyday Life, "it is within the political system."[58] The very power of this system, to make people believe that others believe in it, contains within it the seeds for its own eventual dissipation.

How can there be "cultural politics"? One of de Certeau's last words on the subject leaves the reader with a sense of ambivalence. "It remains to be seen," he wrote, "if the members of a society—today drowned in the anonymity of discourses of which they are dispossessed, and subject to conglomerates whose control exceeds their grasp—will find, along with the power of locating themselves in a game of acknowledged forces, the means of capturing speech."[59]

NOTES

I would like to thank Antol Rosenthal, Erica Windler, Steven C. Topik, Mark Poster, Guido Ruggiero, Claudio Lomnitz, and Miguel Angel Centeno for their kind assistance with this chapter.

1. See David E. Apter, "Discourse Theory and Political Violence," *Times Literary Supplement*, January 16, 1998, 38; Homi Bhabha, "The Commitment to Theory," in *The Location of Culture* (New York: Routledge, 1994), 36.

2. See James C. Scott, *Weapons of the Weak: Everyday Faces of Peasant Resistance* (New Haven, Conn.: Yale University Press, 1985).

3. See Mark Poster, *Cultural History and Postmodernity: Disciplinary Readings and Challenges* (New York: Columbia University Press, 1997), 110.

4. Michel de Certeau, *The Writing of History*, trans. Tom Conley (New York: Columbia University Press, 1988), 69. See also de Certeau's *Heterologies: Discourse on the Other*, trans. Brian Massumi (Minneapolis: University of Minnesota Press, 1986).

5. Luce Giard, "How Tomorrow Is Already Being Born," introduction to Michel de Certeau, *The Capture of Speech, and Other Political Writings*, trans. Tom Conley (Minneapolis: University of Minnesota Press, 1997), x–xi.

6. De Certeau quoted in ibid., xiii. See de Certeau, *Heterologies*.

7. John Beverley and James Sanders, "Negotiating with the Disciplines: A Conversation on Latin American Subaltern Studies," *Latin American Cultural Studies* 6 (1997): 239.

8. Luís Madureira, "Lapses in Taste," in Francis Barker, Peter Hulme, and Margaret Iverson, eds., *Cannibalism and the Colonial World* (Cambridge: Cambridge University Press, 1998), 114.

9. Susan Bassnett, "The Translation Turn in Cultural Studies," in Susan Bassnett and André Lefevre, eds., *Constructing Cultures: Essays on Literary Translation* (London: Multilingual Matters, 1998), 130–31; Beverley and Sanders, "Negotiating with the Disciplines," 237.

10. Randal Johnson cited by Bassnett, "The Translation Turn in Cultural Studies," 128.

11. Tom Conley, "Afterword: A Creative Swarm," in Michel de Certeau, *Culture in the Plural* (Minneapolis: University of Minnesota Press, 1997), 164 n. 8.

12. He also taught at the University of California, San Diego.

13. Some of de Certeau's observations seem to go too far, however. His lament

that historians represent a closed fraternity notable for its narrowness and shared rules surely does describe the wide spectrum among historians and in the historical literature. Surely de Certeau would not have placed in the same "club" the members of Rio's Institute of Geography and History, whose work stands closer to history as practiced in the nineteenth-century, and the Marxist scholars who dominate many, if not most, history departments in many Latin American countries, not the least in Brazil's leading Brazilian federal universities in Rio de Janeiro and São Paulo. Both groups publish extensively, joined by others not at the ideological extremes, but producing published history representing many different approaches, methods, and goals. The lack of a national historical journal in Brazil, in fact, keeps any "club" of the type described by de Certeau from forming and encourages the birth of new and more specialized journals as diverse as the feminist *Cadernos Pagú*, published in Campinas, to the publications by the University of Paraná in Curitiba's center for applied studies of ethnic history.

14. See de Certeau, *The Capture of Speech and Other Political Writings*, chaps. 7–17.

15. Michel de Certeau, "The Guerrilla Martyr," in *The Capture of Speech*, 80–81.

16. Ibid., 83–84.

17. Michel de Certeau, "Hidden Revolutions," in *Culture in the Plural*, 11.

18. Joyce Appleby, Lynn Hunt, and Margaret Jacob, *Telling the Truth about History* (New York: Norton, 1994); and the special issue of the *Hispanic American Historical Review* 79, no. 2 (May 1999), dedicated to Mexico's New Cultural History.

19. De Certeau, *Heterologies*, 44; Poster, *Cultural History and Postmodernity*, 3–5.

20. See Matt Steinglass, "International Man of Mystery," *Lingua Franca* 8, no. 3 (April 1998): 33.

21. Michel de Certeau, *The Practice of Everyday Life* (Berkeley: University of California Press, 1984), xviii.

22. Poster, *Cultural History and Postmodernity*, 116.

23. Kentaro Tomio, "Towards Spatial History: Michel de Certeau and the Practices of Everyday Life" (paper presented at the meeting of the American Historical Association, New York, January 1997).

24. See Henri Lefebvre, *Everyday Life in the Modern World* (New Brunswick, N.J.: Transaction Books, 1984).

25. Conley, "Afterword: A Creative Swarm," 151.

26. Tristan Mendoza, "Modernity, Commodification, and the Spectacle from Marx through Debord into the Postmodern," in Steven Best and Douglas Kellner, eds., *The Postmodern Adventure*, excerpted at http://ccwf.cc.utexas.edu/panicbuy/HaTeMail/marxtopomo.html.

27. Michel de Certeau, "The Language of Violence," in *Culture in the Plural*, 30–33.

28. Translated and cited by Roberta C. Wigder, *Brazil Rediscovered* (Philadelphia: Dorrance, 1977).

29. From pamphlet, "Construindo o Brasil," circulated by the Group for Moral and Civic Education, Rio de Janeiro, Robert M. Levine collection.

30. De Certeau, "The Language of Violence," 29.

31. Conley, "Afterword: A Creative Swarms," 155.

32. Michel de Certeau, "The Soft and the Hard," in *Culture in the Plural*, 134.

33. De Certeau, *Practice of Everyday Life*, 11, 17, 21, 60, 141. See also Michelle Chilcoat, "Walking Rhetoric," http://www.georgetown.edu/labyrinth/e-center/chilcoat.htm; Tomio, "Towards Spatial History," 8, 10; Postner, *Cultural History and Postmodernity*, 133.

34. Roland Boer, "Knockin' on Heaven's Door: De Certeau, Religion and Everyday Life," cited at www.utas.edu.au/doc/humsoc.

35. Beryl Langer, review of *The Practice of Everyday Life*, *Contemporary Sociology* 17 (1988): 123.

36. Henry Jenkins, cited in "Early Critical Theory Approaches to *Star Trek*," http://www.clo.com/rvk/past_res.htm#Textual Poacher.

37. Michel de Certeau, "Words and Representatives," in *Culture in the Plural*, 12.

38. Pierre Nora, *Realms of Memory*, 3 vols., ed. Lawrence Kritzman; trans. Alfred Goldhammer (New York: Columbia University Press, 1996–97).

39. *Midwest Book Review*, cited by Amazon.com European history division (www.amazon.com/exec/obidos/SIN/0231084048).

40. De Certeau, *Practice of Everyday Life*, 15.

41. Ibid., 16.

42. Michel de Certeau, "Les Chrétiens et la dictature militaire au Brésil," *Politique d'Aujord'Hui*, November 1969, 39–53.

43. Ibid. 84.

44. Ibid., 85.

45. De Certeau, *The Capture of Speech*, 200 n. 17.

46. Ibid., 86.

47. Ibid., 87.

48. Erik Erickson, quoted by Robert Coles in *Doing Documentary Work* (New York: Oxford University Press, 1997), 43.

49. See, for example, Emir Sader and Ken Silverstein, *Without Fear of Being Happy: Lula, the Workers' Party, and Brazil* (London: Verso, 1991); John D. French, ed., *The Gendered Worlds of Latin American Women Workers: From Household and Factory to the Union Hall and Ballot Box* (Durham, N.C.: Duke University Press, 1997); John D. French, *The Brazilian Workers' ABC: Class Conflict and Alliances in Modern São Paulo* (Chapel Hill: University of North Carolina Press, 1992).

50. Mary Wilhermine Williams, *Dom Pedro the Magnanimous* (Chapel Hill: University of North Carolina Press, 1937).

51. De Certeau, *Practice of Everyday Life*, xiv.

52. Beryl Langer, review of *The Practice of Everyday Life*, 123.

53. De Certeau, *Practice of Everyday Life*, 16.

54. See "Cultural and Narrative Tactics in Women's, Minority, and Post-Colonial Literature," Society for the Study of Narrative Literature, meeting of the Modern Language Association, Chicago, 1996, http://www.wheatonma.edu/academic/academic.dept/English/text/.

55. Carlos J. Alonso, *The Burden of Modernity: The Rhetoric of Cultural*

Discourse in Spanish America (New York: Oxford University Press, 1998), esp. 33–35. I have extended Alonso's comments to include Brazil as well.

56. Tom Conley, "Afterword: The 'Events' and Their Erosion," in *The Capture of Speech*, 183.

57. Ibid., 188.

58. De Certeau, *Practice of Everyday Life*, 182.

59. Michel de Certeau, "A Necessary Politicization," in *Culture in the Plural*, 121.

Chapter Eleven

NATIONALISM AS A PRACTICAL SYSTEM

BENEDICT ANDERSON'S THEORY OF NATIONALISM FROM

THE VANTAGE POINT OF SPANISH AMERICA

CLAUDIO LOMNITZ

BENEDICT ANDERSON'S *Imagined Communities* probably has been the single most influential work on nationalism of the past two decades. Written with clarity and flair, Anderson's book explains nationalism as a specific form of communitarianism whose cultural conditions of possibility were determined by the development of communications media (print capitalism) and colonial statecraft (especially state ritual and state ethnography, for instance, bureaucratic "pilgrimages," censuses, and maps).

Seen in this light, nationalisms are historically recent creations and yet are terribly successful as cultural techniques that shape subjectivity. In fact, it is nationalism's power to form subjects that truly arrests Anderson's attention: "[Patriotic deaths] bring us abruptly face to face with the central problem posed by nationalism: what makes the shrunken imaginings of recent history (scarcely more than two centuries) generate such colossal sacrifices?"[1] This concern with subject formation and identity is consonant with Anderson's principal innovation, which is to treat nationalism not as an ideology but rather as a hegemonic, commonsensical, and tacitly shared cultural construct.

For Anderson, nationalism is a kind of cultural successor to the universalism of premodern (World) religions. Thus, although he locates the birth of nationalism in the late eighteenth and early nineteenth centuries, the preconditions for its emergence occur much earlier, with Europe's expansion in the sixteenth century. In Anderson's view, European expansion created the image of plural and independent lines of civilizational development, and this pluralism or relativism was eventually transformed into a kind of secular historicism in which individuated collectivities—"nations"—competed with each other.

One of the most surprising turns in Anderson's brief book is that he claims that nationalism developed first in the colonial world and spread from there back to Europe. This move caught Latin Americanist historians off balance, since the historiography of independence up to then was dominated by treatises on the intellectual influences of Europe—of liberalism, of the Enlightenment—on American independence, and not the other way around. Rarely did the Latin American specialist dare to claim much originality for these movements, let alone to suggest that nationalism itself had been invented in Spanish America and was subsequently exported to Europe.

Latin Americanists are collectively in Anderson's debt, for his insistence on the singularity of colonial conditions alone. However, despite this boon to a profession that often aches to claim singularity for itself, developments in the Latin American field were slow to turn in Anderson's direction, with significant works using Anderson as a point of inspiration appearing practically ten years after the book was first published.

The slothful reaction to Anderson by Latin American historians and anthropologists has been due not only to the usual reaction of the subfield's antibodies against brash foreign intruders who do not respect the regnant doxa. It is also the result of considerable difficulty in grappling with the relationship between the book's general proposal on nationalism (which is often inspiring) and the fact that Anderson's view of American independence is incorrect in a number of particulars.

My aim in this chapter is to carry out a comprehensive critique of *Imagined Communities*, by which I mean a critique that interrogates both the conceptual and the historical thesis. I shall do so by way of a close study of nationalism in the Spanish-American republics, and in Mexico particularly. Because this area is, according to Anderson's formulation, the birthplace of modern nationalism, it is a key to his general thesis. On the other hand, the fertility of Anderson's masterful book is such that criticizing its central thesis requires developing an alternative perspective, the seeds of which are also presented here.

REVIEW OF THE HISTORICAL THESIS

In order to understand Anderson's account of the birth of Spanish-American nationalism and independence, we must be clear first on what exactly he is trying to explain:

> The aggressiveness of Madrid and the spirit of liberalism, while central to any understanding of the impulse of resistance in the Spanish Americas, do not in themselves explain why entities like Chile, Venezuela, and Mexico turned out to be emotionally plausible and politically viable, nor why San Martín should decree that certain aborigines be identified by the neological "Peruvians." Nor,

ultimately, do they account for the real sacrifices made. . . . This willingness to sacrifice on the part of comfortable classes is food for thought.[2]

At stake, then, is the explanation of what makes a country "emotionally plausible" and "politically viable" from an internal perspective. In addition, there are issues concerning identity and sacrifice: Why do Indians become Peruvians, and why do privileged Creoles lay down their lives for national independence? Anderson's explanation of why this is so proceeds along three separate lines.

First, in Spanish America colonial administrative practices divided Creoles from Peninsulars by reserving the highest offices of the empire for the latter, thereby fostering a sense of resentment and identity among the former. Second, the fact that Creole bureaucrats were constrained to serve only in their administrative units of origin meant that they collectively shared an image of these provinces as their political territory. The bureaucratic pilgrimage through colonial administrative space allowed for the conflation of Creole national identity with a specific *patria*, or fatherland.

Anderson recognizes, however, that these two factors were present before the rise of Spanish-American nationalisms at the end of the eighteenth century, and he feels that they were insufficient to produce true nationalism. The third, and indispensable, factor was the rise of print capitalism, especially newspapers. These papers allowed for the formation of an idea of "empty time" that was to be occupied by the secular process of development between parallel and competing nations:

> We have seen that the very conception of the newspaper implies the refraction of even "world events" into a specific imagined world of vernacular readers; and also how important to that imagined community is an idea of steady, solid simultaneity through time. Such a simultaneity the immense stretch of the Spanish American Empire, and the isolation of its component parts, made difficult to imagine. Mexican Creoles might learn months later of developments in Buenos Aires, but it would be through Mexican newspapers, not those of the Rio de la Plata; and the event would appear as "similar to" rather than "part of" events in Mexico. In this sense, the "failure" of the Spanish American experience to generate a permanent Spanish-America-wide nationalism reflects the general level of development of capitalism and technology in the late eighteenth century and the "local" backwardness of Spanish capitalism and technology in relation to the administrative stretch of the empire.[3]

Thus, because they emerge so early, Spanish-American nationalisms exhibit an oddity, which is that linguistic identification does not coincide with the territorial consciousness of Creole bureaucrats and newspaper readers, thus allowing for the emergence of both a series of individual nationalisms and pan-Spanish-American quasi-national identity. In most later (European and Asian) cases, linguistic identity would play a more central and defining role: "What the eye is to the lover—that particular, ordinary eye he or she is born with—language—whatever language history has made his or her mother-tongue—is to the patriot. Through that language, encountered at mother's knee and parted with only at the grave, pasts are restored, fellowships are imagined, and futures dreamed."[4]

In short, Anderson explains the rise of Spanish-American nationalisms (Chilean, Peruvian, Bolivian) as the result of a general distinction between Creoles and Peninsulars, a Creole political-territorial imaginary that was shaped by the provincial character of the careers of Creole officialdom, and a consciousness of national specificity that was shaped by newspapers that were at once provincial and conscious of parallel states. Once these early Creole nationalisms succeeded in forging sovereign states, they became models for other nations.[5]

In order to decide whether this theory of the rise of nationalism is an acceptable account, we need to understand precisely what Anderson means by "nationalism," and whether his definition corresponds in a useful way to the historical phenomena that are being explained. For Anderson, the nation "is an imagined political community—and imagined as both inherently limited and sovereign."[6] "Nationalism" is the adherence to and identification with such a community. Although the emphasis on the "imaginary" quality of national communities is redundant—all communities are imaginary constructs—Anderson's emphasis on nationalism's imaginary quality is meant to signal that nations are not face-to-face communities, and therefore involve a characteristic form of abstraction.[7] The imaginary quality of the national community is also underlined for a political purpose, since Anderson is critical of nationalism and so is intent on showing its historical contingency and its "invented" nature.

Understanding the "community" half of Anderson's definition is, perhaps, not as simple a matter, since community takes a specific and limited connotation for the author: "[The nation] is imagined as community because, regardless of the actual inequality and exploitation that may prevail in each, the nation is always conceived as a deep comradeship. Ultimately it is this *fraternity* that makes it possible, over the past two centuries, for so many millions of people, not so much to kill, as willingly to die for such limited meanings."[8]

This association between nationalism and sacrifice is consonant with Anderson's guiding preoccupation, which was the troubling fact that socialist countries were fighting nationalists wars, showing that nationalism could provide a kind of comradery that ran deeper than the solidarities of shared class interest. This led Anderson to investigate nationalism's secret potency, its capacity to generate personal sacrifice. Correspondingly, the question of sacrifice is, for Anderson, the telltale sign of nationalism, a fact that leads him to view nationalism as a substitute for religious community. Let us pause to consider this definition before moving on to Anderson's historical thesis on the genesis of nationalism.

The first difficulty that must be faced is that Anderson's definition of nation does not always coincide with the historical usage of the term, even in the place and time that Anderson identifies as the site of its invention. The subtleties in the usage of the term *nación* can perhaps be introduced through an example. In 1784, Don Joaquín Velasquez de León, director of Mexico City's School of Mining, wrote in *La Gazeta de Mexico*, "I said in my letter of the year 71 that the Machine that is called of fire was easy to use and to conserve; but one year later, that is in 72. the Excellent mister Don Jorge Juan, *honor and ornament of our Nation* in all sciences and mathematics, devoted himself to building that Machine in the Royal Seminary of Nobles of Madrid."[9] In this instance, Mr. Velázquez, who was writing for a predominantly Creole audience in the context of a debate with Father J. Antonio Alzate, a famous Creole scientist, wrote of Jorge Juan that he was "an honor to our nation." The ambiguity of this formulation helps us understand the process of transformation that the semantic field of the term *nation* was undergoing.

In the early eighteenth century, *nación* was defined as "the collection of inhabitants of a province, country or kingdom."[10] This definition is already quite ambiguous. New Spain, for example, was a province (or several provinces), a country (or several countries), and a kingdom, just as Castille was a kingdom that encompassed several provinces and countries. Thus, returning to our example, the Castillian scientist Jorge Juan might not be of the same *nación* as most of the readers of *La Gazeta de Mexico*. However, two further ambiguities in fact make this identification possible.

First, the term *nacional* referred to "that which is characteristic of or originates from a nation." Thus, Mexican Creoles could be of the Spanish nation because they had their roots in Spain, were characteristic (*propios*) of Spain, and so on. A second ambiguity of the semantic field of *nación* stems from the movement of administrative reforms that Spain's enlightened despots set in motion around the middle of the eighteenth century. Among other policies, the Bourbons made a concerted effort to streamline the territorial organization of the empire, undermining the idea of the Spanish empire as being composed of a series of kingdoms.

Thus, from the viewpoint of Spain's colonies of the late eighteenth century, the term *nación* could be used to pit *peninsulares* against Americans as Anderson has suggested. However, it could also be used to emphasize the extension of national identity by way of lines of descent and thus be made into a synonym of *blood* or *caste*, thereby providing a rationale for internal divisions within colonial societies. Finally, the concept of *nación* could be used as a sign of pan-imperial identity, regardless of descent.

Moreover, if the referent of the term *nación* was ambiguous with respect to its connection to territory and to bloodlines, it also had complex connections to sovereignty. This was particularly so in the Americas. So, for instance, if someone took the "bloodline" definition of *nación*, he or she might point to the varying *fueros* (inviolable legal privileges) attached to the Spanish and Indian republics as forms of government and identify two fundamental nations. If, on the other hand, someone identified *nación* with a kingdom or province, he or she could cite the *fueros* enjoyed by the nobility and the citizens of the republic. It is important to note that in both of these cases, sovereignty is not absolute or popular sovereignty, but rather a limited form of sovereignty comparable to that of *pater potestas* or to arenas of individual sovereignty granted by the doctrine of free will.[11]

Thus, whereas Anderson's definition of nationhood involves a sense of the sovereignty of a state over a territory, the Spanish definition vacillated between an (increasingly unified but nonetheless ambiguous) territorial definition and a definition around descent. Both of these forms involved specific *fueros*, in other words, access to limited forms of sovereignty.

It is pertinent to note that this notion survived the American independence movements, for example, in the ways that federalism was interpreted in early nineteenth-century Mexico, in local appeals to ancestral rights and priviledges, in references made to "Indian nations," or in the ambiguous referents of the term *república*.[12]

Due to the ambiguity in the ties between "nation" and "blood," Spanish usage of the term *nación* could be distinguished from a second term, *patria* (or fatherland), in such a way that a single land could be the *patria* of more than one *nación*. This was, indeed, the case in most of the Americas, which were conceived as pluri-national *patrias*. This tense coexistence between a discourse of loyalty to the land and one of filiation through descent is visible in colonial political symbolism.[13] Common loyalty to the land was a concept that was available in Spanish political discourse at least since the sixteenth century, but it was nonetheless not directly assimilable to the notion of nation in the Americas. This ambiguity is at the basis of the category of "Creole" itself, which, as a number of historians have shown, emerged in the mid–sixteenth century but maintained a problematic relationship to Spanishness throughout the colonial period.[14]

The move to associate nation with common subjection to the king was promoted by Charles III, who sought to diminish differences of caste in favor of a broad, homogenized category of "subjects." Thus a tendential identification between "nation" and "sovereignty" was being built up by absolutist monarchs in the eighteenth century, a fact that makes San Martín's dictum that so claimed Anderson's attention ("in the future the aborigines shall not be called Indians or natives; they are children and citizens of Peru and they shall be known as Peruvians") less of a Creole invention than Anderson supposed.[15]

A second significant problem in applying Anderson's definition to the Latin American case is that belonging to an imagined national community does not necessarily imply "deep horizontal comradery." The idea of nation was originally tied to that of lineage; members of a nation could be linked by vertical ties of loyalty as much as by horizontal ties of equality. This is most obviously relevant when considering the way in which age and sex enter the picture of national identity. Women and children could and can very much identify with their nations even though usually they are not their nation's representative subjects. Similarly, a master and a servant could be part of the same nation without having to construct this tie as a horizontal link based on fraternity.[16]

This is a fundamental point for Spanish-American nationalism in the nineteenth century, when corporations such as indigenous communities, haciendas, and guilds were even more salient than they are today. Nonetheless, the point also has broader significance. Jurgen Habermas pointed out that the bourgeois public sphere in eighteenth-century northern Europe (which was tied inextricably to the development of nationalism) was made up ideally of private citizens. Nonetheless, the citizen's "private sphere" encompassed his family, making the citizen at once an equal to other citizens (Anderson's "fraternal bond") and the head of a household in which he might be the only full citizen. It would be a mistake, however, to presuppose that nationalism was embraced only by the citizen and not by his wife and children.

In more general terms, the horizontal relationship of comradery that Anderson wants to make the exclusive trait of the national community occurred in societies with corporations, and the symbolism of an encompassing relationship between citizens and these corporations is critical to understanding the nation's capacity to mobilize its subjects. Nationalists have fought battles to protect "their" women, to gain land for "their" villages, to defend "their" towns. It is just as true, however, that women, servants, family members, and, more generally, the members of corporate communities or republics could send "their" citizens to war. In other words, citizens could represent various corporate bodies to the state, and they could represent the power of the state in these corporate bodies.

In Spanish America the complexities of these relationships of encompassment (between the national state, citizens, and various corporations) have been widely recognized in analyses of conflicts between liberal and conservative factions in the nineteenth century, and in the role of local communities in the wars of independence themselves.[17] Indeed, the relationship between the modern ideal of sovereignty and citizenship and the legitimate claims of the corporations is a central theme in Latin America to this day.

The third, and final, difficulty with Anderson's definition of nationalism is his insistence on sacrifice as its quintessential symptom. The image of nationalism as causing a lemminglike impulse to sacrifice because of its appeal to community is as misleading as the idea that nationalism is necessarily a communal ideology of "deep, horizontal comradery." For in order to comprehend what nationalism is and has been about, one must place it in its context of use. The capacity to generate personal sacrifice in the name of the nation is usually not a simple function of communitarian imaginings of comradery. Ideological appeals to nationhood are most often coupled with the coercive, moral or economic force of other social relationships, including the appeal to the defense of hearth and home, or the economic or coercive pressure of a local community, or the coercive apparatus of the state itself.

Moreover, there are plenty of examples of nationalism spreading mostly as a currency that allows a local community or subject to interpellate a state office in order to make claims based on rights of citizenship.[18] It is misleading to privilege sacrifice in the study of nationalism, since the spread of this ideology is more often associated with the formulation of various sorts of claims vis-à-vis the state or toward actors from other communities.

In sum, I have raised three objections to Anderson's definition of nation and nationalism, noting, first, that the definition does not correspond to historical usage. Second, Anderson's emphasis on horizontal comradery covers only certain aspects of nationalism, ignoring the fact that nationalism always involves articulating discourses of fraternity with hierarchical relationships, a fact that allows for the formulation of different kinds of national imaginaries. Finally, I argued that Anderson makes sacrifice appear as a consequence of the national communitarian imagining, when it is most often the result of the subject's position in a web of relationships, some of which are characterized by coercion, while others have a moral appeal that is not directly that of nationalism.

TOWARD AN ALTERNATIVE PERSPECTIVE

In one of his most brilliant moments, Anderson suggests that nationalism should not be analyzed as a species of "ideology" but rather as a cultural construct that has affinity with "kinship" or "religion."[19] Anderson's selection of "deep horizontal comradery" as the defining element of nationalism is his attempt to give meaning to this proposition. The essence of nationalism for Anderson is that it provides an idiom of identity and brotherhood around a progressive polity ("the nation"). Following Victor Turner, Anderson looks for the production of this fraternity in moments of communitas such as state pilgrimages. He also explores the conditions of possibility of national identity, arguing that nationalism depends on a secular understanding of time as "empty" and of the world as being made up of nations whose progress unfolds simultaneously and differentially through this empty time. Thus, for Anderson, the compelling aspect of nationalism is its promise of fraternity.

I suggested earlier that nationalism is an idiom that articulates citizens to a number of communities, ranging from family, to corporate groups, to villages and towns, to the national state. The connections between these communities is often itself the substance of nationalist discourse and struggle. It follows that the stakes of national sentiment cannot so readily be reduced to the brotherhood among citizens.

In order to define the nature of nationalist imaginings, we must ask questions such as: When and how is nationalism invoked in a man's relationship with his wife? How is it deployed in the dealings between a small-town schoolteacher and his villagers, or between an Indian cacique and a president? For in each of these cases, the ideology of fraternity invoked by Anderson is being used to articulate hierarchies into the polity. The protection of the nation then becomes the protection of the family, or of the village, or of the race.

My first and most fundamental amendment to Anderson is thus that nationalism does not form a single fraternal imaginary community, since it systematically distinguishes full citizens from part citizens or strong citizens from weak ones (e.g., children, women, Indians, the ignorant). Since these distinctions are by nature heterogeneous, we cannot conclude that nationalism's power stems primarily from the fraternal bond that it promises to all citizens. The fraternal bond is critical, but so are what one might call the *bonds of dependence* that are intrinsically a part of any nationalism.

This leads me to a second, though minor and derivative, amendment. The pride of place that Anderson gives to sacrifice in his view of nationalism is misleading, for if we accept that the national community is not strictly about equality and fraternity, but rather about an idiom for articulating ties of dependence to the state through citizenship (fraternity), then the defense of the fraternal bond becomes one possible symptom of nationalism among several others.

In other words, the power of nationalism is as evident in the gesture of a *niño héroe* who wraps himself in the flag and dies for his country as it is in the gesture of the peasant who invokes his citizenship when petitioning for communal land, or the small-town notable who claims that he and his villagers descend from Aztec ancestors when he petitions for a school. In fact, common nationality can even be invoked by a peasant who resists abduction to the army. Finally, the very nature of patriotic sacrifice is easily misconstrued if we do not pay close attention to the bonds of dependence that are central to the national community, for citizens enlisted in World War I not only because of their fraternal ties with other volunteers or conscripts but also because their families might reject them if they did not, or their communities might reject their families, and so on.

In short, instead of saying, as Anderson does, that the nation is a community "because, regardless of the actual inequality and exploitation that may prevail in each, the nation is always conceived as a deep comradeship," I define the nation as a community that is conceived of as deep comradeship among full citizens, each of whom is a potential broker between the national state and weak, embryonic or partial citizens whom he or she can construe as dependents.

This brings me to a final comment regarding the relationship between the analytic definition of nationalism and actual usage of the term. Although my earlier revised definition would still exclude any form of ethnic identification that did not strive for some degree of political sovereignty, I believe that it has a greater capacity to include and distinguish between historical varieties of nationalism. For instance, the ambiguity between a "racial" and a political-territorial definition of *nación* that I cited earlier for the late-eighteenth century Spanish world is a reflection of a specific moment in nation building that should not simply be called "prenational," since it involves a territorially finite state and a sovereign people, even though it tolerated significant differences between stations and even estates. Similarly, the peasant who has never seen a map or aided a census taker, and who has no notion of why, say, "Germany" and "Guadalajara" are incommensurate categories, can still be a nationalist because he makes an appeal as a Mexican, or because he comes home to his wife late and drunk on the night of September 15 (Mexican Independence Day).

Revised General Historical Thesis

The fundamental thing about nationalism is that it is a productive discourse that allows subjects to rework various connections between social institutions, including, prominently, the relationship between state institutions and other social organizational forms. As such, the power of nationalism lies not so much in its hold on the souls of individuals (though this is not insignificant) as in the fact that it provides interactive frames in which the relationship between state institutions and various and diverse social relationships (family relationships, the organization of work, the definition of forms of property, and the regulation of public space) can be negotiated. Thus, one could write a history of nationalism that would have two bookends: one in which societies were not sufficiently dynamic and states were insufficiently potent for nationalism to emerge as a useful space of negotiation and contention, and another in which states were no longer sufficiently potent and complex to be the key actors in the process of regulating what Michel Foucault called "bio-power," that is, the power to administer a "population" and to regulate its habits. Capitalism traverses this history from end to end, and it is therefore misleading to begin the history of nationalism at the end of the eighteenth century, and not at the beginning of the sixteenth century.

Instead of positing the notion that nationalism emerged first in the Americas around the time of independence, with the rise of print capitalism, and that it is therefore scarcely two hundred years old, the Spanish and Spanish-American cases suggest that nationalism developed in stages, beginning with European colonization in the sixteenth century or perhaps in the *reconquista*. In fact, nationalisms developed along different, though interrelated, tracks, such that, as in the analogy between nationalism and kinship, one might locate diverse nationalist systems.

In the rest of this chapter, I shall outline what this alternative perspective reveals for the Spanish-American case. I will argue for several moments in the development of nationalism, each of which involved a distinct interconnection between fraternity and dependency. This reinterpretation of the history of Spanish-American nationalism leads me to identify theoretical mistakes in Anderson's general argument, including false conclusions concerning the historical connections between "racism" and nationalism, as well as between language and nationalism; a misleading emphasis on the idiom of fraternity as the only available language of national identity; and an incorrect or successional view of the relationship between religion and nationalism.

A fundamental error in Anderson's account of the history of nationalism is his insistence on associating it with secularization. In the case of Spain, whose formation as a nation is certainly one of the earliest, the opposite is the case: national consciousness emerges as an offshoot of religious expansionism. I cite from Anderson once again to clarify what is at stake:

> In the course of the sixteenth century, Europe's "discovery" of grandiose civilizations hitherto only dimly rumored—in China, Japan, Southeast Asia, and the Indian subcontinent—or completely unknown—Aztec Mexico and Incan

Peru—suggested an irremediable human pluralism. Most of these civilizations had developed quite separate from the known history of Europe, Christendom, Antiquity, indeed man: their genealogies lay outside of and were unassimilable to Eden. (Only homogeneous, empty time would offer them accommodation.)[20]

This point of view is perhaps a true reflection of the ways in which expansion was assimilated in England and the Netherlands, but it was not the cultural form that expansion took in Spain (or in the Spain's strongest early competitor, the Ottoman empire).[21] On the contrary, both the Spanish *reconquista* and subsequent expansion into Africa and to America were narrated very much in the framework of what Anderson describes in shorthand as "Eden."

It is well known that Columbus and other explorers speculated on their proximity specifically to Eden, and to other biblical sites, when they reached the New World. That they attributed their success to God's design is evident in the ways in which they christened the land: islands and mainland being named alternatively for royal and for spiritual sponsors (Isla Juana, Filipinas, and Fernandina alternating with San Salvador, Veracruz, Santo Domingo, etc.). Neither was this identity between conquest and the broader teleology of Christendom abandoned once colonization set in.

Franciscan missionaries interpreted their evangelizing mission in Mexico in terms that were consonant with the messianic scholastic philosopher Joachim de Fiore.[22] The priest Mendieta, an apologist of Hernán Cortés, derived many a moral from the marvelous fact that Cortés had been born in the same year as Martin Luther, the one to work for God in extending the true faith, the other to work for the Devil.[23] In fact, the whole of the conquistador's "discourse of the marvelous" was peppered evenly with elements of popular literature (Marco Polo, Mandeville, Virgil, chivalry novels) and with biblical stories. One might argue, contrary to Anderson, that the successes of Ferdinand, Isabella, and Charles V gave new life and plausibility to a narrative of Eden that had been much weaker in the days of Mandeville and Marco Polo, when the idea of taking Jerusalem and of achieving the Universal Catholic Monarchy was beyond any realistic expectation.

But even after Spanish expansionism was waning, by the 1570s, the relationship between the true faith and the ways of local heathens was still told as part of the Christian eschatology, as is obvious both in narratives of indigenous intellectuals such as Felipe Guamán Poma de Ayala and in those of seventeenth-century Creole patriots, such as Mexico's Carlos de Sigüenza y Góngora. Both of these argued (in different ways) that the Aztecs and the Inca had been evangelized before the arrival of the

Spaniards and had subsequently been led astray by the Devil, only to be brought back into the fold by an alliance between the remaining loyal Indians (such as the Texcocans or the Tlaxcallans in Mexico, or Guaman Poma's own family in Peru) and the Spaniards. The significance of this point for the history of Creole patriotism has been argued extensively by both David Brading and Jacques Lafaye.

Not only was Spanish expansion told as part of Christian eschatology, but the social organization of the state that was being built during this expansion innovatively identified the Church with a national idea. The earliest formulation of this occurred in the days of the Spanish *reconquista*, with the legal codification of so-called blood purity [*limpieza de sangre*] and especially with the formation of the Spanish Inquisition in the late 1400s. Certificates of blood purity, guaranteeing that the holder was an Old Christian, were necessary in order to hold office, to enter the church, or to enter certain guilds. Although the holders of these certificates were not identified as "Spaniards" but rather as "Old Christians," they were thought of as a community of blood and belief that had privileged access to the state.

The nationalization of the church became much more significant with expansion to America. The whole of the first chapter of the Laws of the Indies is in fact devoted to justifying Spanish expansion to the Indies as a divine grace extended to the king so that he might bring the true faith to those lands. Moreover, holding political office or belonging to the privileged classes was also seen in relation to faithfulness to the church, as is evident in a law that threatens any nobleman or holder of office with the loss of all privileges if he takes the name of God in vain.[24]

Leaning heavily on these formulas, the concept of "Spanish" was created as a legal category of identity in order to organize political life in the Indies. Spanish authority involved moral and religious tutelage over other social categories of persons, including "Indians," "blacks," "mulattos," and "mestizos," and also as a category differentiated from other European "foreigners" [*extranjeros*]. For example, Book 3, Title 3, Law 66, of the Laws of the Indies (first written in 1558) grants "the Viceroys of Peru the faculty to entrust [*encomendar*] any Indians that may be unoccupied [*indios que hubiere vacos*] during their time of arrival to those provinces, or any that may become unoccupied, to the Spaniards [*españoles*] living in them . . . so that they may have them, enjoy their tribute, and give them the good treatment that is mandated in our laws."

Similarly, another law (1608) orders, "Of the people in aid that the Viceroy might send from New Spain to the Philippines, he not allow in any way that mestizos or mulattos go or be admitted, because of the inconveniences that have occurred."[25] Book 3, Title 5, Law 14, orders that arms builders cannot teach their art to Indians; Title 10, Law 7 of the same book prohibits military captains from naming slaves as standard-bearers in the army, while Law 12 (1643) of the same book and title orders army officials not to give "mulattos, dark ones [*morenos*], mestizos" the job of soldier. Book 3, Title 15, Law 33, orders that the wives of the members of the Audiencia hear mass in a specific part of the chapel in the company of their families, civil authorities, or women of rank, "and not Indian women, Black Women or Mulatas." On the other hand, the king ordered that when viceroys and judges named a "protector of Indians" (a kind of free lawyer for Indians), "they should not elect mestizos, because this is important for their defense, and otherwise the Indians can suffer injuries and prejudice"; in other words, Spaniards, not mestizos, are the best and most appropriate defendants of Indians. Examples can be multiplied much further.[26]

In short, a concept of "Spanish" emerged quickly for the colonization of the Americas, and Spaniards were expected to take up a position of spiritual, civil, and military leadership. The notion of Spanishness was formally and legally understood as a question of descent, and it therefore included "Creoles," even though contexts of differentiation and discrimination between American-born Spaniards and Peninsulars did exist from the mid-sixteenth century onward.[27] This process of differentiation was predicated not on blood but rather on ideas concerning the influence of the land on the character, makeup, and physiognomy of those born in the Indies.[28] The term *criollo* had, in fact, a derogatory slant, in that it tended to assimilate American-born Spaniards with other American-born castes, such as slaves or mestizos.[29] Thus patriotism (in the sense of exaltation of the land of birth) became central to the Creoles because it was through a vindication of the true worth of the land that they could fully claim the inheritance of their blood.[30] This tension between a nationalism based on community of descent and a patriotism based on a clear, delimited idea of "Spain" (as opposed both to the Indies and to other European holdings of the Spanish monarch) would remain important in Spain and in the Americas even after independence.[31]

The degree to which Spaniards, Spanishness, and the Spanish language were identified with the True Faith and with civilization comes through in the text of the following law (1550): "Having made a close examination concerning whether the mysteries of our Holy Catholic Faith can be properly explained in even the most perfect language of the Indians, it has been recognized that this is not possible without incurring in great dissonances and imperfections. . . . So having resolved that it would be best to introduce the Castilian language, we order that teachers be made available to Indians who wish voluntarily to learn, and we have thought that these may be the *sacristanes*."

In short, in the colonies the Spanish language was not seen as merely a convenient and profane vernacular, but rather as a language that was closer to God.[32] Language thus reflected the process of *nationalization of the church*, which lies at the center of the history of Spanish (and Spanish-American) nationalisms, a point of departure that is at the opposite of the spectrum posited by Anderson, who imagined that secularization was in every case at the root of nationalism.

The civil leadership of Spaniards over Indians and others is laid out in a number of laws and practices, including in laws concerning the layout of Spanish towns and streets; in the superiority of Spanish courts to Indian courts (Indian magistrates could jail mestizos or blacks, but not Spaniards); and, more fundamentally, in that the laws of Castille served as the blueprint for those of the Indies, and for every other realm in the Spanish domain.[33] In sum, the concept of *español*, as a community of blood associated with a religion, a language, a civilization, and a territory emerged rather quickly in the course of the sixteenth century.

SECOND MOMENT OF SPANISH NATIONALISM

The first moment of Spanish national construction was, then, quite different in spirit and content from that posited by Anderson; Spanishness was built out of an idea of a privileged connection to the church, and Spaniards were a chosen people, led by monarchs who had been singled out by the pope with the title of "Catholic." As Old Christians, they were the true keepers of the faith and therefore the only viable political, moral, and economic elite.[34] The conquistadors were thus instantly a kind of nobility in the Indies, and "Spaniards" were the dominant caste. In short, Spanish nationality was built on religious militancy, descent, and language all rolled into a notion of a national calling to spiritual tutelage in the Americas and throughout the world.

The Spanish language in the Indies was not simply an arbitrary tongue among others; it was the suitable language in which to communicate the mysteries of the Catholic faith. Even today in Mexico, *hablar en cristiano* (to speak in Christian) is synonymous with speaking in Spanish. Similarly, the Spanish bloodline—for Spanishness usually included American-born Spaniards—had a special destiny with regard to the True Faith. Relativism was not at the origin of Spanish nationalism, nor did the discovery of the Indies dislocate Christian eschatology in any fundamental way. "Eden," as Anderson calls it, was maintained as the framework for histories that explained and situated Aztecs, Incas, and the rest of them.[35]

Spain's precocious consolidation as a state allowed for the rise of a form of national consciousness that was distinct from the relativist vocation of Britain and the Netherlands, whose entry to the game of (early) modern state and empire as underdogs made them fertile ground for the development of liberalism and, eventually, of truly modern forms of nationalism that are more akin to those described by Anderson.[36]

On the other hand, Spain's rapid decay in the European theater both consolidated and exacerbated national consciousness in peculiar ways. Horst Pietschmann has summarized the development of Spanish economic thinking of the late sixteenth and seventeenth centuries, arguing that the administrative reforms of the Bourbons in the eighteenth century were not a simple importation of French administrative ideas, but rather that they combined the latter with a native body of economic and administrative theories and projects devoted to finding remedies for the economic decline of Spain.[37] Among these, Pietschmann's summary and discussion of the influential work of Luis Ortiz (1558) is pertinent for my argument here.

Ortiz argued that Spain was poor because it only exported raw materials and then reimported them in the form of manufactured goods. The Spaniards' disdain for manual labor contributed to the underdevelopment of industry, as did the progressive depopulation of the countryside. As a partial remedy, Ortiz campaigned for laws to enhance the prestige of manual labor: "These should be extended even to the extreme that the state force all young men (including the nobles) to learn a trade, under the penalty that they would otherwise lose their nationality."[38]

These recommendations, and others like them, became a staple of seventeenth-century economic projects and studies. Interestingly, they usually call for the strengthening of the crown, the peopling of the country, and the leveling of some differences between the various stations. Such recommendations are conceived as a matter of national interest, and, in Ortiz's case, proposed penalties for failure to comply include loss of nationality.

Three points concerning this intellectual tradition are pertinent for our purpose here: first, a national consciousness was exacerbated by the perception of Spain's increasing backwardness vis-à-vis its competitors; second, the solutions that were proposed (policies concerning trade, population, education, work, administrative rationalization, etc.) also called systematically for a diminution of regional differences and policy reforms that involved conceptualizing a people in a finite territory, under a more streamlined and more equalizing administration; finally, the idea of relative decline and of competition involved a keen sense of "empty time" (i.e., of secular competition between states progressing through time) before the advent of "print capitalism," a fact that is obvious not only in the economic literature but also in all manner of military and commercial policy.[39]

A final citation from Pietschmann, who is my principal authority in this matter, summarizes my point concerning this second phase and links it to national transformation in the eighteenth century: "Together with the affirmation of the Catholic religion (the Spanish Enlightenment was qualified as being specifically Christian, and it had its reformist current in Jansenism), we find also the patriotism of the Enlightened thinkers, a fact that differentiates them from the cosmopolitanism of Enlightenment thinkers in France and other European countries. This patriotism, which gave the Spanish Enlightenment a strongly political character, was expressed in the desire that Spain reconquer its earlier economic florescence and its political position as a power of the first order."[40]

Thus, under the Bourbons, the discussions of the policy makers of the prior century and a half were reanimated, and they generated a series of administrative reforms. These reforms were, once again, built on the patriotic and national conscience that had developed since the conquest, a conscience that simultaneously produced a clearly delimited image of "Spain" as a land and of "Spaniards" as a nation (even though there was no isomorphism between the nation and Spain).[41]

As an example of the Spanish imagined community that was being constructed through these reforms, I offer the following vignette, also taken from La Gazeta de Mexico, describing the celebration of the birth of royal twins and the signing of a peace treaty with France and the United States in Madrid: "Rarely shall there be a motive for greater complacency, nor more worthy of the jubilation of the *Spaniards*, than the happy birth of the two twin infantes, and the conclusion of a peace so advantageous to the *national interests* . . ."[42] Having identified both the subjects of the ritual as Spaniards and the interests being served by the twin birth and by the peace treaty as "national," La Gazeta de Mexico goes on to narrate the public festivities that marked the event, especially the content of a series of allegorical floats [carros alegóricos]:

> The first car is preceded by drums, trumpets, pages, heralds and eight couples of both sexes, six of artisans, one of farmers [hortelanos] and one of field hands [labradores], each with the instrument of its profession. They are followed by the orchestra and immediately thereafter by a super car, pulled like the rest by six horses, in which the Statue of Atlantis, characterized with several mottos, holds the sky. Our August Monarch Charles III holds with his heroic virtues and happy government the *Spanish* Monarchy. The love of the *Spaniards* venerates in its glorious Monarch the Princes and the Royal Family, so worthy also of the love that is bestowed to them by *the Nation*.

Here we have, in an officially sanctioned bulletin published in Mexico City, the portrayal of a Spanish nation—represented by farmers, agricultural workers, and artisans and protected by a national monarch, who holds the sky over their heads like Atlas. Both the monarchy and the people are called "Spanish" here, and the description of this festivity in

Mexico is clearly meant to make this national celebration inclusive at the very least to a Creole audience. Yet the territory of "Spain" is clearly limited in the ritual, in a way that diverges from the potentially more inclusive term *nación*: "The last car . . . is preceded by eight couples on horseback, armed with lance and shield. Then two pages, and nine couples that indicate the different Provinces of Spain, whose costumes they wear. They are accompanied by an orchestra, to which they correspond with dances of their respective provinces."

The description of a series of allegories portraying Spain goes on in detail and is summed up in the following analysis: "The interpretation of this car is easy. Spain is represented in the greatest surge of its happiness due to the birth of the two SERENE INFANTES, by [newly signed peace], by its products, by its main rivers, by its Sciences, Arts, Navy, Commerce and Agriculture, all of which is fomented by our august sovereign, facilitating for this illustrious Nation, the abundance and opulence that is promised by its fertile soil and the constancy of its loyal and energetic inhabitants."

In short, a clear image of Spain, represented by a modern idea of the public good (with great prominence given to arts and industry, to natural resources, and to the customs of the various folk), is present in this state ritual. At the same time, the inclusiveness of the category of "nation" appears to be a sight broader than the Spanish territory that is so clearly delimited, since it includes the readers of the *La Gazeta de Mexico*, who are fully expected to share in the joy of the occasion. Around the time of this festivity, Charles III would try to implement administrative reforms that would more clearly make the territorial image of Spain inclusive of the Indies in a way that paralleled the inclusive potential of the concept of the Spanish nation.

BOURBON REFORMS AND INDEPENDENCE

The high point of this reformist movement, in the late eighteenth century under Charles III, involved trying to make Spain and its colonies into a coherent economic space, with a relatively streamlined administration, an active financial and economic policy, and a decentralized administration and army. This imperial unity was known as the Cuerpo unido de Nación,[43] and its administrative organization was clearly the precursor of the state organizations that were generated with independence.

These reforms were promoted not only as a response to a feeling of backwardness and of nostalgia for past national glories but also to face the political threats posed by both the British navy and the American Revolution. The former threat, in particular, made the decentralization of administration an important strategy for the fortification of the empire. This system of decentralization and administrative rationalization also involved promoting a view of industry and of public interest that is significant in the formation of a modern version of nationalism, based on individual property, a skilled and well-policed workforce, and a bourgeois public sphere.

Two divergent tendencies are produced with these administrative, religious, and educational reforms. On one hand, the formation of the idea of a Grán España, made up of Iberia and the Indies together, with a population of subjects tending toward greater internal homogenization under increasingly bourgeois forms of political identity; on the other, the consolidation of the various administrative units—the viceroyalties and the new "intendencies"—as viable state units, each with its own internal financial administration and permanent army.

These contradictory tendencies are in fact related: on one hand, the administrative consolidation of transatlantic political units was the only logical means to shape a strong Grán España; on the other, the very process of consolidating their viability made independence all the easier to imagine. Alexander Humboldt's voyage and writings on Spanish America are a good example of this conundrum. Whereas in the sixteenth and seventeenth centuries printed materials about the Indies were banned from those lands, and foreigners were outlawed from going beyond the ports of the Indies, Humboldt received carte blanche to travel there, and authorities were asked to give him all their statistics and any information that he might require. Humboldt's publications on the political economy of the Indies followed the spirit of the Bourbon reforms, as well as German Cameralist administrative theory, by treating each principal administrative unit (mainly viceroyalties) as a coherent whole, with a population, an economy, a map, and so on.

The administrative consolidation of viceroyalties, intendencies, and other political units was occurring not as a ploy to keep Creoles boxed into their administrative units but rather to strengthen the general state of the empire and to give each segment a greater capacity to respond to a political crisis. From the seventeenth century forward, the Armada from Spain had to struggle to make successful voyages to the Americas, and there were moments when it was entirely incapable of managing Spanish-American trade. Greater administrative and military autonomy would provide another line of imperial defense.

Thus, at the same time that the "political viability" and the "emotional plausibility" of the viceroyalties were strengthened politically by the new system of intendencies and ideologically through a new emphasis on the public good through industry and education, so too was the notion of a truly pan-imperial identity closer at hand than ever before. These contradictory tendencies are in evidence at the time of independence: first, in the parallels between the American wars of independence and the "war of independence" of Spain against the French invaders; second, in the fact that in the liberal Constitution of Cadiz (1812), "Spaniards" were defined as all of the people who were born in the Spanish territories, with no distinction made between Iberia and the Indies.

The Rocky Road to Modern Nationalism in Mexico

In Latin America, the road to national modernity was particularly cumbersome. This was due to the early date of independence movements, a fact that resulted not so much from the force of nationalist feeling in the region as from the decadence of Spain in the European forum.[44] As a result, the new countries faced stiff internal and foreign relations problems, and it is in the context of these problems that a functioning nationalism developed.

The fourth moment in the evolution of Spanish-American nationalism can best be understood as one wherein the dynamics of independent postcolonial statehood forced deep ideological changes, including a sharp change in who was considered a national and who a foreigner, a redefinition of the extension of the fraternal bond through the idea of citizenship, of the relationship between religion and nationality, and between race and nation. In this final section, I explore the dynamics of these transformations through a summary of certain key events in early independent Mexico (1810–29).

As Anthony Pagden has demonstrated, Creole patriotism was predicated on Spanish political philosophy. In the Iberian world, sovereignty was granted by God to the people, who, in turn, ceded it to the monarch. It is therefore not surprising that the early fathers of Mexican independence Hidalgo and Morelos, who were secular priests, claimed to be fighting for the sake of religion. Here, for instance, is a formulation by Morelos: "Know that when kings go missing, Sovereignty resides only in the Nation; know also that every nation is free and is authorized to form the class of government that it chooses and not to be the slave of another; know also (for you undoubtedly have heard tell of this) that we are so far from heresy that our struggle comes down to defending and protecting in all of its rights our holy religion, which is the aim of our sights, and to extend the cult of Our Lady the Virgin Mary."[45]

Correspondingly, Morelos and Hidalgo accused the Spaniards of betraying their true Christian mission and of using Christianity as a subterfuge for the exploitation of the Americans.[46] To uphold the true Christian faith was also to drive out all Spaniards who had milked the Mexicans of their native wealth and who had driven them down to an abject condition.

These early movements failed. Morelos and Hidalgo were executed, and although some of their followers continued the fight, independence was not to be achieved by this particular ideological wing. Instead, Agustín Iturbide, who had been a loyalist army officer, was able to forge an alliance with both the upper clergy (who never supported Hidalgo and Morelos) and the Spaniards by providing them with ample guarantees of continuity and belonging in the new republic. Iturbide was crowned sovereign of the Mexican empire in 1821, but his reign lasted only one year.

Only eight years after the consummation of independence under the Plan de Iguala, the so-called radical party, which was associated with the Freemasons of the rite of York, supported a movement to expel the Spaniards from Mexico. And yet, these *yorquinos* were not associated with the sort of popular religiosity of Morelos and Hidalgo, instead, favoring the implementation of a system modeled after that of the United States. In short, Mexican nationalism went from excluding Spaniards, to including them, to excluding them again in a very short lapse of time.

The very violence of the ideological transformation of early Mexican nationalism suggests that a general or abstract "nationalism" does not help one understand the specifics of its contents or its dynamics of propagation. In fact, just as the notion of "kinship" is an abstraction of such a general level that it can obfuscate the nature of the practices that are being summed up in the category, so too can we say that Anderson's culturalist reading of nationalism is so general and abstract that it fails to clarify the politics of community production.

The specific formulations of the nature of the nation and of who was included and excluded underwent dramatic shifts that cannot be attributed to changes in consciousness gained by new maps or censuses (Humboldt was still the main source that people drew on in this period). Neither do these shifts respond to an intensification of travel or of the strength of bureaucratic networks across the territory. The formation of Mexican nationalism can be understood in relation to the political conditions of its production. These conditions were determined by the new nation's position in an international order, as much as by the fact that it did not have a national ruling class.

This latter point requires elaboration. At the time of independence, Spanish-American countries did not have a Creole bourgoisie that could serve as a national-dominant class. Domestic regional economies were not well articulated to each other; much of the transatlantic merchant elite was Spanish; mining capital often required foreign partnerships. Thus, the Creole elite was a regional elite, and not a national bourgeoisie. In this context, only two institutions could conceivably serve to articulate a national elite. The military, however, was not a unified body, since it was led precisely by regional caudillos, many of whom controlled their own militias. The church, on the other hand, articulated the national space in terms of clerics, and ideologically vis-à-vis competing Protestant powers, but it could not serve as a national dominant class.

In this context, articulating regional leaders into national factions was necessary. In the early years after Mexico's independence, Freemasonry had precisely this role.[47] It was through masonry that regional elites forged interregional networks that could prefigure the national bureaucracy after independence.

When independence was attained, much of Mexico's political elite belonged to Masonic lodges organized in the Scottish rite. These elites were well disposed to Britain, and, indeed, Great Britain was the first great power to recognize Mexico. Not surprisingly, George Ward, Britain's first ambassador to Mexico, was able to reap numerous economic and political concessions from the government of Mexico's first president, Guadalupe Victoria, so much so that when U.S. ambassador Joel Poinsett arrived on the scene in 1825, he saw gaining some of the terrain that the United States had already ceded to the British as his most formidable task.[48] Poinsett made a sustained effort to build a pro-American party to counter British influence in Guadalupe Victoria's government. Part of Poinsett's well-calibrated strategy included aid in the organization of Masonic lodges to counter those affiliated with the Scottish rite, and he attached these Masons to the rite of York (chartered by the lodge in Pennsylvania). These two Masonic organizations would function as "political parties" throughout this period.

Both the Scottish and the Yorkish Masons tried to monopolize as many government posts as they could. As the competition between the *escoseses* and the *yoquinos* became embittered, the "American cause" (of York) began to identify the Masons of the Scottish rite with imperialist European interests, especially with Spanish interests. This allowed the *yorquinos* to distract attention from the U.S.-British rivalry, and it promised to yield juicy dividends to *yorquinos* in the form of Spanish property, since the Spaniards were still the most prosperous sector of Mexico's population. The *escoseses*, on their part, because they were losing the contest for national power, denounced the role of Joel Poinsett as a foreigner creating the party of *yorquinos* and the very existence of "secret societies."

Thus, it was in the competition between two secret societies for full control over the apparatus of the state that two critical aspects of Mexican nationalism were consolidated: nationalism as an excluding ideology (even as a xenophobic ideology)—seen both in the move to expel the Spaniards and in the move to expel Poinsett; and nationalism as an ideology that made *public* access to the state bureaucracy a cornerstone of its ideology. These aspects of nationalism reinforced one another because neither of the two Masonic parties could afford the luxury of identifying entirely either with foreign interests (since each needed to attack a different foreign power—the *yorkinos* wanted to attack British and Spanish interests, the *escoseses* were opposed to U.S. interests), and neither could they openly admit that they merely wished to control the bureaucratic apparatus.

Finally, the links between religion and nationalism should not be taken as constant. Although early Mexican patriotism was understood as a superior loyalty to the Catholic faith, and thus Mexican nationalism vehemently excluded other faiths, the British and the Americans coincided in their interests in propagating freedom of religion. Consequently, some degree of religious tolerance was necessary to maintain trade with England and the United States. On the other hand, the polarization of the political spectrum soon produced a Jacobin camp. Eventually, church properties would be to Jacobins what Spanish properties had been to *yorquinos* in 1829: a source of wealth that could be their spoils for group expansion in a period of little economic growth.

In this fashion, Mexico consolidated a national state with a nationalism built on three principles: the defense against foreigners, the defense of open publicness (and of an understanding of the state as a normative order rather than as a governing class), and the (uneven) extension of the benefits of nationalism to popular levels (be it through the abolition of tribute, of guild restrictions, of church tithes, of distribution of national lands, the distribution of spoils from the Spaniards, the distribution of goods or new technologies). These three pillars are the product of the contest of two secret societies, supported by two imperialist states, for control over the state apparatus. These secret societies, in turn, functioned thanks to the cleavages of economic and political interests that cut across national lines or that did not reach "up" to the national level at all. In short, the bases of communitarian feeling, the criteria of inclusion and exclusion in the nation, the imagination of a territory, and the very conceptualization of national fraternity were all shaped in the political fray.

CONCLUSIONS

The cultural density of the phenomenon of nationalism lies in the politics of its production and deployment. Nationalism combines the use of transnationally generated formulas, ranging from legal formulations to state pageantry, with a politics that is inextricably local. A dense or thick description of nationalism is therefore a necessary step for understanding its cultural characteristics.

The Spanish-American and Mexican cases present a significant historical problem for Anderson's conceptualization because in Spain national
construction began with an appropriation of the church, not with a rela-
tivization of "Eden." Spanish was seen as a modern form of Latin, and
therefore was more appropriate for communicating the faith than indigenous languages. In a related vein, "race" was central to early modern
Spanish nationalism, insofar as descent from Old Christians was seen as
a sign of a historical tie to the faith, a sign that gave its owners control
over the bureaucratic apparatus of both church and state.

Moreover, the concept of "empty time" was present in the Spanish
world long before print capitalism, beginning with the decline of empire
and Spain's failure to attain a universal monarchy. Thus, Spanish economic thought formulated the notion of a national economy beginning in
the mid–sixteenth century. The administrative constructs that allowed for
the imaginings of a people tied to a territory can be dated to the sixteenth
century, when both colonial expansion and the defense of the empire
against European powers led to the consolidation of the notion of
"Spain" and of "Spaniards." As Spain continued to decline in the European forum, state reforms tended to target political middlemen in an attempt to substitute regional political classes with a bureaucracy, to consolidate an idea of a national territory, and to conform a greater Spanish
nation made up of subjects that tended increasingly toward an internal
uniformity vis-à-vis the crown.

Finally, independence itself, as Anderson recognized, was not the product of cultural nationalism, but rather of the decline of Spain's capacity to
run its overseas territories. As a result, much of the specific contents of
modern nationalist ideology—such as the notion that politics should be
public, or that religion should not be a criterion for choosing a trading
partner, or that a Spaniard is not a Mexican even if he sympathizes with
the Mexican cause—were the cultural products of independence, and not
its precondition.

On the theoretical front, the Latin American case leads me to modify
Anderson's definition of nationalism in order to stress both fraternal ties
and bonds of dependence in the imagined community. It is in the articulation between citizenship and nationality that various nationalisms derive
their power. As a result, sacrifice is not the quintessential feature of nationalism but rather is one of a number of possible signs and manifestations.

In addition, since Anderson's ideas concerning the necessity of cultural
relativism as a precondition for nationalism are incorrect, it follows that
his theoretical emphasis on the centrality of language over race in nationalism can also be questioned. In the case of Spain, at least, "racial" identity (in the sense of a bloodline) was coupled with linguistic identity for

the formation of an opposition between "Spaniards" and "Indians," and it was descent from Old Christians who had fought holy wars that made Spaniards a chosen people.

Like kinship and religion, nationalism has come in various strands. In the early modern period, we must distinguish between the nationalism of a chosen people, such as that of Spain, and the defensive nationalism of the British or the Dutch, who created nationalist ideals in order to affirm their right to maintain and to sanctify their own traditions. Both of these forms contrast with the highly unstable nationalist formulations of early postcolonial Spanish America. Nationalism's family tree reaches back to the very birth of the modern world, and ideas of political community that have emerged since then are both more and less than a cultural successor of the religious community.

Notes

1. Benedict Anderson, *Imagined Communities* (London: Verso, 1983), 7.

2. Ibid., 52.

3. Ibid., 62.

4. Ibid., 154. Anderson goes even further and denies that racial identity and racism are connected in any essential way to nationalism: "The fact of the matter is that nationalism thinks in terms of historical destinies, while racism dreams of eternal contaminations. . . . The dreams of racism actually have their origin in ideologies of class, rather than in those of nation" (149–50). I shall argue later that this assertion is untenable in the Iberian world.

5. Ibid., 82.

6. Ibid., 6.

7. At times Anderson appears to believe that there is such a thing as a "concrete" versus an "imaginary" community: "The relatively small size of traditional aristocracies, their fixed political bases, and the personalization of political relations implied by sexual intercourse and inheritance, meant that their cohesions as classes were as much concrete as imagined. An illiterate nobility could still act as a nobility. But the bourgeoisie? Here was a class which, figuratively speaking, came into being as a class only in so many replications" (ibid., 77). Although Anderson is shrewd in searching for differences in the social organization of communication in various classes as a key to understanding nationalism, he incorrectly assumes that some forms of community are "concrete" while others are "imaginary." All communitarian relationships are based on an idea of the social whole that is imaginary; and "the nobility" of his example was much more reliant on systemic "replications" than Anderson imagines. So, for example, all legitimate descendants of the conquistadors and early settlers of the Indies were officially considered nobles [*hijos dalgo*] (*Leyes de Indias*, Book 4, Title 6, Law 4). Likewise, it was policy to recognize and maintain the status of the Indian "nobility" (*Leyes de Indias*, Book 7, Title 7, Law 1). In short, the nobility of the

Spanish colonial era played as systemic a role as the bourgeoisie, which meant that it burgeoned wherever it was needed to maintain a local hierarchy and state organization. The grandees of Spain were surely as ignorant of the identities of the descendants of first settlers or of Indian nobles in Chile as the members of the bourgeoisie of Barcelona were ignorant of the identity of their class counterparts in the Rio de la Plata.

8. Anderson, *Imagined Communities*, 7; my emphasis.

9. *La Gazeta de Mexico*, September 8, 1784, 13; my emphasis.

10. Real Academia Española, *Diccionario de la lengua castellana en que se explica el verdadero sentido de las voces* (Madrid, 1726–39).

11. For an illuminating discussion of the relationship between ancien régime and modern ideas regarding sovereignty in the Spanish and Spanish-American world, see Francois Xavier Guerra, "De la política antigua a la política moderna, la revolución de la soberanía," in F. X. Guerra and Annick Lampérière, eds., *Los espacios públicos en Iberoamérica: Ambigüedades y problemas, siglos XVIII–XIX* (Mexico City: Fondo de Cultura Económica, 1998), 109–39. The whole of Guerra's oeuvre has demonstrated that throughout the nineteenth century Spanish America combined elements of an ancien régime and of a modern polity. A similar point has been made by Fernando Escalante, *Ciudadanos Imaginarios* (Mexico City: El Colegio de Mexico, 1992). Twentieth-century Latin America is also not without examples of tensions from competing claims between state sovereignty and the traditional rights of corporations and communities.

12. See Annick Lampérière, "República y publicidad a fines del antiguo régimen," in Guerra and Lampérière, *Los espacios públicos en Iberoamérica*, 55–60.

13. A good case in point is the use of the eagle eating the serpent as the symbol for Mexico City. Florescano, who has studied the evolution of this symbol, shows that the Aztec symbol was used preferentially over the coat of arms that was assigned to the city since the early seventeenth century. This use of this indigenous symbol also buttressed Creole identity. The symbol was eventually written into the flag of Mexico in lieu of Hidalgo's Virgin of Guadalupe, or of Morelos's "Viva la Virgen María." Enrique Florescano, "Indian, Spanish, and Liberal Iconographic Traditions in Mexico and the Creation of National Symbols" (ms. presented at the Getty Center for the History of Art and the Humanities, Los Angeles, May 14, 1996).

14. Key works on this matter include David A. Brading, *The First America: The Spanish Monarchy, Creole Patriots and the Liberal State, 1492–1867* (New York: Cambridge University Press, 1991); Jacques Lafaye, *Quetzalcoatl y Guadalupe: La formación de la conciencia nacional en México* (Mexico City: Fondo de Cultura Económica, 1977); Bernard Lavallé, *Las promesas ambiguas: Ensayos sobre criollismo colonial en los andes* (Lima: Pontificia Universidad Católica del Perú, 1993).

15. Anderson, *Imagined Communities*, 49–50. Indeed, the Spanish constitution that was promoted in Cadiz in 1812 defined Spanish citizenship in such a way as to include in equal terms those born in any part of the Spanish dominion. Article 18; in Felipe Tena Ramírez, *Leyes fundamentales de México, 1808–1957* (Mexico City: Editorial Porrúa, 1957), 62. Aljovín discusses the decline of An-

dean Curacas at the end of the eighteenth century in the context of the Bourbon state's goal of eliminating the power of all institutions that brokered the relationship between the state and its subjects. Cristobal Aljovín, "Poderes locales en la primera mitad del XIX," *Histórica* 21, no. 1. (1997): 1–25.

16. For example, in both the Constitution of Cadiz (1812) and Mexico's Centralist Constitution (1836), servants have nationality (Spanish and Mexican, respectively), but in neither case were servants citizens.

17. For the salience of individual communities as primary referents of identity in the wars of independence, see Eric Van Young, "Millennium on the Northern Marches: The Mad Messiah of Durango and Popular Rebellion in Mexico, 1800–1815," *Comparative Studies in Society and History* 28 (1986): 385–413. For the ways in which community or corporate identities interlocked with nationalist discourses, see Florencia Mallon, *Peasant and Nation: The Making of Post-colonial Mexico and Peru.* (Berkeley: University of California Press, 1995), chaps. 5, 7; also Escalante, *Ciudadanos Imaginarios,* 97–119, 193–197. An early formulation of the problem was set forth by Edmundo O'Gorman, who argued that Juárez's triumph over the French in 1867 must truly be considered a "second independence," not simply in the sense that Mexico was freed from a foreign invader but, much more fundamentally, because it represented the triumph of liberal republicanism over a classical republicanism: "We could say, then, that if Miguel Hidalgo is the founder of [our] nationality, Benito Juárez is the founder of republican nationality, which is not, as we know, at all the same thing." (Edmundo O'Gorman, *La supervivencia política novohispana: Reflexiones sobre el monarquismo mexicano* (Mexico City: Condumex, 1969), 86.

18. See, for instance, Florencia Mallon's discussion "of popular liberalism" in nineteenth-century Mexico and Peru (*Peasant and Nation,* p. 130). Contemporary examples abound; see Carlos Vélez-Ibáñez, *Rituals of Marginality: Politics, Process, and Culture Change in Central Urban Mexico, 1969–1974* (Berkeley: University of California Press, 1981).

19. Anderson, *Imagined Communities,* 5.

20. Ibid., 69.

21. See Cornell Fleischer, "The Lawgiver as Messiah: The Making of the Imperial Image in the Reign of Suleyman," in Gilles Veinstein ed., *Soliman le magnifique et son temps* (Paris: Documentation française, 1992), 159–77. Clearly, early modern nationalism differed considerably in England, France, and the Netherlands. Stephen Pincus interprets the Glorious Revolution as the first nationalist revolution, rather than as a religious war. England's early separation of nationalism and religion reflects the fact that it never hoped to achieve a universal monarchy, as Spain and the Ottomans did; thus to a certain degree one could say that a religious nationalism is at the origins of the Spanish imperial state, whereas a revolutionary, secular form of nationalism developed in England. Stephen Pincus, "The English Nationalist Revolution of 1688–1689" (ms., University of Chicago, 1998).

22. John Leddy Phelan, *The Millennial Kingdom of the Franciscans in the New World* (Berkeley: University of California Press, 1970).

23. "It ought to be well pondered how, without any doubt God chose the valiant Cortés as his instrument for opening the door and preparing the way for

the preachers of the gospel in the New World, where the Catholic church might be restored and recompensed by the conversions of many souls for the great loss and damages which the accursed Luther was to cause at the same time within established Christianity. . . . Thus it is not without mystery that in the same year in which Luther was born in Eislebe, in Saxony, Hernando Cortés saw the light of day in Medellín, a village in Spain; the former to upset the world and bring beneath the banner of Satan many of the faithful who had been for generations Catholics; the latter to bring into the fold of the church an infinite number of people who had for ages been under the dominion of Satan in ideolatry, vice and sin" (Fray Jerónimo de Mendieta, *Historia eclesiástica indiana*, 3 vols. (1596; Mexico City: Editorial Joaquín García Icazbalceta, 1876), 3:174–5.

24. Book 1, Title 1, Law 25.

25. Book 3, Title 4, Law 15.

26. Book 6, Title 6, Law 7. Laws distinguishing subjects of the Spanish crown from foreigners were equally precise (e.g., Book 3, Title 13, Law 8). The fact that these laws were not always put into practice is not relevant to the matter at hand, which is that there was a concerted effort to create a category of "Spaniard" and to make Spaniards the standard-bearers of the faith.

27. It should be noted, however, that these processes were by no means a simple constant, and that the politics of differentiation between "Peninsulars" and "Creoles" responded to varying kinds of interests (including, for instance, interests in prolonging *encomendero* privilege after the second generation; interest in keeping Creoles out of certain religious orders or away from certain political posts). These interests waxed and waned at various times and places, in such a way that there were places and times when a "Creole" was simply a Spaniard, other moments when "Creole" was used principally as a discriminatory term, and yet others when American-born Spaniards tried to affirm the equality, and even the superiority, of their land with respect to Spain, Rome, or other European locations. See Lavallé, *Las promesas ambiguas*, passim.

28. Although it is important to note that the nature of American lands and of their influence on the character of the Americans was a polemical subject in scientific circles from the time of initial contact to the early twentieth century. See Antonello Gerbi, *The Dispute of the New World: The History of a Polemic, 1750–1900* (1995; Pittsburgh: Pittsburgh University Press, 1973); and Gerbi, *Nature in the New World: From Christopher Columbus to Gonzalo Fernández de Oviedo* (1975; Pittsburgh: Pittsburgh University Press, 1985).

29. Lavallé, *Las promesas ambiguas*, 20.

30. The literature exalting American lands at times also refashions the connections between the Americas and "Eden." This has been studied in detail for Mexico by Lafaye, *Quetzalcoatl y Guadelupe*, chap. 1 and by Brading, *The First America*, chaps. 14, 16. In the Andean world, Lavallé notes, "Many Creoles believed that their patria could be compared to the Elisian Fields, with the Bible's Paradise. There was in this, for some, a mere literary style. . . . For others, there could be no doubt: America should not be *compared* to paradise, it *was* the earthly paradise of the Scriptures" (*Las promesas ambiguas*, 122; emphasis in original).

31. Raphael Semmes, a soldier in the U.S. army, described the reception that

was given to U.S. troops by Mexico City's elites in 1847: "The Calle de Plateros, through which we marched to the grand plaza, is the street in which all the principal shops are found; and although these were closed, gay curtains fluttered from the balconies above . . . (almost every house had prepared and hung out a neutral flag, English, French, Spanish, etc., as a means of protection), and the fashionably dressed women, who showed themselves without the least reserve at doorways and windows, gave one the idea rather of a grand national festival, than of the entry of a conquering army into an enemy capital." (Cited in Luis Fernando Granados, "Sueñan las piedras: Alzamiento ocurrido enla ciudad de México, 14, 15 y 16 de septiembre, 1847" (Licenciatura thesis, UNAM [Mexico], 1998). The "neutral flags" were meant to signal to U.S. soldiers that the families in question were also foreign nationals by descent.

32. Charles V is said to have claimed that whereas German was appropriate for speaking to horses, and Italian was ideal for courting women, Spanish was for speaking to God. The term *ladino* also provides a clue to the sacralization of Spanish, since it was used to refer to Jews, Moors, African slaves, or, later, Indians, who spoke (neo-)Latin, that is, Spanish (Lavallé, *Las promesas ambiguas*, 19). A discussion of the history of the title "Rey Católico" and of its significance for Spain in its competition with France can be found in Pablo Fernández Abadalejo, "Rey Católico": Gestación y metamorfosis de un título," in Luis A. Ribot García, ed., *El Tratado de Tordesillas y su época* (Madrid: Junta de Castilla y Aragón, 1994), 1:209–16. Jaime Contreras argues that Spain's persecution of heresy under the Reyes Católicos can be understood as a political appropriation of the church: "The so-called heresy, which was but a little elf in its beginnings, thus was transformed into a fundamental support for the Crown's law." Jaime Contreras, "Los primeros años de la inquisición: Guerra civil, monarquía, mesianismo y herejía," in Ribot García, *El Tratado des Tordesillas*, 2:681–703. On the identification between Christianity and Spanish civilization in the so-called spiritual conquest of Mexico, see Peggy Liss, *Mexico under Spain, 1521–1556: Society and the Origins of Nationality* (Chicago: University of Chicago Press, 1975), esp. 77–82.

33. Book 2, Title 1, Law 2: "That the Laws of Castille be kept in any matter not decided in those of the Indies."

34. Antonello Gerbi remarks that Fernandez de Oviedo contrasted the grandeur of Spain with that of ancient Rome, noting that Spanish Goths were Christians and were martyred while resisting Roman paganism. Thus, in the sixteenth century, Spain's national identification with Christianity was made to rank higher even than Rome's (*Nature in the New World*, 267–68).

35. Pagden has shown that talk of a universal monarchy was never thoroughly accepted in Spain itself, and that it was extinguished as an impracticable ideal by end of the seventeenth century. However, he also argues that Spain's ideological role as guardian of universal Christendom "formed an important part of the ideological armature of what has some claims to being the first European nation state." Anthony Pagden, *Spanish Imperialism and the Political Imagination* (New Haven, Conn.: Yale University Press, 1991), 5.

36. The Laws of the Indies provide an interesting example of how Spain reconciled the simultaneous development between empires through time with a Catholic universalism. Much of the legislation that was promoted by Philip IV (at a time

of intense imperial decay) shows punctilious concern with public oration and repentance for public sins, as mechanisms to reanimate the empire and, perhaps, also as potential explanations of its political shortcomings. For example, Book 1, Title 1, Law 23 (passed originally in 1626) orders viceroys and church authorities to celebrate November 21 of every year with a mass to the Holy Sacrament, in which priests call on everyone to reform their "vices and public sins" in order to thank God for his clemency in allowing Spanish ships to reach the Indies unharmed.

37. Horst Pietschmann, *Las reformas borbónicas y el sistema de intendencias en Nueva España: Un estudio político administrativo* (1972; Mexico City: Fondo de Cultura Económica, 1996), 18–24.

38. Ibid., 19.

39. "In all of the authors [writing on economics and administration in the mid-sixteenth and seventeenth centuries] we find an awareness of the economic decadence and a negative consensus concerning Spain's policies. In addition, it is interesting to note that a great proportion of these planners were well informed of the realities that existed abroad. In many of their writings we find references to the economic situation, to the systems of taxation, to the discoveries and methods of labor in industry and in the trades existing in other European states. It also appears that these ideas concerning the economic troubles of the country had a truly wide audience, since the majority of their projects were printed, and we even find their ideas repeatedly in the works of writers like Cervantes." Ibid., 23.

40. Ibid., 25.

41. Domínguez Ortiz illuminates this situation: "The social thought of enlightened Spaniards was not radical. It did not claim the total suppression of barriers between the estates, because these were crumbling on their own account. Instead, it seemed more urgent to struggle against economic differences that condemned a great portion of the population to misery. This does not mean that pride in nobility had disappeared . . . but they no longer tolerated nobility titles as excuses to refuse common charges; privileges could only be justified if they were employed for the good of the nation." Antonio Domínguez Ortiz, *Carlos III y la España de la Ilustración* (Madrid: Alianza Editorial, 1989), 120–21. Domínguez discusses the significance of state projects and knowledge production in this period in his fifth chapter. See also Barbara Stein and Stanley Stein, "Concepts and Realities of Spanish Economic Growth, 1759–1789," Historia ibérica, economía y sociedad en los siglos XVIII y XIX (1) (1971): 103–20.

42. *La Gazeta de Mexico*, November 3, 1784; my emphasis.

43. Pietschmann, *Las reformas borbónicas*, 302

44. The fact that a nationalism and a national program were not common denominators even among Mexican insurgents has been forcefully demonstrated by Eric Van Young, who has shown the centrality both of local indigenous revolts whose claims with regards to state building were in fact the opposite of those of the Creole directorate ("Millennium," 386, 412), and of an unideological criminal or brigand element whose participation was entirely opportunistic ("Agustín Marroquín: The Sociopath as Rebel," in Judith Ewell and William Beezley, eds., *The Human Tradition in Latin America: The Nineteenth Century* [Wilmington, Del.: SR Books, 1989], 36–37). The role of opportunistic rogues and the criminal

element in independence is also pungently demonstrated by Christon Archer, "The Young Antonio López de Santa Anna: Veracruz Counterinsurgent and Incipient Caudillo," in Ewell and Beezley, *The Human Tradition in Latin America.* On the other hand, Spanish-American independence was predictable even before indigenous social movements got started and before nationalists really heated up. As early as 1786, Thomas Jefferson's main preoccupation regarding Spanish-America was that it should not fall out of Spanish hands too quickly. The fact that Spain would eventually lose those territories was, for Jefferson, a foregone conclusion. The United States needed time to gain strength in order to annex as many Spanish-American territories as possible. (Cited in José Fuentes Mares, *Poinsett: Historia de una gran intriga* (Mexico City: Oceano, 1983), 34–35.

45. Padgen, *Spanish Imperialism*, 199.

46. For a description that illustrates some similarities between these ideas and those expressed in indigenous messianic revolts of this period, see Van Young, "Millennium," 402.

47. Masons appear to have been present in Spanish America since the 1780s, though in the Mexican case it appears that the deputies who were sent to the Cortes of Cadiz in 1812 were critical in the formation of Mexico's lodges of the Scottish rite.

48. Poinsett to Henry Clay, June 4, 1825, *Dispatches from U.S. Ministers to Mexico.*

INDEX

Adelman, Jeremy, 8, 17, 20
agent state type, 182*f*
agriculture: commercial, 246, 248; labor-repressive, 244, 246–49, 259–61. *See also* landowners
Aguirre, Carlos, 301
Alberdi, Juan Bautista, 36
Allende, Salvador, 121, 127, 250, 253, 322
Allesandri, Arturo, 250
Allub, Leopoldo, 248, 256
Almond, Gabriel, 227, 229
Alonso, Carlos J., 324
Alzate, Father J. Antonio, 333
American Economics Association, 56
Amin, Samir, 84
Anderson, Benedict: alternative perspective to thesis by, 336–38; on construction of Spanish nationalism, 343–46; on development of nationalism, 329–30; historical thesis of, 11, 330–36; limitations of nationalism thesis by, 352–53
Anderson, Perry, 166
Andrews, George Reid, 245
Argentina: development in post-war, 63; Mothers of the Plaza de Mayo, 322; Orden Conservador of, 170–71, 176n.38; state-building in, 159
Aristotelian approach, 180
Arndt, H. W., 107
Arrighi, Giovanni, 84
Asian "miracles," 124, 291, 296
"Asian tigers," 124
Austin, J. L., 313
authoritarian regimes: centralized systems of control by, 322; language used by oppressive, 315–16; Moore study of, 286n.88; risk of forming, 76n.27; seeds of destruction within, 320; "textual poaching" as resistance to, 317–18. *See also* regime formation
Avellaneda, Nicolás, 37

Baer, Werner, 61
Bakhtin, Mikhail, 313
Barran, J. P., 170
Barrios, Gabriel, 191
Bartra, Roger, 192

Bauer, Arnold, 247, 262
Bay of Pigs invasion (1961), 224
Bello, Andrés, 36
Bendix, Reinhard, 20
Bengoa, Jose, 260, 261
Betancourt, Rómulo, 231, 234
Beverley, John, 310
Black Legend of Latin America: confirmed by Latin American nation-state, 155; cultural determinism of, 16; cultural stereotyping of, 301; described, 29; failure to develop institutions by, 10; institutionalism studied through, 34; perceived disciplinary failures of, 290–91; property rights approach challenge to, 41. *See also* history
blood purity legal codification, 341
Bolívar, Simón, 5, 164
Bolivia revolution, 223–24
Bolton, Eugene, 29
Borah, Woodrow, 29
Bourdieu, Pierre, 310, 314
Brading, David, 341
Brazil: bureaucratic-authoritarian regime of, 222; economic reforms (1920s) in, 112; language used by oppressive regime of, 315–16; property rights in slave society of, 37
Brazil Empire, 35, 36
Brazilian Umbanda, 312
Brazilian women's March of the Family for God and Liberty, 315–16
Brazil and Mexico: Patterns in Late Development (Hewlett and Weinert), 61
Brunner, José Joaquín, 311
Brzezinski, Zbigniew, 64
Buendía, Manuel, 190
Burke, Edmund, 139

Cancian, Frank, 83, 89
capital-intensive state-building, 158–59
capitalism: ecological consequences of, 89–90; Latin American exploitation by European, 66–67, 78n.37; Polanyi's study of, 87, 88–95
capitalized coercion state-building, 160–61